Introduction to
Building
Management

FIFTH EDITION

R. E. Calvert
C.Eng., M.I.C.E., F.C.I.O.B.

BUTTERWORTHS
London   Boston   Durban   Sydney   Toronto   Wellington

First published 1964
Second edition 1966
Third edition 1970
Fourth edition 1981
   Reprinted 1982, 1983
Fifth edition 1986

© R. E. Calvert 1986

British Library Cataloguing in Publication Data

Calvert, R. E.
   Introduction to building management.—5th ed.
   1. Construction industry—Great Britain—
   Management
   I. Title
   690'.068   HD9715.G72

   ISBN 0-408-02540-9

Library of Congress Cataloging in Publication Data

Calvert, R. E. (Richard Ernest)
   Introduction to building management.
   Bibliography: p.
   Includes index.
   1. Construction industry—Management.   I. Title
   HD9715.A2C34   1986   690'.068   85-28022

   ISBN 0-408-02540-9

Photoset by Butterworths Litho Preparation Department
Printed and bound in Great Britain by Page Bros Ltd, Norwich, Norfolk

Contents

Part II Management in Practice

Appendices

Preface to Fifth Edition

Anyone who sticks his head above the crowd is liable to be shot at, and this is certainly true for authors. But constructive criticism is healthy, and I am grateful to everyone who has contributed in this fashion and I have incorporated these in subsequent editions wherever possible.

It has been suggested by several commentators that 'management in principle' and 'management in practice' is an artificial distinction and the sections should be integrated; and certainly it is true that theory and practice cannot be separated in our managerial actions. However, for ease of detailed consideration, and to assist the continuity and hence our understanding of underlying causes and reasons, I believe that it is better to continue with this sub-division.

The 'classical' or mechanistic ideas of managerial thinking have been followed by 'social' or participative theories, and these in turn have been quickly modified by more recent 'organic' writings. But a new viewpoint or a more complex theory does not necessarily destroy all the old truths. The Building and Civil Engineering industries still find antiquated tools like the 'organisation chart' very useful, and still find social science very 'avant garde'. I have also kept away from the more mathematical techniques of operational research which I consider are not relevant to practical builders.

At the same time the Chartered Institute of Building, upon whose Final part II examination I originally based this book, has developed a new examination structure. This has split management subjects between Associate level, Member Exam part I and Member Exam part II, adding some new subjects to the latter. I have therefore decided to continue to concentrate solely upon management subjects, regardless of their place in the Institute's examinations, rather than to attempt to cover the new Member Exam part II.

I well appreciate that many of the subjects treated by me in a single chapter are now so specialised that each warrants a complete book in order to properly expound the full implications. But this handbook is only an 'introduction to management' ideas and practices as they apply to building construction. Anyone who develops a deeper interest in any particular aspect is encouraged to study a more specialised treatise.

Moreover, I have omitted the subject of building maintenance despite its importance of being nearly 40% of current U.K. construction value. It is such a specialised sector of the industry that I prefer to recommend *Managing Building Maintenance* from the CIOB, 1985.

Thus, in the 23 years since I wrote the first preface much has changed, yet I hope that many more new readers will continue to find my distillation helpful.

R.E.C.

Framlingham,
Woodbridge, Suffolk.
1986.

Preface to Fourth Edition

I have dodged this thorough revision for a long time, because I thought it might be a big job, but only now can I appreciate the full extent of my task.

The volume of parliamentary legislation was an obvious aspect, but it was more of a considerable addition than a straightforward amendment. Health and safety, industrial relations, and transport management, are now extensive subjects in their own rights.

At the same time, other subjects already well known in manufacturing and commerce have spread their influence to construction, so that we now need to understand discounted cash flow, cash flow forecasting and market research.

Building has been in the forefront of the developing concept of terotechnology; whilst the growing interest in winter building is of course peculiar to ourselves.

The study of the place of industry in society, the expanding influence of organisational development, and the ever growing power of the computer, are developments of the last decade that we just cannot afford to ignore.

Hence, although the basic principles of building management have not changed, and our problems and weaknesses are still the same but accentuated and made more chronic by the current pressures of life, both on site and at head office we have to be aware of and take into account whole new areas of knowledge. I wish particularly to thank my colleague Harry Jakeman for his advice on safety and industrial relations legislation, and my son Andrew for assistance with the finance chapter.

I sincerely hope that the additional material in this book will spread the gospel in certain directions and prove to be of practical assistance to both students and experienced practitioners alike. My greatest reward is still to meet someone who is kind enough to tell me that this particular *Introduction to Building Management* has been of service and value.

R.E.C.

Wombourne,
Wolverhampton.
1980

Preface to Third Edition

Since I first wrote this book in 1962, only 6 years ago, several developments have taken place in the building industry, despite our overall impression that so many desirable changes are still as far away as ever. In 1966 it was necessary to amend Chapters 8, 9 and 11, in order to keep up with the continuing spate of government legislation.

This time I have taken the opportunity to add an extra chapter on Operational Research, because of the significant impact upon project planning and control made by the introduction of network techniques during these last few years. Networks have prepared the way for the application of computers to construction, and this powerful combination presents a potential that we have hardly touched.

Looking to the immediate future, we have the change to the Metric System, which must have a great effect upon the construction industry, but at present only partly understood. Because the economy of the United Kingdom is dependent upon international trade, and an increasing proportion (60 per cent) of our exports are to countries using metric measurements, the Federation of British Industries suggested in 1965 that a change would be beneficial. That year the government announced its support for the replacement of the imperial system by the metric system of measurement, the changeover to be effected by 1975. Although the construction industry is primarily domestic, the need for increased industrialisation and the possibility of combining dimensional co-ordination with the changeover, prompted construction to become one of the first to implement the switch to decimalisation.

In February 1967 the British Standards Institution published a Programme for the Construction Industry (P.D. 6030), together with a Guide for the use of S.I. (Système International) units (P.D. 6031). As from 1 January 1969, new projects intended to start after 1 January 1970 will be designed in S.I. units, and reinforcement steel will be manufactured to metric sizes from 1 March 1969. Moreover, students reading for examinations to be taken after 1969 have already started to use metres, grams, newtons and litres, and so all the examples in this book have been converted to these units. In this task I have found the BSI *New Metric Conversion Slide* and the CIRIA *Metric Conversion Factors* extremely helpful. Acts of Parliament have yet to be translated by the relevant ministries, and for this reason I have included the metric equivalents alongside quoted figures. Words such as mileage and yardstick, which will probably remain as part of our language, I have left unaltered. As an aid to the reader during the transitional phase of this revolution, I have included a table of Metric Conversion Factors which I hope will prove useful.

To all those people who have been kind enough to commend my book I tend my sincere thanks, and hope that these omissions and additions will increase its usefulness.

R.E.C.

Tettenhall,
Wolverhampton.
1969.

Preface to First Edition

Although this project began initially as lecture notes, intended primarily for students reading for the Institute of Builders Part II Final Examination, I have tried to write a book that will be of assistance to all supervisory and executive grades of practising builders. I hope, therefore, that this text book for students will also prove to be a useful work of reference on the site and in the builder's office, and to all those who are concerned with greater efficiency within the building industry. Since the managerial responsibilities of the civil engineer are the same as those of the builder, despite the differences in accent, I trust he too will find much to interest him.

This book is introductory in character, aiming to provide a broad appreciation of management principles, and a grounding in their practical application both at head office and on the contracts. It is not intended to be exhaustive in treatment nor a management course in itself, and I sincerely trust that this introduction to the broad field of management studies will serve to whet the appetite for that wider and deeper reading so rightly recommended by the Institute of Builders.

I have endeavoured to consult all the readily available literature, nevertheless, the views expressed represent the truth as I understand it in relation to the construction industries, and although I intend no criticism of either individuals or organisations, I make no apology for comparing existing conditions with the ultimate ideals. Since it is only in the ordered sequence of writing that man can discover his deeper thoughts and cause them to become articulate, then this survey might also be regarded as a discourse for my own benefit as much as an expression of my personal beliefs for the interest of others.

I should like to take this opportunity to express my sincere thanks to all those Building Colleges who so kindly answered my appeal for help with opinions and suggestions, and particularly for their honest advice and kind encouragement. I must also acknowledge my dependence upon the Institute of Builders' admirable Syllabus of *Management Subjects*, and of the tremendous assistance I derived later from their *Management Notebook*. Without the former this book could not have been written, and indeed would not even have been attempted. Furthermore, I readily own my indebtness to many other sources of information, for which reason I have included a bibliography at the end of each chapter. In addition I have drawn upon my own practical experience as a civil engineer and agent with a national company of building and civil engineering contractors, and I wish to place on record my appreciation of the facilities made available to me. My thanks are also due to those kind friends who helped me with corrections and suggestions or the loan and recommendation of reference books.

Knowing how natural it is for builders and engineers to turn to sketches for explanations, I have included as many diagrams as possible to clarify the text. The majority of my examples have been based upon working experience, except the time and method studies in Chapter 17, which are purely imaginary illustrations and should not be taken as factual standards. All charts and standard forms are proven suggestions but are not in any sense the ultimate or sole possibilities.

Despite certain requests, I have not been able to include exercises or practical case histories for space will just not allow this; moreover, I think this aspect is better handled by individual lecturers and colleges.

There are significant differences between the organisation and practices of building and civil engineering in Scotland, and those of England and Wales, due largely to the emphasis north of the border on the single trade contracting firms. Therefore, while I feel that the basic principles of management are common throughout Great Britain, I have perforce left the interpretation of Scottish procedure to the proper institutions.

Finally, if I have inadvertently fallen behind the times anywhere in my writing, I must entreat the reader's indulgence, for things are changing so rapidly in the construction industries that I have found real difficulty in keeping details up-to-date.

R.E.C.

Codsall,
Wolverhampton.
1963.

To my wife Rosalie

Introduction

The Meaning of Management

In this book the term management refers to the philosophy or practice of organised human activity, while managers are the people responsible for the conduct and control of such an undertaking. As the name suggests, management is a social exercise, part art and part science, involving the organisation of a number of individuals in order to achieve a common purpose. The manager is therefore concerned with *the ways and means of getting a job done,* so that management entails responsibility for

a. planning and regulating the enterprise by installing and operating proper procedures,

b. ensuring the co-operation of personnel by providing the will to work and guiding and supervising their activities.

The field of management is usually divided into general and specialist branches, for each of which there have been developed particular techniques or 'tools', and in each of which a professional institution is to be found. These functions which are broadly common to all industry, together with some of their appropriate tools which are of particular relevance to the building industry, include:

a. *General management* responsible for the formulation of policy, the discharge of legal responsibilities, overall direction and co-ordination of specialist functions; organisation charts and manuals, standard procedures, management ratios, control figures.

b. *Finance* covering the capital and revenue resources, accounting, insurance and costing; budgetary control, cost analysis, cost control.

c. *Design,* usually the reponsibility of an architect in the building industry.

d. *Development* including experimental work and research into both materials and processes; statistical method.

e. *Marketing* concerned with external relations, tendering and the securing of future work; advertising, public relations.

f. Production covering the complete process of planning and co-ordinating the work of construction; planning, programming, progressing, stock control, work study, quality control, accident prevention, sub-contract liaison, communication methods.

g. Maintenance directed towards the upkeep of property, transport, plant and equipment; planned maintenance.

h. Personnel concerned with employment of labour, recruitment and training of staff, welfare services and safety; selection procedures, training programmes, incentive schemes, joint consultation.

i. Office responsible for devising clerical procedures and means of communication; organisation and methods.

j. Purchasing involving procuring supplies, delivery and quality control of materials; supply progressing.

The basic fundamentals of management and detailed operation of techniques can be taught and applied for the most part irrespective of the industry concerned, and, despite the special problems and differences of emphasis of the construction industry compared with others, building managers should understand and master the principles and methods involved. In addition to technical skill and experience, executives require education and training in management to fit them for present day conditions and the complexities of modern building.

In the following chapters the background, development and application of scientific method to the general problems of industrial management are described in the section Management in Principle. In the section Management in Practice are explained those various management functions that are common to all managers, but viewed from the specific standpoint of the several partners in the building team. The third section, Management Techniques, covers those particular management tools that, properly understood and utilised, can help to keep the construction industry abreast of the continually more difficult demands of the nation.

But we must never forget that managers of businesses are fundamentally concerned in performing two basic tasks – preparing goods and services, and selling them. Thus, whilst there is an urgent need for more effective bridges between theory and practice so that they may enrich each other, we must not allow a too-academic or scientific pre-occupation to distract us from the down-to-earth practical aspects of managing building and civil engineering projects.

Perhaps the most significant management change that has been brought about by the oil cartel-induced world-wide recession, and its consequent sharpening of competition, has been the re-awakened interest in marketing. Instead of waiting for enquiries to tender for work, it has become necessary to anticipate the requirements of prospective clients, to prepare organisational resources to meet those needs and then go out to sell the services made available. This philosophy today permeates and colours every aspect of management activity.

BIBLIOGRAPHY

Management Training in the Building Industry, British Institute of Management.
Alistair Mant, *The Rise and Fall of the British Manager*, British Institute of Management 1978.

Part I

Management
in
Principle

Chapter 1

Historical

The contemporary conception of management at different periods is of more than historical interest, because the varying phases over the course of time are none other than stages of the evolutionary process which has produced management as we know it today. At least as far as Great Britain is concerned, industrial management has a long history, but published records and evidence are scanty. Although Sir William Morland in the 1660's was apparently making use of incentive rates for some of the workmen he employed on civil engineering constructions, the earliest reliable and full picture that we have of effective management methods dates back to the end of the eighteenth century, i.e. the middle of the Industrial Revolution.

1. The Industrial Revolution (circa 1750 to 1850)

This may be described as the application of mechanical power to the production of goods, and the earliest efforts to improve management were those concerned with technical issues of production, because the social conscience of the day did not enforce responsibility for personnel problems.

Some early pioneers in the field of management included:

1. *James Watt,* the son of a master carpenter. In partnership with Matthew Boulton he gave to the world the first efficient steam engine, on which modern industry has been built. In 1795 they built their Soho Foundry near Birmingham, where the main interest centred on the efficient use of their large variety of machinery. This entailed the elaboration of Production Management processes such as the layout of plant, the flow of operations, the planning of work schedules, and other technical matters as the standardisation of parts and the

prefixing of dimensions. An inevitable consequence was an emphasis on the adequate training of the skilled craftsman.

2. *Robert Owen*, the pioneer of Personnel Management. He was born the son of an ironmonger, generations ahead of his time. Between 1800 and 1828 as managing director of the New Lanark cotton mills near Glasgow, he successfully put into practice social reforms to remedy the evils that contemporary industry accepted as inevitable. He ceased employing children under ten, reduced the working day for all his workers to 10½ hours and improved the factory conditions. He also started welfare schemes, set up infant schools and a model village, besides agitating for legislation that led to the passing of a Factories Act in 1819. Although he was a highly successful manufacturer it was a hundred years before his ideas bore their full fruit.

3. *Charles Babbage* was among the first to advocate in relation to industrial problems, the fundamental thinking which preceded the formulation of principles of management. His writings told little of the art of management as actually practised in the early nineteenth century, but suggested the scientific or analytical approach to the problems of manufacturing. A mathematician, he designed the world's first programmable computer but Victorian engineering was not up to its construction.

2. Management Evolution

Important as were the technical problems created by the introduction of machinery, the social and organisational problems which it brought in its train were still more pressing. The main difficulty lay in training human beings to denounce their desultory habits of work, and to identify themselves with the unvarying regularity of a factory discipline.

By the middle of the nineteenth century, questions of wages and working conditions had become predominant, particularly in connection with the evolution of a Trade Union system and the means of negotiation in collective bargaining. Parallel with this another aspect was coming into prominence, namely financial administration, made necessary by the increasing demand for capital and the provision of finance for industry through the limited liability principle.

Towards the close of the nineteenth century the main problems were beginning to concern the processes of marketing or distribution, to meet the emerging competition of growing industrial countries in Europe and elsewhere. In consequence, questions of the cost of production and of estimating prices were beginning to loom large. As more and more people were trained in the applied sciences, and particularly engineers became intimately acquainted with industry and its problems, it was inevitable that some of them should attempt to apply to these problems of conducting work the kind of thinking in which they had been trained as technologists. A group of engineers in the United States, among whom Taylor, Gantt and Gilbreth were the most distinguished, founded a movement in 1910 to which they gave the title of *Scientific Management*.

Some of these later pioneers were:

1. *Frederick Winslow Taylor,* the Father of Scientific Management. He began his studies into better methods of doing work in the Midvale Steel Works in the 1880's, as chargehand of the lathe operators. By detailed analytical experiments he investigated problems of industrial organisation such as the relationship between a foreman and his work, and what constitutes a 'fair day's work'. He was acknowledged as a high speed tool expert and gave his name to a bonus system, but his teachings of "a mental revolution for both employer and worker" were misunderstood by management and opposed by organised labour in this country until after his death in 1915.
2. *Henry Lawrence Gantt* was a close associate of Taylor both in consultancy and teaching work, but his writings emphasised the human interest. He is remembered chiefly as the inventor of the Gantt chart for graphical planning.
3. *Frank Bunker Gilbreth,* pioneer of motion study, devoted the greater part of his career to the search for 'the one best way to do work'. As a young bricklayer in America in 1885, he experimented with trestles and new designs of hods to eliminate unnecessary movement and effort from bricklaying. By 1904 the original eighteen motions necessary to place a brick had been reduced to four or five, so that, without undue fatigue, Gilbreth's men were able to handle 2,700 bricks per man per day. After allowing for the smaller American bricks this still compares favourably with today's standard of 400 to 800 in this country! Gilbreth went into the contracting

business but continued his studies, and in 1912 introduced the science of micromotion study. The ultra-small basic elements of body movements he called 'Therbligs' (an anagram of his name) and the books written in collaboration with his wife, Lillian, remain largely the classic works on this subject.

4. *Henri Fayol,* while General Manager of a large French iron and steel combine, read a paper in 1908 reviewing the processes that went to make up his everyday practice as chief executive, namely, forecasting, planning, organising, commanding, co-ordinating and controlling. He was the first to analyse and explicitly lay down a set of principles of management but he added nothing further and it was eighteen years befoie it appeared in English. He was a firm advocate of the principle that *management can, and should, be taught.*

5. *Elton Mayo,* with North Whitehead and their associates of the Western Electric Company of America, set out in 1924 to study the effects of lighting on output at their Hawthorne plant. To the amazement of the investigators they found that human emotions could play havoc with the results of carefully planned and controlled scientific experiments. Their results interpret management as the leadership of people and a social task of human beings among other human beings.

6. *Hans Renold* founded in Manchester a company for the manufacture of driving chains and sprockets, that was an example of British scientific management a generation ahead of its time. In 1913 he read a paper on Engineering Workshop Organisation, based upon his own firm, which described enlightened principles and methods that even today sections of British industry have not yet learned to apply. The company's organisation structure was based upon functional specialisation; certain of the younger staff were trained in management, whilst monthly balance sheets and returns facilitated the preparation of the annual stock-taking and yearly balance sheet within a few days. He enjoyed good work and believed that 'the working of an efficient system requires men of tact and power to lead'.

7. *B. Seebohm Rowntree* was director of the Industrial Welfare Department of the Ministry of Munitions, founded in 1916 to infuse into war production factories some understanding of the personnel and welfare aspects of management. When he left the Ministry he initiated the Oxford Management Conferences, which still aim to teach the essentials of effective human management to those directly in contact with

the rank and file. As a successful business executive at York he turned ideas into realities, and made industry a human thing with a purpose of service to the communtiy.

3. The Development of the Scientific Aspects of Management

A scientist proceeds by systematic reasoning, and the scientific approach to the various aspects of management has developed those modern methods whereby we try to substitute,

    a. in plans and decisions, investigation and knowledge for individual judgement or opinion;

    b. in practice, the intelligent and critical use of 'tools' for hunch or instinct; and

    c. on the human side, fairness and trust in place of bias and suspicion.

In the years that have intervened since the work of these pioneers first became known, there has been built up a very large body of knowledge bearing upon the *processes of management,* irrespective of the field of industry to which they are applied. In some degree this knowledge has to be applied to every task involving the control of other people, and much of this can be the subject of theoretical study. To the ideas of Babbage, the teachings of Taylor and the principles of Fayol must be added the early textbook of J. Slater-Lewis in 1896, the human writings of Mary Follett in the 1920's, the numerous publications of Colonel Urwick, and the recent literature of Sir Walter Puckey, E. F. L. Brech and Sir Frederic Hooper. Yet, despite the professional outlook in the technical spheres, the training of the technician in management is a story that even today is only beginning. The inclusion of Management subjects in the Final Examination of the Institute of Builders* in 1961 is part of this first chapter.

The *tools of management* are many and varied, ranging from Gantt charts to Gilbreth's motion-study, and include such recent developments as management audit and statistical method. Following the practical examples of Boulton and Watt, and Hans Renold Ltd., British industry has many notable examples of progessive managements including Imperial Chemical Industries and Marks and Spencers Ltd. But in this country the construction industries have hitherto failed to make the fullest use of these tools, and as the Building Productivity Team report (1949)

---

*Now the Chartered Institute of Building.

highlighted, here lies an opportunity to secure higher productivity and greater efficiency through their more effective and widespread application.

An historical account of the unfolding of industrial management in Great Britain is the story of the personnel function, the *human factor* in management. The old, old lesson of Owen, that personnel management pays, has been demonstrated in two World Wars, by Rowntree in 1916, and a Chief Inspector of Factories in 1941. The tenet that no system of management can be sucessful that is not based on the human element in the organisation, has been amply illustrated by Cadbury Brothers Ltd., and described by Mayo. This element in the executive process forms the thread linking the successive scenes into a continuous story, which today emphasises as the most essential feature of modern management, the exercise of leadership in a group of persons collaborating towards a given goal.

This story teaches one great lesson, that those who follow in the footsteps of the management pioneers, must be patient and persevering to a degree demanded by few other tasks.

4. Management and the Social Sciences

The social sciences include sociology, social anthropology, social psychology, political science, branches of psychology and economics. Industrial social scientists are particularly interested in:

1. The problems of organisation structure.
2. The nature of conflict and cooperation in organisations.
3. Human motiviation, satisfaction and incentives.
4. The communication of ideas, orders and information.
5. The relation of physical and mental health to the physical and social environment.
6. Technical and administrative change.

Since the Hawthorne experiments, most of the theoretical research on organisation and management has been done by social scientists from universities rather than by practising industrial managers. The chief contributors to the development of suggested patterns of organisation and management which would release individual potential were Argyris (1957), McGregor (1960) and Likert (1967). British researchers have played a leading role in the study of organisation and techology, notably Scott *et al.* (1956), Burns and Stalker (1961), and Woodward (1965). Technical procedures and equipment might limit organisation alternatives or influence human interaction and thus affect satisfaction and morale. The study of social groups in industry has been continued by the University of Michigan and the Tavistock Institute of Human Relations; and by individuals in Britain and the U.S.A., e.g. Roy (1954), Sayles (1958), Wilson (1962), Lupton (1963) and Cunnison (1965). However, in Britain the Chairman of the Glacier Metal Company, Wilfred Brown, has written from his own managerial experience and from the research undertaken in his organisation by the Tavistock Institute and Elliott Jaques.

Some individual studies are typical of the social scientist's work, in his effort to explain and predict the outcome of particular human activities in industrial organisations. Gouldner, an American sociologist, studied a Gypsum factory over a period of three years, and in 1955 showed how useful the notion of role expectations can be, and in particular that regularity and predictability in social relationships are highly valued by individuals. In 1952 Walker and Guest reported upon their investigation into assembly line work. Jobs which provided opportunities for social interaction were desirable; whilst machine pacing, repetitiveness and social deprivation were unsatisfactory. Satisfaction found its expression in behaviour as well as in attitude. Joan Woodward's aim was to test management theory against business practice. Her major conclusion argued in 1965 was that there seemed to be a pattern of organisation appropriate to the technology employed. A study by Burns and Stalker (1961) elaborated this same point, recommending a flexible 'organic' organisation for situations of rapidly changing objectives and technology; and a more formal 'mechanical' kind of organisation where objectives and technology are well established and not subject to rapid changes. A Liverpool University study of a large steel plant concluded in 1956 that although the effects of technical innovation may be to change radically the social structure, it is possible, given time and appropriate machinery for the redress of grievances, to assimilate it smoothly. The fashion for productivity agreements was largely created by managers at the Fawley Refinery of the Esso Company. In his book describing the Fawley Productivity Agreements (1964) Allan Flanders argued that managers ought to take the initiative in proposing changes in working practices to improve efficiency, and in working out the implications of such changes for wages, earnings, differentials and so on.

Social Science must be seen by managers as a method of analysis and of suggesting courses of action and decision. In particular the following problems are amenable to its concepts:

i.   Industrial conflict,
ii. Joint consultation and industrial participation,
iii. Incentive and motivation, and
iv. Technical and administrative change.

There is also now a good basis of Organisation Theory and experience in its practical uses. Much of this is described in greater detail in Chapter 19, Organisational Development.

BIBLIOGRAPHY

Urwick and Brech, *The Making of Scientific Management,* Pitman.

Vol. I.   *Thirteen Pioneers.*
Vol. II. *Management in British Industry.*
Vol. III. *The Hawthorne Investigations.*

Chapter 2

Processes

1. Seven Major Processes as Outlined by Fayol, Urwick and Others

Since Fayol first laid down a set of principles deduced from an analysis of his own practical working as a manager, the subject has been revised and added to by Urwick and others, so that the outlines of seven major processes of management are now recognised. The aspects of management known as the planning and executive functions have been sub-divided as follows:

Forecasting or predicting ⎫
Planning   ⎬ Planning function
Organising or preparing ⎭

Motivating or commanding ⎫
Controlling   ⎬ Executive function
Co-ordinating   ⎭

Around and through these six processes runs a seventh, communicating or explaining which may be likened to the life-blood without which the highly complicated heart of management will not beat (see Fig. 2.1). Each process is composed of two elements in varying degrees, the human element dynamics and the technical element mechanics, although by an over simplification the planning function is considered to be more concerned with things and the executive function with people.

A suggested mnemonic for remembering the names of these processes is the jingle 'Fond Parents Often Molly Coddle Children's Circulations'. The total task of management may be summed up as responsibility for welding into a single working force the three constituents, people, ideas and things; and how each process discharges part of this responsibility is, to begin with, better studied separately.

11

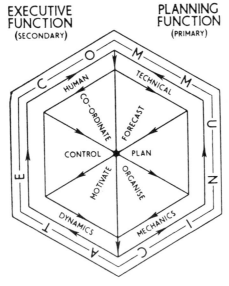

EXECUTIVE
FUNCTION
(SECONDARY)

PLANNING
FUNCTION
(PRIMARY)

Fig. 2.1. The heart of manage-
ment. Circulations of com-
munications around the various
processes, conveying planning
instructions outwards and feed-
ing back information on results
to improve the next cycle

2. Forecasting

Forecasting or looking ahead is generally the prerogative of the
Principals or Board of Directors, although it can enter into
decisions at any level. The interpretation of the objects of an
enterprise, the setting down of the main lines along which activity
to fulfil those aims is to be directed, comprises the formulation of
its policy. Policy is the very foundation of an organisation, and
must be based upon an adequate assessment of all the relevant
facts from without and within the company. The only reliable
method of arriving at important policy decisions is the systematic
approach based upon a precise diagnosis of the situation, the
collection and tabulation of all the facts, a dispassionate consideration and prognosis and the formulation of a logical conclusion. In
the simpler terms of a military appreciation the stages of looking
ahead are:

  i. Objective,
 ii. Information,
iii. Factors involved,
 iv. Possible alternatives and
  v. Plan selected.

Objectives may be as widely varied as economic forecasting, i.e. how much capital is required and which is the best source, estimating margins for tenders, the alternatives of buying and hiring plant, or the selection of an executive. Information may be in the form of trends indicated by control figures, market research results or interview tests. The final outcome may involve insurance cover, prices, estimated labour requirements or staff promotions.

Competent direction is an essential factor in efficient management, and requires the qualities of broad vision, clear and incisive thinking, courage, self-confidence, and a good judgement of men and situations.

3. Planning

The realm of direction is succeeded by the sphere of administration, where the ideas of policy laid down by the Board are interpreted by the managers and translated into instructions for action. Planning is that aspect of administration concerned with the particular rather than the general and is dependent upon reliable and accurate information and standards. By determining the broad lines of operations, the strategy or general programme, and choosing the appropriate methods, materials and machines for the most effective action, so planning issues the orders as to how, when and where work is to be carried out. Once again the military sequence for briefing is logical and complete:

i. Information on background,
ii. Intention proposed,
iii. Method to be adopted,
iv. Administrative details and
v. Intercommunication systems.

The process of planning usually refers exclusively to those operations concerned with, and the department responsible for, determining the manner in which a job is to be executed, i.e. the preparation of construction programmes in relation to time, method statements, drawing schedules, etc. However, the word 'planning' in the sense of forethought, can also include such activities as market research, training schemes and the recording of plant locations and availability. To be really effective planning must be simple, flexible, balanced and based upon accurate standards of performance determined by systematic analysis of observed and recorded facts. Planning is perhaps the most important tool of management, requiring intense application, precise attention to detail, imagination and a sound knowledge of technical theory, but is always a means and not an end in itself. In its application, full regard must be paid to the human needs of the organisation, for neglect may completely nullify an otherwise indispensable technique.

4. Organising

Organising provides the framework of management, the basic structure upon which the succeeding executive and supervisory functions can build in accordance with the policy principles determined by the directors. This is the other aspect of administration complementary to planning, and concerned with the more general selection of the people and the *modus operandi* necessary for the discharge of managerial responsibilities.

The process of organising or preparing comprises:

a. the definition and nominal distribution of the responsibilities and duties of the various executive and supervisory personnel forming the establishment of the enterprise,

b. the recording of the types of formal relationships existing between individual appointments, the pattern of accountability and theoretical paths of contact,

c. the formulation and installation of standard procedures, preferred methods of working and operating instructions for standard techniques.

Certain guiding principles can be discerned for designing the organisation structure, as follows:

i. Schedules of responsibilities, the organisation chart and standard procedures, should preferably be written down and distributed so far as applicable, for general reference purposes, to allow revision, and to preserve continuity despite transient personnel.

ii. When increasing size dictates the sub-division of responsibilities, this should be determined by functional or operational specialisation.

iii. A single head executive should be responsible to the policy-forming body for the carrying-out of all the operations of the business.

iv. Decentralisation of decision should be provided by the adequate delegation of responsibility, and any limitations should be specifically mentioned.

v. Clear lines of accountability should link the chief executive with all points of the organisation, and the integration of specialists should not interrupt the lines of command.

vi. The structure must be flexible enough to facilitate adjustments when circumstances change, but since endurance is the ultimate test of an enterprise's success, a formal outline and code are necessary to assure the continuous and effective function of the whole body despite fluctuating and mortal members.

vii. There is no typical organisation since consideration must be given to the individual characteristics of each undertaking. Similarly, since the personalities of key men provide the driving force of any living organism, adaptations must be found to utilise their strengths whilst protecting against their weaknesses.

In practice, organisation is a process of compromise calling for attributes of thoroughness, logical reasoning and patience.

5. Motivating

After direction and administration follows the more dynamic phase of executive function and supervision, each process the logical counterpart or corollary of those preceding. Thus it is useless to forecast or direct, without the supporting process of motivation to command the rank and file members of the team to pull their weight wholeheartedly. Without the willing co-operation or will to work of the workers, their desire to give of their best and enthusiasm for the aims of the venture, the brightest ideas of the directors and cleverest schemes of the planners and organisers, will be doomed to frustration and failure. Motivating is essentially a social process, the executive function of cultivating morale, inspiring loyalty to the leaders, and producing an emotional climate conducive to the proper fulfilment of all the tasks undertaken by the group.

A man is motivated when he actively *wants* to do something, and motivation covers all the reasons which underlie human behaviour and actions, including the negative fears of unemployment or punishment. The need for strict discipline in a commercial organisation is an indication that morale (or spiritual condition) is too low, and the positive incentive of reward is much the better method of improving the psychological situation. In order to achieve this desirable state of high morale it is necessary to:

i.   Arouse interest by keeping everyone informed of proposed developments and the progress of activities.
ii.   Foster enthusiasm by forwarding the attainment of legitimate personal and social satisfactions.
iii. Develop harmony and a sense of participation by joint consultation.
iv.   Enlist co-operation by providing reasonable continuity of employment and security for the future.
v.   Secure loyalty by studied fairness in allocation of duties, distribution of rewards, and administration of discipline, etc.
vi.   Promote keenness by fostering a sense of competition and group or personal achievement.
vii. Encourage self-discipline by developing a sense of responsibility and the enjoyment of trust.
viii. Inspire confidence and respect by fair judgement and impartial dealings with subordinates.
ix.   Ensure acceptance of the necessary rules and regulations by inspiring a sense of duty and a responsibility for the affairs of the organisation.
x.   Assist ambition by encouragement and the affording of opportunities for individual development.
xi.   Prevent frustration by providing a sympathetic and effective outlet for grievances and misunderstandings.
xii. Supply incentives by the introduction of financial rewards or status symbols.

Motivation can influence all fields of management, and take innumerable forms, from architectural competitions to company symbols, and joint consultation to bonus schemes, each facet designed to initiate a specific desire for action. To use a musical analogy, every form of motive is a variation on one of four themes: the love of accomplishment, affiliation, service and self, all potential springs of response in everybody. Finally it must be remembered that the tone of any undertaking is largely a reflection of the personality and outlook of its leader, for an organisation cannot fundamentally be better than its chief executive.

6. Controlling

The obverse of planning is the process of controlling, i.e. the comparison of actual performance with the planned standards, the application of corrective measures when and where necessary, and the recording of results so obtained to serve as future planning data. Whereas previous processes have been largely concerned with strategy, controlling is the tactical sphere of management, checking current achievements against predetermined targets and adjusting the deployment of resources to attain the desired objectives.

Such major fields as finance and production must be constantly inspected to ensure that working capital is being put to the most profitable use, and that programmes are adhered to in terms of output, cost and quality. Normally the board of directors are responsible for financial review, while more junior executives supervise production activities. Controlling comprises the functions of accounting, budgeting, costing and recording, all dependent upon the gathering and assessment of reliable information, whether to prompt short term reactions or provide long term experience.

Control information must

i. be separated according to responsibility,
ii. present results in a consistent manner,
iii. represent an appropriate time period,
iv. be available in time for effective decisions to be taken,
v. divert the minimum energies from primary functions,
vi. show clearly the deviations from plan or the exceptions to allowed tolerance.

Unnecessary information should be avoided since it is both wasteful and a hindrance.

Although control is effected via procedures and techniques, the human element is predominant, for the guidance and supervision of the field forces and their supporting services calls for quick decisions, a sense of fair play, the 'common touch' and unbounded tact.

7. Co-ordinating

The essential follow-up of organising is the process of co-ordinating, the linking together of the various members to constitute a practical ensemble, and the balancing of resources and activities to ensure complete harmony at every performance. Major aims of co-ordination are the prevention of separation into water-tight compartments as a consequence of specialisation, and the preservation of a recognisable unity throughout the framework of the enterprise. This tendency to separate into individual functions increases with the size of the organisation, so that

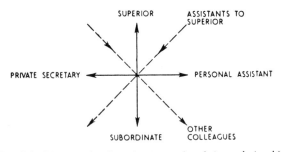

Fig. 2.2. Diagram showing the network of interrelationships

Fields / Processes	Finance	Design	Development	Marketing
Forecasting	Financial policy Investments Insurances			Sales policy Estimating
Planning	Cash requirements Supply of working capital Financial budget	Drawing schedule Accommodation schedule Cost analysis		Market research Advertising campaigns
Organising	Shares register	Check lists Standardisation		Check list for site visit report
Motivating	Dividends	Competitions	Sense of leadership in the industry	Advertising Public relations Discounts
Controlling	Useful ratios Accountancy Cost control Standard costing	Site reports Cost planning		Successful tenders percentage
Co-ordinating	Bank accounts	Comparison of drawings with bills of quantities	Seminars	
Communicating			Published papers Lectures to institutions	

Fig. 2.3. The responsibilities of management, showing the interrelation of

keeping the team together may become a vital task for a general manager.

Deliberate co-ordination of management may require specified mechanisms such as regular meetings to integrate ideas and actions, the establishment of additional communication systems for greater clarity and the pictorial presentation of responsibilities to assist co-operation between individuals. In particular the various functions and sub-functions must be correlated by the delegation of degrees of authority according to divisions of work, and the resulting network of interrelationships (Fig. 2.2) is an important factor in achieving union.

Successful co-ordination requires early introduction, direct personal contact, a reciprocal activity and continuous operation, but is achieved in the main by the efforts and skill of the individual manager with due regard to the overriding human factors involved.

Production	Maintenance	Personnel	Office	Purchasing
Output standards Labour require- ments	Buy/hire plant	Interviews Promotions Labour policy		Stockpiling Provisional orders
Construction pro- gramme Method statement Site layout Short term plans Method study	Plant availability	Training schemes Executive develop- ment Staff availability	Wall charts Office layout	Delivery pro- gramme Sub-contract time- table
Job specification Process chart Site organisation Work measurement	Planned mainten- ance lists Hire rates	Organisation chart	Forms design Office procedures	Standard procedures for inviting prices, ordering, progres- sing and hasten- ing
Working conditions Site welfare "Plan for Safety"		Incentives Company morale Company symbols Profit sharing		Penalty clauses
Progress record Plant utilisation Quality control Statistical methods	Spot inspections	Personnel reports Merit rating	Site office inspec- tions	Stores control
Site meetings Productivity committees		Suggestion box Joint consultation		Progressing deliveries Comparison of tenders

management processes with industrial divisions or fields.

8. Communicating

Finally there is that common denominator of every group activity, the need to transmit and share information, that makes communicating the ubiquitous handmaiden of the other six processes of management. Communications are the means employed by the leader to make known his predictions and inspire the necessary efforts, by executives to pass on their plans and instructions for action, and by the supervisors to co-ordinate activities and control operations. A means of contact between departments and individuals, and a channel for the distribution of knowledge are obvious fundamentals of management, but other equally important aspects of communicating are not always fully appreciated. To promote a better understanding by describing what is being done and why, and permit free expression of suggestions by all levels of personnel, encourages a sense of participation and prevents the friction of suspicion and misunderstanding, thus contributing to the maintenance of healthy morale. The circulation of knowledge, ideas, decisions and feelings, conveys essential blood to the living organs; while the two-way traffic of intelligence provided by the explaining of orders and the reporting back of progress, supplies the vital oxygen to the corporate body.

Although the process of communicating is never more than the indispensable 'tool' of leadership or supervision, nevertheless the ability to convey messages clearly, vividly and convincingly, by either speech or writing, is the key to the exercise of power among civilised people. The spoken word is more infectious and particularly useful for short term persuasion, while the written word is more permanent and hence more suitable for long term directions. To be effective both arts necessitate the possession of accurate facts, the use of simple, precise language, and the fluency of expression developed by constant practice. It is therefore essential to good industrial management, that every executive and supervisor should consciously, and regularly, cultivate proficiency in speaking and writing good, unambiguous English.

9. The Pyramid of Management

In conclusion, it should be appreciated how these individual processes support the eventual edifice of management. Each process stems logically from its forerunner, so that the gradual development of ideas, via the transition of means, proceeds to the ultimate transformation into deeds. Thus the overall manoeuvre of combining the individual components into one solid achievement, that is consequently greater than the sum of the separate units themselves, is accomplished by the various managerial levels as illustrated by Fig. 2.4 below.

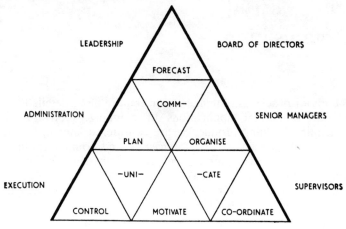

Fig. 2.4. Pyramid of management

This analogy also serves to show how motivation may be reserved as a function of the leaders.

The way in which the various processes are interwoven into the complete fabric of managerial responsibility, and affect the working of all fields of industrial activity, is demonstrated by the Schedule compiled as Fig. 2.3. This list of examples is not intended to be exhaustive, but merely to indicate the difference between fields of activity and management processes, and to show how the latter fulfil the functions of the former. Like the spectral colours of the rainbow, processes overlap or merge into one another, and the perfection of white can only be produced by the full utilisation and correct blending of all seven constituents. The criteria of successful management are:

a. achievement of the undertaking's prescribed purpose,
b. comparative productivity of the enterprise,
c. the contentment of the staff and employees. Although often considered last, the true satisfaction of the members of an organisation is all important, for a manager can only achieve his goal through the work of his subordinates.

BIBLIOGRAPHY

E. F. L. Brech, *Management, Its Nature and Significance*, Pitman, 1959.

Chapter 3

Organisation

The major processes of management require more detailed study, and the particular applications of planning, motivating and controlling building production are considered later in Chapters 13, 17 and 15 respectively; forecasting and communicating are enlarged upon in Chapter 4 under the headings of policy making, report writing, effective speaking and effective reading. Organisation, the basic structure underlying all management activities, deserves our first attention.

1. The Span of Control

As a business enterpise grows in order to undertake more work, and consequently employs more labour, the problem of co-ordinating the various activities and numerous personnel gradually expands beyond the capacity of one individual. It becomes necessary to delegate authority to assistants, so that first-hand information concerning operations is no longer entirely within the province of one man, but must be obtained by reference to others. The manager who has delegated responsibility to two subordinates remains accountable for their twin performances, and if their activities are interdependent, then he must also correlate the secondary relationship existing between the two of them. The total combination of such primary and secondary inter-relations that must arise between interlocking executives, increases progressively in the order 1, 3, 6, 10, 15, 21, 28, 36, 45, 55, etc. (see Fig. 3.1). Since there is a practical limit to the number of separate items to which the normal human brain can attend at any one time, there must be a definite limit to the span of responsibility that the average manager can competently control.

When deciding the range of a particular span of control consideration must therefore be given to the following factors:

a. The actual time required for giving decisions and guidance to subordinates.
b. The relative geographical location of subordinates and the consequent travelling time involved.
c. The complexity and variety of responsibilities concerned.
d. The personal character and emotional stability of the particular manager.

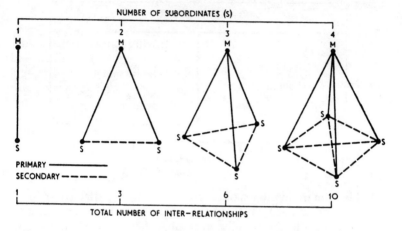

Fig. 3.1. The increasing span of responsibility

The specific span of control for a particular set of conditions thus requires considerable thought, and the resulting decision will largely depend upon a sound appraisal of the personnel aspect; but a total of 5, 6 or 7 is generally regarded as the maximum range under normal circumstances.

2. The Structure and the Parts of Division of an Undertaking

The organisation structure of an undertaking is the supporting framework designed to fulfil the twin functions of management, i.e. the planning and execution of that particular work for which the enterprise was intended. All of the general and specialist fields of operation must be allocated to a particular executive or supervisory post, so that nothing is overlooked nor yet overlapped.

In a one man firm, all the activities of management may be concentrated in one person, as illustrated in Fig. 3.2.

As the small business expands, the owner finds that he cannot control everything himself, so he engages staff and divides his responsibilities among them. The most logical division is into the specialist operations, the functions of general management perhaps being retained by the principal himself.

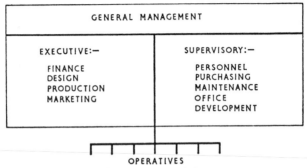

Fig. 3.2. Concentrated functions

This form of division is of course limited by the effective span of control permitted by circumstances, but certain fields of activity e.g. production, are usually more important than others so that sufficient grouping of ancillary functions can be achieved. A new chart of activities might be drawn as Fig. 3.3 which depicts the much larger and more complex structure now required to meet the different situation.

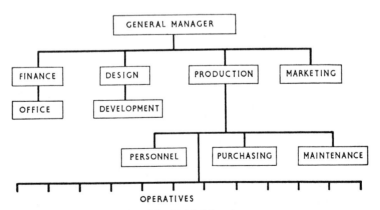

Fig. 3.3. Divided functions

With further expansion and additional staff, each of these main functions may be sub-divided into individual elements, e.g. marketing into estimating, public relations and quantity surveying. The still comparatively simple Fig. 3.3 would thus become much more complex, with each distinct function growing additional branches as shown in Fig. 3.4.

Fig. 3.4. Subdivision by elements

In a larger organisation it might become desirable to delegate responsibility for one or several major activities, by individual products, so that further subdivision could be as shown in Fig. 3.5.

When an enterprise has grown to national status it may be necessary to open branch offices and so delegate by geographical areas. Overall responsibility for certain functions may be retained at head office, with other functions reproduced at each area office as shown in Fig. 3.6.

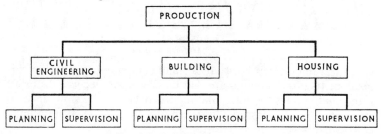

Fig. 3.5. Subdivision by products

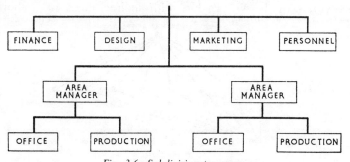

Fig. 3.6. Subdivision by areas

Just as the extent of an undertaking's divisions may vary, so may the form of its organisational structure differ. Since the purposes and personnel of different enterprises are peculiar to themselves, typical patterns can only be superficial, but three separate components can be identified.

The simplest form is commonly called the military pattern since it resembles the old-time army organisation. There is a direct line of authority from manager to workman, and Fig. 3.7 shows the

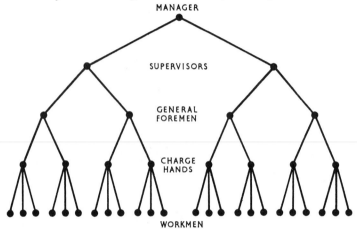

Fig. 3.7. Military pattern

structural lines of authority of a small company organised in this fashion. Its disadvantages are that messages can become distorted if the chain line is too long, and reports back may be slow since no stage can be by-passed. Furthermore the whole system may collapse if a key man is lost.

At the other extreme is the pattern of functional *specialisation* pioneered by F. W. Taylor, with indirect lines of authority

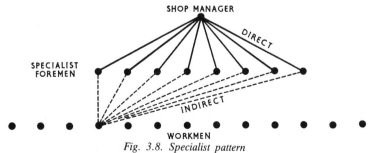

Fig. 3.8. Specialist pattern

between manager and workmen. The arrangement of authority as applied by Taylor to his machine shop is shown diagrammatically in Fig. 3.8, the foremen being individually responsible for separate aspects of planning and supervision. Despite the theoretical advantages of specialisation and a larger management staff this system is too complicated in practice and it is easy for a man with eight masters to evade his responsibilities.

A third form of organisation which combines features of the two previous alternatives, is that known as the line-and-staff pattern. This, like the military system, has a direct line of authority from the general manager to each workman, but in addition each executive has the assistance of functional specialists who are responsible for sections of the staff work. Modifications of this form of structure have been used in many large engineering works, and the scheme of authority illustrated in Fig. 3.9 is an example only of how it might be adapted for a medium sized building firm.

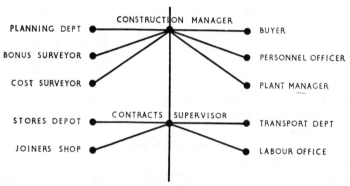

Fig. 3.9. Line-and-staff pattern

In practice, most organisation structures combine elements of both military and line-and-staff patterns, but from the preceding examples it will be evident that every company tree eventually resembles a pyramid, which may be either shallow or deep, depending upon the number of intermediaries in the chain of command between manager and operatives. A shallow structure possesses easy communications but is weaker managerially, and might be suitable for a firm manufacturing breeze blocks, where a proportion of faulty products would not be vital. But a company constructing mechanical excavators, where fine limits are essential and no rejects can be allowed, would require additional stages of supervision and inspection so that its structure would be deeper by

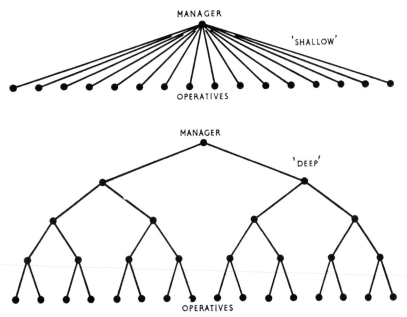

Fig. 3.10. The organisation pyramid

comparison. This relative peculiarity of an undertaking's skeleton is demonstrated in Fig. 3.10.

3. Direct, Lateral, Functional and Staff Relationships

An organisation structure containing any or all of the pattern features described previously, implies the existence of certain relationships between individual members. These relationships are part of the integrated plan for the working of the management machine, and the fulfilment of the co-operative task requires both the delegation of authority, and the allocation of responsibility. Four distinct types of relationships are recognised: direct, lateral, functional and staff, and one individual may have different relationships with different people.

1. *Direct relations* are those existing between superior and his subordinates, and involve the giving of instructions and the obligation to carry them out. This is a line relationship where the senior's authority is direct and his responsibility is general, and may occur at any level in the organisation and in every department.

2. *Lateral relations* are those which arise between executives or supervisors on an equal level of responsibility and answerable to the same superior. This is the reciprocal relationship apparent between working colleagues, responsible to a common senior for different divisions or separate elements of the enterprise. As equals they have no rights of authority, but must collaborate on matters of mutual interest and so co-ordinate their related activities.

3. *Functional relations* occur between a specialist and any other members of the organisation, in the course of his advisory duties. The specialist executive exercises only indirect authority over everyone but his own particular departmental subordinates, and gives his service usually through the line superior of the member concerned, and limited strictly to his isolated subject. This is a functional relationship with specialised responsibility, such as obtains between a technical expert and a production unit.

4. *Staff relations* imply no delegation of authority and carry only advisory responsibility. This relationship occurs mainly within the higher levels of an organisation, arising from the appointment of a personal assistant to an executive such as the managing director. A personal assistant represents his chief, and assists him to discharge the responsibility for co-ordinating line and functional executives by dispensing advice on his behalf, but it is only with his chief that there exists any formal relationship.

Relationship	Authority	Responsibility
Direct	Direct	General
Lateral	Equal	Co-operative
Functional	Indirect	Specialised
Staff	Representative	Advisory
Personal Staff	Nil	Personal

Fig. 3.11. Relationships in organisation

In addition there is the personal staff relationship such as exists between an executive and his private secretary, but no authority is involved and responsibility is purely personal.

A comparative table of relationships is given in Fig. 3.11, and a part of an organisation chart is depicted in Fig. 3.12 to show typical examples of these relations between members.

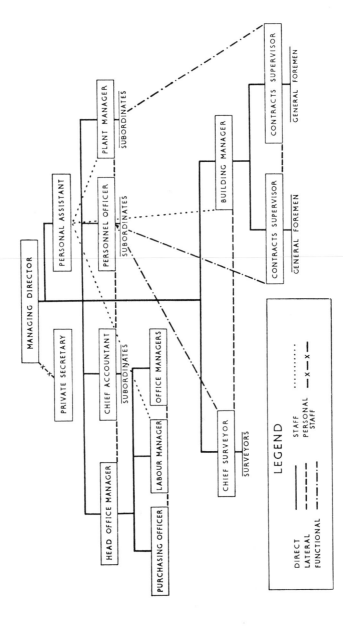

Fig. 3.12. Part of an organisation chart illustrating the coexistence of different relationships

4. The Nature of Responsibility, Authority and Accountability

To be given *responsibility* is to be commissioned or entrusted with a charge for which one must give an account; moreover one must answer for the manner of execution of those duties assigned. A manager is responsible for the forwarding of company policy, for the actions of every member of the organisation, and for the corporate results achieved. Real responsibility involves both a burden and a risk for it carries with it the corollary of personal sanctions of penalty or reward, and the former cannot exist without the presence of the latter.

In order to fulfil the obligations of his responsibilities an executive must at the same time also be invested with the requisite *authority*, the power to act and the right to enforce obedience to his commands. Responsibility without authority is frustrating, and authority without responsibility is pernicious: authority and responsibility must therefore correspond. The delegation of particular authority is one means of securing the co-ordination of individual efforts, by allotting the right to make decisions and to issue instructions governing the work of others.

When an executive deputes certain of his responsibilities to assistants, he retains full responsibility for due performance of the tasks devoluted and also for the acts of his subordinates. Thus he remains obligated to his own superior, and must decide how best to ensure that his subordinate does effectively perform those duties entrusted. This *accountability* can never be delegated nor divorced, and hence accountability to higher authority for the decisions and actions of subordinates is absolute and permanent.

5. Definition of Responsibilities

Since it is essential that responsibilities should be carried by individuals who receive the rewards for success and pay the penalties for failure, it follows that their duties must be clear-cut and well defined. Uncertainty about authority and responsibility always causes trouble, and it is more important that everyone should be fully acquainted with the organisation structure, than that it should be theoretically perfect. Efficient management requires a precise framework to obviate overlapping and duplication of effort, or the omission of essentials and other misunderstandings. The existence of a known stable structure designed specifically to perform an express purpose, provides a secure foundation for detailed planning and contributes to effective co-ordination and healthy morale.

Although an organisation chart is an illustration of the division of responsibilities, and gives a pictorial indication of the relationships arising, only the codified writing down of the tasks allocated to the various members of the enterprise, and of the formal inter-relations intended, can constitute the actual organisation structure.

Definitions should be drawn up for each individual officer, detailing his responsibilities, immediate superior and subordinates, any special duties and limitations, relevant functional contacts and compulsory membership of committees. These statements together with the organisation chart will then form the organisation manual, of which a personal copy should be given to every executive and supervisor. This manual will inevitably require continual amendment as the company develops, but its scope and value will increase with the size and importance of the undertaking.

6. Qualities of Management

In the previous chapter, reference was made to certain personal qualities that are desirable and helpful in executives, when fulfilling particular processes of management. All virtues would obviously find some place in the physical, mental and spiritual make-up of a manager, but a number of basic character traits are essentials. Such qualities as accuracy, determination, enthusiasm, initiative, integrity, loyalty, resourcefulness, self-confidence, and a balanced temperament are pre-eminent advantages, for the man at the top is peculiarly lonely and often self-dependent. Complementing these private attributes, is the vital ability to work in harmony with other people and contribute as a member of a team. One of the biggest problems is that of personal dealings with fellow executives, due to the conflicting human reactions that may arise between ambitious equals.

Nevertheless, the key quality required of a manager is that of *leadership*: the ability to inspire self-confidence among subordinates, to choose capable staff and knit them into a team with a common purpose, and to evoke by one's personality a loyalty which will make men follow and give of their best. From the leader must come the example, for his moral attitude will set the tone and his actions will be copied by the lower levels of supervision. The knowledge of how and when to praise or reprove, and the courage to admit an error and make necessary changes, are integral hallmarks of a true leader of men.

Since self-discipline by subordinates is not inherent, it is the manager's responsibility to engender and exact willing and intelligent obedience by the *development of good morale*. Morale is the human facet of management, a reflection of the contentment of the people composing an organisation. This is nowadays recognised to be of such importance that the personnel function is often reserved for a director. Human contentment is not ensured solely by wages and conditions, but by the overall climate of work so that the complete manager must also possess social skills. Mutual confidence requires full and frank information as to what is being done and why, an understanding of the other person's point of view, the judicious use of joint consultation, and participation in off-duty activities both educational and social. Employees must find satisfaction in their work, learn to feel that they matter, and have a conscious sense of personal dignity in their employment. The craftsman's pride in self-expression and creative achievement is an example of this factor. Finally a man's work should have a real meaning for him, and he must feel part of a purposeful and successful, co-operative undertaking.

To some extent qualities of character must be in-born, but latent attributes and skills can be developed by study, coaching, the exchange of views and opportunities for experience, with an increased professional competence as a result.

BIBLIOGRAPHY

Frederick Hooper, *Management Survey,* Pelican Books, 1960.

Chapter 4

Other Aspects

1. Policy Making

A Memorandum of Association (see Chapter 6) states the objects for which a limited company has been formed, thus explaining the commercial or industrial purposes of the enterprise, e.g. to design, build and sell houses. The interpretation of this charter constitutes the formulation of policy, which is the very corner-stone of management. Policy includes both the ethical principles on which the relations and conduct of the undertaking will be based, and the organisational structure that will be utilised in its business operations. Each element must be considered from two aspects, *a.* in relation to the outside world, and *b.* with respect to the people comprising the organisation.

Policy making is the responsibility of top management, usually the principals of a small firm, or the Board of directors in the case of a Company. Each major function should be represented on such a policy planning group, and if necessary heads of departments and other specialists should be co-opted to cover all relevant company activities. While the formulation of general policy may be an intermittent responsibility, in that formal Board meetings are usually held at intervals, e.g. monthly, it is nevertheless essential that policy should be kept flexible by continuous review without sacrificing consistency and stability.

Company policy is usually required for four main objectives: Finance, Sales, Personnel and Production (see Chapters 6, 7, 9 and 13), and must be founded upon consideration of factual information. Contributions may include records of past experience, the specialised knowledge of staff, technical and financial statistics, the results of market research or joint consultation, cost and output data, or reports of particular committees.

Policy decisions should be carefully defined in writing and personally explained to all concerned. They should indicate the main lines of sectional working and, wherever possible, include departmental budgets. As chief executive it will be the task of the Managing Director to reinterpret particular points, issue further instructions and make adjustments of *ad hoc* decisions when necessary, as part of the continuous process of communicating policy to subordinate levels.

The clear formulation of policy is the foundation of effective management, and contributes in many ways to the promotion of sound employee relations. It also provides a basis for assessing the results of management, by providing budgets and other criteria for measuring the achievement of purpose and the effectiveness of operations.

2. Investigating a problem

The factor common to all processes and activities of management is that of investigating a problem, so that the adoption of the correct procedure here is essential for optimum success. A snap judgement based on incomplete knowledge or personal instinct is risky, and may often be inaccurate and unfair.

A more effective approach is that of the scientist, who proceeds systematically to gather all the relevant data, analyse and classify his observations, develop a hypothesis that fits the known facts, test this conclusion by experiment and make any necessary modifications, formulate a law and use the final answer to predict what will happen in given circumstances. This method of reasoning, from the particular observation to the general law, is known as inductive thinking. Alternatively, to accept another observer's general hypothesis, and by reasoning backwards to deduce a particular consequence, is deductive thinking.

The scientific approach when applied to management problems, produces an ordered sequence of analysis that may be recommended:

1. *Define* the problem—a clear and accurate statement of the object or purpose of the exercise is essential.

2. *Obtain* the facts—all the relevant information, data, records and opinions concerning both the problem itself and all relevant factors.

3. *Examine* the facts—each piece of evidence must be critically but impartially weighed, and considered in relation to one another.

4. *Consider* the alternatives—the arguments for and against each line of action open, and each possible plan, must be thoroughly explored before finally deciding which course to adopt.

5. *Act* on the decision—ways and means must be settled, and the selected plan developed in sufficient detail as to how, when, where and who, to enable clear instructions to be issued for its execution.

6. *Check* the results—it is important to check that the correct action is taken, and to follow up the development to ascertain that the desired result is actually achieved.

This sequence resembles the form of a military appreciation, and the headings used there: object, information, factors, courses and plan, can provide an easy way to remember the proper steps for everyday use.

3. Taking Decisions

The aptitude for taking decisions is the chief quality that distinguishes a manager from a technologist, for decision is an indispensable part of leadership. Investigating a problem should approach to a science, but ultimate success will still depend upon the art with which a decision is taken, for the final hurdle of choosing between this, rather than that, is usually the hardest test. Moreover, as every sea bather knows, the longer a decision is deferred, the more difficult it becomes to resolve.

It is seldom possible, nor is there always the time, to obtain all the relevant facts, so that a decision is often a choice betwen alternative risks or probabilities. Indeed there are times when it is more important that some decision shall be made, rather than that the decision itself shall be perfectly correct. Making a rapid decision calls for a certain amount of moral courage, and this is even more apparent when it becomes necessary to stick to that decision in the face of criticism or opposition.

Making up one's mind in this fashion demands the ability to comprehend clearly, and assess accurately, a wide range of factors and alternatives, so that intense concentration is required for a short period. This sudden concentration of thought can be cultivated by practice, while the ability to sense a situation and exercise a right judgement will improve with experience.

Making known a decision should follow the sequence of military orders, i.e. information, intention, method, administration, inter-communication and questions, with the accent on explanation of full facts of the situation. In industry, however, it is advisable to request or suggest rather than instruct, and people will follow more readily when they understand the factual background and believe in the necessary action.

4. The Use of Committees and Groups

There are three alternative ways of dealing with a situation or settling a problem:

1. by imposing a solution either from above or below,
2. by accepting a compromise reached by bargaining,
3. by agreeing to the best answer arrived at after joint discussion.

The first method implies the use of force, which emphasises a permanent division, since it represents either a victory to be maintained or a defeat to be revenged at the next opportunity. Equally, method two is an uneasy armistice decided by relative powers, rather than upon true assessment of the facts. By contrast, the employment of discussion ensures a genuine solution based upon conviction, with the maximum chance of acceptable and harmonious action. Thus committees or informal group meetings can play an important part in the organisational structure.

Committees can be used for different purposes with appropriately varied membership as follows:

a. as an advisory body such as a site safety committee, with elected representatives from each activity, for the purpose of deliberating on particular problems and so assisting an executive by combining the total knowledge and experience of its members,

b. as a means of consultation, e.g. a planning meeting, where the members appointed by reason of their individual functions, contribute their different viewpoints and so ensure that all aspects are properly considered,

c. as a channel for information and a method of communication, usually between a superior and his immediate subordinates, as for example when a contracts manager meets his supervisors to receive their weekly progress reports and pool their resources,

d. as a process of co-ordination usually between a specialist and several production units, such as a transport manager allocating his daily vehicle tasks to meet the requirements of the respective general foremen.

It is important that the number of members on a committee should be kept to the minimum for optimum results, and that everyone, especially the chairman, understands the correct procedure for the conduct and recording of formal meetings. Moreover, it must be remembered that committees cannot take decisions, and the person responsible must issue instructions and be accountable for the results. When used properly, these committees can fulfil a vital role in judicious management.

5. Using the "Exception" Principle

It is essential, particularly in a large concern, to protect the management from being swamped by detail, and this can be achieved by employing the *exception* principle to separate routine work from the exceptional. By establishing standards, it is possible to concentrate attention on deviations from standard, or the exception, thereby limiting the need for investigation to the essential points. A manager should receive only condensed, summarised and comparative reports, preferably vetted by a subordinate, with all the exceptions to the past averages or to the normal clearly indicated, both the especially good and the particularly bad deviations. This will allow him to review the whole position in a few minutes, and so leave him free to attend to the broader issues of policy and personnel.

Another example of the use of the exception principle is provided by the instance of foremen whose respective duties make regular contact, but who usually manage to sort out their differences themselves. Only in the exceptional case of their failing to reach agreement, do they refer to a superior for arbitration. Most wall chart systems and other forms of comparative progress

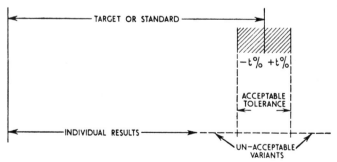

Fig. 4.1. Production tolerances

equipment, also employ the exception principle in a visual form, by exposing a brilliant colour or an unusual design to catch the eye, and so drawing attention to any deviations, while leaving the *as programmed* part unemphasised.

Other applications of the exception principle include: minimum levels for prompting the re-ordering of general stores, standard costs, production tolerances (see Fig. 4.1), concrete aggregate sieve analysis specifications, British Standard engineering brick sizes, and numerous other similar techniques.

The common aim of all these exception principle applications is to single out the exceptions for attention, correction, or rejection.

6. Reports and Report Writing

Written reports are an essential part of good communications, the life-blood of business management (Chapter 2), and serve two main purposes:

a. Regular condensed reports for comparative purposes, as mentioned in the previous section, and

b. Occasional fully documented reports to guide major policy decisions as referred to in section 1 of this chapter

Condensed reports, like military reconnaissance reports, are intended to supply the important ideas as quickly as possible, with details afterwards if required. They should therefore be divided into two parts:

1. A brief summary of the principal points.

2. The detailed information, arranged under headings, and shown where possible in tabular form.

Documented reports should be composed of five parts:

1. An introduction giving—reason for the report—purpose of the report (terms of reference)—source of facts if historical—method of securing facts if by research—statement of main ideas.

2. A summary of parts 3 and 4.

3. The main body divided into sections and subsections each accompanied by its own relevant data.

4. General conclusions reached, and any recommendations.

5. Appendices such as tables, specimen forms, sketches, etc.

Reports generally should include the name of the author, the date, an appropriate Title page, and an index if necessary.

The use of plain and direct English in report writing is as important as the structure, if the object of transferring ideas from one mind to another is to be fully achieved. A golden rule is to select those words that exactly convey the meaning of the writer, and use no others. Use short compact sentences, and omit superfluous words or padding.

When writing, it is essential to imagine the reaction of the intended reader, so that nothing is taken for granted. Only by thinking for others, by simplicity, and the correct use of vocabulary, is it possible to avoid that confused expression or unintelligible jargon that inevitably leads to misunderstanding.

Having chosen the right words, it is still necessary to arrange them in an orderly fashion, to observe all the grammatical conventions, and finally to employ good English idiom so that the composition, while correct, is also human and lively. Correct spelling, and clear punctuation should complete the written presentation of our knowledge or ideas.

A good report, like a successful fashion model, requires both the correct shape and the right clothing.

7. Effective Speaking

Speaking is the universal means by which we convey information, thoughts and ideas to the minds of other people. Speech is the every day vehicle for inter-communication whether it be a conversation between friends, a business conference or technical report, the patter of a salesman or a public lecture. A knowledge and understanding of the basic principles underlying this particular accomplishment may mean the difference between success and failure in a manager's career. The qualifications of a successful speaker include:

    a. personality and determination,
    b. faith in himself and his message,
    c. an ability for composition and delivery,
    d. a sound knowledge of his subject, and
    e. a large and varied vocabulary.

Of these the latter three can be developed by constant practice.

Vocabulary includes both a knowledge of the meaning of words and of their correct pronunciation. Exercises such as appear in certain magazines can materially help to increase one's word power. Choice of words is of the highest importance and should always be specific, personal and appropriate to both the speaker and the listener. Words that imitate the idea they convey or are suggestive of their meaning, e.g. bang or shudder, add vividness and clarity to vocal expression.

All forms of speech are essentially attempts to persuade other people to adopt or confirm a certain belief, or to begin or continue a particular course of action. The minds and hearts of others can be influenced through the use of the techniques of persuasion in five principal ways, by

1. the personality of the speaker,
2. the use of explanation,
3. the force of logical reasoning,
4. the power of suggestion, and
5. psychological appeals to human needs, wants, desires, instincts and sentiments.

Although combinations of all these methods may be used at any occasion, each is peculiarly applicable to a particular form of verbal activity.

Conversation, the basic source of all effective speaking, is primarily a spontaneous exchange of ideas between two or more persons. Nevertheless the basic rules of this type of situation should be studied, if the essential qualities of personality are to be developed for more formal occasions. The rules for a good conversationalist are to:

1. Ask questions, to make the other person feel important.
2. Discuss common topics to avoid confusion and stealing the limelight.
3. Be brief at each opportunity, and so maintain interest.
4. Be a good listener to improve one's acceptability.
5. Be complimentary but always sincere, and relationships will improve.
6. *Do not* argue, correct another speaker, or score off others.

Industrial conferences are arranged for the purpose of accomplishing specified business objectives. The essential elements here are detailed organisation, a carefully chosen presentation to suit the particular members attending, and precise instructions and explanations. Exposition, the chief facet, can be assisted by examples, statistics, illustrations and visual aids.

Oral reports are usually of a technical nature and require the gathering and presentation of either historical or research data. The logical consideration of evidence and deduction of proof should follow the same pattern as recommended in section 2.

Modern advertising makes continual use of the power of suggestion, by presenting stimuli to conjure up pleasurable or desirable associations in the mind of the prospective buyer. The salesman, having obtained an interview by his pleasing personality, and after convincing himself by a thorough knowledge of his product, suggests confidence by his direct manner and positive language. Subtle suggestion may imply that because a popular sports idol uses a certain commodity then every aspiring sportsman should do the same, or associates a particular brand of article with an attractive film starlet. The art of selling also includes appeals to human needs, e.g. food, clothing or shelter, and human wants such as luxuries, material possessions and status symbols.

Public speaking is the culmination of a speaker's training and requires all the previous techniques of persuasion. In addition, the orator may directly or unobtrusively, appeal to the human desires for power or self-esteem, and the instincts of self-preservation or curiosity, or call upon the energy of emotions, the compulsion of convention or the urge for unity.

A successful public speech requires careful and detailed preparation, beginning with the collection and sifting of available material, suitable illustrations and authoritative quotations. Then the outline must be constructed, stage by stage, i.e. title, general and particular objectives, means of attaining the purposes, introduction, main and supporting points of discussion, and conclusion. Upon this skeleton must be worked the gathered material to produce an effective and well proportioned speech.

Whether a speech should be written out in full or committed to memory is largely a matter for personal choice. Writing facilitates criticism and rehearsal and is essential when an address must be word perfect, while extemporisation is more flexible and allows advantage to be taken of atmosphere and inspiration. If notes are used they should be brief, a synopsis of main headings, and should be consulted openly.

To summarise, an effective speaker should

a. have something worthwhile to say,

b. think out and prepare his words before delivery, and

c. remember that only constant practice will create perfection.

8. Effective Reading

Few people read at the level of skill and speed that their innate capacities make possible. Inefficient reading results chiefly from bad habits, incomplete concentration and an unnecessary time-lag between the act of seeing and the mental interpretation of what is seen.

With intensive training it is possible to increase one's general reading rate by 25 to 100 per cent and simultaneously to sharpen comprehension and strengthen retention. For a business executive with scores of papers to peruse each day, e.g. reports, trade journals, minutes of meetings, etc., such increased efficiency could well be worth a few months systematic and conscientious training.

During recent years, colleges, big business and the armed services in the United States have developed reading clinics for improved reading habits, with the emphasis on comprehension, efficient techniques, retention and recall, perception training and vocabulary study.

Methods of achieving faster comprehension are:

i. Make time for more reading and allocate regular periods for concentrated practice.
ii. Aim to find the author's main theme and follow his pattern of thinking, ignoring the details and concentrating on ideas.
iii. Exercise your intelligence by tackling more profound or difficult books.
iv. Budget your time by setting targets for completion.
v. Pace yourself by keeping up throughout to a measured potential speed.
vi. Develop habits of immediate concentration by purposefully looking for broad concepts and quickly finding an interest in a book.

Better techniques of reading include:

i. The elimination of bad habits such as inner speech, lip movements or whispering, and regression or unnecessary checking.
ii. The cultivation of an aggressive attitude, to strip a page down to its essentials and to grasp its total meaning rapidly and accurately.
iii. Skimming where possible by ignoring unimportant, linking words, without missing anything of crucial importance.
iv. Reading critically, sceptically, resisting the mesmerism of print and developing a touchstone for judgement by wide reading.

The eye moves across a printed line in a series of jerks and only sees when it stops. Beyond the narrow area of focus is a larger field of vague peripheral vision. Perception can be trained to make greater use of peripheral vision, to increase the span of recognition and to reduce the fixation time.

A larger vocabulary can be built up by conscious study, and retention and recall improved by practice and tests. There are several good training manuals that will repay the student for careful study and considerable practice, but more effective reading is a continuous, never-ending process.

9. Social Responsibility

The industrial manager has obligations to three different social groups:

    a. the shareholders or directors who have appointed him,

    b. the human beings whose labour he manages,

    c. the general community, both local and national.

To his employers a manager has a two-fold responsibility, to safeguard the capital invested in plant, machinery, etc., and to earn profits as interest on money loaned to the enterprise. These fairly obvious responsibilities are discharged by means of various administrative procedures or control techniques, such as accountancy. It must be remembered however, that industrial activities are subject to the same moral code which governs all other aspects of life, so that the manager must ensure that his business policies do not conflict with his other obligations.

With his employees the manager must preserve the dignity of human labour, and determine his dealings with equity and justice. Moreover, work must be arranged so that it requires some measure of initiative and responsibility, in order to provide the worker with social satisfaction and status. Again, the individual's contribution to the total effort must be openly recognised so that pride in work and the creative instinct are given outlets.

Effectiveness and economy of operation must be attained by the promotion of co-operation through the personnel function, by an understanding of the part played by human emotions, and by the provision of improved working conditions. Finally, the manager must inculcate in his workers a sense of their own responsibilities, for effective results require the combined efforts of both capital and labour. The manager's obligation to his employees can be summed up as the promotion of their happiness and contentment, or morale.

From the community, management has received labour, materials and amenities, and hence owes a responsibility to supply goods or services of the right quality at reasonable prices. This involves an obligation to ensure the maximum utilisation of the undertaking's productive potential, and the most effective use of its resources, in order to satisfy the current needs or desires of the community and to maintain a proper balance between the various consumers. To the local community, the manager must recognise his responsibility to provide suitable and regular employment for the citizens, and to respect or improve the physical and social amenities of the district, when considering such matters as waste disposal and building design.

Some of these latter obligations are not so immediately obvious, or require such a high level of competence, that this particular field is a good example of the need for training for management.

BIBLIOGRAPHY

Sir Ernest Gowers, *The Complete Plain Words*, H.M.S.O., 1960.
Norman Lewis, *How to Read Better and Faster*, Thos. T. Crowell Co.
Peter Westland, *Teach Yourself Public Speaking*, English Universities Press.
Huston, Sandberg & Mills, *Effective Speaking in Business*, Prentice-Hall.

Chapter 5

The Purpose of Industry in Society

1. The Demands of Society

The ever-changing economic climate, the world energy crisis, Britain's membership of the European Economic Community, the demand that organisations should be socially responsible, and the insistence that the whole decision-making process in business be shared, have led to much new thinking about the purpose of industry in society.

The frontier discussion meeting on 'Industrial Growth and the Demands of Society' held in 1973 by the B.I.M. was announced as follows:

'The last decades have seen a remarkable growth of the economies of the industrialised areas of the world, but resulting affluence has brought its own problems. Social demand, for example in relation to education, health, urban renewal, transportation, housing and environment, is becoming the major claimant for public investment in most of the 'developed' countries and could easily absorb all the products of increased economic growth to be expected in the present decade. In addition, problems of scale and excessive centralisation of government activity is producing in many affluent societies an increasing alienation of the individual, with difficult manifestations which range from apathy to violence. As prosperity grows, aspirations become generalised both within and between countries, leading to strong currents of equalitarianism. Technological development, on which growth of the economy depends, is increasingly distrusted, especially by the young, and social environmental obstruction of plans for power stations, nuclear reactors, pipelines and oil refineries may well delay general solutions of the energy problem. These matters are of deep concern to industry and necessitate much re-thinking in terms of long-term self-interest; they demand also a new type of relationship between industry and government in which firms can be seen to be contributing more directly to the attainment of national goals'.

The speaker, Dr Alexander King, Director General for Scientific Affairs O.E.C.D., proposed that 'The real limits to growth are not likely to be material, but social, political and managerial'.

This interest in social values has come out of the impact of social and behavioural sciences, and one result of the soul-searching and questioning in Great Britain has been that private enterprise is increasingly being attacked. In a period of recession a section of public opinion holds business responsible for failing to meet its expectations; and high prices, unemployment, and a lower standard of living may be seen as measures of business and management failure.

What is the case for business, and how can management set the record straight?

2. The Role of Industry

Dr. A. C. Hutchinson, managing director of B.D.H. Chemicals, in a lecture given to the Institution of Works Managers, described 'The Role of Industry in Society' in terms of conflict theory. The business situation is illustrated in the diagrams (see Figure 5.1) where six groups exert pressure on a company, each offering a contribution, and each deriving benefits to satisfy its particular needs. All groups – government, community, customers, shareholders, employees and suppliers – share a common interest that the

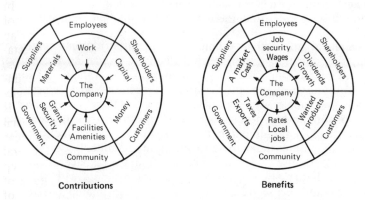

Fig. 5.1. The role of industry in society (after A. C. Hutchinson)

enterprise will continue and grow, so that they will share in the increased prosperity. No group therefore can afford to be too greedy, and hence a dynamic equilibrium is established between the contenders, based upon a controlled conflict of interests. Only one group (the employees) is in touch with all the others; hence they must hold the balance although they are an interested party. In a modern company all up to and including executive directors are employees, and must share in the arbitration role. Since the end of the 1939/45 war, governments have increasingly taken over this role, by price, wage and dividend restraints, and this distortion has damaged both industry and commerce, and inhibited growth and investment.

3. The Function of Profit

Britain enjoys a mixed economy, where private enterprise and public authorities operate side by side in the national interests. Industrial enterprises such as manufacturing, construction, agriculture and quarrying produce the required goods, and commercial institutions like insurance, banking and building societies provide the necessary services. This is the wealth-producing sector that funds the Welfare State, our cultural life and all the advantages of an advanced technological civilisation. This small over-crowded island of necessity must import a large part of its food and raw materials, and our balance of payments is dependent upon both the visible and invisible exports of industry and commerce. Monopolies and restrictive practices are controlled by legislation, whilst free competition ensures that failure to maintain an output greater than the input leads to liquidation or bankruptcy.

Central and local government, health authorities and centres of higher education, are supported wholly or in part by taxation or rates levied upon private individuals and corporations. Nationalised industries and public utilities, such as coal, electricity, railways, canals, water boards and the Post Office, are required to be profitable and produce a modest return on their investments, but there is no similar penalty for failure. Their monopolistic positions allow them to raise prices unrestrainedly despite user councils, or else to demand subsidies from the taxpayer. Competition with the State is restricted, as for example with the Post Office, and this sector already absorbs approximately 60% of the gross national product. The experience of the building industry *vis-à-vis* local authority direct labour organisations, and the civil service revelations made by Leslie Chapman in his book *Your Disobedient Servant,* suggest that there is no effective alternative to the discipline of competition. The measure of success in a capitalist society is of course profitability, and boards of directors are responsible to their shareholders for keeping the company solvent and ensuring an acceptable return on their capital. But in both private and state-owned companies employees must appreciate that their living standards and their security of a good life are equally dependent upon the successful management of productive enterprises. Similarly, executives, supervisors and workpeople must understand that profit is a real and necessary condition for the survival of every company. Provided that a business is run in socially acceptable ways (more of this later), profits are a guide to efficiency, a sound test of performance and a stimulation to management morale. Profit may also lure capital onto untried trails, so that research and invention are encouraged, and innovation rewarded. It is no coincidence that the French word for contractor is 'entrepreneur', for the construction industry is truly the epitome of private enterprise.

Profit is what is left after all costs and overheads have been deducted from the price or contract sum. Being also the product of turnover multiplied by the profit margin, it is difficult to increase overall profit by maximising the one without damaging the other component. Since the would-be entrepreneur must provide the correct product/service, at the right time, at a price that the market is prepared to pay, maintaining the optimum balance is a constant pre-occupation of the commercially minded manager. Moreover, there are other more subtle factors such as reputation and public responsibility (e.g. safety) which must be fulfilled to ensure long-term profitability.

Much of the present-day controversy surrounding profit is not about the making but the distribution. Examination of the public accounts of almost any sizeable company will show that the shareholders receive a modest return on their risked capital, whilst the lion's share goes to the government in taxes, and what is left is necessarily ploughed back into the business to furnish new investment. A typical example is shown in Fig. 5.2.

Perhaps the cause of much dissatisfaction lies in the apparently insoluble desire to combine maximum personal liberty with a continued expansion of general prosperity, and the elimination of those inequalities which generate so much envy. It would seem that the U.S.A. has attained immense prosperity and apparent

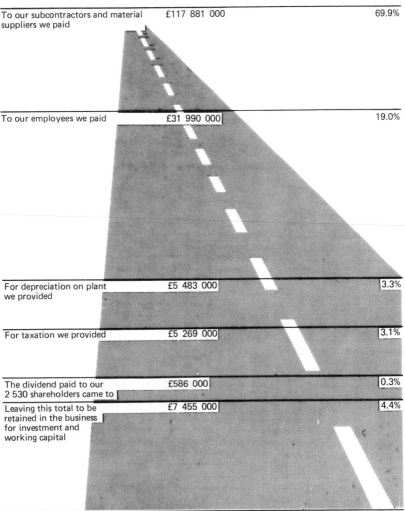

Our turnover was £168 664 000

To our subcontractors and material suppliers we paid	£117 881 000	69.9%
To our employees we paid	£31 990 000	19.0%
For depreciation on plant we provided	£5 483 000	3.3%
For taxation we provided	£5 269 000	3.1%
The dividend paid to our 2 530 shareholders came to	£586 000	0.3%
Leaving this total to be retained in the business for investment and working capital	£7 455 000	4.4%

In this diagram, the figures are represented by areas of the road in perspective.

Fig. 5.2. Where does the money go? (from Sir Alfred McAlpine Goup of Companies Report to Employees 1977)

liberty but at the expense of inequalities like poverty and rebellious minorities. At the other extreme the rival world power, the U.S.S.R., has achieved technical and military prosperity with nominal equality, but at the near total loss of freedom to choose. Great Britain appears to have fallen in between, still with personal liberty and comparative equality, but a will-o'-the-wisp prosperity.

4. The Social Conscience

Profit then is but one objective among many, for through the framework of law, the development of mass education, and more rapid communication, companies are being held accountable for the quality of peoples' life and its values. There is strong pressure for industry to demonstrate its increased awareness of social responsibility, e.g. the quality of environment, job security and satisfaction, opportunities for the underprivileged, and consumerism, and policies and actions must not only be right, but must be capable of being convincingly defended before reasonable men. Moreover, a good board of directors must be sensitive to the need to carry their employees with them in most of their important decisions. This social responsibility is both a corporate and a personal matter, and each individual manager must contribute to the development of the aims of his own community. A truly professional manager should play an active part in both social and political activities, and contribute his time, his acquired knowledge and his accumulated experience to the solution of the problems of the community as a whole. American corporations particularly set a good example of service to the community, and by so doing transform their public relations from publicity into genuine concern with the public. In the years ahead few companies will be able to develop and prosper unless they take full account of the human factors, and interpret their business objectives in ways that also make sense in social terms.

Yet this proper anxiety about industry's social conscience must not be allowed to obscure the fact that specific policies on such issues as pollution control, the employment of minorities, and safety at work, are properly the responsibility of government and Parliament. The prime duty of industrial management, within the context of its general obligations to society and enacted legislation, must remain to deploy and operate the assets under its control to their maximum economic advantage – in the interests of us all.

5. Putting the House in Order

When a company becomes very big and hence very powerful, it runs the danger of developing a contempt for criticism – perhaps even from its own customers. The new generation of young people who have been specifically trained for management may also show a certain arrogance, through feeling that they are the only ones who have been specially educated. Both of these pitfalls must be avoided, and management must realise that its privileges of power and protection must be exercised with great care if they are to be preserved. The need to include social as well as financial considerations when it comes to defining the modern ideal of corporate responsibility, means that major companies should spell out the business code they practise. If the image of management is to show any marked improvement, then it must define its aims for business growth, and involve more people intelligently in the economic and social changes that are taking place. Only in this way can it encourage trade unions, which are naturally resistant to change, to become more receptive and co-operative. Since business is central to the general standard of living and quality of communal life in an industrialised society, good relationships in this field will also influence practices in many other spheres of human endeavour. There must therefore be an ethical dimension in corporate activity, and it is must be seen to be there.

6. Getting the Record Straight

The lack of any coherent input from the business community into the nation's economic policies has for too long allowed destructive propaganda full reign. Many people assume capitalism is a vicious and outmoded way of running things, simply because they have never heard the other side of the argument. This dangerous trend must not be allowed to go on, and more industrialists (like the group Aims of Industry) ought to be organising support for their beliefs, and helping to thrash out policies designed to achieve profitable goals in the true interests of the nation. The distorted image of industry is a prime cause of poor recruitment to production engineering and construction, and there is an urgent need for better communication between schools and commerce and industry. The lack of true knowledge in schools about the industry that supports us all, requires a serious public relations programme to polish the tarnished image of manufacturing and industrial management among most school-leavers.

It is a trait of human nature to be suspicious of what it doesn't understand, and false basic assumptions have led too many students and academics to condemn industry and commerce. Business men need to do a far better job of explaining the true purpose of industry, and closing the attitude gap. The wealth-creating activities of industry and commerce in fact sustain the arts and scholarship; and industry must now accept a large part of the responsibility for convincing the rest of the population that the future prosperity and welfare of this country are in the hands of those who work in productive industry and creative commerce. True comparability between public service and private industry must also reward the engineers rather than the bureaucrats. Only in this way can we attract sufficient talent away from the administrative public service and into productive industry, the true servant of society.

The continuing world-wide recession of the 1980's and the resulting scourge of massive redundancies are combining to teach the public at large the 'fundamental and essential role of business as the prime creator of wealth and, therefore, of employment in our society'. This was the aim of the Business Education Campaign launched in 1978 by Denys Randolph, Chairman of Wilkinson Match, and the Institute of Directors. In the words of Bill Moore, president of the Contractors Plant Association, in his new year message via *Contract Journal*, January 3 1980, 'Protracted and serious inflation and events in the oil supply world . . ., have at last brought home the fact that across-the-board economic growth cannot be assumed to go on for ever. The country now has painfully to choose between rival growth priorities, on the basis of genuine principles and of true merit, and this is, I believe, a fundamental change of attitude that will increasingly be seen throughout the next decade'.

It is Government's responsibility to create the environment within which industry and the services can operate effectively, and to achieve this it must be counselled by those whose special skills and knowledge are crucial to the production of the nation's industrial and commercial wealth. For this reason the British Institute of Management produced the Managers Manifesto in 1978, to urge on the political parties the need to create the right environment to enable managers to raise the commercial, industrial and administrative performance of the nation. 'Good management for a prosperous Britain' sets out those policies that managers want to see included in the manifestos of all the political parties, and followed, steadily and consistently, by Government.

The Industrial Society has produced 'The Challenge of Industry' Programme, a series of highly participative two-day conferences for sixth form pupils of secondary schools. The aims are: to increase understanding of the necessary place of industry and commerce in the creation of the nation's wealth; to present the need in industry for able young people to tackle the problems and thus make a contribution to economic prosperity and the need for a positive and open-minded attitude toward industry; to recognise that in a free society, the need to manage and lead by persuasion and consent and to understand and accept the right of employees to have their interest represented by trade unions; and to build a closer relationship between schools and industry. The success of these conferences depends upon the hard work and enthusiasm of group advisers, line managers seconded by member companies and practising trade unionists, who lead the examination of subjects relating to problems that arise in the management of people at work.

In 1981 the Institution of Metallurgists published the proceedings of a conference that it held on the subject of 'Reversing Britain's Industrial Decline'. One of the many positive papers, by Kenneth Adams, suggested that the engineering professional institutions who are now taking a greater interest in general social and economic problems, hold one of the keys to stemming the decline. He wants them to communicate with the public at large, so that attitudes can be changed. Adams points out that 'When we British recognise the necessity, the value and the virtue of our work we perform it as well, and often better, than any other nation. Our farming performance demonstrates this.' One very obvious demonstration of changing attitudes is the way in which many different areas of the country, via newspapers and postal cancellations, vie with each other to attract industry by means of grants, loans and rent concessions.

7. The Place of Construction in the Community

As well as providing employment for many people (11% of the gross national product in 1973), the construction industry also extends and improves the fabric and facilities of society. In the words of H.R.H. the Duke of Edinburgh at the start of 1984's celebrations of the 150th Anniversaries of The Chartered Institute of Building and the Royal Institute of British Architects: 'Everything in our surroundings that is not part of the natural environment belongs to what has been described as the built environment. Most of the built environment in which most people have their being, is the product of builders and architects and that is the measure of the influence of building on the human community.' Similarly, the Institution of Civil Engineers which marked the 150th Anniversary of its Royal Charter in 1978, adopted Thomas Tredgold's definition of civil engineering as 'the art of directing the Great Sources of Power in Nature for the use and convenience of Man'. Construction thus meets the most fundamental need of the community for shelter, whilst also providing the material rewards of applying scientific knowledge and method to the practical benefit of mankind.

Since the constructor – be he architect, builder or engineer – is concerned with the fundamental development of modern civilised society, he must therefore carry a great responsibility for the direction and speed of evolution of our civilisation. In 1966, the Council of Engineering Institutions reognised the responsibilities of engineers as members of society by setting a compulsory paper on 'The Engineer in Society' in part 2 of their examination. The purpose was to show the wider implications of engineering by introducing the student to his responsibility for the social and economic results of technological decisions. Whilst the technical ability of the craftsman is still essential to industrial prosperity, the role of the professional constructor requires much more. Since 1974 The Institution of Civil Engineers has included 'Place of the engineer in the community' topics as part of its Professional Interview for corporate membership.

'The engineer in the community' part of the essay examination is subdivided as follows: the engineer as a professional; economics; politics, environment; and working overseas. All three learned societies, C.I.O.B., I.C.E. and R.I.B.A., publish their own 'Rules for professional conduct', but no code can hope to encompass every situation, e.g. military growth or work for an evil regime, and ultimately each case becomes a problem of personal ethics. The impartiality of professional contract administrators is en- shrined in the various Conditions of Contract, and yet contention is rife and arbitration a growing sector. When the professional is a full-time employee of the promoting authority, what happens to independence? Engineers as well as architects must take account of the aesthetics of a structure. But should one innovate when in Thomas Edison's opinion 'invention is one part inspiration and 99 parts perspiration', and the path from conception to delivery is often long and nerve-racking, and any financial rewards doubtful?

Any professional must also be aware of the views of society which may change ahead of legislation.

The need to develop skills in the management of construction projects is generally accepted, but involvement in top-level decision making and control of capital expenditure is also needed. One definition of an engineer is someone who can do for the price what any fool could do for twice as much. With limited resources and a proper interest in 'value for money', it is right to save the client's money – but not at someone else's expense or safety. Both consultants and contractors have to be financially and commercially aware, for we now have a very expensive labour force and cost-control is essential. Moreover, the industry has for some time been used as an economic regulator by both major political parties.

Development is fraught with contradictions since the balance between man, nature and society is so delicate, and often little understood. The simplest project may generate unintended effects which may be good or bad, e.g. loneliness or lack of identity in high-rise flats, or the build-up of bilharzia in slow-moving irrigation canals. Major civil engineering projects not only confer great benefits upon the community, but may also produce less pleasant side-effects such as dereliction, pollution and adverse sociological change. People are quite rightly concerned with the quality of the built environment, and this puts an added responsibility upon the construction team to maintain the safety and quality of life whilst meeting the conflicting needs of modern society. Satisfying our ever-growing energy requirements can be particularly divisive e.g. the Vale of Belvoir coalfield or the second nuclear power station at Sizewell; and the roles of pressure groups and of public participation must therefore be understood. H.R.H. Prince Philip in his introduction to the C.I.O.B. 1984 Building Tomorrow's Heritage project, said 'Building has become one of the most important factors in our national life. The quality of life in the home, in offices, in factories and in other places of work and leisure depends directly on the quality of the buildings. Furthermore, we all have to live with our total urban and industrial surroundings.'

In the view of Sir Monty Finniston 'The great issues of the future are likely to have very large and ever-increasing technological content, and it is here that policy decisions must give greater weight to the views of those who both conceive the changes and implement them rather than to the non-technical beneficiaries'. Sir Alan Cottrell giving the 1976 Graham Clark lecture asserted that 'We need to engage more of the brain-power and expertise that

exists in the country', and this requires Builders and Civil
Engineers outside the government service 'to help find solutions to
social and political problems which combine both social and
technological factors'.

There is also a need for a much better-informed public, and this
calls for the professional constructor not only 'to advise on the
expected effects of industrial and technical developments, and the
anticipated influence of world trends', but also 'to join actively in
the great national debates on public policy'. The professional's
trained mind 'is especially valuable in the battle against the
sloganeer and the hidden persuader.' Sir Monty believes that 'A
positive attitude based on knowledge, experience, commitment
and responsibility is required to counter the clamour from
'anti-movements to progress in society', and the disproportionate
influence, often based on dogma or ignorance, of fringe pressure
groups.

In order to influence policy decisions and not just respond to
them, professionals must become involved in political argument
and not merely remain as technical advisers. This means entering
the political field and taking a more prominent part in running the
communities in which they live. The Federation of Civil Engineering Contractors recognised their need to boost political muscle
when, in 1980, they decided to conduct a 'low-budget exercise' in
order to influence government policy on expenditure. They
believed that if civil engineering was given the degree of priority in
public affairs which its fundamental importance to the economy
merited, other industry objectives might be more readily achieved.
The Institution of Civil Engineers also believes that the Institution
should play a greater role in shaping the destiny of society,
politics, and national economics. Ian Campbell in his 1981
Presidential address called for the abandonment of a passive role
by members, but expressed his disappointment that the I.C.E.'s
suggestion to the Prime Minister that there should be an
infrastructure planning board to co-ordinate national long-term
strategic issues, had produced no more than curt acknowledge-
ments. Obviously we still have some way to go, either in
promoting the prestige and social status of engineers, or their
ability to communicate their thoughts with laymen.

Although a number of firms have a long tradition of working
overseas, the substantial decline in the construction work-load in
Britain has resulted in a significant increase in the amount of
overseas work carried out by British designers and contractors.
The invisible earnings gained by these activities are an important

contribution to the U.K. economy. Questions worthy of consideration in this field must include those of assistance to developing countries and the suitable type of design solution (appropriate technology) when labour may be cheap and plentiful but plant and materials are scarce. As with all of the other sub-divisions surveyed every point is only a focus for discussion, for every factor has two sides each with its proponents, and unlike most technical problems there is no agreed best answer.

8. Our Changing Society

Having reviewed the demands of our industrialised society (1), and the general role of industry in that society (2), we then discussed the particular place of construction within our civilisation (7). Now it is necessary to consider the changing attitudes of present-day society and the prevailing economic climate. In 1970 in his book 'Future Shock', Alvin Toffler looked at the powerful currents of change that were already rocking our institutions and shifting our values. The Wind of Change named by Harold Macmillan, the growing Social Conscience (4) and the Permissive Society are but three instances. Although we have so far escaped the futility and hopelessness foreseen by George Orwell in his book '1984'; in the face of the accelerating world arms race, the ineffectiveness of the United Nations and the disunity of the European Economic Community, who can say with certainty that we are not heading for catastrophe?

But ten years later in his new book 'The Third Wave', Toffler argues that 'beneath the clatter and jangle of seemingly senseless events, there lies a startling and potentially hopeful pattern'. 'The Third Wave' stands for the third wave of change in the history of civilisation; the first change was the introduction of Agriculture ten thousand years ago, and the second was the Industrial Revolution circa 1750–1850. The new era we have now entered has been variously described as the 'Space Age', 'Information Age', 'Electronic Era' and the 'Technological Revolution'. Toffler believes that what we are experiencing now is not merely the disintegration of an old society, but the creation of the foundations for a new civilisation; and the human story, far from ending, has just begun. The growing awareness that 'Small is Beautiful' is perhaps another encouragement for optimism.

It is impossible to divorce social change from business life, and there is no doubt that moral decay has been an important contributor to our economic problems. Asking fundamental questions about our future is not a matter of intellectual curiosity but a matter of survival. If today's political structures are obsolete, and our institutions, designed for a much slower and simpler society, are swamped and out-of-date, it will require imaginative leadership to bring about the necessary changes. Hence, the Institution of Civil Engineers has appointed a Corporate Planning Group to produce a consultative document, in order to stimulate debate amongst its members about the ways in which the institution needs to develop to deal with the challenges of the future.

The researches of Charles Darwin showed that if systems failed to adapt to change they would cease to exist. However, evolution does not work to a rigid timescale, nor is it measurable until after it has happened, but we all know that we are moving at an every-increasing speed into a world that as yet we don't know how to cope with. These, then, are some of the patterns of the future that constructors, along with other industrialists, may need to take into account when considering their own way ahead.

In the Spring of 1983, Spencer Stuart Management Consultants commissioned Francis Kinsman to sound out the opinions of 30 very senior people intimately connected with the leading edge of British management. His book 'The New Agenda' records their answers to the question: 'What do you imagine will be the most important social issues facing British managements by 1990?' The perspectives covered provide a detailed guide to our profoundly changing social environment: unemployment, the social responsibility of business, the pensions dilemma, the involvement of business with Government, the Third World and the environment, the marketplace and the consumer, management and the employee, the unions, changing work patterns, training and education, young people, the role of women, class, the manager and the organisation, and finally the potential harvest of change. Every manager wishing to ride these changes and survive this turbulent decade must resolve to seek the answers to these matters.

BIBLIOGRAPHY

A. C. Hutchinson, 'The Role of Industry in Society', *Works Management*, February 1977.
Kenneth Adams, 'Code of Corporate Business Practice', *Management Today*, August 1973.
'Manufacturing's tarnished image needs polishing', *Works Management*, February 1976.

H.R.H. Prince Philip, 'Key to prosperity is held by engineers', *New Civil Engineer,* 2 June 1977.
Keith Elliott, 'Management by Subjectives', *Management Today,* September 1975.
Guides to Good Management Practice, British Institute of Management, July 1974.
The Enterprise and Factors Affecting its Operation, International Labour Office, 1965.
Good management for a prosperous Britain, British Institute of Management, 1978.
Harold R. Pollard, *Further Developments in Management Thought,* Heinemann, 1978.

PART II

Management
in
Practice

Chapter 6

Finance

1. Legal Requirements to Keep Accounts

Every company *must* keep proper books of account with respect to:

    a. All sums of money received and expended by the company and the matters in respect of which the receipt and expenditure take place.

    b. All sales and purchases of goods by the company.

    c. The assets and liabilities of the company.

The Companies Acts 1948/1967 attempt to define 'proper books of account' by saying 'such books as are necessary to give a true and fair view of the state of the company's affairs and explain its transactions'. The books must be kept at the registered office 'or at such other place as the directors think fit', and must at all times be open to inspection by the directors.

'If any person being a director of a company fails to take all reasonable steps to secure compliance by the company with the above requirements, or has by his own wilful act been the cause of any default by the company thereunder, he is, in respect of each offence, liable on summary conviction to imprisonment for a term not exceeding six months, or to a fine.'

Moreover, '. . . if where a company is wound up it is shown that proper books of account were not kept by the company throughout the period of two years immediately preceding the commencement of the winding-up, every director, manager, or other officer who was knowingly a party to or connived at the default of the company shall, unless he shows that he acted honestly or that in the circumstances in which the business of the company was carried on the default was excusable, be liable to imprisonment for a term not exceeding one year.

'For the purposes of this section, the company shall have kept such books or accounts as are necessary to exhibit and explain the transactions and financial position of its business, including books containing entries from day to day in sufficient detail of all cash received and cash paid, and statements of the annual stocktakings and of all goods sold and purchased, showing the goods and the buyers and sellers thereof in sufficient detail to enable those goods and those buyers and sellers to be identified.'

It will be obvious from these statutory provisions that every company must keep adequate books of account; and in fact only by means of a complete set of books on the double-entry system can this be assured.

2. Forming the Undertaking's Financial Policy

When a contracting business is established, funds are required for the acquisition of buildings, machines, raw materials, etc., and for the payment of wages and salaries, the expense of lighting, heating, carriage and a host of other things incidental to construction. Answers must, therefore, be found to the questions:

  i. How much money will be required?
  ii. From what sources are the total funds to be raised?

In solving these problems, the first step is to discover the potential market for the product which it is proposed to build. The scale of operation and hence the finance necessary, will depend entirely upon the volume of work which may reasonably be expected – not only in the immediate future, but over a period as long as the business in its proposed form is likely to last.

The second step is to determine the amount which must be spent on:

  a. More or less permanent things like land, premises, plant, equipment, furniture and so forth,
  b. Things like materials, fuel, etc., which will be used up during the course of construction,
  c. Wages, petty cash and other expenses.

A builder is basically an investor, not in stocks and shares, but in plant, equipment, materials and services. Quite naturally he expects to make a return on these investments, the amount of the return depending upon the relation of the sum invested to its utility in the enterprise. He therefore wishes to know whether it will pay to invest in either materials, equipment or services. Frequently there are two or more choices, and again he asks

'Which will give the greatest return on the money invested?'
Having made his decision, he is faced with the problem of making
the investment pay what he anticipated.

The third consideration is the source of the funds required to
provide fixed and working capital, and this will depend upon the
type of constitution which the firm is to adopt. In the case of sole
proprietorship or partnership the money will come from the
private pocket of the owners, but where the capital involved is
considerable, the incorporation of the business as a company, the
members of which have limited liability, is desirable. Again, when
the company purchases materials on credit, normally paid for at
the end of the following month, it has the use of money equal to
the value of these materials. The agreements entered into with
those who supply the money, establish the economic conditions of
the business and fix the character of most of its financial
obligations.

3. The Provision of Capital

Whether it is a private or public company the money invested in
the company is obtained through the sale of securities, and the
money thus raised becomes either the permanent capital of the
company or its long term obligations. The company gives either
preference or ordinary shares in exchange for its permanent
capital, which may be divided into the following various classes.

a. Authorised (*nominal or registered*) *capital* is the maximum
amount of capital which a company in its Memorandum takes
power to issue. A statement of this capital, made on the statutory
form, must be registered with the Registrar and, in addition to
registration fees, capital duty at the rate of 50p per cent must be
paid on it. The authorised capital may be increased or decreased
only in accordance with the provisions of The Companies Act.
This nominal capital is divided into shares, the denominational
value of which are decided by the promoters of the company;
shares of £1 each are the most common but values varying from 5p
to £100 may be seen. The authorised capital may or may not be
wholly issued.

b. Issued capital is that portion of a company's authorised
capital which has been issued to the public for subscription, or to
the vendors as fully or partly paid in exchange for assets acquired
by the company. All the capital issued, however, may not be taken
up.

c. Subscribed capital consists of that portion of the issued capital which is actually subscribed for by the public, or allotted to vendors in respect of assets conveyed to the company. Very frequently the subscribed capital is less than the authorised capital, either because the whole authorised capital has not been issued for subscription, or has not been fully subscribed for by the public. Only the capital actually subscribed can be shown on the Balance Sheet.

d. Called-up capital is that part of the subscribed capital which has actually been called up. The uncalled part of the subscribed capital, which represents the contingent liability of the shareholders on the shares, is known as the *uncalled capital*

e. Paid-up capital is that part of the subscribed capital which has been called up and actually paid by the subscribers. The paid-up capital may be somewhat less than the called-up capital by reason of the failure of subscribers to pay the calls on shares for which they have subscribed. The difference between the called-up and the paid-up capital represents calls in arrear.

f. Companies may also issue *debentures,* which are acknowledgments of money borrowed; debenture-holders are thus creditors of the company, and not owners like the shareholders.

4. Forming a Company

Any seven or more persons may combine to form and register a *public* company; any two or more may form and register a *private* company.

The usual steps in the formation of a *public company* limited by shares are to prepare:

1. The Memorandum of Association, and the Articles of Association.
2. The preliminary contracts.
3. A statement of the nominal capital.
4. A list of the directors.
5. The directors must sign and file a written consent to act as directors, and the Memorandum or a contract to take and pay for their qualification shares.
6. The statutory declaration that all the requirements of the Act have been complied with.

All the above documents must be duly signed, stamped and lodged with the Registrar of Companies, who issues a certificate that the company is incorporated and is limited.

The next step is to obtain the necessary capital, by the preparation and issue of a *Prospectus,* inviting the public to subscribe for the company's share capital or debentures. Should the issue prove successful, i.e. should the minimum subscription be taken up by the public, and the amount payable on application on each share (not less than 5 per cent of the nominal value) be received, then the directors may proceed to allotment.

A statutory declaration must be filed that: *a.* the minimum subscription has been allotted, and *b.* that every director has paid in cash the same proportion on their qualification shares, whereupon the Registrar will certify that the company is entitled to commence business.

a. Memorandum of Association, the company's charter, must state:

1. The name of the company with 'Limited' as the last word.
2. Whether the registered office is in England or in Scotland.
3. The objects of the company.
4. That the liability of the members is limited.
5. The amount of share capital and the division thereof.

b. Articles of Association comprise the rules and by-laws which regulate the internal government of a company and its members.

c. Preliminary Contracts are agreements entered into prior to the formation of a company between vendors of property to be acquired by the company and the company itself.

d. Directors are appointed to manage the affairs of a company on behalf of the general body of shareholders. Every public company must have at least two directors and every private company one, who need not be a member of the company and come up for re-election in order of rotation.

e. Common Seal with the company's name engraved thereon is the company's official signature and is impressed upon all share and debenture certificates, and upon all contracts executed under seal.

f. The Secretary is a statutory office, and he must sign the annual return and certify the accompanying Balance Sheet.

5. Description of Limited Companies

(i) *An Incorporated Company* consists of a body of persons united for certain definite purposes under royal or legislative sanction, in such manner that they form a corporate body, i.e. an entity recognised in law as a distinct legal personality capable of holding property in its own right, of incurring obligations, and of suing and being sued in its own name. Subject to its Memorandum and Articles of Association, a Limited Company has the same contractual powers as a firm or private person. Companies may be incorporated in one of three ways, namely, by

a. *Royal Charter* – e.g. The Hudson's Bay Company.

b. *Special Act of Parliament* – e.g. The Bank of England.

c. *Registration under The Companies Act,* 1948.

There are three classes of Incorporated Companies, namely:

a. Companies limited by *shares.*

b. Companies limited by *guarantee.*

c. Companies the liability of whose members is *unlimited.*

Class *b* is quite unsuitable for commercial undertakings. Class *c* is more common since the Companies Act 1967.

Registration as a Company confers many advantages not possessed by a firm or sole trader. Registration facilitates the raising of fresh capital, increases financial resources, and so enhances credit, expedites extensions and amalgamations, and permits arrangements to be made for employees to acquire an interest in the business. The death or bankruptcy of members does not affect a company's existence, neither does the transfer of its shares from one person to another. Most important is that no member of a company limited by shares can be called upon to contribute any sum beyond the nominal value of the shares he has agreed to take. He may lose the capital he has invested should the company fail, but no matter how involved in debt the company may become the amount of his subscription to the capital fund marks the limit of his liability.

Following the EEC second directive on the harmonisation of company law, the name of a company must clearly indicate that it is a public, as opposed to a private, company.

(ii) *Partnership* is the relation existing between persons carrying on business in common with a view to sharing profits. No partnership, other than banking, may have more than twenty partners, and the objects of the business must be legal. If the partnership is for a period of more than one year, then by the provision of the *Statute of Frauds,* the agreements must be in writing. Persons who have entered into partnerships are called collectively a 'firm', and the name under which the business is carried on is the 'firm name'. Under the *Registration of Business Names Act,* 1916, there must be registration to any firm name which does not consist of the true surnames of all the partners, disclosing the business name, the nature of the business, the place of business, and each partner's name, nationality and residence.

The Law of Partnership has been consolidated into *The Partnership Act,* 1890, and *The Limited Partnership Act,* 1907, which makes it possible to limit the powers and liability of certain partners. Nevertheless the relationship between partners may be whatever the partners mutually agree between themselves that it shall be.

(iii) *Sole Trader.* When a business belongs to a single owner, he is said to be a sole trader.

6. Provision and Types of Shares

When the shares issued have been fully paid, share certificates usually signed by two directors and the secretary, are issued to members. The *Share Certificate Book* consists of pages divided into three parts. The first counterfoil records details of the certificate, the name and address of the shareholder and the number of shares; the second is a form of acknowledgment to be signed by the shareholder; and the third part is the certificate itself.

Various classes of shares are commonly met with:

1. *Preference shares.* These usually rank first both as to payment of dividend and return of capital. If they carry both, then: (i.) the fixed rate of interest attached to the shares must be paid out of profits before the ordinary shares rank for dividend, (ii.) in the event of the company going into liquidation, preference capital has the right to prior payment before other classes of shares, should funds be available after payment of debts.

1a. *Simple or non-cumulative preference shares.* Carrying a preferential right to dividend out of the profits of each year only, these shares have no claim on the profits of succeeding years should the profits for any year be inadequate to pay the dividend.

1b. *Cumulative preference shares.* With this class the preferential rights to dividend accumulate from year to year in the event of the non-payment of dividend, the arrears of one year being carried forward to the next. Thus if a company made insufficient profits to pay the dividend upon them for four years, it would have accumulated a liability to pay four years' dividend as and when sufficient profits were available to meet these claims, before any dividend could be paid to the holders of subordinate classes of shares.

1c. *Participating preference shares.* In addition to the advantages attaching to 1b, these shares carry a right to a stated share in the surplus profits after payment of the fixed dividend to which they are entitled, usually after a certain minimum has been paid on the subordinate classes.

1d. *Pre-preference (or first preference) shares.* For the purpose of raising urgently needed capital, these shares are sometimes issued with the consent of the preference shareholders. The rights of the holders of such shares in respect of dividend and capital repayment stand in front of those of holders of all other classes of shares.

1e. *Preferred ordinary shares.* Holders of these shares have the right to a fixed dividend after the claims of the preference shareholders have been met, and before the ordinary shares rank for dividend. They are always non-cumulative.

2. *Redeemable preference shares.* A company may, if so authorised by its Articles, issue preference shares which are to be liable to be redeemed. Redemption may be out of the profits of the company or out of the proceeds of a fresh issue of shares made for the purpose. When redeemed otherwise than by a fresh issue, there must be set aside, out of the profits which would otherwise be available for dividend, an equal sum to a reserve fund called the Capital Redemption Reserve Fund. It may then issue shares up to the nominal amount of the shares redeemed, and then apply the capital Redemption Reserve Fund in paying up unissued shares of the company to be issued to members as fully paid bonus shares.

3. *Ordinary shares.* The bulk of shares issued by most limited companies are of this class. They carry no special rights but, generally, they are entitled to the surplus profits remaining after the prior fixed dividends have been satisfied.

4. *Deferred ordinary shares.* If these exist they are deferred in favour of prior classes of shares.

5. *Deferred management or founders' shares.* These shares are usually issued as fully paid to the promoters, or managers, of the issuing company, possibly in payment for goodwill. Regarding dividends, they usually stand aside until an agreed dividend has been paid on the ordinary shares, but

the voting powers which they command and the profits they share may be considerable.

6. **Bonus shares.** Successful companies sometimes issue shares in lieu of increased dividends. The usual procedure is to declare a dividend, credit the shareholders with the dividend, and then to issue shares in discharge of it, no money passing on either side. Bonus shares may be of any of the classes described above.

7. **Co-partnership shares.** These shares are sometimes issued to a company's employees in order to give them an interest in the concern. Frequently such shares carry no voting power. They are usually entitled to the same dividend rights as the ordinary shares, but their transfer is usually under the control of the company and effected at a fixed price.

7. Assets

(a) **Fixed.** Generally, any property, including resources in the form of building/engineering works or components created by capital expenditure, are termed 'assets'. Those assets of a more or less permanent kind that are *not* held for sale or for conversion into cash, but are retained solely as instruments of production or in order to earn revenue, are known as 'fixed assets'. Of such are land, buildings, machinery, furniture and the like.

(b) **Current.** Assets made or acquired for sale and conversion into cash as raw materials, fuel, partly manufactured stock or work in progress, goods for resale, trade and sundry debtors, temporary investments, and cash in hand and at Bank, are known as 'current assets'. Because they are constantly changing and going through a process of conversion from cash into stock, stock into debtors and debtors into cash again, they are sometimes called 'floating assets'.

Working Capital is the amount by which the readily convertible, liquid, or current assets of a concern exceed its current liabilities. Thus, the total of a company's cash, investments, bills receivable, stock, book debts, and similar floating assets *minus* its trade creditors, bank overdraft, bills payable, and similar floating liabilities represents the 'circulating' or working capital of the company. In calculating such capital, the more or less permanent fixed assets, and long or fixed-period loans and similar 'fixed' liabilities, are excluded.

8. Useful Ratios

In the day-to-day management of a business, there is little time for the study of detailed records relating to operating costs and revenue. It is therefore necessary to devise means for conveying to those who have to take decisions the information upon which those decisions have to be based, in a form which permits an almost instantaneous grasp of the essentials of the situation. Management relies very largely, therefore, upon summarised statements, charts and ratios.

There are many ratios which provide indices of management efficiency and financial stability, among them the following:

1. *Current assets to current liabilities.* This is sometimes known as the Working Capital Ratio, since the difference between the two items represents working capital, and is generally considered to be an indication of the ability of the firm to pay its current debts promptly. Although it varies between different businesses, a ratio of 2 : 1 should be looked for here, and a fall should be taken as a sign of insufficient working capital. However, since current assets include cash, accounts receivable, stock and work-in-progress, a firm with current assets mainly in cash is in a far different position from one having current assets mainly in work-in-progress and stocks of material, although the two ratios may be the same.

2. *Liquid assets to current liabilities.* Liquid assets are current assets less stocks and work in progress, i.e. those assets which can quickly be turned into cash. Here a ratio of 1 : 1 is essential if commitments are to be met without delay. But because of the nature of the building industry, a company having work-in-progress in the form of contracts long since completed but not finalised, cannot be said to have a current asset which is readily converted to cash. Therefore, by itself this test is not a conclusive indicator of a building firm's current position.

3. *Outstanding debtors to sales.* If the previous ratio is unsatisfactory, the explanation may be that clients are not settling their accounts quickly enough, and the cash position is therefore strained. If two months' credit is usual, this ratio should be about 18 per cent. In the construction industry this really amounts to the ratio of outstanding retentions to annual turnover, and may be helpful since it measures to some extent the diligence of the surveyors responsible for measuring interim payments and finalising accounts for completed jobs.

4. ***Stocks and work in progress to sales moving annual total.*** This ratio is particularly important where ratios 1 and 2 give cause for concern, and an increase will mean that an unduly large amount of capital is becoming tied up in stocks and work in progress. The 'Z' chart described in Chapter 16 would be suitable for showing this factor.

5. ***Cash to current liabilities.*** The cash position of a company established by this ratio, is usually considered satisfactory if it is about 25 per cent.

6. ***Current profit (or loss) to invested capital.*** In the final analysis, the value of a business is measured by the profit that is made, and this is probably the ratio most used today. It has the advantage of reflecting the turnover of the capital, and therefore of giving a better measure of the final result; besides making it possible to forecast the probable return of an investment in a given section of the business.

7. ***Current profit (or loss) to sales.*** This alternative ratio is also useful and has gained popularity during the past few years.

8. ***Direct labour to turnover.*** For a building firm engaged purely on new work this figure should be less than 15 per cent, which envisages a turnover of over £40 000 per operative, whether employed direct by the company or as a member of a labour-only sub-contract gang. A figure for alterations and jobbing work may vary with the type of work undertaken, but as a general rule direct labour and its associated overheads such as fares, overtime, NI and HWP should not exceed 30 per cent.

9. ***Average credit period.*** This information is ratio 3 in another form, that of the number of weeks which elapse between completion of a job and payment of the final account.

10. ***Overhead percentage.*** Although often related to turnover, the ratio of overheads to direct labour is more constant, easier to calculate and more closely related since overheads can only be recovered by time spent on productive work.

In general these ratios should be compared for a series of balance sheets to determine the tendencies of a business. The figures for a number of years have to be available before a definite trend appears. Since 1962 when seven firms took part in a pilot scheme, regular comparisons of management ratios have been organised for the Construction Industry by the Centre for Interfirm Comparison Limited.*

*In 1969, the second scheme sponsored jointly by the E.D.C's for Building and Civil Engineering and the C.I.T.B., involved 76 companies. By 1979, over 150 individual companies had co-operated in these surveys.

9. Dividends and Profits

When the profits of a limited company are divided amongst the proprietors the portion of such distribution received by each shareholder is termed a *dividend*. Almost invariably companies frame special articles governing the payment of dividends. These usually provide as follows:

 a. dividends are to be declared in general meeting, and no dividend may exceed the rate recommended by the directors
 b. interim dividends may be paid
 c. no dividend may be paid except out of profits
 d. dividends may be paid only on the actual amounts paid up on the shares
 e. calls paid in advance carry no right to dividend
 f. directors may make such reserves as they deem proper prior to the declaration of a dividend.

What constitutes the profits of a company available for dividend is a large and involved question, but the following is a brief summary of the rules laid down:

 a. dividends may not be paid out of capital
 b. loss or depreciation of fixed capital does not prevent payment of a dividend, but loss of circulating capital *must* be made good before a dividend is paid
 c. sums written off for depreciation, and profits written off against goodwill, may be applied as profits, if in fact no depreciation has taken place
 d. profits carried to reserve are still profits unless capitalised.

Net *profit* may be defined as the amount available for distribution to the proprietor, partners, or shareholders of a business, after all charges that have been incurred in the earning of the revenue for the period under review have been taken into account, and the shrinkage in the value of the assets held by the business has been allowed for.

The directors must submit to the Annual General Meeting a report with respect to the state of the company's affairs, the amount, if any, which they recommend should be paid by way of dividend, and the amount, if any, which they propose to carry to any of the company's reserves. To this report must be attached the balance sheet and a profit and loss account.

10. Trading Accounts

The final accounts are compiled from a large number of individual accounts kept in what is known as the ledger. By the convention of double-entry book-keeping, when value is received the account concerned is debited, and when value is given it is credited. If then the totals of the various ledger accounts are listed, the total debits and the total credits must agree. In practice, only the balances on the accounts are extracted, and the resulting list known as the *trial balance* (see Fig. 6.1) is the information from which the profit and loss account and balance sheet may be drawn up. It will be noted that every item in the trial balance appears again in one or other of the final accounts.

When an agreed trial balance has been extracted from the books at the close of a financial period, the next step is to ascertain the

A. Building Contractors Ltd.

TRIAL BALANCE
as on December 31, 19—

Where shown in final a/c's	Name of account	Dr £	Cr £
BS	Share capital account		500 000
BS	Freehold premises	100 000	
BS	Office furniture and fittings	40 000	
TA	Stock (stores and materials Jan. 1)	30 450	
TA	Purchases (stores and materials)	406 000	
TA	Work certified		1 443 450
BS	Bills receivable	5 570	
BS	Bills payable		10 000
P & L	Discount received		5 000
P & L	Head office salaries	70 000	
TA	Site salaries	25 000	
TA	Workmen's wages	210 000	
P & L	General expenses	4 000	
P & L	Rates and insurance	16 000	
P & L	Carriage and postage	1 050	
P & L	Joinery shop a/c (loss)	4 000	
P & L	Plant department a/c (profit)		10 000
TA	Sub-contractors account	505 000	
TA	Contract expenses	30 000	
TA	Work in progress (Jan. 1)	33 000	
P & L	Directors' fees	10 000	
BS	Sundry debtors	4 430	
BS	Plant and equipment	245 000	
BS	Cash at bank	102 000	
BS	Cash in hand	29 000	
TA	Plant hire charges	99 950	
A	Profit and loss a/c balance (Jan. 1)		2 000
		£1 970 450	£1 970 450

Fig. 6.1

trading results achieved. This may be done by preparing a single profit and loss account, but more frequently by dividing the account into sections in order to show:

a. the gross profit or earnings,

b. the real or net profit for the period, and

c. how the net profit for the period has been appropriated.

It is essential in a building business, if an efficient check upon the production process is to be maintained, to show the gross profit earned by construction, i.e. by a *trading account.*

Unlike other industrial concerns the builder usually keeps separate accounts for each sizeable contract, and another account for all the jobbing work. These are in effect individual trading accounts, and every cost which can be directly identified with a particular job is debited to the account for that contract. Similarly, work certified is credited to the appropriate project and the value of uncertified work in progress, estimated at cost, is carried down. The difference between these two sides of the contract account therefore represents the gross profit or loss realised on the current year's working.

The 'working' or trading account will be confined to those items which directly affect the prime cost of construction, and all estimating, service departments and head office charges will be dealt with in the profit and loss account. The trading account (see Fig. 6.2) should include, on the debit side:

a. initial stock and work in progress,

b. construction materials purchased,

c. site wages and expenses and supervision salaries,

d. plant charges,

e. site overheads;

and on the credit side:

f. payments certified, and

g. final stock and work in progress.

This is therefore an overall summary of the information provided by the individual contract accounts.

Where a firm undertakes several types of work, e.g. building, civil engineering, housing, jobbing, handled by separate departments, it is customary to prepare the trading account on departmental lines.

Contracting businesses have at the close of the year a certain amount of work in hand, which will not be completed till the next financial year. The valuation of 'work in progress' requires the utmost care, and in general the value of the work taken credit for in the trading account should not exceed its actual cost, i.e.

A. Building Contractors Ltd.   Trading Account for the Year ended December 31, 19—

Dr.					Cr.
1978		£	1978		£
Jan. 1	To Stock	30 450	Dec. 31	By Work certified	1 443 450
Jan. 1	,, Work in progress	33 000	Dec. 31	,, Work in Progress	45 000
Dec. 1	,, Purchases	406 000	Dec. 31	,, Stock	26 000
Dec. 31	,, Site salaries	25 000			
Dec. 31	,, Workmen's wages	210 000			
Dec. 31	,, Plant hire charges	99 950			
Dec. 31	,, Sub-contractors	505 000			
Dec. 31	,, Contract expenses	30 000			
Dec. 31	,, Balance, being gross profit for the year carried to the Profit and Loss Account	175 050			71 000
		£1 514 450			£1 514 450

Fig. 6.2

materials, wages and apportionment of oncost. Where the work is within sight of completion, and the final cost can be exactly estimated, a measure of profit may be added to the valuation, if possible contingencies are also taken into account.

The *profit and loss account* proper constitutes the net operating profit or loss after making provision for depreciation, or other liability (see Fig. 6.3).

An *appropriation of profit account* shows how the net profit for the year, together with any balance brought forward from the previous year, is to be utilised. Part must of course be set aside to provide for the estimated liability for taxation on the current year's trading. It is also usual to set aside certain sums as reserves for the future, and to show the provisions for dividends which the directors propose to pay (see Fig. 6.3).

The Companies Act 1976 laid down additional requirements in respect of the preparation and filing of accounts, accounting records and disclosure of interests in shares. Recognised qualifications for the auditor are listed, notifications are required of changes of directors and secretary, and the penalties for non-compliance with the Act are substantially strengthened.

11. Balance Sheets

When the figures necessary for the compilation of the trading and profit and loss accounts have been extracted from the trial balance, the remaining items together with the balance from the profit and loss account form the framework of the balance sheet. Items of a like nature are grouped together, since the totals only of the generic groups can be dealt with in the balance sheet. The balance sheet or capital statement sets out the financial position of the company as on a definite date, and does not cover a period as does a profit and loss account (see Fig. 6.4).

The Companies Acts 1948 and 1967 lay down a comprehensive schedule of the information to be afforded by a balance sheet, including:

i.   A summary of the authorised share capital
ii. A summary of the issued share capital
iii. A classification of reserves, provisions, liabilities and assets
iv. Identification of the fixed, current and other assets and a statement of how the values of fixed assets have been arrived at
v.   The holding of shares in subsidiary companies and the indebtedness to and from such companies

Profit and Loss Account for the Year ended December 31, 19—

Dr.		£		Cr.	£
1978			1978		
Dec. 31	To Head office salaries	70 000	Dec. 31	By Balance brought down from the Trading Account	175 050
Dec. 31	,, General expenses	4 000		,, Discount received	5 000
Dec. 31	,, Rates and insurance	16 000		,, Plant department (balance)	10 000
Dec. 31	,, Depreciation:				
	Plant and equipment 11% 26 950				
	Office furniture 5% 2 000	28 950			
Dec. 31	,, Carriage and postage	1 050			
Dec. 31	,, Directors' fees	10 000			
Dec. 31	,, Joinery shop (Balance)	4 000			
Dec. 31	,, Balance carried down being net profit for the year	56 050			
		£190 050			190 050

Appropriation Account

Dr.		£		Cr.	£
1978			1978		
Dec. 31	To Provision for Corporation Tax	15 000	Dec. 31	By Balance brought forward from last year	2 000
Dec. 31	,, Transfer to reserve	10 000	Dec. 31	,, Balance brought down	56 050
Dec. 31	,, Proposed dividend on Ordinary Shares, 5%	25 000			
Dec. 31	,, Balance carried down	8 050			
		58 050			58 050

Fig. 6.3

A. Building Contractors Ltd.   Balance Sheet December 31, 19—

	£	£		£	£
Capital			*Fixed Assets*		
Authorised: 1 000 000 Shares of £1 each	£1 000 000		Plant and equipment at cost	245 000	
Issued: 500 000 Shares of £1 each fully paid		500 000	Less Depreciation	26 950	218 050
			Freehold premises		100 000
Revenue Reserves			Office furniture at cost	40 000	
General reserve	10 000		Less Depreciation	2 000	38 000
Corporation Tax	15 000				356 050
Profit and Loss Account (balance)	8 050	33 050			
			Current Assets		
			Work in progress	45 000	
Current Liabilities			Stock (stores and materials)	26 000	71 000
Bills payable	10 000		Sundry debtors	4 430	
Proposed dividend	25 000	35 000	Bills reeivable	5 570	10 000
			Cash at bank	102 000	
			Cash in hand	29 000	131 000
					212 000
		£568 050			£568 050

Fig. 6.4

vi.   Details of unquoted investments
vii. The total remuneration paid to directors if not already disclosed in the profit and loss account
viii. The basis on which any amount set aside for Corporation Tax has been computed

12. Taxation

There are two very big claims upon the money which flows into a company. Firstly there is the money which must be set aside each year to maintain the company's plant and premises in good order, called depreciation. The tax system in this country is so arranged that a company can charge a certain amount of depreciation each year as a legitimate expense of its business and this amount can be set aside from the profits without any tax having to be paid on it. In its accounts the company can write off its assets at its own discretion, but this amount is disregarded by the Inland Revenue (i.e. added back to profit) and replaced for taxation purposes by *capital allowances.* In the case of plant and machinery the full capital cost may be claimed as a deduction from profit for the year in which the expenditure is incurred. Certain assets, notably motor vehicles and computers, which do not qualify for the first year allowance, instead attract a writing-down allowance of 25% calculated each year on the reducing balance. New industrial buildings (but not shops or offices) receive an allowance of 40% in the first year, and additionally both new and second-hand industrial buildings attract writing-down allowances which effectively write off the whole of the original expense over 25 or 50 years. This system of capital allowances, by allowing substantial tax relief early in the working life of a capital asset, acts as an incentive to investment, because capital expenditure on the right (i.e. eligible) assets effectively reduces the company's tax liability in the short term.

Other government incentives to encourage modernisation and re-equipment in industry include *Regional Development Grants.* These are cash contributions to the cost of investment expenditure, made to companies resident in certain areas of the country which have been designated as 'special development', 'development' or 'intermediate areas' requiring assistance. Where a Regional Development Grant has been received in respect of certain capital expenditure, the full cost of the asset is still eligible for the normal capital allowances.

The second and bigger claim upon the profits of a company is for *taxation* made by the Inland Revenue acting as agents for the Treasury. A company is not taxed on all the profit it makes, for legitimate expenses incurred in making this money can be set against the gross profits. In addition to depreciation, deductions are allowed for fees paid to the directors and the auditors, the interest paid on any bank overdraft or loans such as debenture stock and the contributions made to a pension fund for its staff. When all these expenses have been deducted from the gross trading profit the remaining item is called taxable profits which is then subjected to the process of taxation.

Companies pay corporation tax (currently 52%) on their profits (trading profit, capital gains and investment income). There are several minor differences between a company's taxable profit and that recorded in its accounts. For example, expenditure on entertaining is not an allowable deduction for tax purposes unless it is for foreign customers. However, the tax system recognises the burden imposed by inflation upon the financing of stocks of materials and finished goods. Stock relief provides relief from corporation tax on the nominal increased value of stock during the financial year.

Corporate tax used to discourage the payment of dividends, but since April 1973 the introduction of the imputation system has neutralized this effect. When a company pays a dividend, it has to pay Advance Corporation Tax to the Inland Revenue, at a rate equivalent to the basic rate of Income Tax on the combined dividend plus A. C. T. i.e. currently 30% on a notional 'gross' dividend. The shareholder thus receives a payment which is net of basic rate income tax. Of course, he is still liable to pay the difference if he is in a higher tax bracket. The company however, is able to set off the A. C. T. which it has paid, against its liability to mainstream Corporation Tax i.e. it is treated as a payment on account.

13. Depreciation

Fixed assets do not retain their productive powers indefinitely and a charge must therefore be made against profits each year to cover the estimated amount by which the value of the assets has deteriorated in the current year. The permanent wastage of the cost of an asset due to wear and tear, obsolescence, deterioration or any other factor is known as *depreciation,* and provision is made by charges against revenue which, within the effective life of the asset, are sufficient to write off its initial cost, less, when considered necessary, its residual or scrap value.

When the amount of the depreciation has been assessed, the following methods may be employed for its distribution over the life of the asset.

1. *The straight-line method.* Also known as the 'fixed-instalment' method, the original value of the asset is divided by the number of years of its estimated working life, and an equal part of the cost is debited each year of that life to revenue, repairs and renewals also being charged to revenue. Advantages are:

   a. its simplicity, and

   b. that the asset is completely eliminated at the close of its life.

   Objections include

   a. the question of interest is ignored, and

   b. the burden of repairs falls more heavily on the later than the earlier years of the life of the asset.

1A. *The working hours method.* An alternative is a modification of the straight line method, whereby the expected life of a machine is assessed in terms of working hours, and the depreciation is proportional to the number of hours that have been worked up-to-date. This method is unsatisfactory for a builder since a piece of new plant may spend a large amount of its time idle, so that the written down value on the company's books will be very much higher than its current market value.

2. *The diminishing balance method.* Probably the most popular way of allowing for depreciation of mechanical plant is to write off a fixed percentage from the diminishing balance of the asset account every year. The advantage of this constant ratio method is that the revenue charge is equitably averaged, since when the machine is new the depreciation charge is heavy and the repairs and maintenance charge light, whereas in the later years when repairs are heavy the depreciation is light. Care must be taken to ensure that the percentage rate employed is sufficiently high completely to eliminate the asset at the close of its life. A suitable rate of depreciation for plant with a reasonably long working life such as mixers, excavators, small dumpers, etc., is 25 per cent per annum, but for items with heavier wear, such as bulldozers and tractor shovels, it is normal to allow a larger

Year	Depreciation for the year	Total depreciation	Balance at end of year
	£	£	£
1	250	250	750
2	187·5	437·5	562·5
3	140·6	578·1	421·9
4	105·5	683·6	316·4
5	79·1	762·7	237·3
6	59·3	822·0	178·0
7	44·5	866·5	133·5
8	33·4	899·9	100·1
9	25·0	924·9	75·1
10	18·8	943·7	56·3

Fig. 6.5. Method 2

amount such as 33⅓ per cent. A typical calculation based on 25 per cent is given above (Fig. 6.5).

3. **The depreciation fund method.** A fixed proportion of the initial cost is transferred each year from revenue account to a depreciation reserve which, if it were allowed to accumulate with compound interest on successive instalments, would at the end of the life produce the initial cost less scrap value. This is the only convenient method for the depreciation of a normal civil engineering asset such as a railway line, and a typical calculation is tabled below (Fig. 6.6).

3A. **The sinking fund method.** This is a variation of 3 where the annual charge is invested in Stock Exchange securities. The advantage of this method is that it provides the actual cash wherewith to replace the asset.

Year	Payment for the year	Interest for the year	Depreciation for the year	Fund total at end of year	Balance at end of year
1	71·6	0	71·6	71·6	928·4
2	71·6	4·3	75·9	147·5	852·5
3	71·6	8·8	80·4	227·9	772·1
4	71·6	13·7	85·3	313·2	686·8
5	71·6	18·8	90·4	403·6	596·4
6	71·6	24·2	95·8	499·4	500·6
7	71·6	30·0	101·6	601·0	399·0
8	71·6	36·0	107·6	708·6	291·4
9	71·6	42·5	114·1	822·7	177·3
10	71·6	49·4	121·0	943·7	56·3

Fig. 6.6. Method 3

3B. ***The insurance policy method.*** This is another form of sinking
fund but a capital endowment policy is taken out with an
Assurance Company for the amount necessary to replace
the asset, maturing at the close of the life of the asset. The
advantage is that the exact sum required will be forthcoming, whereas Stock Exchange securities carry the risk of
market fluctuations. It will be noted that methods 3, 3A, 3B
and 3c are more complex variations of the straight-line
method but they take into account the question of interest.

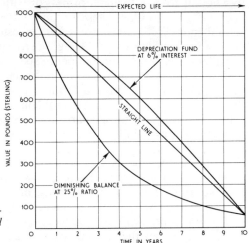

Fig. 6.7. Graphical com-
parison of most useful
methods of depreciation

3C. ***The annuity method.*** The constant annual depreciation
charge is ascertained from tables, and is calculated so as to
eliminate the asset, together with interest on the capital
sunk, at the close of the life of the asset. This is a most
scientific system but objections are:
a. that when additions are made to the Asset Account,
revised calculations must be made, and
b. that in the early years the book value may be in excess of
the real value.

4. ***Valuation method.*** Depreciation may be determined by the
process of actual re-valuation of the asset at the close of
each financial year. Such valuations are useful as a
periodical check upon other methods, but this method is
not suitable for heavy fixed assets such as buildings.

However, it is particularly suitable for loose tools, copy-rights and patents, animals and containers like sacks or bottles.

A graphical comparison of the three most usual methods is shown in Fig. 6.7, using the examples given earlier.

14. The Appraisal of Investment Policies

A building company is frequently faced with making a decision as to whether to invest capital or not, or with the equally important decision of choosing between alternative investments. Large capital sums of money are often invested in plant, and the alternative methods of buy, lease, borrow or hire may need to be considered. A property developer or speculative house builder will wish to compare the merits of various sites or projects. Since most business enterprises have a limited amount of capital at their disposal, the general financial problem facing management is to select those uses for the available funds which will give the highest anticipated profitability in terms of either monies returned or saved.

Some of the commonly used approximations for appraising capital investments have been giving way to the use of more sophisticated and accurate methods, and a comparative study is necessary for their proper understanding.

    a. The *rate of return* method assesses the average rate of return by expressing the monies earned as a percentage of the capital invested. Such rates of return calculated for alternative investments may be compared directly, but the method has the disadvantage that it does not take into account the timings of the receipts obtained.

    Since a pound today is worth more than a pound in the future, then the 'fourth dimension' of time must be considered in economic studies. With high interest rates and endemic inflation, the factor of time is a most important element in any investment decision.

    b. The *pay-back* method compares the calculated number of years over which a capital investment will be paid back by the profits from the project. This method has the disadvantage that it does not consider any returns made beyond the initial period, and although it might be suitable for very short-life, highly profitable investments, it is not satisfactory for longer-term projects usual in building works.

c. The *present value* (or worth) method converts all income and expenditure items to equivalent lump sums at the present time. The initial investment is of course already in these terms, but other payments are calculated from a formula.

This technique is also known as *discounted cash flow* analysis, because the future cash flows are discounted, i.e. given present worth, in order to equate them with the initial capital investment.

Discounted cash flow (D.C.F.) is based on the reciprocal of compound interest. The future value of an investment for any number of years at various rates of compound interest can be calculated by the formula:

$Fv = Pv (1 + r)^n$ (see Fig. 6.8)

where Fv = future sum or value or worth

Pv = present sum

r = rate of interest (expressed as a decimal)

n = number of years hence.

Alternatively, the future value may be discounted back to the present value by transposing the formula to:

$$Pv = \frac{Fv}{(1+r)^n} \text{ (see Fig. 6.8)}$$

To avoid tedious calculations we may use published discount tables, which give the present value of £1 due at the end of a number of years for various rates of interest.

Years	5%		10%		15%	
	Compound interest	Discount factor*	Compound interest	Discount factor*	Compound interest	Discount factor*
1	1.0500	0.9524	1.1000	0.9091	1.1500	0.8696
2	1.1025	0.9070	1.2100	0.8264	1.3225	0.7561
3	1.1576	0.8638	1.3310	0.7513	1.5209	0.6575
4	1.2155	0.8227	1.4641	0.6830	1.7490	0.5718
5	1.2763	0.7835	1.6105	0.6209	2.0114	0.4972
6	1.3401	0.7462	1.7716	0.5645	2.3131	0.4323
7	1.4071	0.7107	1.9487	0.5132	2.6600	0.3759
8	1.4775	0.6768	2.1436	0.4665	3.0590	0.3269
9	1.5513	0.6446	2.3579	0.4241	3.5179	0.2843
10	1.6289	0.6139	2.5937	0.3855	4.0456	0.2472

* Present value of £1 to be received in one payment at the end of a given number of years.

Fig. 6.8

To use the present value method, management must first set the minimum rate of return below which they will not approve capital projects. This rate will be based upon the actual cost of capital to the company – or the interest that could be earned by present funds elsewhere – suitably adjusted for the risk or uncertainty inherent in the proposal. As an example, suppose that we wish to purchase a new item of plant and there are two suitable models available. Assuming that the criterion rate of return of 10% has been decided, and the respective cash flows anticipated are as follows, which one should we buy?

		Model A	Model B
Capital cost now		£30 000	£40 000
Net revenue	1	6 000	5 000
during year	2	8 000	6 000
	3	20 000	9 000
	4	3 000	18 000
	5	3 000	22 000
	Totals:	£40 000	£60 000

By 'discounting' at 10% we shall obtain the following net present values:

10%	Discount factor	A actual	Present value	B actual	Present value
Now	1.0000	30 000	30 000	40 000	40 000
Year 1	0.9091	6 000	5 454.6	5 000	4 545.5
2	0.8264	8 000	6 611.2	6 000	4 958.4
3	0.7513	20 000	15 026.0	9 000	6 761.7
4	0.6830	3 000	2 049.0	18 000	11 294.0
5	0.6209	3 000	1 862.7	22 000	13 659.8
			£ 31 003.5		£ 41 219.4

Both of these projects are viable since in each case the total present worth of the net returns is greater than the amount of the original investment.

The profitability index of each project may be calculated as follows and ranked in order.

$$A = \frac{31\ 003.5}{30\ 000} = 1.0334$$

$$B = \frac{41\ 219.5}{40\ 000} = 1.0306$$

The weakness of this method is that it is limited to showing whether or not a particular scheme is viable at a particular interest rate. It may not always be possible to establish such a rate with certainty, or the rate may vary over the period under consideration.

d. The *internal rate of return* establishes the 'true' present value and hence enables ranking to be carried out directly. The method does not require the pre-selection of an interest rate in order to make the necessary calculations, but instead establishes a *yield rate*. The yield rate on a capital investment is obtained by discounting the cash flows (both in and out) at such a rate that the present value of the balance of income over expenditure exactly equals the value of the initial capital outflow. This rate of discount is the internal yield, or the internal rate of return at which capital expenditure is exchanged for an annual income. By estimation or trial and error we can ascertain that the yield rate required to precisely equate the present worth of the total cash flows to the original investment lies somewhere between two figures. For example, our previous figures can be discounted at 11% as follows:

11%	Discount factor	Actual A	Present value	Actual B	Present value
Now	1.0000	30 000	30 000	40 000	40 000
End of year					
1	0.9009	6 000	5 405.4	5 000	4 504.5
2	0.8116	8 000	6 492.8	6 000	4 869.6
3	0.7312	20 000	14 624.0	9 000	6 580.8
4	0.6587	3 000	1 976.1	18 000	11 856.6
5	0.5935	3 000	1 780.5	22 000	13 057.0
			30 278.8		40 868.5

and again at 12%:

12%	Discount factor	Actual A	Present value	Actual B	Present value
Now	1.0000	30 000	30 000	40 000	40 000
End of year					
1	0.8929	6 000	5 357.4	5 000	4 464.5
2	0.7972	8 000	6 377.6	6 000	4 783.2
3	0.7118	20 000	14 236.0	9 000	6 406.2
4	0.6355	3 000	1 906.5	18 000	11 439.0
5	0.5674	3 000	1 702.2	22 000	12 482.8
			29 579.7		39 575.7

In both cases the yield rate lies somewhere between 11% and 12% and can be determined by interpolation as follows:

$$A \quad \text{True rate} = 11 + \frac{278.8}{278.8 + 420.3} = 11 + \frac{278.8}{699.1}$$

$$= 11.3988$$

$$B \quad \text{True rate} = 11 + \frac{868.5}{868.5 + 424.3} = 11 + \frac{868.5}{1292.8}$$

$$= 11.6718$$

Thus, a comparison of these different methods of appraisal applied to this example gives the following different results:

a. *Rate of return*

$$A = \frac{40\ 000 \times 100}{30\ 000 \times 5} = \frac{400}{15} = 26.67\%$$

$$B = \frac{60\ 000 \times 100}{40\ 000 \times 5} = \frac{600}{20} = 30.00\%$$

B is preferable to A.

b. Pay back

A = something less than 3 years.

B = something less than 4 years.

A is preferable to B.

c. Present value
Both A and B are viable, and the difference in profitability is infinitesimal.

d. Internal rate of return
B is marginally better than A.

Investment decisions – whether to go ahead or not, which alternative to choose, or how best to fund the project – must ultimately be taken upon sound economic criteria, and the use of some analytical tool is therefore essential. Of course, there are also often other less definable factors involved, e.g. appearance, morale or safety; but as with other long-term planning, incomplete information is never a valid reason to omit the planning process.

15. The Need for Financial Planning

The management of finance is not a static responsibility but one which requires constant appraisal and review. The appraisal of investment policies has already underlined the long-term fact that 'a bird in the hand is worth two in the bush,' but we also need to consider the factor of short-term liquidity. Liquid assets are those like cash in hand, or a credit account at the bank, which can be used to settle urgent and immediate demands for payment. Those readers who have played the family game of Monopoly will know the feeling of despair when one is faced with a demand for rent on an opponent's hotel, but one's money is tied up in land and property. Many an otherwise profitable business has been forced into liquidation because calls for wages or bills for materials could not be met at the critical time, although substantial assets were frozen in long-term investments. It is perfectly possible for the profit and loss account of a company to show an apparent profit, when in fact the firm is struggling to maintain a sufficient cash flow to allow it to continue trading. It is also accepted that far more companies go out of business because they are not solvent, than fail because they are not profitable.

Government statistics deployed by Dr. Pat Hillebrandt show that the chance of a company in the construction industry becoming insolvent is nearly twice as high as in other industries. The reasons include: the high risks involved, e.g. uncertain ground conditions, unpredictable weather and variable labour availability; the necessity for pricing the product before it is produced; competitive tendering as a means of pricing; the low fixed-capital requirements which result in over-competition; a tendency to operate with too low a working capital; and the ease of entry to the industry which encourages inefficient contractors at a time of boom. The risk of overtrading, i.e. of increasing turnover too fast or too far, whether as a means of expansion at a time of plentiful work or to increase total profit when margins are depressed, can also lead to cash control problems. Increased turnover requires more finance for materials and labour and increases general indebtedness.

Construction suffers from several peculiar delays to its cash-inflows, namely retention monies, seasonal effects on output, preliminary expenses, contract extensions, the valuation of variations, and the settlement of claims.

- *a. Retention monies* are deducted from interim valuations to provide a reserve for possible unsatisfactory work and maintenance. The GC/Works/1 form of contract retains 3% of valued work and 10% on unfixed components and materials. The Standard Form of Building Contract provides for up to 10% on both works and materials subject to a maximum of 5% of the contract sum. This typical funding of the contract is illustrated in Fig. 6.9 with the release of retention in two halves at start and finish of the maintenance period. Ideally, it would be a good time to start a new contract at either of these cash inflow points.

- *b. The seasonal effects* on construction work are shown in Fig. 14.1 both as a monthly histogram and as a cumulative graph. The effects of winter and the Christmas holiday are apparent, and the improvement during spring. The hidden effects of holidays during the months May to September are real nevertheless, and explain the peak of October. Since work must of necessity be priced on averages, the cumulative curve shows how the loss sustained during the winter is gradually recovered by the 'haymaking' during the hoped-for summer. Inevitably the start date and duration of a contract will determine the net pattern of seasonal effects, which will vary with each individual project.

c. Preliminary expenses can be very high during the first few weeks of a contract, when office accommodation, materials stores, concrete batching plants, and possibly extensive temporary works, are all required in the initial set-up but only recovered during the span of the project. Provision for this particular peak capital demand has been made in the Fifth Edition of the civil engineering conditions of contract, but is not recognised in the two building forms.

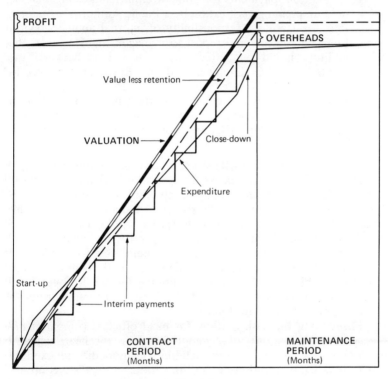

Fig. 6.9

d. Contract extensions of time for inclement weather, lack of progress by nominated sub-contractors, and other reasons, do not usually include recompense for the additional site on-costs incurred, and requests for such payments are likely to be left unresolved until the practical completion of the works.

   e. The valuation of variations, if not readily agreed immediately, is similarly liable to be left unsettled until the end of the job.

   f. Settlement of claims for changes in quantity, quality or conditions, is almost invariably put aside until the contract completion. Then compensation for additional time expense, special rates for new or varied items of work, and miscellaneous claims in general, may be considered, argued, compromised and eventually settled maybe months or even years later.

   g. In addition, payments for both variations and claims may be held up pending verification by a Public Authority's *Auditor.* It is the statutory responsibility of internal audit to review financial controls and report to management. However, the auditor should not affect the relationships between the Contractor, the Employer and the Engineer/Architect as defined in the Contract. The joint statement (1983) by The Institution of Civil Engineers and the Chartered Institute of Public Finance and Accountancy, should help to resolve problems as they arise and not after the final account is submitted.

Thus the peculiar financial structure of construction companies, together with the unique external factors of uncertainty and almost inevitable delays, mean that most contractors will run short of cash at critical times and many will experience liquidity problems. The result is that the construction industry has the highest number of company financial failures of any major British industry.

Nevertheless, if likely cash flow problems could be identified well in advance, it should be possible to plan cash requirements to avoid bunching, or to arrange additional finance to meet peak demands and many failures could be averted. The answer lies in some sort of cash flow forecast.

Forecasting the cash outflow for head office is comparatively easy, since the majority of payments for staff, rent, heat, light and telephone etc. are only too predictable. The more difficult exercise is to assess the cash flows in and out for each separate contract. The basis for a contract flow forecast must be the contract programme and the priced bill of quantities. From these two documents we can build an anticipated valuation graph, as described in Chapter 13 and illustrated in Fig. 13.8. A break-down of the contract sum is also required, and taking the contract for forty houses already referred to, let us assume that the following figures result from the estimator's analysis of the Bill of Quantities:

Head Office and profit say 9%	81 000
Maintenance allowance say 1%	9 000
Labour (inc. site staff) and plant	275 000
Materials	225 000
Sub-contractors – nominated and domestic	232 000
Fixed price allowance	78 000

Contract Sum: £ 900 000

If the contract had a price fluctuation clause, then the non-recoverable element allowed would be substituted for the fixed price figure. To avoid unnecessary complications we could assume that increased costs and the recoverable payments were self-cancelling, and so ignore this factor.

Let us also assume that the retention is 10% up to a maximum of 5% of the contract sum, and will be released half at practical competion and half at the end of the six month maintenance period. We also need to know the dates of valuations and the period for honouring them. Let us say that valuations will be made at the end of each calendar month, and payment will be received one month later. Let us also assume that wages and plant costs are paid at the end of the month, whilst subs and material bills are debited one month later.

We can now draw up a cash flow chart (see Fig. 6.10) in the following manner, using the cumulative valuation from the graph (Fig. 13.8) as our starting point for both cash flows 'in' and 'out'. The Head Office and profit plus the maintenance allowance amount to 10% of the contract sum, and can therefore be calculated as a proportion of the valuation. Official labour rates will rise at discrete steps on fixed dates, but in fact they tend to slip and escalate over a period. Material prices also tend to escalate over a period, and so it is fair to spread our increased costs allowance on a rising figure of $1 + 2 + 3$ etc. Subtracting these two items from the valuation will leave our basic costs.

The basic costs can be proportioned between labour and plant, materials and sub-contracts on the basis of the estimator's analysis. In this case it is realised that sub-contractors will not be involved during the first three months. Alternatively, sub-contracts could be assessed as a separate exercise by pricing the programme as for the total valuation graph. Retention of course is withheld from the sub-contractors and released later exactly as for the main contractor.

The various components of expenditure can now be listed in the months that they will be paid out: labour and plant and increased

	Oct	Nov	Dec	Jan	Feb	Mar	Apr	May	Jun	Jul	Aug	Sep	Oct	Nov	Dec	Jan	Feb	Mar	Apr
Valuation	1 500	4 000	9 000	18 500	24 000	36 000	45 000	56 000	70 500	82 000	88 000	90 000							
H/off. profit main.	150	400	900	1 850	2 400	3 600	4 500	5 600	7 050	8 200	8 800	9 000							
Increased costs	100	300	600	1 000	1 500	2 100	2 800	3 600	4 500	5 500	6 600	7 800							
Basic costs	1 250	3 300	7 510	15 650	20 100	30 300	37 700	46 800	58 950	68 300	72 600	73 200							
Labour and plant	687	1 815	4 125	5 868	7 537	11 363	14 137	17 550	22 106	25 613	27 225	27 500							
Materials	563	1 485	3 375	4 805	6 171	9 302	11 574	14 368	18 098	20 968	22 288	22 500							
Sub-contracts				4 977	6 392	9 635	11 989	14 882	18 746	21 719	23 087	23 200							
S.C. retention				– 498	– 639	– 964	–1 160	–1 160	–1 160	–1 160	–1 160	– 580							
Owed to subs				4 479	5 753	8 671	10 829	13 722	17 586	20 559	21 927	22 620							
Labour and plant	687	1 128	2 310	1 743	1 669	3 826	2 774	3 413	4 556	3 507	1 612	275	212						
Materials		563	922	1 890	1 430	1 366	3 131	2 272	2 794	3 730	2 870	1 320	693						
Subs – retn.					4 479	1 274	2 918	2 158	2 893	3 864	2 973	1 368							
Increased costs	100	200	300	400	500	600	700	800	900	1 000	1 100	1 200							
Maintenance													150	150	150	150	150	150	580
Expenditure	787	1 891	3 532	4 033	8 078	7 066	9 523	8 643	11 143	12 101	8 555	4 163	1 055	150	150	150	150	150	580
Valuation	1 500	4 000	9 000	18 500	24 000	36 000	45 000	56 000	70 500	82 000	88 000	90 000							
Retention	– 150	– 400	– 900	–1 850	–2 400	–3 600	–4 500	–4 500	–4 500	–4 500	–4 500	–4 500	–2 250						
Certified	1 350	3 600	8 100	16 450	21 600	32 400	40 500	51 500	66 000	77 500	83 500	87 750							
Prev. payment		1 350	3 600	8 100	16 450	21 600	32 400	40 500	51 500	66 000	77 500	83 500							
Income	–	1 350	2 250	4 500	8 350	5 150	10 800	8 100	11 000	14 500	11 500	6 000	4 250						2 250
Net cash flow	– 787	– 541	–1 282	+ 467	+ 272	–1 916	+1277	– 543	– 143	+2399	+2945	+1837	+3195	– 150	– 150	– 150	– 150	– 150	+1670
Cumulative C.F.	– 787	–1 328	–2 610	–2 143	–1 871	–3 787	–2 510	–3 053	–3 196	– 797	+2148	+3985	+7180	+7030	+6880	+6730	+6580	+6430	+8100

Contract Period ← → | Maintenance Period ← →

Fig. 6.10. Cash flow forecast for 40 houses (in £10's)

costs in the month they are incurred; materials and sub-contracts (less retention) one month later. Maintenance will be spread over the appropriate six months. Total expenditure can then be added up as shown. Beginning once again with the valuation, we deduct retention as 10% up to a maximum of 5% of the contract sum, with half released on substantial completion and the remainder after the maintenance period. The amounts certified are paid one month later, and the individual monthly income is calculated by deducting the previous payment.

Income (positive) and expenditure (negative) are now added together to give the net cash flow for each separate month. By accumulating these cash flows we end up with £81 000 in credit – our anticipated Head Office overheads and profit. It will be noticed that it has been necessary to fund the contract for the first ten months, before the cumulative cash flow became a net inflow. This is not unusual, but it is very illuminating if the situation has not been appreciated before.

If cash-flow forecasts are prepared for every contract, then they can be added together with Head Office requirements to provide an overall picture of the company's finances. A cash forecast will enable the Finance Director to:

 a. Ensure that cash is available to meet day-to-day require-ments.
 b. Meet periodic demands such as tax.
 c. Plan payment for heavy outlays like plant.
 d. Repay loans as soon as possible.
 e. Transfer surplus cash to earn interest.
 f. Ensure that temporary credit arrangements are available when required. The benefits of cash planning will be evident from the more efficient running of the business and a more stable financial structure.

16. Sources of Finance for Construction

Changing patterns of economic, social and political climate have direct and irresistible implications for the building and civil engineering industries. In the decade since the early 1970's the total workload has dropped 20% in volume. No-one builds a new factory, when manufacturing in general is operating well below capacity. Since 1973 there has been a significant switch from new works to repair, maintenance and improvement. The relative shares have changed from 75/25 in favour of new work, to 60/40 or closer. There has also been a marked decline in the public sector client as a source of work for the industry. Central and local government, which accounted for 45% of contractors' workload in the mid-1970's, have fallen to 38% in the mid-1980's. Civil engineering and local authority housing have been particularly affected.

Characteristic sources of finance for construction include insurance companies, building societies and government. *Insurance companies* offer two main types of insurance, General Insurance and Life Insurance. General insurance exists to protect assets by providing compensation for unexpected happenings like fire, burglary or accident. These policies are short-term and premiums may vary from year to year. Life insurance protects by providing a sum of money on death; or, in the case of endowment policies, after a specified period of 10, 15 or 25 years or earlier death. These policies are essentially long-term, offering the accumulation of capital in addition to life protection. Premiums are invested in a mix of property, ordinary stocks and fixed interest securities. It is from their investment portfolios that insurance companies finance prestigious office blocks, town centre developments and occasional factory estates. The trustees of pension funds and trust funds may similarly invest in 'bricks and mortar', as a sure haven for their money.

Building Societies have two principal functions. They act as depositories for the savings of individuals, and provide loans to people buying their own homes. The earliest recorded society was founded in 1775 in Birmingham as a building co-operative: but during the nineteenth century societies stopped building and instead became suppliers of finance. Since the 1950's expansion has been rapid so that by 1983 total assets exceeded £86 000 million, and 5 928 000 borrowers were advanced £19 357 million. Investors total 37 713 000, but largely because of amalgamations the numbers of societies have fallen from 2286 in 1900 to a present 206. It can be seen that the building societies have a vital function in the savings/investment equilibrium of the house building industry. Building societies are uniquely constituted, and subject to The Building Societies Act 1962 are managed on conservative lines, so that there is a minimal risk to either investors or borrowers.

Government financial assistance to industry is enormous and varied, much of which stimulates demand for construction. Action to alleviate locations of severe unemployment include the nomination of Assisted Areas e.g. Northern Ireland and Merseyside etc., where special incentives are offered to attract new business. Regional Development Grants and Regional Selective Assistance made under the Industry Act 1972 are also available to safeguard jobs. Aid is also offered to particular sectors of industry, including: Hotels under the Development of Tourism Act 1969, Government Factories in the assisted areas, various schemes for Manufacturing Industry, grants for converting redundant Farm Buildings, and help towards the cost of particular research and development projects largely provided under the Science and Technology Act 1965. There is also a wide range of Government Agencies in different parts of the country, chiefly directed to help in the development of smaller firms. In addition, assistance is available from Local Authorities including New Towns, whose incentives vary greatly from area to area.

Additional capital for expansion or speculative development may be raised by a fresh issue of shares, or the arrangement of a loan. However, additional shares may result in some loss of control by the owners, unless restricted to a script issue. A temporary loan in the form of a bank overdraft may be agreed in advance with one's bank manager, who will always set a limit. If this is insufficient either in amount or period of time, then debenture stocks may be the answer. For a fixed period of years debenture stock holders become long-term creditors, but do not own any part of the business. The owner of a building may consider a mortgage, or as a last resort 'sale and leaseback' from an insurance company or pension fund. These alternative methods have their pros and cons, and their relative merits need careful consideration.

The *capital structure* of a company, as defined by the 'gearing ratio' of loan capital:issued share capital, is a measure of the company's borrowing capacity. High gearing is vulnerable to market changes and is therefore associated with high risk, and a ratio of 1:1 is often considered prudent. On the other hand, low gearing may mean that insufficient funds are available to take advantage of sudden opportunities. The right balance of borrowing is therefore important, ensuring that short-term needs are financed from short-term monies and long-term projects from long-term funds.

BIBLIOGRAPHY

An Introduction to Engineering Economics, The Institution of Civil Engineers, 1969.
P. T. Pigott, *Finance for Builders – Cash Flow Planning*, An Foras Forbartha Construction Division Pamphlet, Number 7 (1), 1971.

The Principles of Cash Forecasting, C.I.T.B. Training Aid B/13.

L. R. Creasey, 'Economics and engineering organisation', *Proceedings Supplement (i),* The Institution of Civil Engineers 1970.

Clive Woodcock, *Raising Finance: The Guardian Guide for the Small Business,* Kogan Page. 1982.

Accounting Methods for the Small Builder, The National Federation of Building Trades Employers, 1962.

Annotated Bibliographies No. 30 Finance, The Institute of Building, 1978.

Chapter 7

Marketing

Although the building industry is admittedly the most difficult in which to ensure a controlled and regulated turnover, nevertheless a business policy is required irrespective of the outstanding work load or of whether the intention is to expand or not. The largest firm can have specialised departments and outside public relations consultants to help in carrying out this policy, while for the smallest it is a matter for the Principal himself. Marketing is just as much a function of management in building as in any other industry – selling the company, its services and its good name.

Marketing is defined by the Institute of Marketing as 'that management process responsible for identifying, anticipating and satisfying customer requirements profitably.' Marketing has two distinct but complementary functions:

1. *Marketing strategy* – finding out what people need or want, organising the resources of the firm to fulfil these needs or wants, whilst determining suitable policies so that both the buyer gains and the seller profits from the transaction.

2. *Selling tactics* – the executive task of employing appropriate techniques to sell the product or service, i.e. obtain orders or contracts.

1. How Policy is Determined

The marketing function is primarily concerned with the formulation of the overall sales policy under the following headings:

    a. Product – what type of work is required and what value of each type, e.g. building, civil engineering, housing or jobbing? Which is best suited to the company's experience, resources and organisation? Reasons for changes in types of work. What ancillary services will be offered, e.g. concrete design and testing laboratory, site investigations and soil mechanics laboratory, architectural and/or structural design office, plant hire?

b. *Customer* – is the company selling to architects, quantity surveyors, consultants or the public? Which architects – local authority, private, local or national? Which public – general, commercial, industrial, local authorities or nationalised industries?

c. *Distribution* – the areas in which work will lie – local, specific regions or country wide. Reasons for any changes in working areas. Should more work be taken at one time of the year than at others? Will the company try to get on to tender lists, or will it aim at negotiated contracts? Who will be responsible for getting work?

d. *Price and Profit* – from an analysis of the jobs completed over say the last five years, which is the most profitable field? Shall the company try for large percentage profits, or a smaller percentage over a larger turnover? What are the oncosts borne by labour, materials and sub-contractors; and what separate percentages will be added to each of these components?

e. *Advertising and Promotion* – will this activity be someone's part-time duty, the responsibility of a specialised department, or will outside public relations consultants be employed? Will the company buy space in the national press or trade journals, or have a spread in the local paper as and when contracts are completed? Companies building houses for private speculation may employ an estate agent. What is the company policy concerning nameboards, site hoardings, painting of vehicles, viewing platforms, Christmas gifts, etc., and entertainment of clients? Some companies adopt a personal symbol and use it on postage cancellations and the windows of completed projects as well as in the other forms of advertising. Others produce sales brochures and issue house magazines.

2. How Building Undertakings Obtain Business and Secure Opportunities to Tender

After the sales policy has been established, selling activities must be organised to carry these plans into effect. The organisation structure of the sales department will depend upon the size of the firm, the chosen spheres of work and its method of distribution. A speculative house builder may employ a full time sales manager and staff, while a jobbing builder may just wait for enquiries. Whatever the sales personnel may be, however, the responsibilities and duties of each person should be clearly defined so that control is simplified and made more effective.

Methods of obtaining business may also vary as follows:

a. *Speculation.* Risking one's own money to build houses, flats, or even factories for sale to an estimated demand.

b. *Arrangement.* Standing agreement with a chain store to erect all their new premises, or with an organisation who sells a design and construction service for specialised plants or council houses.

c. *Reputation.* A few firms can rely upon their name for service or quality, built up over a long period of years;

or *Recommendation* by a satisfied client to his friend.

d. *Negotiation* with someone known to be considering a new building or extension. Contact may be made by the company's public relations officer upon a basis of cost plus, cost plus fee, fixed sum, schedule of rates, or one's own form of negotiated contract.

e. *Tender,* a more competitive opportunity secured in a variety of ways including:
  i. Rotation. Government departments maintain tender lists of approved contractors, and share their invitations to tender a number at a time.
  ii. Selection. Local authorities, nationalised industries, and large commercial concerns invite tenders from around 6 to 12 contractors who have carried out previous work or are known by reputation.
  iii. Invitation. Architects usually invite tenders from perhaps 3 to 6 builders who are known to them or thought to be capable and interested.
  iv. Request. The builder hearing of projected work may write and request permission to be included in the list of invitations.
  v. Open tender in answer to advertisements in the local or national press or trade journals. Being open to 'all-comers' this is the most competitive field, although evidence of experience and ability may be demanded.

3. How Builders Maintain Their Reputation and Service

Reputation as such is of little commercial value unless it is made use of and exploited in the best sense of the word. Activities designed to maintain and foster a company's reputation, to put an attractive image over to its public, comprise that branch of marketing known as *Public Relations*. Builders go into their clients' premises and display their competency for all to see, so that clean and tidy sites, well maintained plant and vehicles, and attractive signboards and hoardings are important. Keeping noise, dust and spillage to a minimum, providing adequate footwalks with overhead protection and lighting when necessary, and proper explanations of unavoidable delays or nuisances, help to give a good name. A firm and friendly contact with the local press is of course essential in order to avoid bad or unfair publicity and ensure that, whenever possible, someone else will blow the firm's trumpet for them. Fast building, new techniques, complicated operations, hazardous operations, saving money, and local or national importance are all good news value. Articles in the technical magazines are invaluable for impressing clients. Topping-out as a public relations exercise is gaining greater popularity these days, perhaps because, with the advent of the high building, it presents an opportunity of discovering splendid new views of the surrounding district. These informal ceremonies, at which the operatives take part, are worthwhile in demonstrating a pride in achievement, and derive from the ancient custom of hoisting a flag, a young fir tree or sheaf of corn when the highest part of a building is reached. Finally it must be remembered that the industry as a whole is judged by each individual project and contractor.

Since it is impossible to sell a bad product for any length of time, a building organisation must promote the qualities of reasonable efficiency and a high standard of integrity. First impressions are often vital so that attention must be paid to the courteous reception of visitors, a polite and effective telephone procedure, prompt acknowledgments and business-like correspondence. Improved efficiency in organisation and construction, particularly completion on time, will not only bring the direct rewards of reduced costs and higher profits, but also additional business from satisfied clients and impressed by-standers. Some form of a follow-up after completion is a worthwhile service in almost every type of building project, for no effort is wasted if it ensures a satisfied customer.

Adherence to a high standard of integrity and professional conduct is the foundation upon which public relations depend. By subscribing to the principles laid down in the Chartered Institute of Building's Memorandum of Association, and by active participation in the affairs of the Institute, building managers can supply the salt with which to savour the whole building industry. The tangible results would be better support for trade associations and more whole-hearted efforts for the promotion of industrial safety.

4. How Tenders are Handled

Enquiries from widely differing sources may in practice be handled in many different ways so far as detail is concerned, dependent upon their relative size, value and importance; the time and staff available; and the type and nature of the particular project, whether usual or unique. Nevertheless, ideally all tenders should follow the same logical pattern of sequence from receipt to submission, in order to ensure that nothing is overlooked and to promote a coherent and regular standard of estimating. The usual stages are as follows:

1. *Enquiry summary.* A summary of the major details, e.g. client, architect, general construction, contract conditions, etc., is prepared, together with an approximate estimate of the total price based upon either a summary of the major quantities of work or upon unit prices per square metre or m^3. From this overall picture the senior estimator decides basic principles such as profit margins on materials and sub-contractors, sources of plant and the extent of sub-letting, and the general treatment of pricing to be used.
2. *Analysis of bills of quantities.* Material enquiries and sub-contract invitations can then be sent out, the various bills or trades may be shared between the estimators, and specified responsibilities allotted, e.g. site inspection. This stage is dealt with in greater detail under the heading of pre-tender planning in Chapter 13.
3. *Pricing of rates.* The bill of quantities items are broken down into their component parts, and each priced separately. Material elements are built up from suppliers' quotations, handling and wastage allowances, conversion factors for mixing or consolidation, and profit margin. Labour and plant elements may be compiled from a library of output standards,

schedules of standard rates or constructed from basic principles by the individual estimator. Standard hire rates for either the company's or outside plant are generally available together with either measured (by work study) or empirical output figures. Bill rates are then synthesised and filled in ready for extension and totalling by comptometers or computer.

4. *Financial analysis.* On completion of the actual pricing it is then necessary to produce a financial analysis of the preliminary tender total, showing the relative figures for the firm's work broken down into labour, plant, material and profit, sub-contractors' work and profit, prime cost and provisional sums with profit, and preliminaries.

5. *Final consideration.* This financial analysis together with a summary of the build-up of major items can then be considered by the directors. Such factors as the ruling market trends, the firm's outstanding work load, availability of labour, plant and materials, and any other particular aspects can be carefully weighed, and any necessary modifications decided upon.

6. *Records.* The actual tender figures submitted are carefully recorded, together with any news of the ultimate placing of the contract and competitors' estimates. Subsequently it is extremely useful to analyse this information in order to watch any trends in the success percentage, and to compare company tenders with the general market level.

5. The Consumer and Market Research

The speculative house builders, the city property developers, and the investors in factory estates or shopping centres, have always been market-orientated; but it is only in recent years that general contractors have addressed themselves to the deliberate act of seeking out new business. Under the stress of a prolonged depression they have become more and more involved in the development of new markets, and in learning the techniques of persuading prospective clients to buy their products and services.

In order to identify and satisfy a customer's need at a profit, it is necessary to have an intimate knowledge of the consumer, to analyse the history and character of the firm, and to find the best markets at a particular time. Market research can be used to assess possible future markets for the company's activities; to discover whether the anticipated building pattern is compatible with the company's resources, expertise and experience; and indicate those particular areas where too many builders are competing unprofitably to serve too few customers. It may identify what is wanted and where, so that plans can be made to meet those requirements when they are needed. Perhaps through the recognition and anticipation of the potential for innovation, completely new markets may be discovered and pioneered through the exploitation of technical developments. An examination of the company's past and present activities should determine what are the organisation's strengths and weaknesses in respect of physical resources, management, finance and know-how. It is essential to discover, from a factual analysis of past results, precisely in which area of the construction market, and on what type of contract we perform best. We shall also learn the optimum size of project for which our particular organisation and training are most cost-effective. In the pursuit of a more efficient interaction between producer and consumer we shall find that specialisation by size or type of work is of great advantage to a firm. Research by Dr. Martin Barnes on behalf of the Builders' Conference has made it clear that overall profitability is more closely linked with 'specialisation' than any other factor.

An essential prerequisite to any effective marketing action is a comprehensive knowledge of the construction market. Keeping a watchful eye on the overall market conditions is a responsible and time-consuming occupation. Monthly statistics gathered by the Department of the Environment are essentially historical, but they do give an idea of sector size and trends. Useful forward indicators are (i) the R.I.B.A. figures on new commissions and work entering the working drawing stage, (ii) the C.B.I. surveys of investment intentions, and (iii) the N.F.B.T.E. quarterly State of Trade Inquiries. The N.E.D.O. also produces summaries of Construction Industry Prospects, as well as forecasts for both the Building and Civil Engineering industries on a yearly subscription basis. Various organisations specialise in supplying sales intelligence gleaned from the local authority planning registers. Market research in depth and detail can be fairly expensive, but a growing demand for information and guidance has produced at least one specialist building management and marketing consultancy. Pressure upon the Government by the industry's Group of Eight has resulted in a detailed breakdown of construction capital expenditure being included in the annual Finance White Paper on public expenditure.

Traditionally, most contractors bring themselves to the notice of potential clients by keeping their names on the 'approved lists' maintained by public authorities. But faced with Government expenditure cuts and long-term recession, it has been advocated that the construction industry should take more positive action to influence the level of consumer demand. According to Mr. Warren Evans, 'Our customers' interest in our products must be deliberately engaged, and we must find ways of placing our wares before them.' This go-out-and-sell theory – the direct appeal to persuade the customer of the advantages of buying a new building – has been actively investigated by the Civil Engineering Economic Development Committee. Their report on Construction for Industrial Recovery spearheaded a promotional effort to convince industrialists that modern buildings add substantially to efficiency and profitability.

An aggresive marketing policy, following upon consumer and market research, should aim to develop a profitable relationship between the company's resources of men and money, and customer's satisfaction. Managers and staff need to be trained to be more aware of the changing business environment, of their clients and their competitors, and of the opportunities available to those who look creatively into the future.

6. Sales Policy and Promotion

After marketing strategy has been decided, and an appropriate management organisation set up, we are left with the tactical task of obtaining contracts, or at least opportunities to tender. The company's services, resources and achievements will have been brought to the notice of prospective clients by advertising and a variety of promotional activities – see section 1e, earlier in this chapter. A favourable climate, comprising an attractive image and a good reputation, will have been created and maintained by suitable public relations work as described in section 3. In addition to the traditional methods of obtaining business described in section 2, it is now usual for larger and medium sized firms to employ salesmen or representatives. By means of letters of enquiry and regular visits, they hope to keep the estimating department supplied with sufficient and suitable invitations to tender.

Many contractors now advertise alternative forms of tender, which offer clients specialised services to suit particular conditions e.g. Lump Sum, Design and Construct, Prime Cost plus Fee and

Management Contracts. The shortage of general work has also tempted some firms to branch out as developers, with mixed results. Success can bring high profits, but there are so many aspects to be brought together correctly that this is a specialised and very risky business. Some of the larger British firms have also ventured overseas, but what was once a comparatively easy and lucrative field has now become a fiercely competitive world, often requiring very complex financial packages to swing the sale. In many industries e.g. consumer goods, the training of salesmen in technique is given great prominence; but in the general contracting sphere a good presence, technical knowledge and the ability to communicate well, seem to be the essential requirements. Most building and civil engineering contractors now seem to have grasped the vital fact that, as the N.H.B.C. poster declares, 'a customer is the most important person in any business'. Yet the need for a separate 'marketing division' was expounded by L. F. Urwick in his book 'Management of Tomorrow', published in 1933.

BIBLIOGRAPHY

J. M. Beirne, *Marketing*, The Chartered Institute of Building Site Management Information Service, No. 22, 1968.
Marketing for the Building Industry, National Federation of Building Trades Employers.
Marketing and Selling, Diagnostic Checklist, C.I.T.B, 1979.
W. B. Jepson and M. P. Nicholson, *Marketing and Building Management*, MTP Construction.
Building Management Notebook — Appendix, Institute of Building, 1975.
A. B. Moore, *Marketing Management in Construction*, Butterworths, 1984.
Code of Estimating Practice, The Chartered Institute of Building, 1979.

Chapter 8

Design, Research and Development

1. Architect/Builder Relationship

Both the architect and the builder have reciprocal legal obligations to the client, which are delineated in their respective forms of agreement and contract, The third side of this business triangle, the architect/builder relationship, is formally described in the conditions of contract and upon the quality and strength of this vital link rests the stability and harmony of the enterprise. Inevitably the really successful and efficient building project depends on the highest degree of co-operation, at every stage and between all levels, but none more so than between the two functional partners.

This essential *entente* is, unfortunately, sometimes weakened by the hypothetical distinction between the professional class and the rest, and by baseless suspicion born of mutual ignorance. Building is still too rigidly compartmented, whereas in the civil engineering field there is more freedom of movement for individuals to and from the professional and contracting sides, resulting in a tendency towards a more sympathetic attitude to the other man's point of view. Ironically the builder may also be an engineer and it is greatly to be hoped that the Chartered Institute of Building with its new membership structure, will eventually take its rightful place as an equal co-partner with the other professional institutions. It is important that builders should be fully aware of the problems confronting the architect in his office. Likewise an understanding by the architects of present day production problems, and an appreciation of the use by a builder of enlightened management techniques, should result in improved collaboration arising naturally out of respect for each other's competence.

When an architect comes on to a job he will treat all alike with courtesy and is entitled to the respect of everyone on the site. But he must be careful to observe the proprieties and give all his orders or directions through the clerk of works to the general foreman, and never to individual workmen. He can do much by his personal influence to make the contract a happy one, and by his knowledge of and interest in the various trades and crafts and their materials, he can stimulate the pride of the operatives in producing work of good quality.

2. Architects' Organisation and Procedure

No person is now able to practise or carry on business under any name, style or title containing the word 'Architect' unless he is registered under the Architects (Registration) Acts, 1931 and 1938. The majority, but not all, are members of the Royal Institute of British Architects and observe a strict Code of Professional Conduct, governing the obtaining of work, remuneration, advertising and other matters.

An architect is employed by the building owner to look after his interests and become his general agent for all purposes relating to designing, obtaining tenders for, and superintending the building of the work for which he has been commissioned. He is therefore vested with considerable authority which is usually described in the Conditions of Contract, but equally he assumes great responsibilities for legal, financial and technical aspects, and under the Statutes of Limitation his liability for negligence only terminates at the end of six years from the date of such an act.

Although an architect's first duty is to his client, by his Principles he must act honestly and impartially in all questions arising between the employer and contractor, and he is often called upon to act as an arbitrator. Essentially, however, he is an artist, and the Copyright Act of 1911 protects his design as an 'Architectural work of Art'.

Upon receiving his initial instruction the architect begins by agreeing an accommodation schedule with his client, and prepares a programme for both his own preparations and eventual construction. Sketch plans and perspectives are produced and preliminary application made to the Local Authority.

When the final sketch design has been approved and planning approval in principle obtained, he proceeds to prepare working drawings and general details. After settling matters of services and prime cost items, and constructing a specification and schedules of finishes, etc., everything is handed over to the quantity surveyor so that he may prepare bills of quantities.

The architect then invites tenders, and upon their receipt advises the building owner as to the selection of the successful contractor. Contract documents are prepared and signed and the contractor's programme agreed, whereupon construction may commence.

To assist in controlling and supervising the progress of the works to ensure that they are carried out in accordance with the terms of the contract, the architect may appoint a Clerk of Works, who will be under his control but paid by the client. The architect checks weekly site reports from the works and attends regular site meetings to maintain good progress and settle outstanding problems.

Architects also issue variation orders for any additions to, or omissions from, the Contract, notify the client of interim certificates as payment for work done, and approve the final account. The architect may also be called upon to inspect the report upon existing buildings, and prepare valuations or schedules of dilapidations and repairs.

3.Planning and Programming the Supply of Working Drawings

Working drawings, with the specification and bills of quantities, form the chief part of the contractor's instructions, and it is therefore essential to ensure that they are received in good time and in the right order, if building work is not to be carried out from hand to mouth followed by the inevitable claims for extra time and costs. Money can be saved by speedy building, but speed can only be obtained by very careful preparation and the avoidance of subsequent variations.

The architect usually begins by preparing a preliminary drawing schedule, often with the help of standard check lists, in order that he can plan the work load for his drawing office and allocate proper priorities as between different contracts or various construction stages. In theory, full working drawings and general details should be available to the quantity surveyor for his preparation of bills of quantities, but in practice, too often, this is not the case. The client is impatient for work to commence, with the result that drawings are incomplete and quantities only provisional, so that everyone must make the best of a bad job.

With the architect, like everyone else these days, often understaffed, it frequently happens that information is still not complete when the Contract is awarded, despite the principle of 'complete documentation' agreed by the Joint Consultative Committee of Architects, Quantity Surveyors and Builders, and endorsed by the Ministry of Works. But it is useless for the builder to blame the architect for failing to understand the problems of those receiving his drawings and instructions, and the contractor should inform the architect as early as possible after the contract is placed, of what he requires to enable him to comply with the agreed construction programme. This can be accomplished by either:

a. The incorporation of symbols on the programme chart to indicate dates when particular drawings or schedules are required (see Figs. 13.9 and 13.16).

or b. A schedule of outstanding information listing all the necessary drawings and giving the latest dates by which they must be received (see Fig. 13.15).

The dates for commencing each item of work will of course be derived from the programme, but the prior periods necessary for ordering materials or making other preparations, and thus the dates when information is required, should be mutually agreed between the architect and the builder.

Copies of this list should be distributed to everyone concerned, and can then be added to as and when additional queries are raised. These will eventually provide a record of details requested and received, should there be the need to substantiate a claim for delay in issuing instructions.

Because of the disproportionate costs in terms of site labour, occasioned by lack of planning or minor variations in design, it is to be hoped that the universally accepted recommendations of The National Federation of Building Trades Employers as to the obligations of both the contractor and the building owner in firm price tendering, will eventually be included in the standard conditions of contract.

4. Advantages of Liaison at Design and Tendering Stages

Building is an unusual industry in that design and production have by tradition been divorced and conducted separately. This gulf between the builder, and the architect and his client, the idea that the contractor begins where the architect ends, is responsible in part for certain inefficiencies of the industry. The contractor has a big contribution to make at both the design and tendering stages if prejudices and suspicion can be overcome.

The standard method of competitive tendering (contract in series) suffers from many inherent disadvantages: it precludes the reciprocal exchange of technical knowledge and information; it tends to create an atmosphere of hard bargaining, which is not conducive to the development of good relations; it places a strain upon the architect's office by aggravating the irregular flow of work; it is wasteful of the quantity surveyor's time and money and inhibits his role in cost planning. Incomplete details with inevitable revisions, provisional quantities and rushed tenders make it most unsuitable for certain commercial and industrial projects, where an early completion date is even more important than the cost.

Alternatively, negotiated contracts (parallel working) provide a basis upon which every member of the building team may co-operate from the outset, so that construction proceeds concurrently with design and pricing. As soon as the basic design is settled, a construction programme agreed and drawing office work synchronised with it, work on the site can start almost immediately. The contribution of the quantity surveyor becomes more valuable because he has much more material to draw upon for his calculations and reviews. To the contractor it means that each stage of construction can be planned well in advance, materials ordered in good time, and the whole job programmed to ensure a steady flow of work and the avoidance of non-productive time. The growing use of prefabricated materials accentuates the importance of this point.

The effect of design on productivity is considerable, and, particularly as buildings become more complex, liaison at the design stage allows the architect as leader, to give the best possible service to his client by taking full advantage of the capabilities of each member of his team. Enlistment of the builder to give advice upon the latest construction methods and techniques, e.g. simplicity of forms, repetition, prefabrications and standard units, can result in savings and improvements and reduce variations; while his knowledge of the availability of craftsmen and demarcation problems, and the supply of materials or components may well effect design economies. Similarly the experience of structural and services engineers can save time or money, and new techniques devised by them may allow the production of new forms of architecture.

Liaison at the tender stage not only cuts out the non-productive tendering period, but because the contractor is familiar with the requirements of the job from the outset he is enabled thoroughly to plan his operations before site work starts, to allocate manpower and plant and earmark supplies in advance. This is particularly important where sub-contractors are concerned, for they are frequently appointed far too late to play their proper part in planning. Advance and certain information also facilitates more precise and realistic costing.

Resistance to the negotiated contract with its obvious attractions is largely due to fears of over-charging and the desire for safeguards of fair prices. There are however numerous methods of giving a client the protection he requires, including 'net cost' bills of quantities drawn up in association with the quantity surveyor, target costs with shared savings, and schedules of prices based upon a comparable contract awarded in open competition. But co-operation and goodwill are a much better formula and the careful choice of a contractor is a better guarantee than a bond. When builders are selected for negotiated contracts by reputation, i.e. recommendation or repeat order by a satisfied client, they have every incentive to please the owner and preserve their good name. The principle of competition has only shifted from price to performance, and can prove to be the more reliable safeguard.

An architect while approving the principle of closer collaboration, might still distrust negotiated contracts, perhaps fearing the growth of package deals or 'turnkey' contracts and the loss of artistic independence. In fact the greater integration of construction produced by parallel working should strengthen his traditional position as leader of the design function, while increasing the responsibility of the builder as the co-ordinator of production.

Moreover, the three cardinal principles of design, i.e. simplicity, symmetry and continuity, seem to be ideally fulfilled by a scheme of parallel working. Surely the best should be achieved both in terms of time and money, purpose and appearance, when the two partners intimately understand each other's contribution, and by close co-operation share the load equally from start until finish.

5. Research and Development

1. *The purpose.* No industry or business can stand still, but must continually improve or amend its products or services in order to keep abreast both of the times and its competitors. Change

is inevitable, but while some notable discoveries have been accidental the majority have been the result of specialised and constant activity. The endeavour of the research and development process is to discover facts by scientific study, and thence to bring new ideas from the latent to the active state. New ideas when properly applied can help to make cheaper and better products, and it has been estimated[1] that work done in the Building Research Station saved £300 m. over 12 years in the school building programme.

However, new ideas must first be recognised and used, and, as National Productivity Year 1963 highlighted, the danger of falling behind lies not in the inability to find new methods, but in the failure to apply them. Development must be someone's definite responsibility, although all must be prepared to give up old privileges and to abandon old practices. Secondly, as has been pointed out in the Emmerson report, there is a need for a change of emphasis in the building industry research effort, from the past concentration on materials and structural aspects towards the more practical matters of site organisation and human relationships.

a. *Pure research* is concerned with searching after the fundamental laws of cause and effect, and the pursuit of theoretical knowledge for its own sake without conscious regard to practical applications. Such basic truths might include the principles of soil mechanics or philosophical treatments of structural analysis.

b. *Applied research*, by distinction, is engaged in courses of critical investigation into the practical applications of learning, and is trying to find ways of putting known information to particular uses. Inquiries into the problem of noise, and earthwork construction in wet weather are current examples of this field.

c. *Operational research* is a particular branch of applied research, in which scientific techniques are used to provide executives with a quantitative basis for their decisions. It is also a social science, whereby working methods and processes are investigated in an effort to improve productivity, and the 1964 pilot study[2] of communications in the building industry, commissioned by the National Joint

---

[1] Viscount Caldecote in the House of Lords on 15 November, 1961.
[2] "Interdependence and Uncertaintity" by The Tavistock Institute, 1966.

Consultative Committee, indicates the growing importance of this type of work.

2. *The organisation.* At Government level various Ministries are responsible for maintaining fifteen laboratories including the Hydraulics Research Station, the Building Research Station and the Road Research Laboratory. They also grant financial aid to over fifty Research Associations which have been set up voluntarily by groups of firms to serve particular industries or common services such as glass, lime, paint, tar, timber, and heating and ventilating. Grant-aid is also given to the Construction Industry Research and Information Association which was begun by the Institution of Civil Engineers, the Federation of Civil Engineering Contractors and the Association of Consulting Engineers. The Department of the Environment has responsibility for the direction and funding of research in the areas of planning, construction, transport, pollution and water. A Director-General of Research co-ordinates research input to the industry directly via B.R.E., T.R.R.L., and the major grants to such bodies as C.I.R.I.A., B.S.R.I.A. and T.R.A.D.A. Since 1972 the Building Research Establishment – an amalgamation of the Building Research Station, Fire Reseach Station and Forest Products Research Laboratory – has maintained close consultation with the industry in its efforts to seek improvement of the environment; value for money and efficiency; health, safety and amenity; and resources.

Universities also carry out research projects such as the three-year study of the structure and economy of the building industry, which has been undertaken by the Manchester College of Science and Technology, while many Trade Associations and Development Councils investigate specific materials including aluminium, cement and concrete, copper, lead, and zinc. A few of the larger and more progressive contracting companies also have research units, primarily directed to their private problems although some work is undertaken for clients.

3. *Sources of information.* The dissemination of technical information within the industry is still largely unco-ordinated, which partly explains why 'neither the professions nor contractors make anything like full use of all the information at present available'.[1]

[1] The Building Research Board Annual Report, 1961.

The Government maintains a National Lending Library for Science and Technology, a Technical Inquiries Service in London, and Regional Technical Information centres. H.M.S.O. distributes Road and Building Science Abstracts together with other Government publications, while the Building Research Station publishes monthly Digests, National and Factory and Tropical Building Studies, as well as certain reference books. B.R.S. also runs an annual course for building teachers, and an advisory service on construction topics.

Six Building Centres display materials and plant and issue manufacturer's data sheets, Trade Development Associations operate information services, and the British Standards Institution is a most useful source of knowledge. The National Federation of Building Trades Employers operates a technical inquiry bureau, reviews research news in the *National Builder* and endeavours to keep its members up-to-date through the Building Advisory Service. Certain management consultants also provide advice and training in building management. Other sources of information include technical and professional journals, the monthly *British Technology Index* and annual publications like *Specification*, and trade literature services such as Specifile Ltd. and Barbour Index Ltd.

Since 1964, the National Building Agency has operated as an official advisory body for building, responsible to the D.O.E. Initially grant-aided, it is now entirely fee-earning; and in addition to helping local authorities with their house-building programmes, its sphere is now much more varied. N.B.A. did much to publicise line-of-balance planning.

4. *Development.* Although there remains this problem of how to inject effectively the results of scientific research into the blood-stream of such a traditional industry, many practical applications have been tackled, although not fully worked out.

   a. *Standardisation* of materials, components and procedures would contribute to productivity by reducing variety, and this might stimulate standardisation of detailing and specialisation by designers.

   b. *Modular co-ordination* of dimensions for building components and designs has been brought a little nearer by the recommendation of a 4in./10cm standard unit by the R.I.B.A. Council. Work by the European Productivity

Agency and others on systems of Preferred Dimensions, and the British Standards Institution two Drafts for Development show some progress in this direction.

c. *Prefabrication* or the off-site preparation of building units has been held back largely by the cost of factory overheads and transport, as shown by the post-war Temporary Housing Programme. However, many items are now available, ranging from water tank laggings to precast concrete buildings and packaged bathroom units.

d. *Industrialisation* of the building process by the use of large factory-produced components was expected to be accelerated by reason of the positive encouragement given by the Ministry of Public Building and Works in the 1960s. Several systems of large unit construction for multi-storey flats were pioneered by British firms, although many of them were of continental origin. But the social reaction against high-rise dwellings, the Ronan Point disaster, and more recent maintenance problems have effectively stopped this development.

e. *Mechanisation* of building operations is inevitably linked with design, and the progress of the previously mentioned developments will speed up the substitution of machine power for manual work. The Lift Slab method and climbing formwork systems are efforts by designers to take advantage of mechanisation.

f. *Development groups* composed of consortiums of local authorities now include CLASP and SCOLA for school construction, and the numerous combinations for housing. These are attempts to rationalise design through the adoption of standard fittings and components, co-ordination of dimensions, greater use of prefabrication, and factory production. In addition, the larger market allows bulk ordering with its consequent economies.

g. *Interchangeability* of labour is required if technical changes are not to lead to demarcation disputes. The introduction of more prefabrication and mechanisation will certainly affect the craft structure of the industry, even if it does not lead to the radical revision suggested by Sir Richard Coppock.

h. *Terotechnology* is officially defined as 'a combination of management, financial, engineering and other practices applied to physical assets in pursuit of economic life-cycle costs.' In building practice it is concerned with the specification and design for reliability and maintainability, including contractor involvement in the design process; determination of the optimum life span; and feedback on costs and performance of buildings in use.

Once again, the basic tenets of good design can be discerned in these trends of technical development, for simplicity, standardisation and repetition are the same objectives under slightly different names.

5. *Application.* It is a generally accepted fact that, while this country probably undertakes more research than any other (except the U.S.A. and the U.S.S.R.), and we make more than our share of important discoveries, we somehow exploit less than our share of the results.

Certainly the construction industry does appear reluctant to make effective use of many of the technical advances made by research and development establishments. The architect and the structural engineer have to design their buildings/structures when they are required, using the best information readily available at the time. They are often interested in the basic problems involved but cannot wait until they are completely solved. This tends to produce a conservative attitude, but since public safety is often involved this is probably inevitable in any event. Unfortunately this favouring of tradition has been reinforced recently by the highly publicised structural failures, resulting in the setting up of a Building Integrity Division at the Building Research Establishment. With the present speed of scientific advance it is impossible for the practitioner to be fully informed of the latest knowledge, and the explanation of new information, techniques and materials is not an easy task without a heavy investment in specialised staff.

Nevertheless building is in the process of transition from a craft to a technologically based industry, and R & D must guide and promote this change, most importantly in new ways of thinking. The aim of building research must be a dual one, to help provide better buildings and to promote more efficient building. Like all applied research, in order to serve its particular ends it must find its outlet to those who will use its results. The designer must apply the results of research on the physical environment and the needs of users, on materials and structures. The contractor must make use of research on management, site organisation, mechanisation, maintenance and other matters. Unfortunately, the research effort tends to be heavily biased towards design and manufacture to the disadvantage of the builder. According to a Ministry of Public Building and Works working party report in 1964, the balance was: materials 41%, design and engineering 38%, construction 16%, and operations and management 5%. It is certainly true that research into all areas can bring direct benefits to construction itself. However, a more equal share of the national research effort must be focused on the methods and techniques used in the actual processes of construction, if increased productivity is to be achieved. Design and construction must be recognised as partners, two intimately connected and interdependent parts of the total process of building. More needs to be done to reduce costs and labour content, and to improve the speed and quality of construction, despite the obvious difficulties of research into construction methods and management.

Despite a tremendous background of research, and the quantity and quality of work by B.R.E., C.I.R.I.A. and others the results have not yet reached the right people. Although the presentation of research information could frequently be in a form more acceptable to the practising builder, something else is evidently required if we are to effectively bridge the gap between the research laboratory and the construction site. Proposed by the Woodbine Parish working party in 1966, and again by Dr. John Weston, Director of the Building Research Station, in 1968, there is a need for regional advisory offices on the lines of the National Agricultural Advisory Service. A more personal, man-to-man advisory service would be more likely to disseminate the results of building research to the places and people where it matters most. Improved communication between the research worker and those in need of the information would also provide guidance from the industry as to the real problems requiring investigation. The potential benefits of applied research to construction could prove to be an essential prerequisite to that much desired regeneration of British industry in general.

BIBLIOGRAPHY

The Architect and his Work, R.I.B.A.
The Building Owner and Planning in Advance, R.I.B.A. and the The National Federation of Building Trades Employers.
The Planning of Building Operations, The Royal Institution of Chartered Surveyors.

Mary Haddock, 'Services for the building industry 7. National Building Agency', *Building,* 16 July 1971.

Terotechnology in buildings: a report by the Building Terotechnology Group, P.S.A., Department of the Environment, Department of Industry, July 1977.

F. M. Lea, *Research for a Changing Industry,* Building Research Current Paper Supplement 4, 1964.

F. M. Lea, *The Users of Building Research,* Building Research Current Paper Supplement 5, 1964.

Building on Banwell: Teamwork gets results, The National Federation of Buildings Trades Employers 1969.

House's Guide to the Construction Industry, 8th edn., Van Nostrand Reinhold, 1985.

Chapter 9

Personnel

1. Personnel Policy

Despite the great advances made in the utilisation of mechanical plant, building seems certain to remain a high labour-content industry, so that the personnel function is of necessity a most important factor in construction management. This is even more obvious in the case of staff or key personnel, for a contractor's business consists solely of the experience and skill of his executive, technical and supervisory employees. With no permanent factory, materials bought specifically for each contract and both labour and plant taken on or hired as required, a contented and loyal staff are the essential nucleus without which no contracting firm can exist for very long. Yet the Central Council for Works and Buildings reported in 1944 that 'the selection and education of personnel managers is one of the aspects of the building industry in which there is most room for improvement'.

A *personnel policy* must be the responsibility of the highest authority, and for this reason many enlightened Chief Executives reserve personnel questions to themselves. Such a policy should be founded on the following principles:

i. justice must be given, and be seen to be given to all,
ii. basic remuneration must be adequate, with prompt and suitable adjustments for merit and service,
iii. every employee must be given the opportunity and encouragement to develop his capabilities to their limit.

The scope of the personnel function is naturally related to the size and operating policy of a company, but many leading builders are now following what is common practice in manufacturing industry, and developing full-time personnel officers or specialist departments. The service provided by a personnel department to general management can greatly assist in securing better utilisation of scarce and expensive labour, and it is to be hoped that many more of the techniques accepted by manufacturing industries will sooner than later be applied to the construction industry. In this connection it is encouraging to remember the Personnel Management Advisory Service set up by the Ministry of Labour in 1945 to provide advice and information on personnel management to all employers.

Personnel activities are generally classified under the following broad divisions:

  a. Employment.
  b. Education and training.
  c. Health and safety.
  d. Employee services or welfare.
  e. Union negotiations and joint consultation.
  f. Wages.

2. Employment

Consideration of the following headings will readily indicate the more obvious advantages of a centralised personnel department, i.e.: greater efficiency, the application of specialist knowledge and up-to-date methods, and disinterested judgement.

  1. ***Recruitment*** of personnel may be from a variety of sources, depending upon local conditions and the class of labour required, e.g.:
     a. Casual enquiries at the site are common for labourers.
     b. Skilled operatives may be transferred by the contractor from one site to another.
     c. Personal contacts by foremen may often succeed when all else has failed.
     d. Introductions from friends or relatives already employed are of great importance from the point of view of company morale and goodwill.
     e. Close contact with local grammar schools and colleges is necessary to attract young technical trainees.
     f. The local Youth Employment Officer can be of great assistance in filling juvenile posts.
     g. Advertisements in the local press for scarce tradesmen, or in the national newspapers and periodicals for staff and executive appointments, require particular attention. An

attractive company image is most helpful; very careful wording is necessary and guaranteed confidence essential for all staff vacancies.

h. Institutions and Professional Registers are useful for finding qualified technical and commercial staff.

i. The main source of supply, however, is usually the local Department of Employment's Job Centre where details of vacancies are filed in occupational order. A worker calling for a job is first interviewed and classified by the counter clerk, and passed on to the placement officer for a confidential talk. The Ministry issue an introduction card addressed to the firm notifying a vacancy, and an applicant is usually offered two or three jobs before he is registered as unemployed. Technical or managerial grades are referred to the Appointments Department, which maintains a Professional and Executive register, pre-selects suitable applicants and arranges for interviews by appointment.

2. *Selection* procedures comprise a variety of techniques to help select the most suitable candidate for a particular position. These include:

a. Interviewing either by an individual or a panel, chiefly for executive and staff appointments. The need here for methodical procedure is self-evident when it is realised that the cost of recruiting and selecting a management trainee may be £1500 or more. Foolproof routines should be designed for each stage, in order to minimise delays or confusion and hence maintain the Company's reputation, e.g.

  i. A job specification is necessary to determine the minimum qualifications, experience, etc., and personal attributes needed.

  ii. A method of recording and classifying written applications is desirable for effective control (see Fig. 9.1).

  iii. Standard application forms simplify the comparison of applications, and prevent relevant details being overlooked (Fig. 9.2).

  iv. Applicants graded as possibles should be invited for early interview, those living locally first, at times convenient to their circumstances. Rejected candidates should be courteously notified.

  v. Throughout any interview the roles of host (employer) and guest (applicant) should be strictly respected.

		Grading			Action Taken					
Name of Applicant	Date Received	Likely	Possible	Useless	Reject	Enquiry	Acknowledge	Interview	Short List	Re-Interview	Remarks
A. Smith	1/3		✓			2/3					
C. Jones	3/3			✓	4/3						
B. Hall	4/3	✓				5/3		12/3			

REGISTER OF APPLICANTS

For Appointment of Contracts manager

Fig. 9.1

Interview assessment forms (see Fig. 9.3) are most helpful, particularly in conjunction with some type of interview rating scale which describes typical grades under the various headings. Assessments must then be carefully compared with the job specification.

vi. Two or three interviews may be necessary, possibly culminating in a short list. The eventual letter of appointment should fully specify all the terms and conditions of engagement. This is a suitable opportunity to fulfil the requirements of the Contracts of Employment Act, 1972, which obliges an employer to provide a written statement covering remuneration, hours of work, holidays, sick pay, pension and length of notice.

As with all methods of selection it is impossible to sum up human individuals within fine limits of accuracy, and the effectiveness of any interview will depend upon the competence of the interviewer.

b. *Group exercises* under observation are another form of interview, but both more extended in time and exhaustive in its demands. Candidates perform tasks, take tests and conduct discussions within a group, while being rated by skilled observers. This type of technique, developed by certain government departments, selection boards and others, can be particularly useful when considering applicants for supervisory or junior executive posts abroad where social acumen and temperament may be important.

FORM OF APPLICATION FOR TECHNICAL STAFF

Surname_____   Christian names_____

Address_____   Nationality_____

Age_____years   Date of birth_____   Place of birth_____

Any physical disability_____

Married or single_____   Number of children_____   Other dependants_____

Are you prepared to travel?_____

GENERAL EDUCATION

Primary school_____

Secondary school_____

Certificates & Subjects_____

College or University_____

Qualifications other than technical_____

National Service_____

Hobbies/Sports/Languages_____

TECHNICAL QUALIFICATIONS

_____

_____

_____

RECORD OF EMPLOYMENT

From	To	Employer	Name & Address	Business	Position

TECHNICAL EXPERIENCE

_____

_____

Any other information that you consider relevant

_____

_____

Position applied for_____

Present salary_____   Notice required _____

Fig. 9.2

INTERVIEW ASSESSMENT			
Applicant: D.E.F. Green		Appointment: Buyer	
Attribute	Satisfactory	Doubtful	Inadequate
Manner and Appearance	✓		
Self Confidence	✓		
Verbal Expression	✓		
Comprehension	✓		
Response			
Native Intelligence	✓		
Resourcefulness		✓	
Initiative		✓	
Co-operativeness			
Stability			
Technical Ability		✓	
Executive Experience			✓
Sense of Humour	✓		
General Impression	a good salesman!		
Interviewed by: J. Smith		Date: 5 may	
Notes			

Fig. 9.3

c. *Formal tests* of both mental and physical abilities which have been designed as supplements to the previous procedures. Such tests are limited in objectives but are well justified if thoroughly understood, the main categories being:

  i. *Intelligence tests.* These are intended to measure the level of inherited intelligence or the ability to apply knowledge. Two main types are in general use, one involving the use of words and/or reasoning from given facts, and the other using patterns or figures. In both, instructions are given and questions asked together with a number of alternative answers from which the correct one must be selected. Time limits are imposed and the score, depending upon the total number of correct answers given, is an indication of the individual's mental age. Up to the age of adolescence, beyond which basic intelligence is assumed not to develop further, a comparative Intelligence Quotient is often calculated by expressing mental age as a percentage of actual age.

ii. *Aptitude tests.* These include tests for manual dexterity and precision, co-ordination of hand and eye, mental concentration and memory, estimation of speed and distance, visual recognition of shape, size and spatial relationship, and understanding of mechanical assemblies and transmission systems, etc. Performance tests which may be either analogous, e.g. typing a set piece, or analytic when based upon an analysis of the separate activities involved, have been used successfully in suiting 'round pegs for round holes'. In addition, observation of a candidate's method and approach may reveal qualities of intellect and character.

iii. *Psychological tests.* Although there is a good deal of scepticism regarding the practical value of both Personality and Projection tests, it is claimed that under the control of a qualified psychologist personality factors can be identified by examination. The former consist of questionnaires which must be answered 'Yes' 'No', or 'Uncertain', within a time limit. Scores are marked by means of a template, and indicate character traits such as self-assurance or enthusiasm. The other variant may be either the Rorschach Ink Blot or a Thematic Apperception test. A standardised 'inkblot' is presented, and questions are asked concerning the mental image produced. Alternatively a picture is shown and the subject is asked to tell a spontaneous story inspired by it. In both cases the interpretations claim to reveal both conscious and sub-conscious emotions.

3. **Placement** is the opposite of selection, being the placing of a particular individual in the most suitable employment. Employment Exchange methods of finding vacancies for unemployed operatives and/or qualified specialists looking for more senior appointments have already been described under Recruitment (see 1. *i*). A more particular aspect is that of vocational guidance, which although it has no age barrier, is especially suitable for helping the young person to choose the career for which he is best fitted. 'Once and for all' scientific tests measure interests, aptitudes and facts about personality, which are then 'scored' and analysed by industrial psychologists. Combined with personal interviews, the information is used to advise students to qualify or apply for the occupation which best suits their individual personality.

4. *Induction* or the introduction of new entrants to an organisation is often a haphazard affair, and some proper reception
procedure is essential if the newcomer is to become an
effective member of the working force. Methods, of course,
vary with age and grade of the employee, but every worker
must first know what the Company does, where he fits in, and
what are the general rules and working conditions. It is a good
practice to present this information, together with details of
employee services, social activities, etc., in a company
hand-book. The next step is to introduce the employee to his
supervisor who in turn will instruct him in his job and its
environment. Special care should be taken wih juveniles, and
older men of mature character should be encouraged to
sponsor youngsters and act as guides, philosophers and
friends in the master and apprentice tradition. During the
critical first few weeks the personnel department should
'follow up' the introduction, to gain the confidence of the new
man and promote a true sense of co-operation. On the
national level there are organisations such as the Industrial
Christian Fellowship, whose major concern is the smooth
transition from school-leaving to employment.

5. *Records* of personnel histories and movements are essential
for management information and the smooth working of the
complex personnel function. Individual data, details of
further education and training, apprenticeship indentures and
student agreements, medical reports on young persons, and
wage/salary changes are obvious examples. Statistical returns
of time lost through absence, injury and sickness can be
investigated to find remedies, resulting in reduced time lost to
production. Movements of labour are sufficiently important
to warrant separate consideration under each heading.

   a. *Transfer* within the construction industries is both inevitable and frequent for staff and key workmen, and the
   recording of movements between various contracts is
   usually a fundamental task of the wages department.
       Management, however, must also be appraised of this
   migration in order to staff new contracts economically, and,
   more importantly, to look ahead and foresee the need for
   future work to maintain full employment. Monthly returns
   from sites and a wall chart are a convenient means of
   fulfilling this need.

Ideally, as high a proportion as possible of the hourly paid operatives should also be employed on a regular and continuous basis, and certain companies have organised registers or central records offices in an effort to attain this desirable objective by transferring workmen from site to site wherever practicable. Regrettably the problem of wasteful and despiriting labour turnover remains the greatest obstacle to real progress by the twin industries – see 5, *d*.

b. *Promotion* opportunities should be related as closely as possible to individual merit, and it is important for morale that there should be a known and regular scheme for staff assessment. The underlying principles of such a policy would be to fill all appointments from within the organisation whenever there is a suitably qualified candidate, and properly to study and develop to the full the potential of every individual. A system of measurement is thus necessary to assess capabilities for promotion, involving two distinct procedures.

   i.   *Job grading* or evaluation sets out to compare differing jobs on a common basis, by grading them according to the difficulties, responsibilities, and experience that each entails. In this way the calibre and experience of available personnel can be matched to the requirements of a task, and the various grades also provide a convenient basis for salary scales.

   ii. *Merit rating* analyses the quality of performance of a worker on a given task, suggested ratings being novice, qualified, experienced, superior, superlative. From 'experienced' onwards, an individual might be promoted to the next higher grade as a 'novice'.

Such a system requires the fullest possible co-operation from every supervisor, but is an essential factor in a successful personnel policy.

c. *Withdrawal* by an employee may be natural on reaching retiring age, or due to a variety of unsatisfactory causes.

   i.   *Retirement* should be an important and pleasant occasion, perhaps marked by a souvenir presentation. Thanks to National Insurance developments the financial problem has been largely removed, and the more important aspect is perhaps a moral one. After legal obligations have ceased, an attitude of consideration and a willingness to extend a helping hand to a faithful servant contibutes greatly to the morale of the company.

ii. *Other causes* should be carefully investigated, either to reduce the potential labour turnover or remove any underlying disgruntlement. Dissatisfaction with conditions, progress, or treatment may reflect upon the morale within the organisation.

d. *Dismissal* by the employer may be for a variety of reasons but the employee must always leave with a sense of justice in the decision so that even his former colleagues bear no resentment.

i. With the skilled man-power shortage, wastage of workmen can be a source of serious loss and management must therefore continually watch the percentage labour turnover, both at company level and on individual contracts.

ii. When the conclusion of a contract brings *redundancy*, it is usual for 'last to come first to go', although credit must be given to those workers with a good record. But the basic problem of casual employment is an evil that must be eliminated, if the building and civil engineering industries are to recruit the quality of workmen necessary to achieve greatest productivity. At company level also it is short sighted to invest heavily in better management techniques, greater mechanisation, etc., when the hoped-for results depend upon the skill, training, co-operation and loyalty of workers who can be dismissed at two hours notice any Friday. The minimum periods of notice of termination required of an employer by the Contracts of Employment Act, 1972[1], and the terms of the Redundancy Payments Act, 1965[2], both help to foster more continuous employment; but cannot give a complete answer to the employer's discrete and fluctuating level of activity, and the employee's traditional independence in migrating to the highest bidder. Although a few progressive firms have introduced policies aimed at minimising the worst effects of a nomadic occupation, an industrial solution *must* be found at national level in order to meet the rising demands of scientific advance and the higher standard of living.

[1,2] Both repealed by the Employment Protection (Consolidation) Act 1978.

3. Education and Training

After the quality of personnel, nothing is more important for the future of the construction industries, including the professions, than their education and training at all levels. If contracting is to gain prestige and build up a properly trained labour force, then certain aspects must be developed more closely along the lines already adopted by manufacturing industries. This is important regardless of the size of the building concern, and a full training programme might include any of the following procedures:

a. *Introductory courses* for new employees need not be lengthy, but should cover background information referred to under Induction.

b. *Further education* is considered to be necessary for all juveniles in order to increase their later usefulness. Because evening classes after working all day may impair their working efficiency, many firms prefer to send their youngsters to school for a full day a week, despite the obvious disadvantages.

c. *Part training* of semi-skilled workers could be a valuable advantage in the building industry where an increased proficiency of only 10 per cent would mean a considerable gain in productivity. Traditionally, semi-skilled jobs are 'picked-up' from others, including of course any bad habits and their rate of working. The part method analyses an operation into its component parts, then each element is taught in graded stages. Instruction includes both general knowledge concerning the work, and specific tuition in performance. Formal training, in all its forms, should be planned and controlled in the following sequence:
   i. Explanation to the learner,
   ii. Demonstration by the instructor,
   iii. Practice by the learner with correction from his tutor,
   iv. Repetition to establish correct performance,
   v. Testing to ensure success.

d. *Practical training* in clerical work should not be underestimated, for accurate paper work is necessary to support maximum production. Skilled instruction in operating office machinery is also essential.

e. *Apprenticeship schemes* for traditional crafts are well developed within the building industry, but the high proportion of non-indentured learners has prompted the National Joint Council to review the normal period of apprenticeship.

Furthermore, developments in building techniques and the introduction of new materials, appear to call for radical reappraisal of the whole system. The civil engineering industry has its separate training schemes for plant and maintenance mechanics; these two complementary arrangements for engineering tradesmen and building craftsmen, could be interpreted as a sign of the need for rationalisation within one national construction industry. Each firm should contribute its fair proportion of skilled operatives.

The prolonged recession in the industry has prompted the Manpower Services Agency to sponsor additional trainees under the Youth Training Scheme, in the hope that employers will be able to take them on as second-year apprentices once they are capable of contributing more on site.

f. *Technical education* and training for students under written agreements is readily available for architects, civil engineers and quantity surveyors. The nearest approach for a builder however, is an industry-sponsored candidate for the Diploma in Technology sandwich course. Nevertheless, in theory at least, the Dip. Tech. student probably gets nearest to gaining the broad experience usually associated with technical apprenticeships in other engineering industries.

g. *Supervisor training* is an integral part of industrial progress, and there is still a great need in the construction industries for adequately trained foremen. The City and Guilds of London Institute covers both building craft and general foremanship education. The Chartered Institute of Building/National Federation of Building Trades Employers Site Management Education and Training Scheme begun in 1977 was an effort to encourage study courses for general foremen. The Construction Industry Training Board has since assumed the responsibilities of the Building Employers Confederation; and an Open Tech version of the scheme was introduced in 1984 to try to provide an answer for those who have difficulty in attending courses at colleges.

In the Federation of Civil Engineering Contractors training schemes, a system of 'job training' is designed to enable mechanics to advance to supervisory grades. The overall conclusion to be drawn is that although the present leaders of both industries are aware of the need for further training, and are taking action, many firms have still to be convinced of the benefits to be derived from the technical education of their foremen.

In industry generally the Industrial Welfare Society, the Institute of Industrial Administration, and the scheme of Supervisor Discussion Groups have all made important contributions to the training of supervisors. The Department of Employment adaptation of the *Training Within Industry* programme for supervisors, is based upon the principle that the greatest benefit is drawn from a scheme that links up with their own daily tasks. T.W.I. programme also includes a method of Job Instruction Training, which teaches foremen the value of discharging their own responsibility for the systematic instruction of subordinates.

h. *Executive development* must be more widely practised if the general efficiency of the industry is to be improved by more competent management. In the long run, the progress of any organisation depends upon the quality of its leaders, and it should therefore be a prime responsibility of top management to pick and train its own potential successors. Confidential assessments by direct seniors should be periodically appraised and rated for performance, character, initiative, co-operation and ability to communicate. Suitable encouragement to study part-time for a professional qualification should improve performance, and opportunities for individual development may be given by job rotation, interdepartmental transfers, special assignments, conferences and courses. The Member part II examination of the Chartered Institute of Building is intended to be a stage in this continuous process of management growth.

The Industrial Training Act 1964, was intended to ensure an adequate supply of trained labour, to secure an improvement in the quality of training, and to provide an equitable distribution of the costs of industrial training. Since the Construction Industry Training Board was established and its levy/grant scheme approved, there seems little doubt that the greater attention to the amount and quality of training at all levels, from operatives to managers, has improved the efficiency of the building and civil engineering industries. All forms of further education, industrial training and management development still have their parts to play, and enlightened managements have been quick to develop their individual lines of action whilst co-operating to the full with the Board.

i. *'Continuing Professional Development'* (C.P.D.) is becoming an accepted phrase in the United Kingdom, covering the activities of both professional development and involvement in public or community service. Following formal education and training, continued competence relies upon the professional's voluntary acceptance of his duty to keep abreast of new developments in his profession, and to widen his general knowledge by a conscious mix of work experience and continuing education and training. We are never too old to learn, and in our rapidly changing world we must respond in order that we may better serve consumers and clients. Society also expects professional people to demonstrate a strong sense of public duty, and the range of activities available is sufficiently wide to cater for an individual's personal preference, personality, available time and work situation.

The objectives of C.P.D. are not new, but the increased international emphasis now being given to this particular challenge is a response to rapidly changing circumstances. In 1972 the Architect's Registration Council of the U.K. (A.R.C.U.K.) published a report on continuing education based mainly on the experience of architects. At the same time the Presidents' Committee for the Urban Environment (P.C.U.E.)* was also thinking about continuing education for the building professions. In the event P.C.U.E. backed the A.R.C.U.K. project and in 1975 jointly created the York Centre for the promotion of multi-disciplinary C.P.D. When sponsorship came to an end in 1980, these institutions† decided to continue research into the subject and in 1981 set up the C.P.D. in Construction (C.P.D.C.) group. Both the Institute of Chartered Accountants and the R.I.C.S. (1980) have introduced C.P.D. on a compulsory basis. The Chilver Report produced by the I.C.E. on its education and training standards (Revised 1981), pointed out that 'Training does not stop at entry to Membership, and . . . emphasised the need for continuing education . . . keeping up with new developments through training at all stages of a civil engineer's career'.

Structured C.P.D. – whether compulsory or voluntary – should positively help individuals to develop their careers, and organisations to develop their employees' potential. The

* P.C.U.E. was an informal committee of the presidents and chief executives of the I.C.E., I.H.Y.E., I.O.B., I.Struct.E., R.I.B.A., R.I.C.S. and R.T.P.I. convened by Sir Hugh Wilson.

† Members of the Presidents' Committee for the Urban Environment now comprises R.I.B.A., R.T.P.I., I.Struct.E., R.I.C.S., C.I.O.B., C.I.B.S., Building Centre Trust and A.R.C.U.K.

benefits of modern technology will not be fully utilised unless we are committed to training in its use. After research has been carried out it is important that the results are communicated to practitioners, in order that they may be applied where appropriate. In many areas of construction there has been no shortage of research, but rather a failure of application. There is a crucial role for the go-between – able to understand the needs of a practical problem and quick to locate the relevance of research; an obvious field for C.P.D.

Similarly, there is a need for much closer links between educationalists and industry to the benefit of both. Mid-career further education, through participation in university departmental summer schools, can both disseminate new knowledge and also influence the direction of research. The problems of professional collaboration in the building industry are still with us – 20 years after the recommendations of the Banwell Committee in 1964. Since 1978, the Midlands and East Anglia Study Centres and others inspired by York, sponsored by P.C.U.E. members, have run courses for multi-disciplinary mid-career education. Such C.P.D. must have spin-off for mutual understanding and co-operation. The C.I.O.B. set up a working party in 1981 to develop an institutional strategy for C.P.D. During 1984, selected major teaching institutions in the U.K. were appointed as C.P.D. Study Centres in the Institute's Regions and Branches, to provide short courses open to all in the industry.

4. Employee Services

The moral obligations of management have already been referred to in Chapter 4.9 and this must include a responsibility for the physical well-being of all employees. Environmental factors such as heating, ventilation and lighting must usually be accepted on building sites, but fortunately fresh air and sunlight are better than any air conditioning plant. However, the more active promotion of health and safety, and the provision of better amenities and welfare facilities are worthy of greater attention.

   1. *Health* services should be concerned more with preventive than curative medicine, and a personnel department must therefore be able to advise on the following matters:
      a. Medical examinations. These are becoming an integral part of selection procedure, since they prevent people from

attempting to do work for which they are physically unsuited. Juveniles are required by law to be examined periodically; it is wise to check employees reporting back after illness, to ensure their recovery and prevent possible spread of infection. Co-operation with local mass radiography projects and blood transfusion centres are particularly worthwhile.

b. *Personal hygiene.* The importance of cleanliness, particularly in the handling of food and the treatment of sanitary accommodation, must be stressed at every opportunity, and the improvement of personal habits must be encouraged by example and education.

c. *Disabled persons.* Many contractors employ the standard 3 per cent of disabled persons as a condition of executing Government contracts, and particular attention needs to be paid to their effective use and possible greater accident proneness.

d. *First aid.* The Construction (Health and Welfare) Regulations 1966 demand provision of First Aid equipment for the treatment of minor injuries and attendance to accidents, but there is a need for many more trained first aiders. On larger sites, moreover, there is ample scope for the introduction of clinical services such as dentistry, chiropody, inoculation, etc., on the lines of many factories.

2. *Welfare* provisions must necessarily be on a different scale from factories and offices, but the standard of mess rooms and toilet facilities on many building sites is primitive compared with other industries.

a. *Canteens.* Regulations demand a supply of drinking water and covered accommodation with furniture for taking meals. The normal contract may only require a 'tea-boy' and facilities for boiling water, but on many there are opportunities for the supply of hot meals with or without the help of professional catering contractors.

b. *Amenities.* Adequate arrangements should be made for:
   i. Suitable shelter during bad weather.
   ii. Cloakrooms or kit lockers and means of drying wet garments.
   iii. Washing facilities before meals, with special provision for painters, fitters, etc.
   iv. Hygienic lavatories are important to both health and morale, and this aspect often reflects the attitude of management to personnel policy in general.

v. Protective clothing is particularly necessary on construction sites, because of weather conditions and prevailing accident hazards (see also pages 150 and 246).

c. *Hostels.* Billets are frequently required on large or remote sites, and these need specialised supervision.

d. *Transport.* For out-of-town jobs either travel allowance or conveyance is essential these days, and the safety and status differences between an open tipper and a comfortable mini-bus are obvious.

e. *Sports and Social Clubs.* These are rare in the building industry, but have an influence on recruitment and fostering of *esprit de corps.*

3. *Safety* at work is the concern of all ranks in industry, management, supervision and labour, but, as in other fields, the lead, example and drive for greater safety must come from the top. Despite the sincerity and enthusiasm of many Accident Prevention Groups, the disturbing fact remains that the number of reported accidents on building operations has increased steadily over the last decade, with appalling costs to the victims, the firms and the nation. Analysis of the causes of accidents has shown that they do not just happen – they are caused, usually by the coincidence of human faults with unsafe actions or conditions. Despite the inherently hazardous nature of many construction operations, no management can remain complacent in the face of the realities of human suffering which lie behind the annual statistics (see Fig. 16.5).

a. *Accident prevention.* The first steps towards reducing the accident rate down to the average for manufacturing industry, are the realisation that accident prevention is a function of management and the adoption of a company policy to ensure that as much attention is paid to safety as to other factors of production.

Practical effect must then be given to this policy by an active consideration of regular reports on safety measures, the encouragement of safe working methods, plant safety devices, and safety education, and above all by personal example.

b. *Statutory safeguards.* The safety, health and welfare legislation detailed in section 7 (p. 146) applies to both the building and civil engineering industries, and provides adequate legislation for safeguarding working places and the conduct of work. If full compliance with these legal obligations is regarded as a minimum requirement by every contracting firm, then the challenge of making and keeping building work safe will have been accepted.

c. *Safety supervision.* The appointment of experienced persons as safety officers or safety supervisors to supervise conduct of work, is now obligatory to check the adequacy of safety arrangements and to ensure compliance with the Statutory Regulations. Both co-operative schemes and the employment of safety consultants are practical alternatives, and on larger contracts safety committees can aid efficiency. A safety officer's duties should also include the introduction of protective clothing, and propaganda and education by posters, lectures, and films.

d. *Accident proneness.* Human fallibility is one of the main factors of industrial accidents, and consequently solutions must be devised which compensate and allow for human error and failure. New workers are more prone to accidents, and training in tested safe methods, and improving the skills of operatives are a second line of defence. However, it is now known that some people are exceedingly accident-prone and such persons must be removed to less dangerous situations, for the safety of both themselves and their fellow-workers. Selection tests of temperament and speed of reaction, etc., can avoid the engagement of the accident-prone, and so reduce the average number of accidents per man.

e. *Determination.* Accident prevention is good business practice, and all operatives must be made aware of the firm's determination to prevent accidents. Above all it is a positive and continuing process, and everyone must be taught to cultivate an awareness of the potential hazards in work, to spot the dangers and to use their common sense.

5. Industrial Relations

The responsibility for the conduct of relationships between employers and workers rests equally on both sides of industry, but the creation of conditions in which good relationships can be developed is recognised as a major function of management. An atmosphere of mutual trust and understanding has more influence on smooth labour relations than any legal[1] system. Most larger

[1] See section 8, p. 152, for industrial relations legislation.

firms have a specialised branch concerned with industrial relations as a distinct aspect of personnel work, and the Department of Employment maintains a separate Industrial Relations Department. The main functions of this Department, besides general advice on personnel management, are to assist in the:

a. Formation and maintenance of joint voluntary machinery in industry,

b. Prevention and settlement of trade disputes,

c. Administration of wages councils policy.

1. *Joint consultation* schemes seek to bring employees into full and responsible participation in the activities of an enterprise. These arrangements often take the form of advisory committees, usually with fewer management than employee representatives. The object of Joint Committees or Works Councils is to weld both sides into a team, with a common purpose; and to provide a means of exchanging views and information between the various functions of the organisation. Subjects usually covered by consultative committees include:

a. Changes or improvements in methods of production, and suggestions for improvements in related matters,

b. Safety, health and welfare arrangements,

c. Education, training, discipline and other similar personnel problems.

It has become increasingly common for management to keep their employee representatives informed on the state of trade, and even to provide information about the firm's financial position.

2. *Trade unions* in the building industry were co-ordinated by the National Federation of Building Trades Operatives, until disbanded in 1973 when ASWW and AUBTW became UCATT. Many trade unionists, like Sir Richard Coppock, believe that only a true amalgamation can solve the problems of demarcation disputes, falling union membership and the need for development of the industry.

a. *Negotiation*. Both the building and civil engineering industries have been well served by joint machinery of long standing, the National Joint Council for the Building Industry and Civil Engineering Construction Conciliation Board. Major reforms carried through include the holidays with pay scheme, and payment for time lost through inclement weather, etc., under the guaranteed minimum week. Yet the existence of two negotiating bodies covering virtually the same group of workers and providing differing agreements on terms and conditions of employment, has in the past caused some confusion and a unified code has much to recommend itself.

b. Conciliation. The construction industries have been singularly free from major industrial disputes, and labour problems have been settled without Government intervention. This has been largely due to the regional and national joint conciliation panels provided by the National Working Rule Agreements.

The Department of Employment normally assists in the settlement of unresolved issues by the following progressive alternatives:

   i. *Conciliation* through the personal intervention of a regional industrial relations officer,[1]

   ii. *Arbitration* with the consent of both parties, either by reference to the Industrial Court or to single arbitrators or arbitration boards appointed by the Minister,

   iii. *Inquiry and investigation* as a last resort. When the facts are considered to be of public interest a court of inquiry must report to both Houses of Parliament, otherwise a more informal committee of investigation may report to the Minister.

3. **Remuneration** is the most obvious factor governing industrial relations, although, subconsciously, security of employment may be a more powerful motivation. The normal individual seeks to be rewarded fairly on his merits; this implies that there should be a fair and logical structure both for wages and salaries. Of course a wage structure must have regard not only to the conditions in a particular firm, but to the relative productivity of the industry, and the national economic position. A number of industries have revised their wage structures within recent years; but the present pattern of building wages cannot be described as rational when tradesmen can receive over 100 per cent more than the nationally agreed rate. Particular features of such a structure warrant individual consideration.

a. Basic rates. Minimum wage and salary scales are necessary for different grades, properly based upon the current cost of living, with due regard to the criteria mentioned earlier, and ideally in conformity with a national wages policy.

[1] See A.C.A.S. on p. 153.

b. *Differentials*. In addition to the previous minima, 'plus' rates are required for specific jobs, dependent upon both the required qualities of the operative and the inherent conditions of the operation. Special attention must be given to the differences between craftsmen, tradesmen and labourers, if recruits are to be encouraged to apply themselves to the training disciplines necessary for up-grading.

c. *Allowances*. Appropriate recognition should be arranged on a systematic basis for shift work, overtime, long service, special part-time responsibilities, etc.

d. *Incentives*. While it must always be remembered that with good leadership and worthwhile objectives, men can be effectively motivated by incentives other than financial reward, nevertheless a scheme of scientifically based bonus payments is the only sure way of keeping productivity and earnings in step. For more senior supervisory staff a system of merit payments may be more practicable than measured 'payments by results'. (See also Chapter 17.)

e. *Assurances*. Monetary rewards include pension and life assurance arrangements, which appeal directly to the innate human desire for security. Accepting the aim that building should be a pensionable career, the National Federation of Building Trades Employers, through its contributory Staff Scheme and non-contributory Operatives Scheme, has provided a means whereby its members can make provision for their key personnel. Sick pay arrangements, holidays with pay, the guaranteed week and a redundancy policy may all be included under this heading.

6. The Human Factor

Despite the increasing rate of the discovery and spread of knowledge, little practical application appears to have resulted from the torrent of literature on management, to judge by the present day industrial unrest and the unsolved problem of how to expand productivity adequately. This has mainly been because 'scientific' managers failed to show sufficient regard for the human factor in industrial relationships; this is borne out by the prevalent arguments as to whether management is an art or a science, and whether managers are born or made. Certainly the basic principles of organisation, and the techniques, methods, and managerial tools are capable of scientific analysis and explanation, but a cornerstone of management technology must be an understanding of people, their motivations, philosophies, and beliefs (see Chapter 19, Organisational Development). Although the management of contracts is now a science, the management of men remains an art because we know comparatively little about their unpredictable, and often misunderstood, natures.

Present day research and technical education places much more emphasis on physical laws than upon the humanities, although it is certain that the human sciences such as psychology, sociology, etc., hold the promise of unlimited rewards. In the meantime managers must take into account many of the shortcomings of human beings, and draw out the best from the personnel available; while man himself, the most complex of machines and the greatest untapped source of power in Nature, remains with a comparatively low utilisation factor. The psychological needs and satisfactions vary with the different spheres of human activity, i.e. individual and collective.

1. *Ergonomics.* The acceptance of the truth that the machine was made for the operator and not *vice versa,* has led to a renewed interest in the improvement of efficiency by fitting the job to the man. Ergonomics is a combined effort by psychologists, physiologists, anatomists and engineers, to develop principles of human behaviour which, when applied to the design of equipment and the working environment, will reduce the amount of mental and physical effort and/or improve the standard of performance. Studies of human problems associated with work such as the shape and size of dials, the legibility of lettering, the positions of control levers, and the dimensions and shapes of furniture, have already led to accepted recommendations for good design.

2. *Morale.* The achievement of an individual is determined by the sum total of his ability plus motivation, and it is the prime responsibility of management to promote that indefinable spirit which impels a human being to work with a will. As Napoleon said, morale is more important than material strength, and conversely unhappy or unsatisfied staff are liable to make mistakes, cause accidents or lose time due to sickness. Moreover, many changes and developments in industry, particularly the more mechanised techniques, tend to minimise a conscientious and personal interest by the operative in his job. The National Trades Technical Society keeps its members up-to-date with industrial progress and

counteracts this tendency by regular meetings for study courses, discussions and works visits. Large scale attitude surveys have shown that the most important factors influencing employee morale are those of justice in rewards, security of health and employment, opportunity for training and advancement, and purpose by those in authority. Since a majority of the male working population are in fact breadwinners for family units, the necessity for security is nowadays accentuated by hire purchase and house mortgages.

3. *Group psychology.* Man is a social animal, and members of a gang or department are profoundly affected in their daily thoughts and actions by the group's own psychological characteristics and its particular code of conduct. The desire of fellow-workers to be regarded as members of an important group, needed by the wider concern, and engaged in activity useful to local or national society, was first demonstrated by the famous Hawthorne experiments in the late 1920's. Contrasting conditions and fringe benefits accorded, for example, to manual and clerical workers can set up resentments, and lead to symptoms such as status symbols. Co-operation and the team outlook can be encouraged by suggestion schemes and joint consultation.

A proper understanding of the wider implications of work, calls for better communications within the building industry at both national and company levels. Everyone likes to belong to a successful team; propaganda to instil pride in the organisation and its product and encourage satisfaction in craftsmanship, can be presented through conferences, trade competitions and house magazines.

4. *Leadership and loyalty.* Efficient production requires good management, and the management of human beings, personnel management, is now recognised as the most important part of a manager's responsibilities. Although many of the more routine duties of the personnel function may be delegated to a 'service' department, the senior executive must nevertheless fulfil the role of leader, whose task it is both to make the arrangements and to see that the remainder of the organisation carries them out. Leadership demands the ability to persuade people, and the happy knack of choosing the right subordinates and being able to weld them into an enthusiastic team. The manager must have an active personal interest in people, a strict sense of fairness, the ability to teach by

example or otherwise, and the power not only to drive others but also to praise and encourage generously.

Employees at all levels need to work for someone they can respect, and the boss must therefore inspire confidence by his integrity and evoke by his own personality a loyalty and devotion which makes work worthwhile. Free men, like a chain, are easier to pull along than to push, and respect and confidence must be earned by the maintenance of a high personal standard at work and at home. Mutual trust between the employer and the workers will in turn develop self-discipline, contentment and a sense of co-operation, so that eventually leadership and loyalty will together add up to a rewarding team spirit.

7. Safety, Health and Welfare Legislation

The findings of the Committee on Safety and Health at Work which was appointed in May 1970 under the Chairmanship of Lord Robens, resulted in:

1. *The Health and Safety at Work Act 1974.* The 1974 Act is an enabling measure made up of four parts:

    Part I   Health, Safety and Welfare at Work.
    Part II   The Employment Medical Advisory Service.
    Part III   Building Regulations.
    Part IV   Miscellaneous.

    The general purposes of Part 1 of the Act are stated as follows:
    a. Securing the health, safety and welfare of persons at work.
    b. Protecting persons other than persons at work against risks to health and safety arising out of work activities.
    c. Controlling the keeping and use of dangerous substances.
    d. Controlling the emission into the atmosphere of noxious or offensive substances from certain premises.
    There are also provisions for the making of health and safety regulations, and the preparation of codes of practice, with a view to progressively replacing any existing relevant statutory provisions. Meantime, the duties under existing health and safety legislation remain in force.
2. *The Health and Safety Commission* representing employers, employees and local authorities, is charged by the Secretary of State to:

a. Further the purposes of the Act.

b. Arrange for research, and the provision of training and information.

c. Provide an information and advisory service.

d. Make proposals for regulations.

A Health and Safety Executive exercises the functions of the Commission and gives effect to any directions given to it by the Commission. The Act is enforced by the Factory Inspectorate or local authorities as directed by the Secretary of State. Inspectors may issue either (i) an Improvement Notice requiring any infringement to be remedied within three weeks; or (ii) a Prohibition Notice requiring an immediate stop to the activities contravening a relevant statutory provision. Conviction of offences against the Act may be penalised by fines up to £1 000, or imprisonment up to 2 years, or both.

3. *The general duties of employers to their employees.* It is the duty of every employer to ensure, *so far as is reasonably practicable,* the health, safety and welfare at work of all his employees and in particular to:

a. 'Provide and maintain plant and systems of work that are safe and without risks to health.' Since nearly 25% of the reportable accidents in the construction industry are attributed to plant, machinery and transport, it is important that the contractor should provide adequate information on the safe use of various items of construction plant, supplementing wherever necessary that advice contained in manufacturers' handbooks. Most accidents connected with plant and machines are caused by failure to observe the basic safety precautions. In particular, the observance of one simple rule would prevent many accidents: 'never attempt to clean, oil or adjust a machine in motion.'

It is a statutory requirement that all moving parts of any machine, power-driven or not, must be properly guarded. Guards removed at any time for maintenance or repair must be put back before the machine is used again. The Woodworking Machine Regulations 1974 cover the general requirements of all woodworking machinery and circular saws in particular.

Certain construction operations and particular items of plant or equipment are required to be tested, examined or inspected at specified intervals, and these must be recorded as laid down in the Construction Regulations of 1961 and 1966 and the Factories Act 1961.

Because of damp conditions and the need for frequent repositioning of cabling and equipment, temporary electrical supplies on construction sites require special attention. In particular, all portable lamps and hand tools should be operated on the reduced 110 voltage. Overhead electricity supply cables are a frequent hazard and special precautions are required by the Construction (General Provisions) Regulations 1961 and the Electricity Regulations. The use of 'goal posts' for plant travelling beneath overhead lines is mandatory. Underground electricity supply cables must be protected from accidental damage by excavation, and close co-operation with the local Electricity Authority is necessary to guard against this danger to life and property.

Accidents associated with temporary works or falsework have received particular attention, culminating in the Bragg Report in January 1976 and the B.S.I. Draft Code of Practice for Falsework 1975. Pending final ratification, the chief recommendations adopted by responsible contractors are (i) practical training for skilled operatives and supervisors, and (ii) the nomination of a temporary works co-ordinator on each site, to ensure that proper procedures are followed, inspections carried out, and to authorise loading or striking.

b. 'Arrange for ensuring the safe use, handling, storage and transport of articles and substances.' Material and equipment must not only be loaded in a safe manner, but also with due regard to the safe unloading at its destination. The Petroleum (Consolidation) Act 1928 and subsequent statutory rules, orders and regulations, provide for the licensing and precise use of petroleum spirit on sites. Gas-oil installations also require special care in the siting of a tank and the possible retaining of spillages. With the increase in the use of flammable liquids – such as white spirits, paints and adhesives – the Fire Prevention Association has produced a guide on their fire safety. Bottled gases, commonly used on construction sites, also require the same careful attention to safe practices.

The 1969 Asbestos Regulations require precautions to be taken by workers who use asbestos-based materials, e.g. asbestos cement pipes and sheeting, insulation boards and lagging.

The Control of Pollution Act 1974 also applies to waste disposal, and since 1976 its deposition has required a 'disposal licence' except in certain described situations.

c. 'Provide such information, instruction, training and supervision necessary to ensure their health and safety at work.'

The provision of information, and its systematic updating, needs to cover the regulations themselves, recommended safe practices, and specific advice about various items of plant and potentially hazardous materials. This is usually achieved through safety bulletins that can be retained in a loose-leaf cover for reference.

Notice of risks arising from particular operations on each individual site, and the precautions to be taken, should be circulated together with details of the site safety organisation.

All plant operators must be properly trained, experienced and careful, and this requires some form of authorisation to drive. Rough terrain fork lifts pose particular problems, and require specialised training, either by a qualified safety officer or an appropriate consultant. The Abrasive Wheels Regulations 1970 require all operators to be properly trained in the safe use of grinding machines, and suitable courses are readily available.

The Woodworking Machine Regulations 1974 insist that no-one shall be employed on such a machine unless he has been sufficiently trained and instructed, except under adequate supervision.

Since 1 January 1979 the Construction Industry Scaffolders Record Scheme has required specific training and experience for the categories of trainee, basic and advanced scaffolder.

The use of films is a most powerful training aid, and the Construction Industry has produced a number of excellent examples.

d. 'Maintain any place of work under the employer's control, in a safe condition, without risk to health, and maintain a means of access to and egress from that is safe and without risk.'

Special fire precautions are necessary on construction sites and advisory leaflets are obtainable from the Fire Protecion Association. Particular attention is required in planning offices, huts and canteens; disposal of rubbish; smoking; heating appliances including oil stoves; gas cylinders, flammable liquids and gases; machinery; oil paints and thinners; flame-producing apparatus, e.g. blow lamps and welding appliances; and bitumen.

The Fire Certificates (Special Premises) Regulations 1976 may require fire certificates for temporary premises unless exemption is granted in appropriate cases.

Access may involve ladders, scaffolds or hoists, for which legal provisions are contained in the Construction (Working Places) Regulations 1966.

e. 'Provide and maintain a working environment that is safe, without risk to health and adequate as regards facilities and arrangements for welfare at work.'

The minimum legal requirements of welfare facilities to be provided on sites, are set out in the Construction (Health & Welfare) Regulations 1966. These cover first aid and ambulances, shelters and accommodation, washing facilities and sanitary conveniences, protective clothing and proper paths. In addition to protective jackets and trousers for those who must continue working in rain, snow, sleet or hail, peculiar construction hazards require the issue of safety helmets and boots, and the provision of goggles where required by the Protection of Eyes Regulations 1974.

4. *Employer's Statement of Policy.* 'Except in such cases as may be prescribed, it is his duty to prepare and revise as necessary a written statement of general policy with respect to the health and safety at work of employees, and the organisation and arrangements made to carry out the policy, and to bring the statement and any revision to the notice of all employees.'

It is usual practice to issue a copy of the general Statement of Policy to every member of the staff, and every timebook-paid employee upon joining the company. A more detailed description of the safety organisation including the name of the Director with particular responsibility for health and safety policy and training, should be made available at Head Office and on each contract site. Provision may be included for the addition of any particular site hazards, the precautions to be taken, and duties of persons responsible, to be inserted by site management.

Under the Social Security Act 1975 all accidents on site must be entered in the Accident Book (Form B1 510) and the employer might also deem it prudent to maintain a separate Notification of Accident Book for his own purpose.

5. *Appointment of safety representatives and Safety Committee.*
Since 1 October 1978, regulations under the enabling act have
provided for the appointment by Trades Unions of safety
representatives, to represent employees in consultations with
employers with a view to making and maintaining arrangements for efficient co-operation in the promotion and
development of measures to ensure the health and safety at
work of employees, and to check the effectiveness of such
measures.

A Code of Practice (1977) accompanied by Guidance Notes
have been published by the H & S Commission, to offer
practical guidance on the appointment of safety representatives and their functions. Safety representatives are entitled to
inspect the workplace, for which the employer must allow
time off with pay and provide relevant information.

The H & S Commission have also issued a Code of Practice
(1978) covering time off for the training of safety representatives. If requested to do so by the safety representatives, an
employer must establish a Safety Committee in order to keep
under review the measures taken to ensure the health and
safety at work of his employees.

6. *Duties of employers to persons other than their employees.*
'Every employer and every self-employed person must
conduct his undertaking in such a way as to ensure that he,
and other persons not in his employment who may be
affected, are not exposed to risks to their health and safety.'
In addition, he must give to such persons the prescribed
information about any aspect of the way in which he conducts
his undertaking, as might affect their health and safety.

Obvious implications for the building site would be the
fencing of dangerous excavations and holes, and the protection of the public on disturbed pathways or in adjoining
buildings. A notice to all visitors warning of the inherent
dangers of construction sites is a must. Sites have a particular
attraction for children, and warning notices and specific
precautions to exclude children from playing in danger areas
are covered in a guidance note by the H & S Executive.

The control of noise on construction sites is necessary in the
interests of both operatives and the community. The Control
of Pollution Act 1974 empowered local authorities to lay
down specific noise limits, and to restrict construction
operations that emit dangerous noise levels. The B.S.I. Code

of Practice 5228 is approved for noise control on construction sites.

7. *The duty of manufacturers and suppliers.* 'It is the duty of any person who designs, manufactures, imports or supplies any article or substance for use at work, to ensure that it is so designed and constructed as to be safe and without risk to health when properly used.' In particular they must make available adequate information about the use for which the article is designed and has been tested, and about any conditions necessary to ensure that when put to that use it will be safe and without risk to health.

This of course applies to makers of plant, equipment and machinery used in construction operations, and a wide variety of materials and chemicals. Such information and advice might well be circulated via the Safety Bulletins referred to under 3 (c) earlier. The particular hazards of handling the various forms of asbestos products are well documented by the Asbestosis Research Council. The Asbestos Regulations 1969 are designed to protect workers from the known injurious effects of prolonged inhalation of dust containing asbestos fibres.

The Health and Safety at Work Act of 1974 has attempted to shift the emphasis away from the legal regulation of guarding machines or ensuring safe conditions – necessary though they be – towards the American philosophy of concentrating on making the working man safe. Perhaps a start has been made on the long task of education, training, supervision and improving the attitudes of mind of everyone concerned with reducing the unacceptable accident rate on construction works.

Certainly, amongst those smaller and medium-sized firms who now benefit from a full-time safety advisor, by having joined one of the 50 construction safety groups, safety is now taken very seriously and accepted as an essential aspect of management responsibility. Another encouraging development is the C.I.O.B./B.E.C./F.C.E.C. site management safety training scheme, now adminstered by the C.I.T.B.

8. Industrial Relations Legislation

Over the last decade industrial management has been inundated with complex employment legislation of a revolutionary kind. The process of familiarising themselves with the rapid changes taking place has been given additional urgency by the knowledge that failure to observe the intricate requirements will attract severe financial penalties at Industrial Tribunal hearings. With the principal aims being to increase job security and to give certain statutory rights to employees and their unions, the individual pieces of legislation have been woven into a complex and sometimes bewildering network of industrial relations rules and regulations.

1. *Acts of Parliament.* The more significant of these are as follows:

Industrial Training Act 1964
Redundancy Payments Act 1965; repealed by EPCA 1978
Equal Pay Act 1970
Industrial Relations Act 1971; repealed by TULRA 1974
Contracts of Employment Act 1972; repealed by EPCA 1978
Social Security Act 1973
Trades Union and Labour Relations Act 1974; parts repealed by EPCA 1978
Sex Discrimination Act 1975
Employment Protection Act 1975; parts repealed by EPCA 1978
Trades Union and Labour Relations (Amendment) Act 1975
Redundancy Rebates Act 1977
Employment Protection (Consolidation) Act 1978
State Earnings Related Pension Scheme 1978
Employment Act 1982
Trades Union Act 1984

Codes of Practice have also been published and their recommendations have legal significance in cases brought before Industrial Tribunals, for example:

Industrial Relations Act 1971, sections 40–46 of Code of Practice relating to Status and Security of Employees
Disciplinary Practice and Procedures Order 1977
Time Off for Trade Union Duties and Activities Order 1977

Department of Employment Guides have also been published to provide information on individual aspects of the EPCA 1978.

2. *Statutory Bodies* have been set up to administer this legislation, and their roles are outlined as follows.

   a. The *Advisory, Conciliation and Arbitration Service* is charged with the duty of promoting improvement in industrial relations. It has a chairman appointed by the Secretary of State and a council of nine members, three representing the T.U.C. and three the C.B.I. Besides the general duties of advice, conciliation and arbitration, it has specific responsibilities in disputes over trade union recognition, in claims for recognised conditions, in the affairs of wages councils and the production of codes of practice:

i.   Disciplinary practice and proceedings in employment.
ii. Disclosure of information to trade unions for collective bargaining purposes.
iii. Time off for trade union duties and activities.

On the other hand, the 1984 Trade Union Act stipulates that secret ballots must be held to endorse any strike call, otherwise heavy damages may be awarded.

b. The *Central Arbitration Committee* handles complaints under the recognition and disclosure procedures, or any other dispute referred to it. Its members are experienced in industrial relations and are appointed by the Secretary of State after consultation with A.C.A.S.

c. *Industrial Tribunals* constitute the main machinery for enforcement of the provisions contained in employment legislation. Since they were first set up under the ITA 1964, their jurisdiction has been extended to cover cases under a number of Acts in the employment field. Although the majority of claims heard by them refer to allegations of unfair dismissal, many others under the RPA 1965, the CEA 1972, the HASAWA 1974 etc. are also considered. With a legally qualified chairman they are composed of two lay members, usually one from a panel of employers, and one trade unionist. Following a claim in writing, a conciliation officer will try to effect an equitable agreement. Failing this, the Tribunal will hear the case and announce its decision, which is binding on both parties.

d. The *Employment Appeal Tribunal* will hear appeals (on questions of law only) from the decisions of Industrial Tribunals. They consist of a judge and either two or four lay members.

e. *Trades Unions* have also been given a new privileged status in law, with considerable legal entitlements and powers. A Trade Union is defined as any organisation of workers whose principal purpose is the regulation of relations between workers and their employers or employers' association. To obtain the new rights, a trade union must be 'independent', i.e. not under the domination of, and free from interference by, an employer or association, and must obtain a certificate to this effect from the Certification Officer. Such a certificated independent Trade Union is entitled to:

i. The right to organize where unions are unrecognised, and protection against dismissal for these activities.

ii. Time off for officials, i.e. shop stewards.

iii. Appoint and train Safety Representatives.

iv. Consultation concerning occupational pension schemes.

v. Consultation concerning redundancy proposals.

vi. Receive certain information for collective bargaining purposes.

vii. Statutory support in claims for recognition.

In addition, protection is retained under the 1971 Act against proceedings for inducing a breach of commercial contract or contracts of employment. No court is empowered to compel an employee to attend or perform any work. The use of injunctions in strike situations has also been limited, since the court must satisfy itself that the party against whom the injunction is directed has been given a reasonable opportunity to state his case. On the other hand, the 1984 Trades Union Act stipulates that secret ballots must be held to endorse any strike call, otherwise heavy damages may be awarded to the employer.

3. *Changes in industrial law* have many practical implications for management policy and procedures:

a. In order to carry out the commitment to increased job security, whilst still retaining the right to select the most suitable workmen, a building company must work out a suitable procedure for *labour recruitment*. This usually includes a written application form, possible references from previous employers, and an interview. Sexual discrimination is of course unlawful, and if it is necessary to advertise vacancies, then it must be made clear that both men and women may apply.

b. Every employee should receive a written *statement of particulars* within 13 weeks of commencement of employment, and be informed of any changes within one month of the change. Items to be shown are: job title; date of commencement and any period of continuous employment; reference to the appropriate Working Rule(s) (Civil Engineering or Building); annual holiday entitlements; any incentive scheme; and the company's disciplinary and grievance procedure. Details of site working hours should also be issued in writing and changed in reasonable time, e.g. winter working. Employees are also entitled to receive an itemised pay statement weekly.

c. A general obligation to make *guarantee payments* to employees, in the event of lay-off or short-time working, has been lifted from the construction industry because of the benefits already included in the Working Rule(s). However, particular care is required when labour is laid off due to a prolonged period of adverse weather conditions. A decision must be made whether to lay off for an extended period, or to discharge the labour force with possible redundancy payments and to recruit again at a later date.

d. The Working Rules of the construction industry contain recommended *disciplinary procedures*, but since copies are not always readily available to operatives a detailed disciplinary and grievance procedure should be contained in the Statement of Particulars. It is recommended that a verbal warning confirmed in writing should set out the circumstances of the misconduct and state a period of time in which improvement is expected. If necessary a second written notice should warn that failure to improve within a reasonable time will result in further disciplinary action. When warranted, a third and final warning should make it clear that further failure will result in dismissal. On continued failure the operatives should be dismissed with appropriate notice, again in writing.

Where there has been misconduct which could warrant summary dismissal, he should be interviewed by a senior site manager, allowed to state his case, and advised of his rights under the procedure.

When determining the nature of the disciplinary action, management must satisfy the test of reasonableness in the circumstances, and taking into account any mitigating circumstances.

Particular care is required when dismissing long-term absentees. Prolonged sickness poses two major questions: (i) after what period of absence is it reasonable to dismiss a sick employee; and (ii) should a warning of impending dismissal be given. The Code of Practice (Disciplinary Practice and Procedures) Order 1977 gives practical guidance on these aspects.

e. An employee with 26 weeks or more continuous service is entitled to receive a written statement of the reasons for *dismissal,* and this must be given within 14 days of the request.

Construction employees subject to the NWR or WRA may be instructed to *transfer* from one contract to another. Such instructions should be in writing, with full details of terms and conditions offered on the new site. To avoid difficulties at Industrial Tribunals it is advisable to obtain a written statement of *termination* from an operative leaving of his own accord.

f. Since every construction project has a limited time period, it is inevitable that the majority of operatives will eventually be dismissed for reasons of *redundancy*. Employees are entitled to redundancy payments according to length of service, and the employer can currently claim a rebate of 41% from the National Redundancy Fund. Moreover, the employer must advise the appropriate recognised unions of his reasons, details etc. and consult with them at the earliest opportunity. Under the agreed Working Rules the following unions are recognised: Building – U.C.A.T.T., T.& G.W.U., G.M.W.U. and F.T.A.T.; Civil engineering – G.M.W.U., T.& G.W.U., U.C.A.T.T. and E.E.P.T.U. The Department of Employment must also be notified:

i.   where 10 or more are to be dismissed within a period of 30 days or less, at least 30 days beforehand; and

ii. where 100 or more dismissals are proposed within a period of 90 days or less, at least 90 days before the first dismissal. A proper procedure for redundancy selection must be carried out, otherwise an employee may claim unfair dismissal and demand reinstatement. Unions generally prefer selection on the basis of voluntary redundancy, then 'last in first out.' But in the interests of continuous employment and maintenance of a competent labour force, the employer may take into account:

i   the possibility of transfer;

ii. length of continuous service;

iii. the capability, qualifications and past conduct of the operative; and

iv. operational requirements.

The best defence at an Industrial Tribunal, would be to produce lists and schedules to show that care had been taken in the selection of gangs to stay or to be dismissed.

g. Employers are required by law to *disclose* certain *information* to a recognised trade union, when requested for purposes of collective bargaining. A Code of Practice has been issued on this potentially sensitive obligation.

h. Employees are now entitled to take *time off* during working hours to perform the following public duties:

  i. Justice of the Peace;
  ii. Local Authority member;
  iii. Statutory Tribunal member;
  iv. Regional or Area Health Authority member;
  v. Member of the governing body of an educational establishment maintained by a Local Education Authority;
  vi. Water Authority member.

However, payment is not stipulated for such time off.

Employees are also entitled to reasonable paid time off for specific Trade Union duties and activities. In order to control the situation, it follows that managers must give careful and thorough consideration to all requests for time off, and be guided by the Code of Practice and/or the appropriate Working Rule.

Operatives made redundant after two years' service are entitled to time off with pay in order to find new work.

j. An employee with two years' continuous service is entitled to *maternity* pay for the first six weeks of absence because of her pregnancy, during the 11 weeks before the expected confinement. The employer may recover such payments from the Public Maternity Pay Fund. After pregnancy the employee is entitled to return to work within a period of 29 weeks of confinement, and her employer must honour this right if he has been informed of this intention. Should a woman be obliged by her 'condition' to give up work earlier, then she is entitled to 90% of her usual pay.

k. Building and civil engineering operatives are entitled to *death benefit* cover of £2 000 provided under the appropriate wages agreements. Employers contribute to the Death Benefit Scheme administered by the Holidays Scheme Management on behalf of all parties to the National Joint Council and the Construction Conciliation Board.

Because of the 'enabling act' nature of much of this legislation, it follows that additional sections are continually being brought into effect, new codes of practice being introduced, and further test cases established so that the industrial relations situation is always fluid and changing. For example, the budget of March 1985 changed the qualifying period for employees of larger companies from one year to two years before they are eligible to take their employer to an industrial tribunal claiming unfair dismissal. With a change of government it is certain that some details will be amended, but equally it must be accepted that the general legal background is here to stay.

BIBLIOGRAPHY

Sir Harold Emmerson, *Survey of Problems Before the Construction Industries*, H.M.S.O., 1962
The Placing and Management of Building Contracts (Simon Report), Published for the Ministry of Works by H.M.S.O., 1944
Handbook of Architectural Practice and Management, Part 2, 'Contracts and Conditions of Service', R.I.B.A.
Construction Industry Training Board Guide – No. 1, Construction Industry Training Board.
Notes for Guidance – Training and Development of Managers in the Medium and Large Firm, Construction Industry Training Board.
Safety Precautions for use of Liquefied Petroleum Gas on Building Operations, National Federation of Building Trades Employers.
Prevention of Accidents to Persons Working in the Vicinity of Overhead Electric Power Lines and Underground Electric Cables, Midlands Electricity Board.
Safety and the Law, The Institute of Building Site Management Information Service No. 10.
Leslie F. W. Hayword, *Statutory Regulations Affecting Mechanical Plant Operation On Site*, Site Management Section Information Service No. 26, Insitute of Building.
Construction Safety, N.F.B.T.E. (now B.E.C.).
'Guide to Statutory Tests, Examinations and Inspections', *Building Technology and Management*, March 1974.
The Act Outlined, Health and Safety Commission.
Safety in Construction Work, Booklets 6A – F, Health and Safety Executive.
Noise from Construction and Demolition Sites, measured levels and their prediction, Report 64, C.I.R.I.A.
Safety Representatives and Safety Committees, Health and Safety Commission.
B. D. Cruddace, *Safety Representatives*, Site Management Information Service No. 77, Institute of Building.
Employment and the Law, N.F.B.T.E., 1978.
Industrial Relations Handbook, A.C.A.S., H.M.S.O., 1980.

Chapter 10

Office Organisation and Methods

1. Office Management

The purpose of the office is to receive, record and distribute information on all aspects of the business, and to provide systems of communications for every division of the undertaking. Although it is often closely associated with the accounting or control function, clerical work is not an end in itself, but is essentially a service to the major operations of designing, manufacturing and selling.

A builder requires fundamental information such as cost controls and daywork records so that he can decide his estimating policy, together with cash and material statements and formal financial accounts in order that he may regulate his production. Whether on site or at head office, the efficient communications provided by telephonist and typist, and the reliable records compiled by timekeeper, checker, storekeeper, goods received clerk and cashier, make a very real contribution to building and civil engineering construction.

Furthermore, it must be remembered that clerical activities are not confined solely to the offices, for both technical and supervisory staff are regularly concerned with clerical procedures. Since information is the very basis of modern management, it follows that 'scientific' builders must be sufficiently conversant with office organisation and methods to be able to make proper use of their office services. The particularly high bankruptcy rate in the building trade may be partly due to indifferent records and poor communications.

2. Clerical Functions

The office is the servant of management, its task being to assist others to play their parts more effectively. This secondary but vital function can be analysed under the following headings:

a. Receiving information. Opening and sorting mail, manning the telephone switchboard or a teleprinter, are examples of the passive side of communications, but there is also the duty of ensuring that information is both reliable and complete. Active steps may therefore be necessary to obtain additional facts required by the management, such as historical research or the setting-up of a library.

b. Recording information. The object of keeping records is to enable stored information to be made readily available whenever required, so that any filing system must be both accurate and accessible. This therefore entails the provision of adequate accommodation with visible references, the establishment of a convenient but comprehensive filing classification with an alphabetical index, and the recording of issues. For central technical information the widely adopted SfB–UDC system (Special for Building–Universal Decimal Classification) described in the R.I.B.A. Filing Manual Handbook is eminently suitable.

c. Rearranging information. The information accumulated is gathered together from many sources, and usually requires to be sorted and analysed before it can be presented to the appropriate manager. Invoices are posted to accounts, regular returns from sites are summarised, cash statements are prepared, and timebook calculations have to be made. While much of this rearrangement is routine, this function, which has become one of the most important jobs within the office, requires experienced and properly trained staff. Statistical research and the presentation of reports for the guidance of top level policy decisions are examples of the specialist nature of this service.

d. Presenting information. As required, the office gives out information from its records either verbally or in writing, and this must be neat, understandable and on time. Placing orders for materials, duplicating sub-contract enquiries or operating a central filing department may be of a routine nature, but it is not sufficient blindly to follow the procedure laid down. Those with clerical responsibilities must give intelligent thought to the practical implications of the words and figures shown on records, and inform the management when anything unusual occurs. Stock deficiencies, bad debts, lost records or urgent messages must all be reported promptly so that action can be taken before it is too late.

e. Safeguarding assets. Finally, the office or clerical function has the responsibility for protecting certain assets of the business. Cash must be held in security and banked, vital records need to be protected from loss or fire, construction sites and stock have to be safeguarded by insurance, and office buildings and equipment need to be serviced and maintained in good working order.

3. Organisation and Methods

Organisation and Methods is the title now used extensively in industry and commerce, to describe the study by full-time investigators of clerical organisation structure and methods of procedure. Its aim is the promotion of efficiency in offices by improving organisation, methods and performance, so that the best use is made of clerical manpower, machines and equipment, and accommodation. The service is a tool of the management, to be used for providing adequate and accurate information for purposes of policy making and managerial control. Hence the specialist is an adviser, whose qualifications must be based primarily on practical experience in O. & M. work.

1. *Gathering information.* After being briefed by the management and having agreed upon the precise scope of the investigation, the O. & M. man's first step is to establish what is being done and to record it on paper. A statement of the purpose of the procedure must be defined, the real use of records established, and the existing methods and sources of information should be methodically examined and described. Reports may be presented in either written or diagrammatic form.

   a. A procedure narrative consists of a written account of the full procedure, listing step-by-step the clerk responsible, and the precise nature of each operation.

   b. A method analysis sheet is also a written account, but lists the operations performed on a single document of the procedure. Each step is described together with a symbol indicating the class of operation involved (see Fig. 10.1).

   c. A flow chart is a pictorial representation of the complete procedure which shows the route of each document, with or without a description of the operations. It is particularly useful for a complicated procedure, and may be used either on its own or in conjunction with method *a* or *b* (see Fig. 10.2).

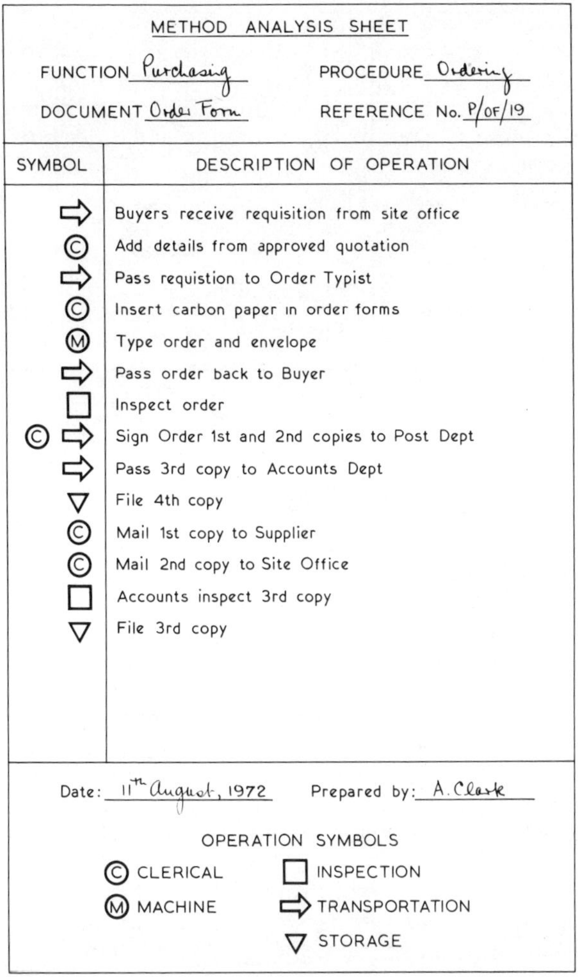

```
                    METHOD  ANALYSIS  SHEET

        FUNCTION Purchasing        PROCEDURE Ordering
        DOCUMENT Order Form        REFERENCE No. P/OF/19
```

SYMBOL	DESCRIPTION OF OPERATION
⇨	Buyers receive requisition from site office
C	Add details from approved quotation
⇨	Pass requistion to Order Typist
C	Insert carbon paper in order forms
M	Type order and envelope
⇨	Pass order back to Buyer
□	Inspect order
C ⇨	Sign Order 1st and 2nd copies to Post Dept
⇨	Pass 3rd copy to Accounts Dept
▽	File 4th copy
C	Mail 1st copy to Supplier
C	Mail 2nd copy to Site Office
□	Accounts inspect 3rd copy
▽	File 3rd copy

```
        Date: 11th August, 1972    Prepared by: A. Clark

                    OPERATION  SYMBOLS
            C CLERICAL          □ INSPECTION
            M MACHINE           ⇨ TRANSPORTATION
                                ▽ STORAGE
```

Fig. 10.1

    d. A specimen chart consists of examples of each document pasted on to a sheet or board, in the order in which they are prepared. Descriptive notes or movement routes may be added as elaboration.

2. *Improving methods.* There is no organisation or set of methods which is suitable for all circumstances, and every contracting business must work out its own compromise solution. The objective is to keep the costs in effort and money compatible

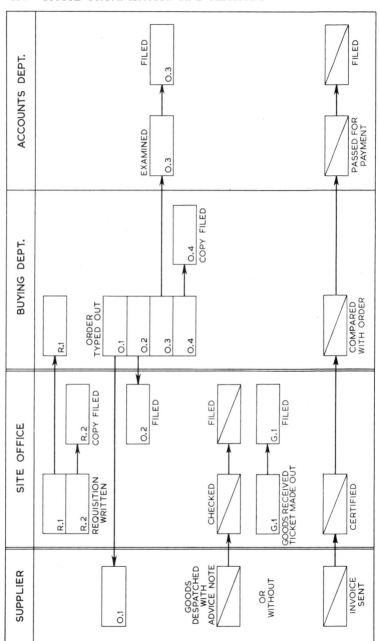

Fig. 10.2. General purchasing procedure

TIMETABLE FOR PREPARATION OF WEEKLY COST/VALUE CONTROL SHEETS

	MONDAY	TUESDAY	WEDNESDAY	THURSDAY	FRIDAY	SATURDAY
COST CLERK	Collect allocations. Calculate Bonus sheet. Price time analysis	— once — Value the cost time. Transfer time analysis to control sheet	— each — Check queries and value additions	— working — Complete cost/value sheet and summary	— day — Transfer from note book to time analysis	Prepare plant allocations
SECTION ENGINEERS	Measure weekly quantities and prepare Bonus sheet	Write out Control sheet				
TIMEKEEPERS	Complete ——	Time ——	Books			
AGENT					Note queries for correction next week	
GENERAL FOREMAN					Examine and investigate cost for improvement	
SURVEYOR						Investigate costs for Variations
COMPLETION DEAD-LINES	Bonus Sheet ↑	Weekly Quantities ↑	Time Books ↑	Control Sheet ↑		

Fig. 10.3

with the staff and resources available. Emphasis is on the work study approach to simplify essential duties, and to eliminate unnecessary movements or processes. In particular, the purpose of each document must be closely questioned for nothing grows more readily than paper work. Improvement may be possible in other directions than by adopting different methods.

   a. *The design of forms* can be an important element in effectiveness and economy. Questions of size, quality of paper, layout and style of printing should be considered, beside the aspects of publicity and standardisation. Recommendations for size and layout are given in B.S.1808.

   b. *Mechanisation* of routine clerical work can be of value in chosen instances by introducing speed, and facilitating progess control and automatic checks. However, great care must be exercised for successes are more usually achieved by revision of manual methods.

3. *Installing procedures.* When the new method has been designed, the agreement of management must be obtained together with the co-operation of those who will operate the system. A method summary or procedure statement should be prepared, both as a record and a means of instruction. In this connection a time schedule is a valuable appendix (see Fig. 10.3) to prescribe the general pattern of the activity, and these documents should be incorporated into a company Manual of Clerical Procedures. The installation plans should include an equipment schedule, a changeover programme and arrangements for inspection during the initial stages.

4. Layout and Working Conditions

1. *Office Accommodation.* The building or civil engineering contractor must consider both permanent and temporary premises.

   a. *Head office* may be either a comparatively spacious modern building designed specifically for office purposes or an older building converted and adapted. The Offices, Shops and Railway Premises Act 1963, which came into operation on 1st May, 1964, lays down standards for the working conditions of office staff. Provisions concerning their comfort and welfare include requirements for cleaning, heating, lighting, ventilation, sanitary conveniences, washing facilities, drinking water, space per employee, storage of clothing, seating, safety and fire precautions.

b. *Site offices* may vary from portable buildings that can be folded and re-erected complete with services within hours, sectional buildings that must be dismantled and rebuilt, or fully equipped caravans constructed for the specific purpose. From the points of view both of efficiency and economy, and possibly of standardisation, these alternatives are well worth careful consideration. The Offices Act 1963, also applies to site offices unless: if movable structures, they are occupied for less than 6 months; if not movable structures they are occupied for less than 6 weeks.

2. *Physical conditions.* Clerical work requires more mental than physical effort, and office working conditions must therefore be conducive to mental concentration. Apart from this efficiency aspect there is also the effect on morale of the health and comfort of the staff.

a. *Cleanliness and tidiness* contribute not only to the health of staff, but also to the neatness and accuracy of their work. Office cleaners should be well supervised and provided with correct equipment and materials. A regular programme should be laid down for 'spring cleaning'.

b. *Decoration* can have a noticeable effect upon the whole atmosphere of an office, for pleasant surroundings usually contribute to good morale. Colours can be either cheerful or cold, restful or stimulating to human emotions, so that a properly planned scheme combining opinions of staff with advice of a specialist, is a good investment.

c. *Heating and ventilation* are associated problems; the aim being an even temperature and a flow of fresh air without draughts. Ideally these conditions are correct when the office occupants are conscious of neither. Air-conditioning is a solution but the expense is seldom justified in a temperate climate. With some exceptions a minimum temperature of 60°F (15.6°C) is stipulated by the Offices Act. It should also be noted that UK Government regulations now demand a maximum of 65°F (18.3°C) in order to conserve energy.

d. *Lighting* is most important to clerical work, for correct illumination is an essential factor in avoiding eye strain and fatigue. Light should be well diffused, adequate for the particular work, and without glare. For natural lighting a northern aspect is best, and windows facing south should be provided with sunblinds. Artificial lighting may cast light directly downwards which produces shadows, or reflect light indirectly from the ceiling which gives better diffusion and less glare. Fluorescent lighting gives a direct and diffused light but with a low ceiling the glare may be a distraction. Supplementary lighting for individual desks is usually necessary for draughtsmen.

    e. Noise is an obvious distraction which can also lead to fatigue. Carpeted floors will absorb the general sounds of office movements, and windows facing busy streets may be fitted with double frames. Telephone switchboards and machine rooms should be isolated, but typewriters, etc., can be muffled by standing them on insulating pads.

3. *Furniture and layout.* The elementary principles of motion study should be applied to both the equipment and arrangement of an office, in order to eliminate unnecessary movement.

    a. Furniture should be standardised where possible in the interest of economy and to permit interchange as work develops. Special desks for typists, calculating machine operators and draughtsmen are the usual exceptions. In general, a working height of 2ft 6in. (762 mm) is normal, and there should be provision for storing personal effects. A properly laid out working area can aid efficiency by

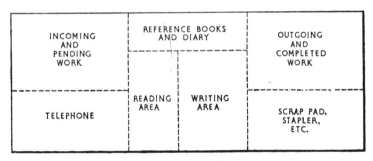

Fig. 10.4. Example of desk layout

encouraging tidiness and simultaneous use of both hands (see Fig. 10.4). Design of chairs is important in reducing fatigue; they should be adjustable for machine operators and revolving where frequent reference to storage space is necessary.

b. *The layout* of an office should be planned in detail to ensure full use of the available floor space, to provide each clerk with the tools for his particular job close to hand, and to streamline the flow of work. Approximately 40 ft^2 (3.72 m^2) of floor space is required for each individual working area including equipment and gangways. A large open office makes for better supervision and flexibility of arrangement, but executives and others whose work is confidential or exacting require private offices.

5. Office Machinery

The extent to which any builder's office can be mechanised depends largely upon the size of the business, but more and more mechanical devices are being used both to save time and mental drudgery and also eliminate much of the erring human element. Machines such as typewriters, letter franking meters, filing and indexing equipment are familiar to everybody but certain aids to general office duties are worthy of special attention.

1. *Duplicators.* There are four main types of machine available for multiplying forms and circulars:

a. *Spirit hectograph* processes are particularly suited to jobs on which relatively small numbers of copies are required, and is the only method which will copy in several colours at one run. The low cost master is written on the glazed sheet by means of a special carbon paper placed beneath it. When affixed to the drum of a rotary machine, spirit dissolves a small portion of the carbon impression which is imprinted on to the copies.

b. *Wax stencils* may be cut on a typewriter or by hand, the ink being pressed through the cuts in the impervious coating. Either flat-bed or rotary models are marketed, the latter often power operated and up to 4,000 copies can be printed. This is a cleaner method than *a,* but since absorbent paper must be used it is not ideal for subsequent pen and ink entries.

c. *Offset litho* duplicators can produce up to 50,000 high quality copies and are therefore often employed on the production of complex forms. Masters are typed or handwritten on thin metal sheets and 'fixed' by means of a chemical wash. The blank portions of the master are wetted by damping rollers and do not therefore pick up the oily ink, whilst the prepared impression rejects water and takes the ink.

  d. *Xerography* is an electrical process which uses a statically charged metal sheet. Exposure removes the positive charge except where covered by the image, so that the remaining impression attracts a negatively charged powder which is again transferred to a positively charged sheet. When heated, the dust particles fuse to give the final copy.

2. *Photo copiers* are used for reproducing small numbers of copies of records or other complicated documents, and are most useful for copying Bills of Quantities or important letters received. There are many variants but every method depends upon the use of light sensitive paper.

  a. *The direct positive* process, like a camera, first produces a re-usable negative through which a light is passed to produce positive copies. Both negative and prints must be developed, fixed, washed and dried, but it is comparatively cheap.

  b. *The transfer* process allows copies to be taken from opaque documents which may have material on both sides. The sensitized paper is placed between the light and the document to produce a negative which is then repeatedly printed on to positive paper and fixed semi-dry in one operation to produce the copies required.

  c. *The dyeline* process is cheaper than the transfer method but the original must be translucent or transparent.

  d. *Drawings* are also reproduced by photographic methods, using a prepared tracing as the 'master'. Developing processes include the wet blueprint, the semi-dry dye-line and the dry ammonia vapour process which obviates any distortion due to shrinkage or expansion.

3. *Adding machines.* After the typewriter this is the commonest office machine in use, and is the basis of all the other computers. Both listing and non-listing types facilitate horizontal casting or the addition of scattered items.

  a. *Listing* machines provide a printed record of the individual items and the totals, usually on a roll of paper. For this reason add/listing machines have many uses in costing and accounting work. Figures are depressed on the keyboard and then transferred to the adding register and printed on the tally roll by the movement of a handle or lever. Keyboards may have a group of ten keys numbered '0' to '9', or several rows of columns each with ten keys. Special features may include two registers for both batch and grand totals, many can also subtract and there are electric models which are both faster and less tiring.

b. *Non-listing* types automatically record the results on dials as the amounts are set up on the keyboard. The vertical rows may include the full '1' to '9' or only the half '1' to '5' keys, the latter case requiring two key strokes for figures above 5. Again models may be electric or have double registers, but subtraction can only be performed by complementary addition. Simple non-listing adding machines can be very useful in estimating, planning or budgetary control.

4. *Calculating machines.* Since these machines multiply or divide by a process of repetitive addition or subtraction, they will not calculate duo-decimal satisfactorily. Duo-decimal and fractional amounts must therefore first be decimalised, a process which requires either the use of conversion tables or a trained comptometer operator to whom the mental operation has become automatic through practice. The calculating machine has become an accepted part of estimating for the purpose of extending and totalling Bills of Quantities, as well as being useful for checking Time Books and other general office operations.

a. *Key-driven* calculators are the non-listing type of adding machine, the commonest and fastest class where calculations and additions have to be performed together.

b. *Rotary* calculators may be either key or lever set, both types recording the results on dials. Primarily intended for multiplication and division only, they do however present a visual check on the factors being used, and require a much shorter period of training and less manual dexterity. For this reason they are suitable for the smaller office.

c. *Printing* calculators list the factors and answers on a tally roll. The first type is a development of the adding listing machine which also prints the number of revolutions during the repetitive additions or subtractions. A second class, fast and automatic, incorporating a typewriter keyboard so that descriptions can be added, is commonly used for keeping stock records.

5. *Punched card systems.* Electro-mechanical punched card machines can be applied to almost every type of clerical operation, but the heavy cost of the equipment must be justified by a volume of detailed work with a high proportion of unchanging factors, so that the same basic information can

be re-used for several purposes. Information is recorded by punched holes in specially designed cards, the position of each hole representing a certain figure or letter in a code system which covers the items or factors for each particular job, e.g. calculation of wages. These holes are sensed either by mechanical operated rods or electrical brush contacts, so that the sorting, adding, printing or other mechanism is automatically actuated at high speed. The range of punched card equipment includes the following:

a. *Punching* machines may be either hand or electrically operated.

b. *Verifying* punches are used to check the punched cards against the original documents.

c. *Multiplying* punches will calculate and punch the product of a multiplier and a multiplicand previously recorded on a card.

d. *Sorting* machines can arrange cards into numerical order for a particular 'field' or group of columns. A collator will compare or bring together cards bearing the same code in a chosen field, from two previously sorted packs.

e. *Interpreter* machines sense the information recorded on cards and repeat it in print so that it may be read.

f. *Tabulators* are adding, subtracting and printing machines which are used to record the final results of the previous operations. An interchangeable control panel is set up to govern the performance of the machine, so that details or summaries of the processed information are printed on continuous stationery in a predetermined order.

6. *Hand-written systems.* Three-in-one manual systems enable three different documents to be completed at one operation, thus saving labour and also providing a means of checking accuracy. All the forms used are designed to be superimposed on one another, so that the collective record is automatically completed when other related statements are made out.

The common basis is a large *posting board,* fitted with pegs or clamps at the sides to hold the papers in place and ensure that entries are accurately aligned and made in correct order. On this board is first placed the largest form in the system and on top of it, interleaved with carbon, are placed the individual record and statement. For example, in writing out a customer's statement, corresponding entries are simultaneously made on the customer's ledger card and the appropriate line of the sales journal sheet. The top two documents are removed and replaced by others which are placed one notch lower on the board, so that the entries appear one after the other on the collective record. Such a system is also suitable for payroll records, in which the summary sheet, the individual's record card, and the payslip can all be completed at once.

A *summariser board* is similar in design but with the pegs or clamps on the top edge. Each completed sheet is folded over so that a selected column of figures appears on its right-hand edge, and the sheets are overlapped so that only the required columns are visible. By moving a horizontal cursor to underline the line under review, it is possible to abstract totals or comparative statistics in this easy way.

7. *Electronic systems.* Both adding and calculating machines, whilst still in use, have been superseded by electronic pocket and desk-top calculators of great variety. Similarly, punched card systems have been replaced by digital computers, which are described in detail in Chapter 20. The silicon 'chip' revolution has given the computer department a status and philosophy of its own.

Communication systems in particular have been revolutionised by electronics, ranging from the simplest 'direct' line telephone; a type commonly used by executives and their secretaries to provide intercommunication without the outside caller hearing the internal conversations; an arrangement with main line(s) and extensions with push-button intercommunication between all extensions; and private branch exchanges (PBX) with multiple lines and extensions. One telephone number only may be given in the telephone directory, but incoming calls are automatically switched to the next free line. Telephone handsets have themselves become much more sophisticated, incorporating push buttons; a memory to store the user's most often dialled numbers or the last number dialled; and a digital display to confirm that the number has been dialled correctly. Machines have also been designed to answer calls in the absence of the subscriber. The simpler type will answer only, and perhaps explain the owner's absence and/or suggest an alternative number or su   'e time to ring again. Another machine will not only answ   with a recorded message, but also invite the caller to leave a message so that the enquiry may be followed up later. There is also the teleprinter, similar in operation to a typewriter but connected via the telephone lines for speedy communication between two points. When a message is typed on the keyboard it is printed simultaneously on both machines, thus providing a record of the transmission.

BIBLIOGRAPHY

G. Mills and O. Standingford, *Office Organisation and Method*, Pitman.
Laura Tatham, *Equipment and Methods for the Smaller Office*, Business Publications.
G. Mills and O. Standingford (eds.) *Office Administration*, Pitman, for the Office Management Association.
Handbook of Architectural Practice and Management, Part 2, 'Office Services, Methods and Aids', R.I.B.A.
The Practice of O & M, Civil Service Dept, H.M.S.O., 1971.
A Guide to the 1963 OSPP Act, Health and Safety Executive, 1980.

Chapter 11

Purchasing

1. Principles of Purchasing

The procuring of materials, equipment and services required for the operation of a business, is essentially a service function: the main object being to purchase at the minimum overall cost consistent with suitable quality and availability. In the construction industries the chief problems have been the acute basic materials shortages, caused by politically induced fluctuations in activity, and the general inability of the building materials producers to conform to the policy of fixed prices for an appreciable period ahead. Since the materials content of a contractor's costs often amounts to 50 per cent or more, the buyer carries a heavy responsibility, and in the face of severe competition and fine profit margins errors here may mean disaster. Moreover it is easier to avoid spending money than it is to recover it later.

1. *Relationships.* Purchasing must be closely co-ordinated with other functions of management for the work of a buying department can be most helpful to other activities of the business.

a. *Policy* decisions are necessary on whether to centralise buying at head office or to decentralise at least for the larger contracts, and whether to buy on contract, i.e. for large amounts or long periods, those materials such as cement or petrol that are commonly required, as an alternative to the more usual current market.

b. *Production* must be kept advised of the current delivery position and of new materials which may interest them. For this reason it is necessary to keep suppliers' records and a good catalogues library.

c. *Estimating* depends upon quotations for tenders, the supply of technical data, and news of price trends and materials shortages.

    d. Accountancy requires legal and other conditions of contract to be checked and invoices to be verified.

    e. Suppliers should be chosen with the sole aim of maximum value for the company, and the ethics of accepting seasonal gifts should be prudently considered. Courtesy and equitable dealings with sales representatives creates goodwill and establishes a desirable co-operation.

2. Purchasing Procedures

In both large and small organisations the same pattern of procedure is followed, whether the operations are the prerogatives of a specialised purchasing officer or allocated to surveyors and site agents. The relevant documents outline a convenient sequence for consideration.

    1. *Requisitions.* Action may be initiated by several sources including:

        a. Estimating department enquiries based upon Bills of Quantities being priced for tenders.

        b. Requisitions from contracts or technical personnel taken-off from drawings, etc. It is desirable to limit the number of persons so authorised, and a ceiling is sometimes placed on the value of such indents unless countersigned by a higher authority.

        c. Instructions by the employing authority nominating suppliers or sub-contractors for Prime Cost items.

    Whatever the origin of the request it is essential that full and accurate information be provided as to quantity and specification of materials, address and realistic dates for delivery, any special inspection requirements and/or contract conditions, purpose or authorisation and the account to be charged.

    2. *Enquiries.* To avoid queries or misunderstandings the supplier should be told as fully as possible what is wanted. For this reason a standard enquiry form is desirable, with a clear title to prevent it being mistaken for an order, and possibly with model conditions printed on the back. Invitations to supply materials or plant may be sent singly since most vendors use their own quotation forms, but it is usual to circulate sub-contract bills of quantities in duplicate so that one can be priced and returned and the other retained for reference. The number of enquiries depends upon the goods required; one for branded articles, three for usual purposes, or more if

considered necessary, but it is wasteful to send enquiries to all suppliers for every order.

The selection of a source of supply is a buyer's most important function, and involves the consideration of whether to purchase from:

i.   A single supplier or from several at the same time,
ii. Manufacturers directly or through builders' merchants,
iii. Local sources or from farther afield.

To avoid negative replies careful selection of likely sources is important, and the experienced buyer relies greatly upon past records. When it is necessary to search for a particular commodity or a new supplier, reference can be made to catalogues, classified directories, professional or trade journals, advertisements, exhibitions, etc.

3. *Quotations.* It is good practice to enter the tenders on a summary sheet so that the important features are set out for easy comparison. Selection of the ultimate supplier depends upon several factors in addition to the quoted price, and these considerations vary with the material or service being examined.

   a. Materials or equipment require the following factors to be taken into account when prices are compared:

   i.   The description and quality of the goods offered, their compliance with specification, and the approval of samples if required.
   ii. The point of delivery, whether quoted ex works or pit, free on rail, free on board or deliverd to site, and the additional cost of carriage if this has not been included.
   iii. The delivery period, including any time required for preparation and approval of drawings. A supplier's past record in this respect should be borne in mind.
   iv. Ability to provide the quantity or rate of delivery required, particularly for such items as aggregates, hardcore or bricks.
   v.   Discounts, including cash discounts for prompt payment, trade discounts where applicable, quantity discounts for bulk orders, cumulative rebates for continued custom, and loyalty rebates for exclusive agreements.
   vi. Technical resources and after sales service, particularly for construction plant, including hired.

   b. Sub-contractors including labour-only and nominated must be carefully chosen for the following qualities apart from acceptable price:

    i. Business integrity and guarantee of service.

    ii. Quality of workmanship which must equal that required by the specification.

    iii. Ability to meet the programmed completion date(s) must be confirmed, and past experience in this respect is invaluable.

    iv. Financial stability or special payment requirements.

    v. It is usual for the Architect's permission to be obtained before work is sublet on a labour-only basis, and sub-contractors must also be approved by the employing authority.

    vi. Details of attendances, facilities, unloading and handling of materials required should be carefully investigated, especially for nominated specialists.

    vii. A proper understanding of the terms and conditions of sub-contract must be ensured, and the main contract conditions must be made available for inspection if desired.

Those contractors with their own trade departments may allow them to compete at this stage with outside specialists, but confidence between the various members of the construction team is essential and any form of 'Dutch auction' must therefore be deprecated.

4. *Orders.* The purchase order is the buyer's offer to purchase, and becomes a legal contract when the seller accepts or acknowledges receipt of the document. Both a written commitment to accept and pay for goods or a service, and an indication of agreement to transfer the property for money are necessary to ensure enforcement of a contract above the value of ten pounds. For this reason an extra copy of the order, or a tear-off portion, are sometimes required to be signed and returned to the buyer. Any differences between 'buyer' and 'seller' conditions must obviously be settled before the order form is made out. To avoid ambiguities later, the specification and price, terms of payment and settlement, details of delivery, and any special clauses of the conditions must be clearly defined. For sub-contractors it is essential that the relevant items of the main contract are passed on in proportion to the value of their work, and a standard Form of Contract such as that issued by the Building Employers Confederation and the Federation of Associations of Specialists and Sub-Contractors, has undeniable advantages. Attend-

ances particularly need to be carefully examined, and a discount or allowance on the National Schedules of Daywork Charges must be agreed if the main contractor requires a profit margin on variations so measured. Unsuccessful tenderers should be notified as early as possible.

Copies of orders should be distributed to the site office, the administration office if elsewhere, the quantity surveyor responsible for measurement and anyone else affected. Apart from special purchases of non-recurring items for individual projects, and quantity orders for basic components such as bricks, orders may be placed for long-term requirements of materials like concrete aggregates where the total quantity can only be stated within limits, while associated items purchased from one supplier, e.g. an ironmonger, may be covered by a blanket order.

3. Follow-up Operations

1. *Progressing.* Since production depends upon the right quantity of components being delivered at the right time, it is essential to organise prompt receipt by following-up or progressing orders. In present supply conditions it is difficult to strike a happy balance between the necessity for ensuring that everything is available on time and the desirability of avoiding double handling. Delivery programmes and schedules should be forwarded to all suppliers, and follow-up action should begin with a reminder, possibly a standard postcard, followed by increasing pressure and personal contact in difficult cases. Should it become necessary to alter or cancel an order, the same procedure of written offer and notified acceptance must be followed to ensure legality.

The simplest form of progressing system is to file outstanding requisitions or orders in delivery date sequence, so that, each morning, deliveries due can be noted and immediate action taken if not received by the afternoon. If a record card is attached to each overdue order then details of chasing action can be entered for information purposes (see Fig. 11.1). Sheets can be refiled in order of revised promises so that a continuous watch can be maintained and action prompted whenever necessary. Suppliers of important items can be reminded at a predetermined check period, to obtain confirmation of delivery dates, or uncover difficulties in time for effective action to be taken. Once again, it is essential that everybody concerned should be advised of the latest position by progress reports.

MATERIALS PROGRESSING RECORD

Material metal Windows Order No. 18/529 Date 21/2/73				
Supplier Steel Products Ltd Quote Ref. ABC/2 Date 10/2/73				
Delivery Due 6 April 63 Quantity 250 no.				
Enquiry Date	Results	Deliveries		
		Date	Qty	Left
7 April	First load promised 13ᵀᴸ	13/4	50	200

Fig. 11.1

2. **Checking.** Apart from specific components that may be inspected during manufacture at works, the delivery of all materials should be checked on site for shortages or damage. Haulage tippers must be inspected to ensure that they are loaded to the capacity being paid for, and meticulous records should be kept for all hired plant. Unloading may be supervised by a storekeeper or materials checker or by foremen, but a clear routine should be established, particularly on the larger or more open sites. Bulk deliveries such as aggregates or ready-mixed concrete should receive spot checks; any goods not examined should be signed for as such

MONTHLY RECONCILIATION OF MATERIALS

Material	Measured Quantity	Opening Stock	Total Receipts	Closing Stock	Actual Quantity	% Waste
Eng. Bricks	100,000	50,000	120,000	65,000	105,000	5%

Fig. 11.2

MATERIALS RISE AND FALL

Invoice Date	Invoice No.	Supplier	Details	Quantity	Price	Cost	Basic Value		Increased Cost	Saving
12 June	4185	R C. Aggregates Ltd	Building Sand	105 tonnes	4.00	420 00	3.75	393 75	26 25	– – –

Fig. 11.3

and checked as soon as possible afterwards. Materials below standard, e.g. dirty sand or deformed bricks, should either be rejected or retained awaiting disposal instructions and the delivery ticket signed accordingly.

In addition, basic building materials including bricks, cement, etc., should be recorded so that periodic reconciliations can be made between deliveries, stocks and usages (see Fig. 11.2) as a check on wastage or other losses.

3. *Storing.* A competent storekeeper is a necessity and an investment on any sizeable contract, both for adequate control of bulk stocks and the identification and location of special components and materials. Activities include the basic recording of receipts and issues, the operation of minimum re-order levels, accounting for returnable packages and empties, transfers between contracts and loan issues to site personnel, disposing of scrap, annual stocktaking, and security arrangements by watchmen or dogs. Standard procedure should be laid down for the efficient operation of these various aspects.

4. *Authorising payment.* Information from the delivery tickets or checkers' notes is recorded by the goods received clerk, and this is later used to verify that the goods charged on invoices have actually been delivered. Invoices are then compared with the original orders to confirm that correct materials have been supplied at the agreed prices, and can then be authorised for payment. Similarly the work of the labour-only sub-contractor is measured weekly and an authorisation issued for cash payment on site. Sub-contractors are measured monthly by the surveyor, and together with nominated suppliers' accounts are included in the interim certificate for payment by the accounts department.

There is however an obverse side to payment, that of ensuring that credit notes are claimed and that contra charges against sub-contractors are recorded for additional attendances or materials supplied. Moreover, when the contract includes cost variation clauses, it is necessary to claim reimbursement for the net variations in the cost of materials. This entails keeping a materials rise and fall record as illustrated in Fig. 11.3, unless a formula reimbursement has been agreed.

BIBLIOGRAPHY

Purchasing for Industry and Public Undertakings, Edited for the Purchasing Association by F. Kay, Pitman.

Chapter 12

Plant and Vehicles

1. Economic Considerations

Plant plays an increasingly important role in building as well as civil engineering operations, and both time and money can be saved by the efficient use of mechanical aids. Yet the full advantages can only be obtained if the plant is well managed, both on and off the site, and this requires a thorough understanding of the economic aspects of using plant and vehicles.

a. *Further mechanisation* of erection is largely influenced by design for the machine needs mass production to pay off, and this requires greater standardisation and repetition. For example, a crane will become expensive if the design does not allow a fairly continuous programme of work while it is on the site. Despite the current recession, an immense task lies before the building industry for many years to come, and to equate reduced national resources with the high cost of labour, new methods must be evolved by which greater and more effective use can be made of mechanical plant.

b. As a larger proportion of the *fixed capital* of the contracting industry is absorbed by plant, it becomes increasingly important that it should be used to its full working capacity and be well maintained, in order to pay for itself and help to reduce construction costs. With the large selection of mechanical plant now available, the most economic choice of machine and method of operation in any situation is not always obvious and must be determined by comparative costing.

c. While it is obviously desirable that a *plant department* should be profitable, this should never be achieved at the expense of contracts, for its primary function must be to provide a service to other divisions of the company. This requires that general management should not only have clear objectives, but also reliable information upon which to base rational decisions.

d. Highly competitive *tendering* relies upon factual costing of plant for estimating purposes, and in civil engineering particularly the choice of method can be decisive.

All these factors underline the necessity for obtaining the true operating costs of all plant.

1. *Costing methods.* In the absence of factual hire rates it is possible to obtain a guide, either from the schedule of rates of hire issued by the Contractors' Plant Association, or from the schedules of daywork charges recommended by the two national employers' organisations.

Although the plant hire industry is generally very competitive, the rates charged do not necessarily reflect the actual cost of operating, for questions of supply and demand or fluctuations of trade may greatly vary the margin of profit made with different types of equipment. Methods based upon the depreciation of plant over a short assumed life such as is used for pure accountancy purposes, not only disguise or exaggerate the actual costs by ignoring certain aspects, but may also prevent the purchase of desirable and truly economical machines. It is essential when calculating and comparing costs to consider the implications of each of the following factors:

a. The working life of any individual item of plant will depend upon its typical characteristics, on the way it is used and on how it is maintained; but eventually further servicing will become uneconomic and the piece of equipment must be scrapped and replaced. Estimates of the average life for various types of machine may be obtained from company records, or plant textbooks, but more valid results were obtained by a Building Research Station survey in 1954.[1]

b. The utilisation of a particular unit of plant must be assessed if the hire charge is to be levied upon the time it is available for work on a contract. Annual usage rates may also be estimated from past experience, although the results obtained from a survey of plant users and tabled in *B.R.S. Digest* 113 can serve as a guide.

c. Market depreciation must be allowed for if it is intended to sell pieces of equipment before the ends of their lives. Low resale values must be expected in the early years for the depreciation rate is steepest in the first year, and still fairly

[1]See *B.R.S. Digest* 113.

steep over the next few years before tailing off. Basic influences are age and use.

d. *Obsolescence* must be borne in mind for new models may be produced with lower relative operating costs. Although this is not generally one of the important factors, machines may become obsolete before they are worn out if they are not used sufficiently.

e. *Replacement costs* should make allowance for inflation because prices often change fairly rapidly, so that the schedule of annual charges might need to be revised annually. If the annual hire charge is calculated as a percentage of the initial purchase price and applied to the current price for new plant, this will overcome the problem.

f. It is necessary to include *interest* charges on the capital loaned to finance the purchase of equipment, either at external mortgage rates or internal profit earnings. Conversely the amounts set aside each year towards replacement should also accrue interest.

g. The standard of *maintenance* and the length of life are obviously related so that cost data must if possible come from the same source. Maintenance costs should include labour, material and full plant department overheads. It is usual for contracts to be responsible for day-to-day repairs but this should be remembered when comparing with outside hire charges.

h. An annual addition must also be made for *insurance, licences* and any administrative overheads.

To the resulting total cost might be added a percentage for contingencies and profit, but because of the difficulty of accurately evaluating the first two items, any comparison with rates quoted outside must be made with reservation.

2. *Management decisions.* Realistic plant charges will allow several important management decisions to be taken as the logical results of scientific analysis.

a. *Source of supply* is a common problem that may give rise to friction between sites and the plant department. Decisions must be taken from the point of view of the economy of the undertaking as a whole, and the majority of contractors supply most of their needs from their own pools. In general it is more economical to own those types of plant most frequently required, and to look to plant hire firms for items that would otherwise stand idle for periods. Ownership, however, brings its own problems of additional organisation and capital, the uncertainty of hiring surplus equipment to other firms, and the temptation to use unsuitable plant from the yard rather than hire a more efficient machine. Plant hire is justified if the changed utilisation rates result in lower hire charges, and hiring from local sources may sometimes obviate high haulage costs from a distant plant depot. On large projects of long duration it may be practical to purchase plant for a specific job and resell at the end of the contract. Advantages of this method include the ability to meet specific requirements and an answer to obsolescence, but fluctuations in prices may make it difficult to forecast costs with certainty. Most builders choose a middle course with the advantage of an organisation under their own control, and the more usual machines readily available. A rule developed by the National Coal Board determines the economic employment of hired plant in a fleet as 1 day in K days, where K is the ratio of hire charges to owning costs. Sufficient machines should be owned to satisfy requirements on the remaining days.

b. *Choice of plant* for a particular operation can only be determined by preparing a programme and costing on the basis of the time allowed and the plant, consumable stores and labour requirements. The total cost must include the hire charge for the full period, the cost of transport both ways and the expenses of setting-up and dismantling. Estimated outputs for a particular piece of plant may be found from text books or based upon experience, but due allowance must be made for the influence of mechanical efficiency, the efficiency of the operator, and prevailing site and weather conditions. Average fuel consumption figures may be taken from manufacturers' data or *B.R.S. Digest* 113. For most types of plant the combined costs are lower for diesel than for petrol driven machines, while diesel and electrical plant are comparable at normal prices.

c. *Internal plant charges* should be foreseeable, and provide incentives to site managements to use equipment intensively, to provide proper care, and to return items promptly. Light plant (static) and tools may conveniently be charged on the basis of an inventory as supplied, being regraded as to its condition when returned, and the contract credited on the re-valuation. The most satisfactory basis for heavy plant (mechanical) is a straight hire rate for each day that the machine is on the site, irrespective of the actual time it is being used. If no hire is payable for periods when the plant is unserviceable, and repairs or replacements are carried out without charge, this will also give the plant department an incentive to supply machines in good working order.

2. Maintenance Organisation

Reliable plant is essential if building and civil engineering work is to be carried out at a fast rate of progress, at low unit cost, and without serious danger to personnel. Systematic maintenance is therefore a matter of prime importance, and since both the life and serviceability of the plant depend to a large extent upon the correct performance of this routine work, effective supervision both in the workshop and on the site is very necessary. Thus whatever the size of the firm, the efficient organisation of the plant department is a vital responsibility.

1. *Repair depot.* It is the normal practice of contractors who possess sufficient plant, to maintain their own yard for storing plant which is not in use, and to employ a plant engineer and fitters for minor repairs and general maintenance. Heavy repairs and major overhauls may be carried out by the makers or specialist firms, but the basic requirements of a depot include the following:

   a. *Workshop facilities* may begin with the minimum of covered accommodation and a concrete floor, with provision for heating and lighting, particularly for night working. Equipment such as benches, hand tools, lifting tackle, welding gear and small power tools may progress to include air compressor, battery charger, lathe, drill etc., as the depot grows.

   b. *Spare parts* must be readily available in order to reduce site delays, and a good service might provide complete assemblies as a service exchange. The size of the store and the variety of quick wearing parts is decided by experience and from repairs records, but standardisation of machines can help to decrease the range required.

   c. *Records* are necessary to progress the work being undertaken, and to ensure that the history of each machine is registered and statistics can be reviewed. A wall chart showing the location of plant on the various sites and their state of serviceability should be checked daily.

The promotion of better relationships between the plant

department and the contracts must be the continual aim of general management, and for this reason clear limits of responsibility must be defined. Sites should be able to call upon a reliable service, but in turn they must clearly requisition exactly what they require and give notice of 'when' and 'for how long'.

2. *Site servicing.* The first stage of maintenance consists of regular attention by the operator to such items as cleaning, oiling and greasing, tightening loose nuts and bolts, etc. Daily routine checks must be made of water, oil, fuel, lights, tyres and brakes (for vehicles), while weekly servicing instructions can be incorporated with the driver's log book to ensure complete coverage. The principle of 'one man to one machine' should be applied so far as possible. Breakdowns will, however, occur on even the best organised site, and unless a black gang is kept available for immediate repairs then the services of a full-time mobile fitter are required. In addition to making minor repairs and adjustments the fitter should also inspect the plant to see that maintenance is being properly carried out, and his selection and training is therefore most important.

3. *Preventive maintenance.* Regular inspection by a competent mechanic is the next stage, to ensure that machines are kept in good working order and thus reduce the number of breakdowns. These checks should preferably take place outside working hours, e.g. week-ends, otherwise the plant will need to be withdrawn at agreed intervals for this purpose. Check lists should be prepared, listing the items to be inspected or adjusted for particular frequencies of mileage or running hours (see Fig. 12.1).

4. *Planned maintenance.* A maintenance inspection may reveal the need for a future major repair, or a periodic overhaul in a workshop may be due when the machine will be completely stripped down and any worn parts renewed. Arrangements for this work and planning so that the minimum production time is lost, the available resources are not over-taxed, and that the anticipated replacement parts are in stock, constitutes the second leg of systematic maintenance known as planned maintenance.

It will be seen that effective plant maintenance concerns the plant department, the site management and the operator, but the vital responsibility for the necessary organisation and co-ordination is that of the highest management level.

Preventive Maintenance Procedure for Water Pumps Every 120 Hours

Plant Number: ....   **Total Operating Hours:** ....

Check and correct where necessary, the following items: Tick if correct, (A) if adjustment is made, (X) if repair is needed, with details.

1. **Engine—check for**
   Fuel leaks ( )
   Oil leaks ( )
   Oil pressure ( )
   Loose holding down bolts ( )
   Tank holding bolts ( )
   Filters and covers on fuel tank ( )

2. **Electric Motor—check**
   Holding down bolts ( )
   Conduit for breaks or cracks ( )
   Slip-rings for arcing ( )
   Brushes and brush holders for wear ( )
   Protective covers for firmness ( )

3. **Electric Starter—check**
   Contacts and clean as necessary ( )

4. **Pump—check for**
   Water leak at gland ( )
   Water leaks at petcocks ( )
   Water leaks at inspection door ( )
   Cracked or damaged pump bodies ( )
   Loose bolts ( )

5. **Stand or Chassis—check for**
   Cracks, fractures or breaks ( )
   Damaged wheels ( )
   Washer and retaining pins in axle ( )

   Additions
   .... ( )
   .... ( )
   .... ( )

   Mechanic ....
   Date ....

Fig. 12.1

3. Statutory Requirements

A detailed knowledge of all the legal requirements associated with plant and vehicles is strictly the province of the plant manager, but a general understanding of the relevant regulations is essential to every builder and civil engineer.

a. Safety precautions. These requirements for plant are an integral part of overall site safety, and although most of them are covered by The Construction (Lifting Operations) Regulations, 1961, the Construction Regulations Handbook (RoSPA) is still an indispensable guide on this subject. Briefly

    i. a crane must be provided with a brake to prevent the fall of the load, be operated by a trained person, and fitted with a cab and an automatic safe load indicator for lifts over one ton (1.016 tonnes),

    ii. lifting gear must be marked with the safe working load,

    iii. any hoist needs to be enclosed, fitted with an automatic device to prevent over-run, and provided with a cage if used for carrying persons,

    iv. items of plant are required to be inspected by competent examiners at stated intervals and prescribed registers and certificates must be kept.

Electrical equipment is subject to the Electricity (Factories Act) Special Regulations, 1908 and 1944, which requires all A.C. portable apparatus (or D.C. above 150 volts) to be properly earthed.

b. Road transport management. In recent years transport management has been faced with the need to implement many new rules and regulations. These have involved change to operating practices and extra costs, but they must be observed since failure to do so will result in severe penalties. It is imperative therefore, that all those responsible for the operation of goods vehicles should fully understand the law and put the legal requirements into practice.

The licensing of goods vehicles is regulated by the Transport Act 1968, the Road Traffic Act 1974 and the Goods Vehicle (Operators Licences) Regulations 1977. A company is required to obtain an operator's licence (O-licence) for all its goods vehicles, except those which never go on the road. Exemptions include passenger vehicles constructed to carry not more than 15 passengers, trailers used in connection with the construction, maintenance or repair of roads, road rollers and trailers, and vehicles not exceeding 1 525 kg (30 cwt) unladen weight, or 3.5 tonnes ($3\frac{1}{2}$ tons) gross weight as shown on the Department of Transport plate. A separate O-licence is needed for each of the twelve Traffic Areas covering the U.K. Every vehicle subject to licensing which is hired without a driver or owned by the company must be specified in detail on the O-licence for the Traffic Area in which it is based. A vehicle may only be on one O-licence at a time, and if therefore it moves from one Area to another for more than three months, then it must be transferred to the new Traffic Area. Similarly, vehicles going off hire must also be taken off the O-licence.

The criterion for securing an operator's licence is to satisfy the Licensing Authority that the vehicles will be operated and maintained safely and legally. This entails regular and effective maintenance, linked with systematic and thorough inspection of vehicles, with records subject to inspection. A very high standard should comply with the Department of Transport *Maintenance Guide Lines*. All drivers are required to inspect their vehicles daily, and to complete and sign a daily inspection report. Preventive maintenance is normally based upon inspection every four weeks coupled with usual servicing. The particular method of inspection should be laid down on a maintenance schedule and record form in conjunction with the Department of Transport *Goods Vehicle Testers Manual*. Where vehicles are based on sites without a fitting shop, arrangements should be made for inspections to be carried out and necessary repairs effected at a local commercial garage.

To ensure that goods-carrying vehicles are maintained in a 'fit and serviceable' condition, tests and inspections may be carried out, either on the roadside or at an operator's premises, by Department of Transport certifying officers, vehicle examiners, or police officers in uniform. Vehicles are liable to spot checks under the Road Traffic Acts 1972 and 1974, or checks on premises under the Motor Vehicles (Construction and Use) Regulations 1973. An examiner who considers that a vehicle is unfit for service may issue either an immediate or delayed prohibition notice, which will continue in force until officially removed by the examiner. Because builders are often inclined to modify their vehicles, they should take particular note of the Construction and Use Regulations and their specifications.

Admission to the occupation of road haulage operator is governed by the Goods Vehicle Operators (Qualifications) Regulations 1977, which was introduced to satisfy an EEC directive. The new system is a modification of the O-licence which is divided into two classes, standard and restricted. A restricted licence entitles the holder to carry goods on his own account only. A standard licence is required wherever goods are to be carried for hire or reward, and applicants must employ nominated transport managers who are of good repute and professionally competent. A transport manager can attain professional competence either by 'grandfather rights', i.e. have been engaged in road transport operations before 1 January 1975, by exempting qualifications, or examination.

The driving of heavy goods vehicles is governed by the Heavy Goods Vehicles (Driving Licencing) Regulations 1975, which requires a driver to hold the appropriate H.G.V. licence. In order to take account of the varying degrees of skill required to drive different types of vehicle, there are eight classes of H.G.V. licence. Listed exemptions include track laying vehicles, road rollers, road construction vehicles, and digging machines. Minimum age limits for various classes of motor vehicle are 17 years for small passenger vehicles (up to 9 persons), 18 years for medium-sized goods vehicles (3.5 to 7.5 tonnes), and 21 years plus H.G.V. licence for other vehicles exceeding 7.5 tonnes or articulated. Should a driver be disqualified from driving, he not only loses his ordinary driving licence but must also give up his H.G.V. licence. E.E.C. regulations have been introduced on a phased basis to regulate drivers' hours for goods vehicles (exceeding 3.5 tonnes maximum weight) as follows:

	Up to 31 Dec 1980	*After 31 Dec 1980*
Maximum driving time	9 h/day	8 h/day
	54h/week	48h /week
	106 h	92 h
	in any 2 consecutive weeks	
Maximum continuous driving time	4½h	4 h
Breaks	One of 30 min, or two of 20 min, or three of 15 min	
Daily rest period	11 consecutive hours	
Weekly rest	29 h immediately preceded or followed by a daily rest period, i.e. 40 h total	

Duty time, spreadover and weekly duty are not covered by E.E.C. regulations, and therefore the rules and concessions laid down in the 1968 Transport Act apply. In the building and civil engineering industries this means that on-duty time including E.E.C. maximum driving time can be extended to 13 h/day, with a weekly maximum of 66 h including E.E.C. Driving Limits.

Passenger vehicles with seats for not more than 15 persons including the driver, on journeys within this country, are exempted from the E.E.C. rules.

Drivers of goods vehicles exceeding 3.5 tonnes plated weight, or 1525 kg unladen weight, and passenger vehicles with seats for 9 or more persons including the driver, are required to keep personal work records covering a period of at least 14 days. The numbered record book (known as E.E.C. type) must be examined and signed by the employer each week, and preserved for 12 months. Employers must also keep a register of all record books issued, and this also must be retained for 12 months.

Speed limits are governed by the Road Traffic Regulation Act 1967. The maximum speed limit on dual carriageways is 70 mile/h (112 km/h) and on single carriageway roads 60 mile/h (96 km/h), unless lower speeds are in force or unless the class of vehicle is restricted to lower limits. Motor vehicles may not be driven on restricted roads at speeds exceeding the specified limits, usually 30 mile/h (48 km/h) or as indicated by traffic signs. Speed limits for certain classes of vehicles are as follows:

Maximum speed 50 mile/h (80 km/h) – goods vehicles not exceeding 30 cwt (1525 kg) unladen weight, and cars or light vans towing trailers and caravans. Maximum speed 40 mile/h (64 km/h) – goods vehicles over 30 cwt unladen weight and articulated vehicles. Maximum speed 30 mile/h (48 km/h) – goods vehicles over 30 cwt unladen weight towing trailers. On motorways the maximum speed limit is 70 mile/h (112 km/h) unless lower speeds are in force. Certain classes of vehicle are restricted to lower limits as follows:

Goods vehicles over 3 tonnes unladen weight, articulated vehicles and drawbar trailer combinations, 60 mile/h (96 km/h). Motor vehicles drawing a trailer which has less than four wheels or is a close-coupled four-wheeled trailer, 50 mile/h (80 km/h). Motor vehicles not exceeding 30 cwt unladen, towing trailers or caravans which do not comply with certain requirements, 40 mile/h (64 km/h).

c. *Excise regulations.* The Vehicles (Excise) Act, 1962 and Customs and Excise Act, 1952 require that any diesel engined road vehicle used on the public highways must be licensed, insured for third-party, equipped with registration plates, a horn and two driving mirrors, have its steering and brakes kept in good order, be driven by a Group 'A' licence holder, and use taxed fuel (D.E.R.V.) for which records must be kept of quantities supplied and hours worked. This chiefly concerns dumpers, for which the licence duty may be remitted if the road distance travelled is not more than 6 miles (9.65 km) in one week. Only in stationary plant and dumpers which are *never* used on the public highway, other than to transfer from one site to another unladen, may untaxed gas oil be used, and the other requirements be exempted.

The Hydrocarbon Oils (Marking of Gas Oil) Regulations 1961 provides that all gas oil delivered from bonded warehouse will contain two prescribed chemical markers as well as a red dye. This is to ensure that rebated gas oil may be distinguished from heavy oils intended to be used as fuel for road vehicles. Under the Hydrocarbon Oil Regulations 1973 Officers of Customs and Excise are empowered to examine any vehicle and sample any oil, and any breach of the law is liable to a penalty of £100.

d. *Fuel storage.* By the provisions of the Petroleum (Consolidation) Act, 1928, not more than 3 gal (13.64 l) of petrol in 1 pt (0.568 l) vessels may be kept, without a licence to be granted by the responsible local authority. However, the Petroleum-Spirit (Motor Vehicles &c) Regulations, 1929, allow up to 60 gal (272.8 l) of petrol intended for motor vehicles or engines to be stored in a suitable place more than 20 ft (6.10 m) from any building, provided that it is prevented from flowing out in case of fire and that notice in writing has been given to the local authority. Otherwise not more than 4 gal (18.18 l) may be kept in 2 gal (9.09 l) containers, which must be marked 'petroleum spirit highly inflammable'. Since the precise requirements of Local Authorities differ from one area to another, it is necessary to check with the local Fire Officer, and also one's Fire Insurance Company.

BIBLIOGRAPHY

Machines for the Modern Builder, H.M.S.O.
'Cranes for Building', *Building Research Station Digest* **129,** H.M.S.O.
'The Costs of Mechanical Plant', *Building Research Digest* **113,** H.M.S.O.
Spence Geddes, *Building and Civil Engineering Plant,* Crosby Lockwood.
The V.P.R. Plant Data Book, Vale's Plant Register.
D. W. Llewellyn, *Plant and the Medium-Sized Builder,* The Builder.
Care of Builders' Machines, Advisory Leaflet No. 33, H.M.S.O.
A Guide to the Law and Diesel Dumpers, Benford Ltd.
The Petroleum-Spirit (Motor Vehicles, &c.) Regulations, 1929, H.M.S.O.
The Contractors' Plant Association Handbook, The Contractors' Plant Association.
A Guide to Maintenance Arrangements and Facilities, prepared by the Ministry of Transport, Federation of Civil Engineering Contractors.
Admission to the Occupation, Freight Transport Association Ltd.

Chapter 13

Construction Planning

1. Production

Scientific management analyses production under three headings:
  i. *Job production,* in which a single product is made, generally to order and often to a specification required by a particular customer,
  ii. *Batch production,* which is half-way between job production and mass production,
  iii. *Mass production,* in which large numbers of precisely similar products, concentrated within a minimal choice-range, and by a complete use of the logic of standardisation and repetition, are made to meet the demands of the general public.

Each of these broad categories of production has its own characteristics, employs different principles, and makes its own special demands on management. In job production the highly-trained craftsman predominates. There is little scope for unskilled workers, except as labourers, and there is a minimum of supervisory staff between higher management and the men on the workshop floor.

In batch production there is less need for the craftsmen, and a greater scope for the semi-skilled worker with the type of skill which can very often be acquired in several months or a year or two, and there is an increase in junior supervisory grades. In mass production skilled workers are fewer still in proportion but are likely to be highly-specialised experts. The bulk of the labour is unskilled, the proficiency required being a matter of dexterity which can usually be imparted by suitable training in a few weeks or months. There is, however, an immense increase in the number and importance of junior supervisory staff, between the worker and the higher executive levels, to meet the needs of co-ordination and the various subdivisions of specialist managerial functions.

The greater part of the building and civil engineering industry is in the category of job production, although certain development companies and to a lesser degree local authority housing estate work, approximate towards batch production. However, it must be noted that so far in these steps towards mass production the change in emphasis from craftsmen to unskilled labour has been relatively unimportant; this may be a measure of the success achieved to-date.

The scientific approach to production begins with a complete analysis of the job, down to its smallest component part. The production of each is planned in terms of the optimum material and taking account of the resources in labour and plant available. The whole is then fitted into a closely integrated programme of production, the ideal of which is that each component should be ready on time, in the correct balance of quantities, at the right place; that the flow of work should be logical and in a single direction; that the distances travelled and the amount of lifting and handling during this flow should be the minimum possible; that machines and men should be employed to capacity without breaks or delays due to shortages or errors in the programme. Supervision of the programme at each point should be adequate and exercise complete control in timing, quality, and quantity. The result is a pattern of very great complexity, always in motion, yet never, in the ideal, allowed to fall out of rhythm or balance.

Production planning of this kind is impossible without the application of scientific methods, and the training for Building Production therefore requires, in addition to technical competence in construction, a mastery of the principles and the detailed knowledge involved by each aspect of the science of production as applied to building and civil engineering. The remainder of this chapter is devoted to these aspects.

2. The Principles and Advantages of Construction Planning

'The term planning appeals by its suggestion of considered, orderly and rational action. It implies tidiness, method, system, discipline, regularity and a measure of exactness. It gives the impression that someone responsible is in charge, has a hand on the wheel, and a sense of direction and destination. It represents co-operation and co-ordination, and contrasts with the inevitable disorder which generally obtains when men act independently in their own interests with no overall framework into which they are constrained to fit.'[1]

[1] 'Now for a Perfect System Nobly Planned' by George Schwartz. – *Sunday Times*, October 1, 1961.

Construction planning is generally concerned with completing a contract in the shortest possible time compatible with economy. Prior consideration must be given to the plan of campaign so that the client can be given the intended completion or handing-over dates, and suppliers and sub-contractors may be notified when their goods or services will be required. Moreover the contractor himself must know what his future commitments will be for staff, labour and plant. It is of the greatest importance that an adequate period, before starting site operation, is made available for the proper planning of equipment and methods, ordering of materials, and preparation of a balanced programme. Obviously the time necessary will vary with the size and nature of the project, but this essential preliminary can affect the whole course of the job.

So far as is practicable, the general foreman should be intimately involved with the planning of his own site. In this way the knowledge gained by research will be available where it can best be put to further use, and confident acceptance of the ultimate programme will be assured. The predominant factor in the erection of traditional houses and flats is normally the output of the bricklayers, or, in the case of reinforced concrete structures, the rate of formwork preparation. However in multi-storey buildings the tower crane considerably influences the production cycle, and in the fields of industrial building and civil engineering it becomes predominantly important fully to utilise expensive mechanical plant. Each operation should commence as soon as possible, without necessarily waiting for the completion of the preceding work, and should continue without interruption at maximum practicable speed. Balanced gangs must be established on repetitive work-cycles, and continuous work made available until each is due to leave the site. High productivity also entails the elimination of double-handling, by the careful timing of bulky material deliveries and the strategic siting of mixing plant, casting bays, hoists and stock piles.

Naturally, the degree of detailed study of the projected works depends upon the time and staff made available, but even broad outline planning can show up possible technical snags well in advance, and thus provide opportunities for their avoidance or solution. Increased productivity made possible by reductions in double-handling, and improved operational methods devised by work study techniques, also result in reduced labour and plant costs. At the same time, the continuity so absolutely essential for the successful introduction of financial incentive schemes, can give a higher level of earnings to the operatives. Faster, more efficient construction means a shorter contract period, with less on-costs and lower overheads, so that the resultant total cost is effectively pruned. Programmes also provide a useful basis for ordering materials, and a comparative reference for assessing progess. To these other advantages must be added the growing record of comprehensive and realistic company standards, made possible by the detailed analysis of achievement against plan for completed jobs, which in due course is reflected in more accurate and keener estimating. This ever-improving cycle of events constitutes the long term benefit of planning, which is indicated diagrammatically in Fig. 13.1.

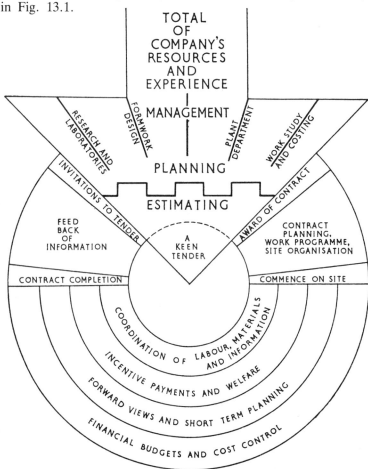

Fig. 13.1. Competition target for building and civil engineering

3. Pre-Tender Planning

Since the character of any construction project is largely predetermined by the priced tender, then it follows that there is a need for concerted discussion and planning at the estimating stage. When preparing a tender the estimator must obviously look into the methods and the timing of operations, and to enable him to consider the contract as a whole rather than as a series of isolated events, he must of necessity prepare an outline programme.

Some of the objectives of pre-tender planning are:

a. to pool the company's past experience and the knowledge of its various departments and specialists,

b. to assist the estimating department by delegating certain tasks to other interested personnel,

c. to eliminate future controversy between estimator and supervisor on such matters as method, output rates, preliminaries and on-costs,

d. to ensure a realistic tender by co-ordinating technical theory with current practice,

e. to improve the ratio of awards/tenders submitted, by reason of the increased attention to detail and the advantages of co-operation.

Such close consultation also helps to create a team spirit and fosters group morale, but naturally the degree of attention must be varied by selection.

Enquiries and invitations to tender should be classified, at director or general manager level, into:

1. those definitely wanted for policy, employment or other important reasons,

2. those desirable at 'the right price',

3. those not obviously attractive.

Only the first group will be accorded 'the full treatment', whilst the others will receive modified shares of the time and manpower left available.

Informal planning meetings should be held as required, a preliminary one for briefing everybody and delegating responsibilities, and perhaps a final one for co-ordinating and approving the ultimate decisions. Consideration may be given to the preparation of the following documents:

a. *Tender summary* of enquiry documents including a directory of the client and his professional advisors, a description of the works, a précis of the contract conditions and any special clauses, and any other aspects of particular importance.

b. *Master file* of correspondence, reports and notes of meetings or conversations.

c. *Site inspection report* on site conditions, access, existing services or facilities, local labour position, any special circumstances, and a map or sketch of the area. For this purpose a standard check list is desirable.

d. *Outline programme* of construction timing, probably plotted in months only.

e. *Methods statement* noting any particular methods of construction or types of equipment assumed for pricing purposes.

f. *Organisation scheme* including schedules of site personnel, accommodation, temporary works, extra labour allowances and any other site on-costs.

g. *Sub-contract tenders* considered or used.

h. *Suppliers' quotations* received for prices and delivery periods.

i. *Financial analysis* of the provisional estimate, listing separately the calculated figures for preliminaries, on-costs, labour, plant and material costs, nominated sub-contractors and suppliers, provisional sums, domestic sub-contractors, overheads and anticipated profit.

The relevance and importance of each of these planning procedures naturally depends upon the individual enquiry and the company's system of estimating, but to some extent each one can contribute to a more realistic and competitive tender.

4. Anticipation of Award

Under the present system of competitive tendering not even the most scientifically precise estimating can totally eliminate the factor of chance, but there is often an intermediary stage before the official award of a contract, when it is reasonably certain that the tender has been successful. During this interval the pre-tender planning may be advanced in the following directions:

1. *Contract pricing notes* can be developed from the original tender summary, to include the price build-up of major rates and the final financial analysis.

2. *Site staff requirements* should be reviewed and available personnel earmarked and warned to be ready. For this purpose a staff availability chart can be invaluable if kept up-to-date by regular monthly returns.

3. *Site telephone arrangements* may be decided and formal application made to the Post Office, because isolated sites may involve several months delay.

4. *Materials in short supply* such as bricks or steel reinforcement when applicable can be reserved by provisional orders.

These preliminary steps will help to ensure a quick, clean start when the contract document is eventually signed.

5. Project Planning

On the award of a contract, the real task of construction planning begins in earnest, but the benefits of any pre-tender planning will now be appreciated to the full. Whereas previously the thoroughness of the technique was selective, it is vital that every project, regardless of its size or duration, should be properly planned from this point onwards. This stage is also known as *contract preliminary planning,* to distinguish it from the short term site planning which follows later as a natural extension.

Project planning may be carried out by a central planning department, or the detail might be done by the site supervisor under the control of a contracts manager. In either situation it is essential that the site agent or general foreman should be seconded if possible, or at least consulted frequently, so that the plan formulated shall be his own.

Overall planning of a building or civil engineering project is carried out, prior to commencement of work on site, in order that management may have a thorough appreciation of the work involved; to allow those responsible for production to sort out its main constituents and decide how, in what order and at what time to do them; and to ensure adequate co-ordination of the labour, plant and material requirements. The procedure can thus be considered in three main stages:

   i. Contract evaluation.
   ii. Work programming.
   iii. Co-ordination and liaison (or scheduling).

6. Evaluation of Contract

In small companies news of the new contract will quickly spread by word of mouth, but in larger organisations it is useful to circulate duplicated copies of a formal 'Notice of Award' to all departmer's and/or executives concerned. This should give the broad details of the job, e.g. name, address, description, job number, approximate value, client, designer and contract dates; and the names of the principal site or supervisory staff.

This should be followed as soon as possible by the *initial planning meeting,* at which more detailed information can be broadcast, the general situation and any unusual implications may be discussed, and individual responsibilities are allocated for specific sections of the contract preliminary planning. The meeting is of a formal nature, with a senior manager taking the chair, and written minutes recorded for distribution. Site management and the estimator concerned must obviously be present, while specialists such as the plant manager or planning assistant are co-opted if required. A standard form of agenda is very helpful when used as a check list to ensure that all aspects are considered, and this might include all the topics mentioned in the remainder of this and the next chapter.

As a result of the earlier pre-tender planning a substantial body of *contract information* may already be available, but otherwise a site inspection report and contract pricing notes must be prepared, and sub-contract tenders, and suppliers' quotations obtained without delay. In addition the various contract documents must be systematically analysed, to yield up their own peculiar contributions to the general pool of knowledge.

1. *Drawings* are all too rarely fully available at this stage of the proceedings, but now is a good opportunity to initiate a comprehensive drawing register and index. A separate register is required for each individual building or separate section, e.g. structural frame, cladding and finishes, roads and drains, etc., with drawings entered in the order they are received. This can be used as an index when setting-out or planning each phase. Information recorded should include the reference number, title or description, main scale, number of copies and date of receipt. If the various amendments are also shown as in the example (see Fig. 13.2), then this document will be a most useful record for the quantity surveyor when he measures the final account. Reinforcement bending schedules can also be registered in a similar fashion. So that drawings may be referred to by number, and their filing drawer located, a drawing index should also be kept. An index should be prepared for each source of issue, e.g. architect, structural engineer, etc., with drawings listed in serial order under their relevant section of the drawing register. A record of the distribution of copies is also useful, particularly when amendments are received. See Fig. 13.3 for a suggested form of this index.

Drawings and bending schedules must be thoroughly sorted and all references carefully checked, and a note made of any details missing.

DRAWING REGISTER
Section: External Services

Drawing			Original		Amendments			
Ref.No.	Title or Description	Main Scale	No.	Date	A	B	C	D
897	Site Layout	1/500	3	3/1/71				
900	Storm Drainage	1/250	3	3/1/71	1 10/1/71			
913	Foul Drainage	1/250	3	3/1/71				
604	Typical M/H Details	1/10	3	10/1/71				
901	Storm Outfall	1/20	2	15/1/71				
E/11	Road Sections	1/10	2	17/1/71				
E/13	Road Elevations	1/200		—	3 20/1/71			

Fig. 13.2

2. **Conditions of contract** provide information concerning the starting date and the contract period. For a complicated contract such as a large industrial installation, start and finish dates are sometimes given for each construction phase, in which case it might be worthwhile to draw a preliminary valuation-of-work chart utilising the individual bills of quantities totals. This enables the overall construction level to be examined, and shows up uneconomic fluctuations. The

DRAWING INDEX
Issued by: Architect

File or Drawer No.	Section or Building									Distribution					
	1	2	3	4	5	6									
Drawing No: (in serial order)	External Services	Basement	Office Block	Canteen	R.C. Details					Agent	Surveyor	Gen. Foreman	Steelfixer		
1001			X							✓	✓	✓			
1002			X							✓	✓	✓			
1003			X							✓	✓	✓			
1004					X					✓	✓		✓		
1005		X								✓	✓	✓			
1007				X						✓	✓	✓			
1008				X						✓	✓	✓			

Fig. 13.3

example depicted in Fig. 13.4 indicates that no time has been allowed for a labour build-up, and also highlights an unwelcome peak during the winter. Although this method is very approximate it does provide a basis for discussion with the client, and helpful modifications may be agreed as a result.

3. *Specifications* must be read, and unusual points noted. References to Codes of Practice should be looked up. and

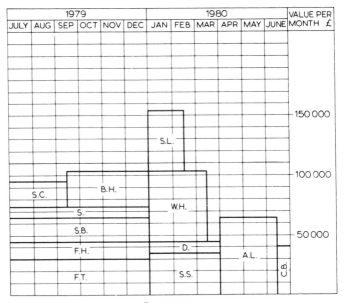

Programme
as required to suit plant deliveries

	Value £	Dates
Site clearance	50 000	1.7.79 to 15.9.80
Air locks	162 500	1.4.80 to 15.9.80
Fan tunnels	180 000	1.7.79 to 31.12.79
Fan house	90 000	1.7.79 to 31.12.79
Shaft lining	75 000	1.1.80 to 15.2.80
Winding house	150 000	1.1.80 to 15.3.80
Sidings	60 000	1.7.79 to 31.12.79
Drainage	30 000	1.1.80 to 31.3.80
Sub-station	105 000	1.1.80 to 31.3.80
Storage bunkers	120 000	1.7.79 to 31.12.79
Boiler house	105 000	15.9.79 to 31.12.79
Car building	20 000	15.6.80 to 30.6.80

Fig. 13.4. Reconstruction for Basic Industrials Ltd. Value of work to be constructed as specified programme

relevant abstracts from the specification included in material requisitions or enquiries. If copies of specifications for nominated specialists, e.g. Heating Engineer, are not forthcoming, they should be requested so that the full story is known. A list of 'materials to be approved' can be drafted, to act as a reminder and a progess record – see Fig. 13.5 for a suggested layout.

4. *Bills of quantities* must be studied until they become familiar, and indexed by margin tags when necessary. Items should be annotated with references to specification, drawing or location where possible, and all discrepancies, queries or further details required must be religiously noted. Separate lists must be made of all domestic sub-contractors and specialists, nominated (P.C.) sub-contractors and suppliers and any provisional sums.

Although materials must be expressly ordered only from drawings, the bills do provide a good guide, and a 'provisional schedule of materials' similar to Fig. 13.6 can be used as a basis for progressing the placing of orders.

For each section of work or each individual building, a list of trades or operations must be drawn up, as far as possible in the anticipated sequence of construction. Certain trades require to be divided into separate operations, e.g. carpenter and joiner into floor joists, roof timbers, first fixings, second fixings and ironmongery. If the bill of quantities value is placed against every operation, the relative importance of each can be assessed and the possible need for further subdivision recognised. These lists will eventually be used to formulate the construction programmes.

Attention to detail is the keynote of contract evaluation, for everything must be checked and cross checked, and nothing taken for granted. Pulling every 'loose end' requires patience and makes this phase of preliminary planning a hard chore, but ironing out problems at this stage will save invaluable time and money during actual construction.

7. Programming of Work

The purposes of a programme are:
   a. to record agreed intentions with the client,
   b. to supply a timetable for co-ordinating the issue of drawings and information, the placing of orders and delivery of

CONTRACT *Effluent Scheme for A.B.C.*   SCHEDULE OF MATERIALS TO BE APPROVED   DATE: 13 June 1980

B of Q Ref.	Material	Location	P.C. Value	Date Submitted	Date Approved	Supplier	Order No.	Remarks
80 e	Blue Eng. Bricks	Acid drain manholes	£150/M	10-7-80	15-7-80	Bricks & Coal Ltd.	101/6	
90 a	C.I. Manhole Covers	All manholes	–					
Spec. 24	Facing Bricks	Pump House	£100/M	10-7-80				Reqd. mid Oct.

Fig. 13.5

CONTRACT *Park Housing Estate*   PROVISIONAL SCHEDULE OF MATERIALS   DATE: 10 Feb. 1980

Material	Description	Quantity	Firm	Date Ordered	Date Required	Date Received	Order No.	Page No. in Bill	Remarks
Hardcore	75mm to 50mm	1000 m³	Brown Transport	12-2-80			3/611		
Portland Cement	Ordinary	150 tonnes	Incorporated Cement Ltd.	"			3/628		
Core. Aggregates			Midshire S & G Co.	"			3/612		
Breeze Blocks	65mm	700 m²			15-4-80			2/60 G	
Sawn Timber	See Spec.				11-6-80				Treated

Fig. 13.6

    materials, and the operations of plant and sub-contractors,

  c. to prepare a basis for the introduction of 'payments by results' or other incentives,

  d. to show the sequence of operations and the total output rates required of labour and plant,

  e. to provide a yardstick for progressing and costing,

  f. to furnish the promoter with the likely financial requirements,

  g. to discourage changes in design by indicating the natural consequences, whilst at the same time facilitating amendments and minimising their harmful effects should contingencies arise.

Hence it is important to *embrace every operation* including preliminaries, temporary works, etc.

In order that proper comparisons may be made between the planned progress and actual achievement, it is also desirable that some standard of *physical measurement* be applied to each item. Quantities by weight, volume, area, length or number can be calculated or estimated; but progress gauged by time, labour or money expended is meaningless. Total figures may be shown in a column down the left-hand side, and/or period figures be superimposed along the operation bars.

The precise form in which the programme is set down on paper may depend to some extent on the type of work being undertaken. Graphs showing quantity against time are simple to understand, and may be convenient for individual operations such as concrete output. Complicated sequences like finishing trades in multi-storey buildings can be explained by exploded isometric drawings, and other pictorial stratagems may be devised for special occasions, but the commonest and most satisfactory method is the *Gantt* or *bar chart*. Charts of this nature are very versatile, but it is usual to list the items of work one below the other on the left-hand side, and show time horizontally. Bars may be suitably hatched or coloured to distinguish trades, or left blank for the future recording of progess. Alternatively, duplicate lines can be left blank, or special percentage columns be provided for this purpose (see Chapter 15, 3, *a*).

The amount of detail depicted on programme charts varies considerably, but three definite scales are distinguishable at project planning level:

i. a broad master programme,

ii. intermediate, section programmes,

iii. detailed operation programmes.

i. *The master or overall programme* covers the full contract period and includes the complete works in broad, overall terms. A master programme does not differ substantially from the outline programme prepared at the time of estimating, although it may be expanded in the light of additional information now made available. Time is usually plotted in months and weeks, with dates and contract week numbers entered. Holiday periods should also be shown, since allowances must be made for these reduced or lost production spells.

It is usual for the site occupation and contract completion dates to be stipulated in the contract, and these can now be drawn either as vertical lines or indicated by appropriate symbols. If the contract period was chosen by the contractor, then it is likely that this includes a small margin for contingencies, so that a separate target completion date may be shown. For various reasons the actual start date may also be deferred. Any other specified or otherwise obvious stage dates should also be marked, e.g. it may be expedient to ensure that a building is weathertight before the onset of winter. If work that is susceptible to frost is proceeding during the winter months, then it is advisable to make some allowance for likely interruptions. This can be arranged either by reducing the output rate where weekly figures are shown, or by arbitrarily designating one or two weeks, perhaps during January or February, when no such work is intended. Although the exact dates of lost time cannot be foretold, the overall position at the end of a 'normal' winter can thus be estimated. Certain civil engineering operations, e.g. earth dams or soil stabilised roads, may have to be completely suspended during certain months and these can be provisionally marked. Planting and seeding which are confined to autumn or spring, may also dictate certain targets. In this way the stage is set.

Every major item or distinct phase of the works must now be listed down the left-hand side, with the more important total quantities where appropriate. The number of titles should not be too numerous, but under inclusive headings the whole contract should be accounted for, including preliminary works. In most instances the 'description of works' given in the bills of quantities, with a little elaboration, is all that is required. For a building project, the usual headings are preliminaries, drains, roads and each individual structure, the latter subdivided into foundations, frame and cladding or superstructure and finishings. Civil engineering undertakings vary considerably, but the same principles apply, although experience is a good guide here. With single buildings or very simple engineering constructions, the master and stage programmes are often combined for reasons of economy and convenience; nevertheless this step by step procedure should be followed.

When the framework has been outlined and the works enumerated, the overall programme can then be drafted, although it may be subject to minor revision after the stage programmes have been prepared. A steady build-up from the start, a constant level of activity thereafter with as few peaks as possible, and a quick run-down at the finish, are ideals to be aimed for: and with the salient dates already mentioned the strategic scheme falls into place like a jigsaw puzzle (see Fig. 13.7 for example).

Once drawn up and approved the master programme becomes in effect a contract document, and should therefore not be altered unless exceptional contingencies arise or a major change is made in the design.

As a check on the financial 'shape' of the contract, it is useful here to prepare a *financial graph* based upon the master programme. This will also provide information to the client as to his anticipated liabilities for monthly payments, and can similarly be used by the Quantity Surveyor as a target or comparison for his interim certificates. Using the figures from the bills of quantities each item of work is valued, and this is then averaged over the weeks allocated on the chart. Each individual week is then totalled up and the cumulative totals drawn as the vertical co-ordinates of a graph, against time on the horizontal scale. The example (see Fig. 13.8) illustrates the typical characteristics of build-up, level of activity and run-down mentioned earlier.

ii. *Phase or section programmes* should now be prepared for every major item that requires more detailed treatment, e.g. each separate building or construction phase of significant size. Each line of the master programme, if required, is magnified so that each individual trade or operation can be distinguished and considered in closer detail. The form of programme chart may be as before, indicating weeks with dates and serial numbers, but covering only part of the contract period. Again holiday periods are shown, and the

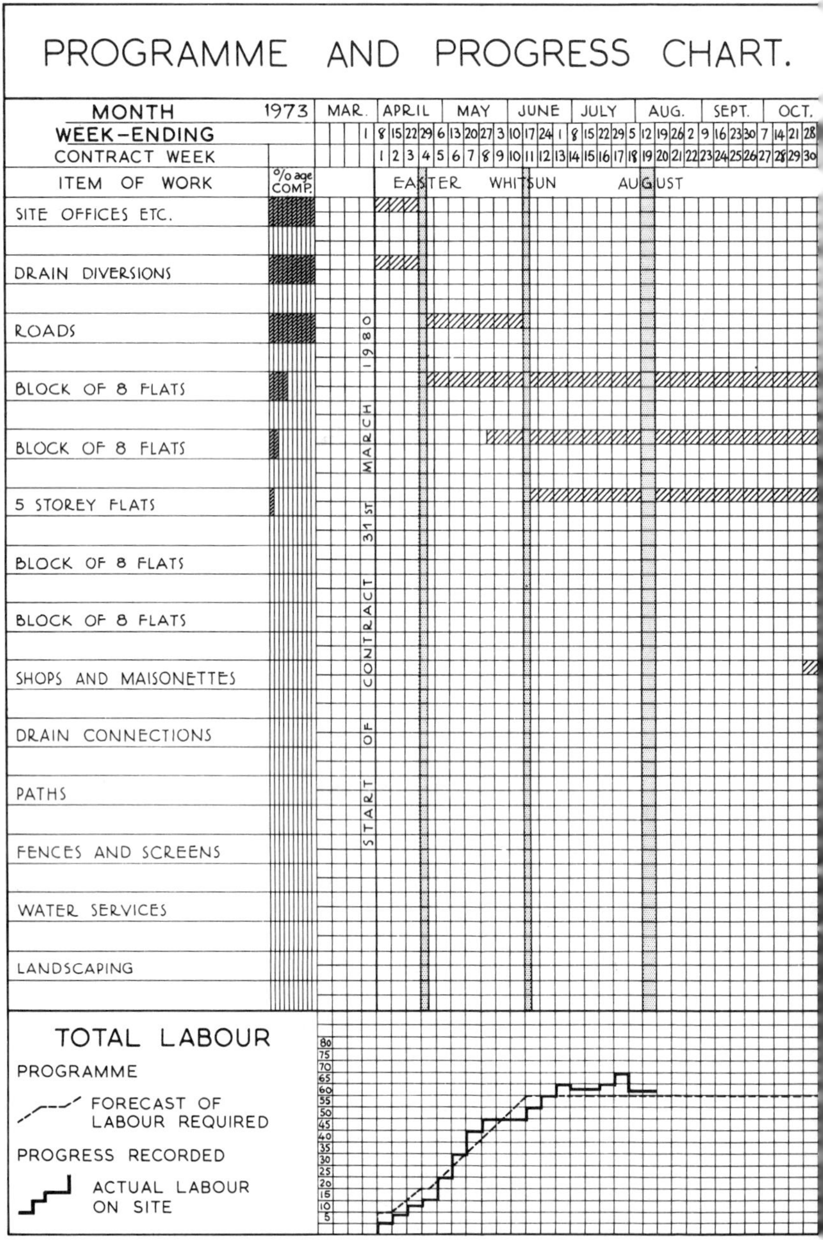

PROGRAMME AND PROGRESS CHART.

MONTH	1973	MAR.	APRIL	MAY	JUNE	JULY	AUG.	SEPT.	OCT.
WEEK—ENDING			1	8 15 22 29	6 13 20 27	3 10 17 24	1 8 15 22 29	5 12 19 26	2 9 16 23 30	7 14 21 28
CONTRACT WEEK				1 2 3 4	5 6 7 8	9 10 11 12	13 14 15 16	17 18 19 20	21 22 23 24 25 26 27	28 29 30
ITEM OF WORK	%age COMP.		EASTER	WHITSUN		AUGUST			

SITE OFFICES ETC.

DRAIN DIVERSIONS

ROADS

BLOCK OF 8 FLATS

BLOCK OF 8 FLATS

5 STOREY FLATS

BLOCK OF 8 FLATS

BLOCK OF 8 FLATS

SHOPS AND MAISONETTES

DRAIN CONNECTIONS

PATHS

FENCES AND SCREENS

WATER SERVICES

LANDSCAPING

TOTAL LABOUR

PROGRAMME

FORECAST OF
LABOUR REQUIRED

PROGRESS RECORDED

ACTUAL LABOUR
ON SITE

Fig. 13.7

CONTRACT: HOUSING ESTATE, MIDTOWN.

DEC.	JAN.	FEB.	MAR.	APRIL	MAY	JUNE	JULY	AUG.	SEPT.	OCT.	NOV.	DEC.
16 23 30	6 13 20 27	3 10 17 24	3 10 17 24 31	7 14 21 28	5 12 19 26	2 9 16 23 30	7 14 21 28	4 11 18 25	1 8 15 22 29	6 13 20 27	3 10 17 24	1 8 15 22 29
37 38 39	40 41 42 43 44	45 46 47 48	49 50 51 52 53	54 55 56 57	58 59 60 61	62 63 64 65 66	67 68 69 70	71 72 73 74	75 76 77 78 79	80 81 82 83	84 85 86 87	88 89 90 91

CHRISTMAS   EASTER   WHIT SUN   AUGUST   TARGET COMPLETION

1974

CONTRACT COMPLETION DATE 31ST DECEMBER

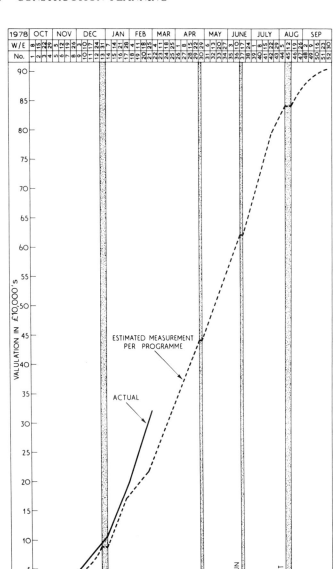

Fig. 13.8. Financial progress chart. (Forty houses for County Council)

start and finish together with any other salient dates, are transferred from the master chart.

Operations are written down the left-hand side, taken from the lists prepared during the examination of the bills of quantities and following in the construction sequence so far as possible. Each trade or sub-trade, each sub-contractor whether nominated or domestic, each nominated supplier or provisional item not covered by another heading, and every major stage must be included. As before, the section programme can then be sketched in, following accepted trade practice for building work sequences or relying upon experience for civil engineering and external works. This is where the practical knowledge of the general foreman or contracts supervisor is indispensable. It is usual for sewers and then roads to be constructed in advance of buildings, but for the connecting drains to be laid after the superstructure has been completed and the scaffolding removed. Main drainage and similar schemes should wherever possible commence from the outfall end: thus innumerable practical considerations virtually dictate the order of progress.

Economic periods for each operation may be calculated from the gang or machine sizes chosen and the anticipated output rates; or the time available for a particular task may be decided by other factors, so that a minimum output is predetermined and the type of machine or number of men required is therefore enforced. Specialists such as steel or R.C. frame erectors, lift engineers, etc., must be consulted as far as possible, to ensure that they are allowed sufficient time and to enlist their full co-operation. Other sub-contractors must be afforded an early opportunity to agree interlocking sequences, and to confirm their ability to make the required labour strength/plant available.

The resulting section programe such as that illustrated in Fig. 13.9 thus presents a fairly comprehensive and detailed picture, from which requirements schedules of information, labour, plant and materials can be derived.

Whilst drafting the master and section programmes consideration will have been given to the methods to be adopted, the types of plant to be used, and the manpower requirements for each key operation. Thus by the time all the section programmes have been finished, a parallel *methods statement* has also been drawn up, recording in detail all the decisions taken (see Fig. 13.10). This document which may

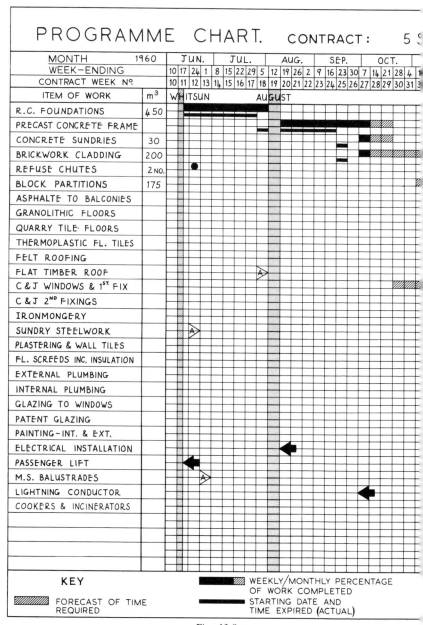

Fig. 13.9

REY BLOCK ~ [SECTION PROGRAMME]

	DEC.	JAN.	FEB.	MAR.	APR.	MAY.	JUN.	JUL.

CHRISTMAS   EASTER   WHITSUN

◄ NOMINATIONS REQUIRED
● WORKING DRAWINGS TO BE APPROVED
▷ ARCHITECTS DRAWINGS REQUIRED

DRG. No. BM/PC/2
DATE. 20TH JANUARY 1973

be the very crux of a civil engineering scheme later serves as a useful reminder and guide for the site management, as well as providing a basis for requisitioning plant and forecasting the labour force needed. Naturally the methods assumed by the estimator will receive first consideration, but with more time available it is possible to explore alternatives and compare them on the basis of cost. The establishment of balanced teams is a pre-requisite for high productivity, and is obvious in the case of a mechanical navvy excavating and loading into lorries for transporting to tip. However, if a central concrete mixing unit is proposed, then deciding its capacity is a little more complicated. Concrete quantities must be abstracted from the separate stage programmes and brought together on one schedule, or superimposed upon a copy of the master programme. If the total quantities are now spread over the allotted time periods, the figures can be added up for each week to show the varying demand for concrete (see Fig. 13.11). A size of mixer may be chosen whose output will satisfy the maximum required, but if there are great fluctuations which cannot be re-arranged more evenly, then it might be more economical to provide for a reasonable average only and import ready-mixed concrete for the extra peaks.

Similarly a forecast of approximate labour requirements can be calculated, from the time shown on the programme against each operation, its total measurement, and the labour output standards used in the tender. For example:

$$\frac{X \text{ m}^2}{Y \text{ weeks}} \div Z \text{ m}^2 \text{ per man week} = \text{No. of men.}$$

They can then be summed up by categories, to show the anticipated total number of men that will be required throughout the life of the contract (see Fig. 13.12). If this is done as soon as the provisional stage programmes have been drawn up, then slight modifications to the programme may avoid impracticable and upsetting fluctuations. This is most necessary for tradesmen such as bricklayers or carpenters and joiners, whose services are at a premium. If the overall labour strength is summarised and charted as a *labour graph*, it is usual to present this below the master programme (see Fig. 13.7). Again this should indicate a steady build-up and an even demand until the fall-off at completion.

CONTRACT *Chemical Factory*

METHOD STATEMENT

DATE: 3 April 1974

Description of Item	Quantity	Details of Method	Plant Involved	Output per Week	Labour Involved	Period Required
Excavate Rising Main	1000 m	Excavate + got out by Navvy.	22 RB trackster	500 m	4 Labourers	2 weeks
P.V.C. Pipes	3,000 m	Lay by roper. Joints by Sub-Contractor	nil	250 m	6 "	12 "
Basement Excavation	5,000 m³	Excavate & load by Navvy.	22 RB dragline & lorry	2,500 m³	2 "	2 "
" Formwork	1,500 m²	8'x4' Timber shutters	nil	150 m²	6 Joiners	10 "
" Reinforcement	5100 kg	Supplied Cut & Bent	nil	1700 kg	2 Steelfixers	3 "
" Concrete	450 m³	Site Mixer supplemented by Ready Mix	14/10 mixer etc.	100 m³	7 Concretors	4½ "

Fig. 13.10

CONTRACT: *Effluent treatment plant*

Description	m³		4	5	6	7	8	9	10	11	12	13	14	15	16	17	18	19	20	21	22	23	24	25
																		Contract Week No.						
Erect and Dismantle			E																					D
Pump House Slab	50			25	25																			
Pump House Walls	440					25	35	55	55	55	55	50	50	30	30									
Pump House Floor	40											20	20											
Pump House Roof	30															15	15							
Sedimentation Ducts	75			25	25	25																		
Tank Foundations	75						15	15	15	15	15													
Tank Walls	440														40	45	45	45	45	45	45	45	40	
Flume Columns	20															10	10							
Measuring Flume	30																	5	5	5	5	5	5	
Various Small Works	140					10	10	10	10	10	10	10	10	10	10	10	10	10	10					
Total	1,340																							
Weekly Output				50	50	60	60	80	80	80	80	80	80	80	85	80	80	80	60	60	50	50	45	

$10/7$ Mixer with 4 min cycle $= 15 \times 4\frac{1}{4} \times 42 = 160 \ m^3/wk$ (approx) i.e. 50% maximum utilisation

Fig. 13.11. *Estimated concrete requirements*

ESTIMATED LABOUR BUILD-UP

CONTRACT: *Effluent treatment plant*

Class of Labour	Qty	1	2	3	4	5	6	7	8	9	10	11	12	13	14	15	16	17	18	19	20	21	22	23	24	25	26	27	28	29	30	Output
Compressor Driver	—										1	1	1	1	1	1	1	1	1	1												—
Outfit A — Drains	1880 m		5	5	5	5	5	5	5	5	5	5	5	5	5	5	5	5	5													$100\,m/wk$
Outfit B — Drains	1,600 m				5	5	5	5	5	5	5	5	5	5	5	5	5	5	5	5												$100\,m/wk$
Backfill Team	—			4	4	4	4	4	4	4	4	4	4	4	4	4	4	4	4	4												—
M.H. Bricklayers	372 m³		3	3	3	3	3	3	3	4	4	4	4	4	4	4	4	3	3	3												$6\,m^3/man\,wk$
Formwork Joiners	3,500 m²					3	3	9	10	10	10	10	10	11	11	13	13	11	11	8	8	7	7	5	5							$20\,m^2/man\,wk$
Steelfixers	—							2	2	2	2	2	2	2	2	2	2	2	2	2	2	2	2	1	1							—
Concretors	1,340 m³				4	5	5	6	6	7	7	7	7	7	7	7	7	7	7	6	6	5	5	5	5	4						$av.\,61\,m^3/wk$
Attd. Plant Erectors	—																				2	2	2	2	2	2	2	2	2			—
Fitter and Office Attd.	—		2	2	2	2	2	2	2	2	2	2	2	2	2	2	2	2	2	2	2	2	2	2	2	2	2	2	2	2		—
Other Works	—			2	2	3	3	3	4	4	5	5	5	5	5	5	5	5	5	5	5	5	5	5	4	4	4	3	3	3		—
Weekly Totals		2	8	15	24	32	33	40	42	44	44	45	45	46	48	48	45	45	43	32	23	20	20	12	8			7	7		5	

Fig. 13.12

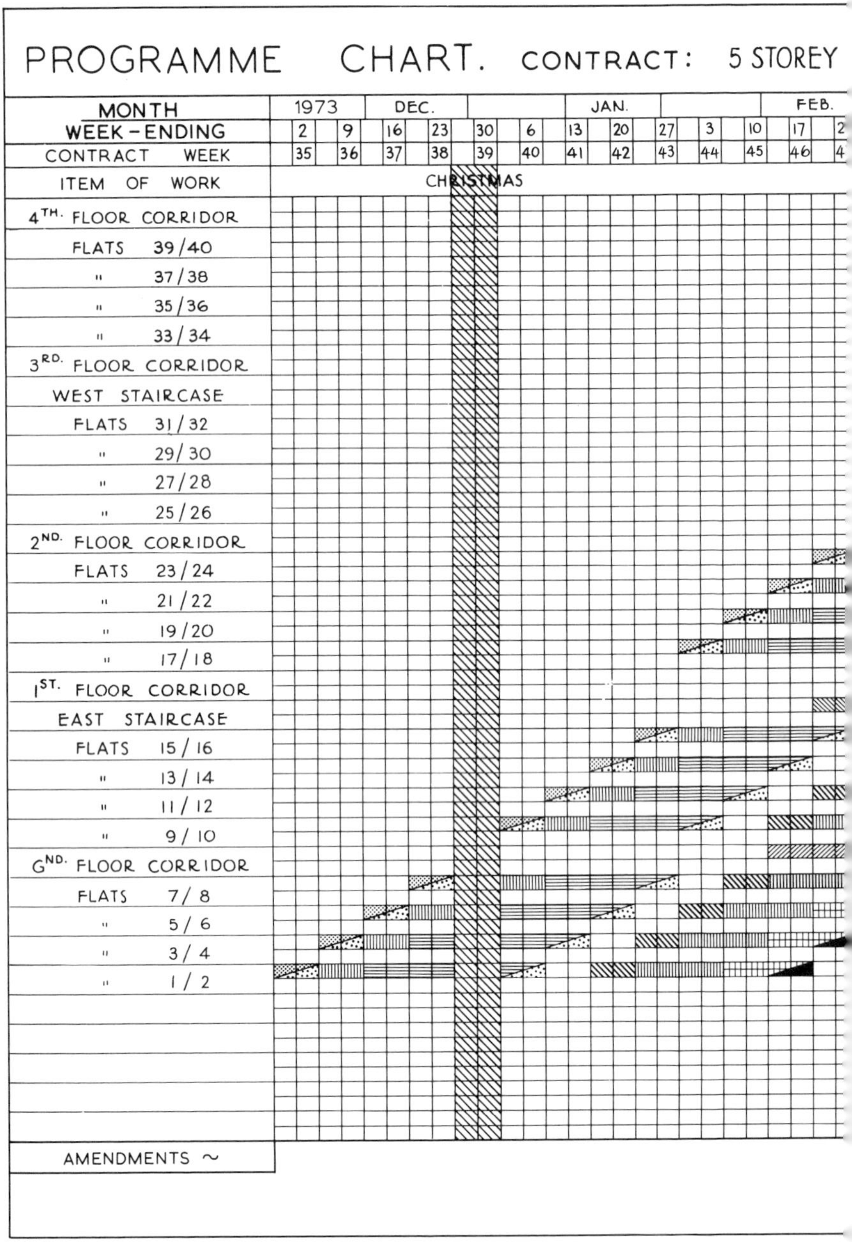

MONTH	1973		DEC.				JAN.					FEB.	
WEEK – ENDING	2	9	16	23	30	6	13	20	27	3	10	17	2
CONTRACT WEEK	35	36	37	38	39	40	41	42	43	44	45	46	4
ITEM OF WORK				CHRISTMAS									
4TH. FLOOR CORRIDOR													
FLATS 39/40													
" 37/38													
" 35/36													
" 33/34													
3RD. FLOOR CORRIDOR													
WEST STAIRCASE													
FLATS 31/32													
" 29/30													
" 27/28													
" 25/26													
2ND. FLOOR CORRIDOR													
FLATS 23/24													
" 21/22													
" 19/20													
" 17/18													
1ST. FLOOR CORRIDOR													
EAST STAIRCASE													
FLATS 15/16													
" 13/14													
" 11/12													
" 9/10													
GND. FLOOR CORRIDOR													
FLATS 7/8													
" 5/6													
" 3/4													
" 1/2													

AMENDMENTS ∼

Fig. 13.13

BLOCK ~ [SEQUENCE CHART]

		MAR.				APRIL				MAY				JUNE		1974
3	10	17	24	31	7	14	21	28	5	12	19	26	2	9	16	23	30	7
48	49	50	51	52	53	54	55	56	57	58	59	60	61	62	63	64	65	66

EASTER

WHITSUN

INDEX

CARCASSING PLUMBER AND ELECTRICIAN	
CARPENTER AND JOINER 1ST. AND 2ND. FIXINGS	
PLASTERING	
FLOOR SCREEDS AND UNDERFLOOR HEATING	
DRYING OUT PERIOD	
SANITARY WARE ETC.	
PAINTING	
THERMOPLASTIC TILES	
QUARRY FLOOR TILES	
GRANOLITHIC PAVING	

DRG. No. BM/PC/3.

DATE. 30TH. JANUARY 1973

iii. *Operation or sequence programmes* are only required when repetitive work-cycles must be established, or when closely interlocking sequences have to be co-ordinated. The finishes of a multi-storey office block, the R.C. frame structure of a tall building, or the turnover of a housing estate are typical examples. Once again particular operations or groups of operations are examined in finer detail, e.g. a typical floor of a multi-storey building may be further expanded to differentiate between the succeeding sub-operations: shutter floor slab, fix floor reinforcement, place concrete, wait for curing, strip formwork, etc. The same chart as before can be used, showing either weeks or days, and probably extending over a part only of the stage programme time period. Once again holidays, start and finish dates, etc., are transferred from the stage programme, and the operations listed down the left-hand side in order of sequence.

The programme chart can then be filled in between the boundaries, jig-saw pattern, following obvious construction sequences or finishing trade procedure. Certain time periods such as the waiting time before concrete formwork may be removed, or the drying time required before following work can be allowed over floor screeds, are either specified or otherwise stipulated, and the remaining time is allocated with available resources in mind (see Fig. 13.13).

For housing contracts the production rate or average 'turn-over' necessary can be calculated by subtracting the waiting period until the completion of the first house, say five months, from the total contract period, and then dividing the remaining period of weeks by the number of dwellings. Similarly for the internal finishes of blocks of flats, by subtracting the overall sequence period required for the completion of one flat, say eleven weeks, from the total finishing period, and dividing the remainder by the number concerned, an average hand-over rate, e.g. two per week, can be determined.

If gangs or teams are to have continuity of work throughout repetitive cycles, then *operations or trades must be balanced* as far as this is practicable. For example, if the cycle is three weeks, then any trade finishing in a shorter period will have to mark time for the remainder of the cycle. Although this may not matter financially in the case of sub-contractors, it may result in their leaving the site and being otherwise involved when they are required again. Since the overall

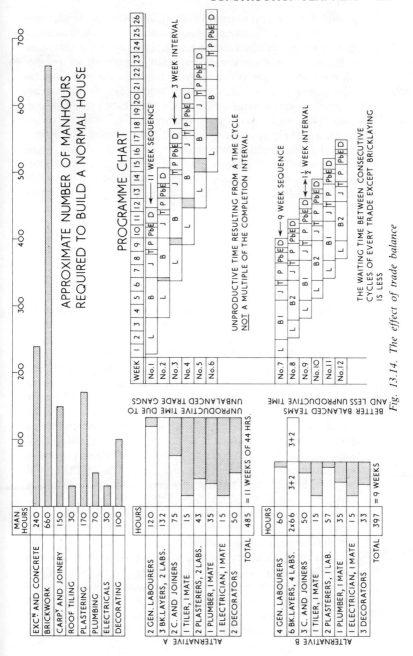

Fig. 13.14. The effect of trade balance

period for the completion of one full sequence is the sum total of the individual cycle times, then it follows that these must be kept within definite limits. Increasing the team size to reduce the time cycle may however result in greater numbers than can be employed together on one unit, in which case two or three smaller teams must work concurrently on two or three units, taking twice or three times as long over each. To obviate unproductive time it is also necessary for every time cycle itself to be a whole multiple of the average hand-over interval, i.e. if flats are being completed at the rate of one a week, then time cycles must not include half weeks. Although the illustrations of haphazard and balanced trade cycles shown in Fig. 13.14 are house building operations, it must be remembered that the principles apply to any type of repetitive work.

8. Co-ordination of Contributors

Having made an appreciation of the project and decided one's campaign for its execution, it is now necessary to co-ordinate the actions of the numerous participants. Building and civil engineering construction is essentially a team operation so that careful liaison between designer, suppliers and sub-contractors, is one of the main contractor's prime functions. Each of the major groups of components – information, labour, plant and materials, must be carefully scheduled to arrive on the site at the right time and in correct quantities.

i.   *Outstanding information* can now be gathered together from the notes made during the investigations of the drawings and bills of quantities, and collected into a schedule as suggested in Section 4A (see Fig. 13.15). Since the architect or engineer will already have prepared a draft list of drawings that he intends to issue, this should be requested and incorporated with the other queries. This schedule will provide an invaluable order of priorities and timetable for the designer's drawing office.

Alternatively, symbols can be added to the programme chart (see Fig. 13.9) to indicate the latest dates by which information or materials must be to hand. A suitable code for this purpose is suggested (Fig. 13.16).

ii. *Plant requirements* can be ascertained from the method statement and together with anticipated dates from the

REQUIRED INFORMATION INDEX

CONTRACT Assembly Factory   SECTION Offices   DATE 1st June 1971

Information Required	From	Dwg. No.	Due to Start	Inform. Reqd. By	Date of Request	Date Received	B/Q Ref.	Remarks
Bonding schedules — roof	Eng.	R/101	1st Dec.'71	1st Sept.'71	1-6-71	8-9-71		3 months delivery for reinf.
Working dwg. metal windows	Supp.		1st Feb.'72	1st Oct.'71	1-6-71		2/41 G	
Working dwg. balustrading	Sub.C.		1st Ap.'72	1st Nov.'71	1-6-71		2/50 F	
Ironmongery schedule	Arch.		10st Jun.'72	10st Mar.'72	1-6-71			
Decorating colour scheme	Arch.		20st Aug.'72	20st June'72	13-9-71			

Fig. 13.15

programme chart incorporated into a heavy (mechanical) plant schedule (see Fig. 13.17). This document can be used to forewarn the Plant Depot and also as a means of progressing plant requisitions. If required a similar schedule may be prepared for light (non-mechanical) plant or tools.

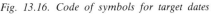

Latest date for drawings,
labelled 'A' for architect 'E' for engineer

Latest date for bending schedules

Manufacturers drawings to be approved

Nominations required

Material samples to be approved

Reinforcement to be delivered

Fig. 13.16. Code of symbols for target dates

iii. *Materials schedules* should be prepared in detail for brick and joinery deliveries, timber cutting lists and reinforcement delivery programmes. Metal windows, sanitary fittings, sundry iron and steel items and any other special materials or components must be precisely phased to suit the agreed programme of work. By these means, bottlenecks will be prevented and wasteful double handling avoided. In these days of unreliable delivery promises, nothing can be guaranteed, but eventually a reputation for 'knowing what you want and when' will produce its just rewards of co-operation and service from suppliers.

iv. *Sub-contractors* must be organised so that their individual start and finish dates dovetail exactly into the overall timetable, and since their efforts in certain classes of building may often account for half the total value of the contract, this liaison is vitally important. A schedule similar to that suggested in Fig. 13.18 will be drawn up from the lists while analysing the bills of quantities, and the appropriate dates taken from the stage programmes. Although these provisional dates are usually incorporated in the sub-contract orders, it is nevertheless desirable that they should be more positively agreed. This may be done by a formal letter of enquiry which has to be signed and returned, or better still by an early site meeting of all key sub-contractors so that necessary labour strengths may also be discussed and any special attendances or other requirements noted. The schedule can also be used as a means of progressing the placing of official orders and the eventual call-up of specialists during actual construction.

CONTRACT *Industrial Insurance Offices*   HEAVY PLANT SCHEDULE   DATE: *11 Jan. 1970*

Machine	Accompanying Equipment	Planned Date Reqd. on Site	Approx. Date of Release From Site	Source of Supply	Remarks (Including purpose for machine)
14/10 Concrete Mixer c/w Scales	Scrape Loud	21-3-70	end Sept. 70	Depot	Electric
20 T Cement Silo	Electric agitator	"	"	"	"
22 RB Excavator	Fitted dragline & backactor	2-2-70	end Aug 70	To be hired	

Fig. 13.17

CONTRACT *Anabilly Factory*   SCHEDULE OF SUB-CONTRACTORS AND SUPPLIERS   DATE 22nd *June 71.*

Remarks	Trade/Material	Sub-Contractor/Supplier	Bill Ref.	Order No.	Estimated			Actual		Called to Site
					Start	Period	Finish	Start	Finish	
	Gas Fitter	Midlands Gas Board	P.C.	121/4	18-9-71		17-1-72			
	Electrician	Socket & Sons Ltd.	P.C.	121/5	18-9-71		17-1-72			
	Plumber	P.B. Lead & Co. Ltd.	41/-	121/8	11-9-71		2-2-72	11-8-71		4-8-71
	Plasterer	Walls & Floors Ltd.	20/-	121/9	25-9-71		29-1-72			
Office only	Floor Tiler	Marble Tile Co. Ltd.	P.C.	121/11		3 month				

Fig. 13.18

9. Short Term Planning

To be wholly effective, planning must be a continuous activity, an attitude of mind rather than a once-for-all operation. Hence the preparatory groundwork of contract preliminary or project planning must be extended by regular short term planning and programming on the site. The purposes of this systematic and analytical pattern of thinking include the following objectives:

a. To encourage the site management to look ahead, to foresee future requirements and hence avoid delays.

b. To review the actual progress achieved, to check performances, and either to take corrective action for shortcomings or to take advantage of any gains.

c. To incorporate any design modifications; or to facilitate improved production techniques in the light of fuller information or further investigation, e.g. work study.

By forecasting for a shorter period of time it is possible to plan in greater detail and with more accuracy, so that the way is also prepared for practical incentive schemes. Master and section programmes are further enlarged, the degree of magnification depending upon the nature of the work, the number and quality of the staff available, and the company's stage of development in these techniques. Although several combinations are possible, the two following alternatives are typical.

10. Monthly Programming

During the last week of each calendar month, a programme is prepared by the site agent/general foreman for the next four or five weeks ahead. Alternatively the period may be varied to coincide with particular stages of the work, e.g. foundations, frame, cladding, finishes, etc., and for this reason it is sometimes more usual to refer to this as a *stage programme* (see Fig. 13.19). The layout of the chart is as before but it shows weeks and days, with week-end rest periods. Relevant operations are transferred from the existing programmes, together with any work outstanding from the previous periods and any additions or items brought forward for any reason. Headings may be further broken down such as brickwork into lifts, and additional minor items can be included. Drafting the stage programme is a technique similar to that decribed for section programmes, but it requires even greater attention to the avoidance of double-handling and the maintenance of continuity of work for both labour and plant.

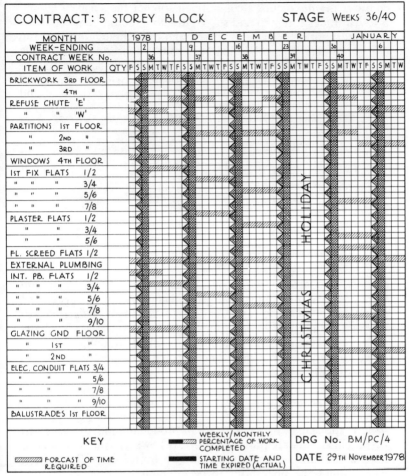

Fig. 13.19. Stage programme

Every operation must then be systematically checked to ensure that the essential information, material, plant and labour is or will be available, and the proper corrections made where necessary. Any sub-contractors not yet on site must be advised of firm starting dates, and any possible bottlenecks or hindrances should be thoroughly investigated and obviated.

Weekly planning meetings are held, perhaps on a Friday, to review the current progress against planned production and to consider the next week's commitments under the stage programme. All trades foremen and sub-contractors should be present, so that interrelations can be discussed and overlapping demands for equipment, etc., can be settled. As a result of these meetings *work lists* (see Fig. 13.20) are prepared for each gang, detailing every task for the coming week. Thus the ganger or chargehand can

WEEKLY WORK LIST

GANG _Jones Bricklayers._   No. OF MEN **4 + 2**   W/E **10th. March 1974**
TRADE

Location	Description of Work	Tick When Done	Foreman's Remarks
F/Drain	Manholes Nos. 3, 4 + 5	✓	
Retg. Wall	Complete both wings	✓	
Canteen	Footings up to D.P.C		Frost delayed strip footings
Gatehouse	Build weighbridge pit	✓	
Office Blk.	1st. floor cladding		
" "	1st. floor partitions		

Fig. 13.20

organise preparatory work ahead and proceed from job to job without delay or waiting for fresh directions. Extra items can of course be added as they arise, and the list can easily be extended to serve either as an allocation sheet for cost purposes or as the basis for a bonus scheme. Completed work is ticked off, and the reasons noted for any task not performed so that the appropriate action can be taken.

11. Weekly Programming

Where applicable, a finer control of production may be achieved by preparing weekly programmes. It is however still necessary to take a *forward view* each month, by listing from the section programmes the operations to be attempted during the coming month, and checking the requirements exactly as before (see Fig. 13.21).

The programme chart is drawn up as before but for one week ahead only and perhaps indicating hours. *Daily planning meetings* are held each afternoon and gang *work lists* (probably with target man hours) produced for the next day's tasks. Obviously this refinement requires some full-time planning assistance and presupposes the existence of reliable output standards, but it does ensure a maximum utilisation of labour and plant and facilitates more accurate and effective incentive techniques.

Northern Counties Power Station

PROGRAMME OF WORK FOR NOVEMBER 1975

Boiler House
Basement floor	Complete concrete to Column 18
Operating floor	Complete concrete to Column 18
	(this depends on structural steelwork being handed over)
Amenities floor	Complete concrete to Column 16
	(N.B. electric supply to hoist)
Fan floor	Complete concrete to Column 16
	(including all plinths)

Turbine House
Basement floor	Complete concrete around No. 4 turbine
North gable	Complete asbestos cladding
No. 5 turbine	Complete block to 8m level

Sewage Works	Complete plant house
Canteen	Complete brickwork
Gatehouse	Install weighbridge
Coal Plant	Complete road to workshop

Fig. 13.21

On this scale of magnification it is useful to prepare *sequence diagrams* (see Fig. 13.22) for repetitive operations, and minutely detailed daily *work schedules* (see Fig. 13.23) for focal plant units such as tower cranes, hoists or central batching mixers. Figure 13.22 shows the order of concreting floor bays where edge formwork cannot be stripped for 7 days. Contract days are given, based on 6 days per week.

12. Conclusion

Proper project planning can have an important influence on labour costs and overall costs, on the level of operatives' earnings and the duration of a job. Detailed planning can also help to eliminate idle and non-productive time of labour and plant, and can anticipate physical difficulties and material shortages in good time for remedial action to be taken. However, it must be remembered that planning is a continuous, cyclical process that requires much more than lip-service if it is to improve the effectiveness of site organisation.

The success of planning does not depend upon techniques but on the correct attitude of mind, and ultimately requires a climate of opinion throughout the industry which accepts and fosters the scientific outlook. Procedure must not become a merely mechanical routine, and the programme must never be mistaken for the end in itself. Although the difficulties themselves are potent reasons

SEQUENCE DIAGRAM

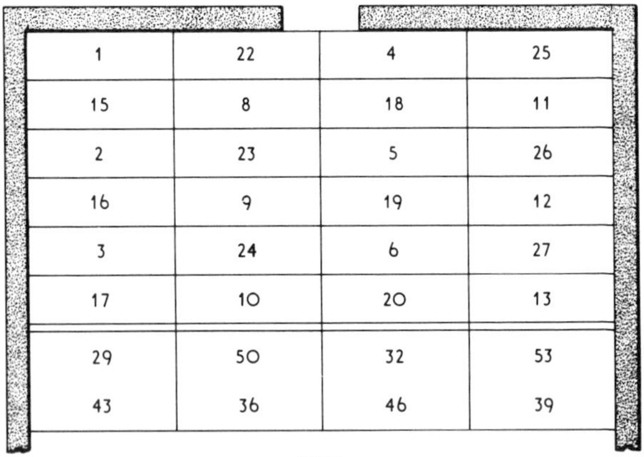

1	22	4	25
15	8	18	11
2	23	5	26
16	9	19	12
3	24	6	27
17	10	20	13
29	50	32	53
43	36	46	39

PLAN

Fig. 13.22

for the necessity of planning and programming, the problem of embracing and reconciling the often conflicting considerations of physical, economic and time factors, should not be underestimated. Planning is an activity requiring a mature and balanced outlook, a thorough knowledge and experience of building technology and practice, and a systematic and analytical approach.

Finally it must be appreciated that the techniques of planning are essentially practical, the means whereby to achieve greater efficiency on site. For this reason planning must not be separated from performance, and responsibility for production must involve at least a considerable share in the evolution of the selected

DAILY WORK SCHEDULE
FOR
TOWER CRANE

DATE: Tuesday 29th. May 1973.

From	To	Gang or Trade	Purpose
8.0 a.m.	10.0 a.m.	Bricklayers	Load-up 3rd. floor
10.0 a.m.	12.0 a.m.	Joiners	Strip staircase shutters
12.0 a.m.	1.0 p.m.	Concretors	Pour lift well 8th. floor
1.0 p.m.	4.0 p.m.	Joiners	Erect columns 8t. floor
4.0 p.m.	5.0 p.m.	Concretors	Pour columns 8t. floor
5.0 p.m.	5.30 p.m.	Steelfixers	Fabric for 9th. floor

Fig. 13.23

programme. Nothing can replace or be a substitute for good supervision, and greater productivity demands higher quality, better-trained site managers.

BIBLIOGRAPHY

Introduction to Programming and Progressing for Builders, Minstry of Works Advisory Leaflet No. 14, H.M.S.O.

The Programming of House-Building, Building Research Station Digest No. 91, H.M.S.O.

Programme and Progress, Ministry of Works Pamphlet, H.M.S.O.

The Organisation of Civil Engineering Work, Post-War National Development Report No. VI, The Institution of Civil Engineers.

Programmes in Construction – a guide to good practice, Chartered Institute of Building, 1981.

Chapter 14

Site Layout and Organisation

The consideration of site layout and organisation from the operational point of view is indistinguishable from construction planning, and since the physical factors of a site often have a direct bearing upon the method and sequence adopted, the two schemes are usually developed in parallel.

1. Layout

A site layout plan should be drawn up showing the relative locations of facilities, accommodation and plant, with the overall intention of providing the best conditions for optimum economy, continuity and safety during building operations. Due regard must be paid to the full implications of tidiness, accessibility and co-ordination of the following features.

    i.   *Access and traffic routes.* Needs vary with the type of project and the stage of the job, but access from the main road should be duplicated where possible, with short direct routes and one-way traffic to encourage 'flow'. Alternative access by rail or canal can be useful for bulk deliveries or lengthy components. Short term approaches may be constructed of hardcore, sleepers, concrete, proprietary track or transportable mats for mechanical navvies, but wherever possible, advantage should be taken of any permanent works for siting temporary roads or hardstandings. Ramps or bridges of interchangeable Bailey units or special fabrications may be necessary, while adequate drainage and maintenance of road surfaces is essential. Similarly, routes to spoil tips must be frequently repaired and attended; cross-overs must be provided for tracked vehicles negotiating metalled roads; and excavated material must be regularly cleared from adjacent highways. Traffic routes may be treated as clearways, or deliberately spanned by cranes for offloading purposes, and, on extensive sites, vehicle check points may be necessary for security reasons.

Permission must be obtained from the Local Authority for access over, or encroachment on public footpaths, and the police must be notified if roads are to be closed or diverted. The erection of fences or hoardings may be required, watching and lighting supplied, rights of way kept open, pedestrian walkways installed or vehicle tracks provided over trenches.

ii. *Materials storage and handling.* The object here is to minimise the wastage and losses arising from careless handling, bad storage or theft, and to reduce costs by obviating double handling or unnecessary movement. Stores and compounds must be provided for tools and equipment, plant spares, and breakable or attractive components or materials. Racks must be constructed for scaffolding and stillages built for oildrums, while storage areas must be designated for bulk items such as bricks. Special attention must be paid to materials like cement or hardboards which must be protected against moisture, and goods which require careful stacking to prevent deformation, e.g. metal windows and stove-enamelled panels. Newly completed buildings or rooms can often be utilised and it may be helpful to construct garages, etc., early in the programme for this specific purpose. A site plan should show not only the locations but sizes of stacks, dates required, planned routes for distribution and the eventual destinations. Methods study techniques such as string diagrams may be used to ensure optimum convenience. Tidiness earns the twin rewards of safety and convenience, by helping to eliminate accidents such as nails in the feet, and facilitating the sorting of 'cut and bent' reinforcement, etc. Sub-contractors' needs must be remembered, and suitable space allotted for their huts and materials.

Economical methods of materials handling include the use of gravity for aggregate feeds and rubbish chutes, the employment of packaged bricks and bulk cement, conveyors, off-loading gantries, stacker trucks, etc., and a minimal unloading gang.

iii. *Administration buildings and facilities.* Environment is of great importance to clerical work, so that the siting of administrative offices both for the contractor and the clerk of works or resident engineer, require due consideration in order to find the right compromise betwen the convenience of a view overlooking the works and freedom from the noise of operations. Size and layout of rooms depend upon the size of staff, but the needs of privacy for discussion and accommodation for site meetings must be borne in mind. Most of the factors reviewed in the earlier chapter on Office Organisation and Methods apply, and it should be remembered that temporary structures may be subject to rating by the local authority. Car parks may be necessary and both the internal and external lighting arrangements should preferably be designed in accordance with the recommendations of the *I.E.S. Technical Report No.* 3.

Welfare facilities also make a real contribution to production so that the requirements of labour camps, messrooms or canteens, drying or changing rooms, and toilets must be properly provided. (See also page 150, *e.*)

iv. *Plant, workshops and services.* The choice of major items of plant is of real consequence on most sites, including weighing the merits of such alternatives as central batching versus individual concrete mixers, and cranes compared with hoists. This has been mentioned earlier under method statement, but their use is of equal importance, involving both the careful balance of plant and manpower for each operation or the introduction of expedients like wet hoppers, and the precise positioning of the machine. Cranes must be superimposed on the scaled plan to ensure that the required reach is available, and drawn to scale on vertical sections to check that obstructions are cleared. The type of scaffold to be used must also be decided, and quantities calculated.

Workshops for joiners and fitters, etc., must be decided and located, balancing easy access and short routes to the scene of construction with the necessity to avoid congestion of the site.

Existing services must be pin-pointed to obviate disruption, and the routes of new ones considered when siting buildings and roads. The installation of temporary petrol pumps, electric power and telephone lines, water and compressed air mains, etc., requires negotiation with the relevant authority and co-ordination with the general scheme of work. Availability of water pressure or electricity characteristics may affect the size and cycle of mixers, choice of drive, and number of hand tools that can be powered.

v. *Security.* The national crime rate has been increasing for some years, and the construction industry is no exception.

Because of the inherent vulnerability and temporary nature of building sites, the accent must be on cost-effective prevention. Early contact with the local Crime Prevention Officer is therefore important, because his advice on any particular hazards in the area will provide site management with a basis for weighing risks against costs.

The first necessity is an adequate perimeter fence with secure entrance gates, and possibly an intruder alarm system. Temporary buildings must be soundly constructed and fitted with mortise locks, wire mesh window guards, and suitable fire fighting equipment. Materials must be protected by strategically sited checkers' huts, the installation of a weighbridge if warranted, compounds for 'attractive' stores, and proper procedures for receipts and issues. Plant and transport need to be immobilised outside working hours, and fuel supplies must be in a sealed compound with padlocked tanks. Small power-driven tools require lock-up facilities, and strict procedures for issues and recovery. Cash should be collected by a security company, and kept in a strong safe which is securely anchored. It is essential that no metal cutting or welding equipment is ever left in the vicinity. All petty cash disbursements and payroll documentation must be properly authorised and supervised to prevent malpractice and deception.

Particular risk periods are the tea and lunch breaks, when all traffic movements should be carefully supervised to prevent thefts via the gates. At night floodlights may be necessary, plus the employment of a nightwatchman, guard dog or visiting patrolman. The form of adequate security will vary from site to site and area to area, but constant vigilance by site management is the only way to maintain the standards set.

vi. *Special problems.* Particular attention may have to be paid to additional factors if special circumstances exist, such as the following:

a. *Confined sites* may involve parking restrictions, one-way traffic on approach roads, restricted delivery time-tables for materials, two-storey offices or gantries over pavements, etc.

b. *Tall buildings* require special arrangements for clocking on and off, the siting of canteens perhaps half-way up, and the installation of passenger lifts.

    c. Staged completions involving the piecemeal hand-over of buildings or sections and the removal or re-location of temporary installations, necessitates detailed planning of the time and manner of such change-overs, in order to avoid double-handling and disrupting delays.

    d. Adjoining property can introduce complications particularly where demolition is concerned, perhaps the diversion of services, shoring or under-pinning, and precautions such as photographs to forestall possible claims for damage.

2. Organisation

After the plant and installations have been arranged, the human organisation must be laid down and equipped. The preliminaries were initiated during the anticipation of award stage but these must be further defined and enlarged.

    a. Staff. Not only the categories and number of staff must be decided but also their responsibilities and relationships, for it is essential that every member should know from whom he must take instructions and to whom he may give them without undue interference. For this purpose it is useful to publicise a diagram indicating the chain of command, and to prepare a chart listing the duties and responsibilities of each individual.

    At the same time banking facilities may be organised if required, office stationery requisitioned, perhaps on a standard check list, and special features advised for insurance purposes.

    b. Communications. Good communication systems are vital to effective control, and nowadays these may range from the shortwave radio or inductive loop system, teleprinter and telephone to the simpler field telephone, the loud hailer or a buzzer for controlling a concrete pump pipeline. The correct postal address and name of the nearest railway station is important to the buying department; for deliveries, adequate notice boards and careful signposting should be provided. When applicable, crane signals must be taught, and the transfer of planning information from management to operatives can be assisted by the issue of prepared location diagrams of the site or building, incorporating a reference code by means of which areas can be pin-pointed or progress recorded.

    On dispersed sites transport such as bicycles or scooters may be necessary for timekeepers or supervisory staff.

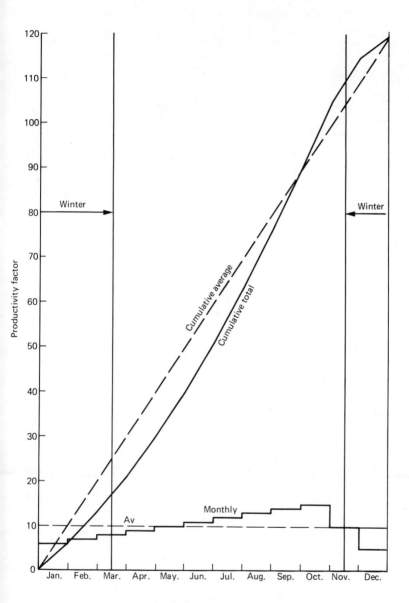

Fig. 14.1. Seasonal effects on productivity

Phenomenon	In conjunction with	Effect
Rain		1 Affects site access and movement 2 Spoils newly finished surfaces 3 Delays drying out of buildings 4 Damages excavations 5 Delays concreting, bricklaying and all external trades 6 Damages unprotected materials 7 Causes discomfort to personnel 8 Increases site hazards
	High wind	1 Increases rain penetration 2 Reduces protection offered by horizontal covers 3 Increases site hazards 4 'Chill' effect on personnel
High wind		1 Makes steel erection, roofing, wall sheeting, scaffolding and similar operations hazardous 2 Limits or prevents operation of tall cranes and cradles etc. 3 Damages untied walls, partially fixed cladding and incomplete structures 4 Scatters loose materials and components 5 Endangers temporary enclosures 6 Dries out earth fill and concrete
High and equatorial temperatures		1 Creates discomfort/danger for site personnel 2 Dries out earth fill and concrete 3 Impedes steel erection and scaffolding
	Rain or humidity	Prickly heat effect on personnel. 'Comfort' index

Low and sub-zero temperatures	1 Damages mortar, concrete, brickwork, etc. 2 Slows or stops development of concrete strength 3 Freezes ground and prevents subsequent work in contact with it, e.g. concreting 4 Slows down excavation 5 Delays painting, plastering etc. 6 Causes delay or failure in starting of mechanical plant 7 Freezes unlagged water pipes and may affect other services 8 Freezes material stockpiles 9 Disrupts supplies of materials 10 Increases transportation hazards 11 Creates discomfort and danger for site personnel 12 Deposits frost film on formwork, steel reinforcement and partially completed structures
Rain	Personnel 'feel' the cold more
High wind	Increases probability of freezing and aggravates effects of 1–12 above. 'Chill' factor affects personnel
Snow	1 Impedes movement of labour, plant and material 2 Blankets externally stored materials 3 Increases hazards and discomfort for personnel 4 Impedes all external operations 5 Creates additional weight on horizontal surfaces
High wind	Causes drifting which may disrupt external communications
Fog	Affects traffic on and off site, and prohibits earthmoving

Fig. 14.2. The effects of weather on building operations

c. Conclusion. Adequate means of control must be ensured by pre-determining the methods and techniques to be adopted. Site safety policy and organisation should be decided, and an effort made from the beginning to foster the attitude of fulfilling the building regulations in the spirit, rather than the letter of the law.

Finally the site layout and organisation are checked against the overall and detailed programmes, to confirm that means and methods are fully integrated and in harmony. This is particularly important when the administrative area has to be moved, either on a large and spread-out site or when phased completions are required.

3. Winter building

a. Effects. Being an outdoor occupation, building construction is vulnerable to weather, although it is hard to quantify the precise effects of natural hazards like rainfall. The British climate, because of its unpredictability, is a major handicap to new work, and inclement weather has long been accepted as inevitable, and therefore to be borne stoically. But the exceptional severity and duration of the winter of 1962–63 prompted builders and clients alike to question the situation, and much can now be done to mitigate the effects of the weather particularly during the period of winter.

A contractor's 'unprotected' monthly turnover will fluctuate cyclically with the season's weather variations. From a peak in October which is about 50% above the yearly average it falls sharply to a trough in December about 50% below average, and then rises steadily up to the next October (see Fig. 14.1). Of course, this cycle reflects the impact of holidays as well as the influence of weather. Thus generally, since many cost factors are fairly constant, site operations tend to lose money from November to April, and builders (rather like farmers), rely upon the 'haymaking' between May and October for their eventual profit. There are wide variations between the more susceptible sites involving earthmoving, and the more pro-tected building projects; between the various stages of construction; and between a mild or severe winter, as well as for different geographical locations. Nevertheless, there is a lot of scope for increasing production output during the worst months, and so improving company profitability and service to the client.

b. Causes. The main weather factors which inhibit construction in Great Britain are rain, frost, wind and daylight. The effects of weather upon building operations are summarised in Fig. 14.2.

Rainfall varies from the drier East to the wetter West, and tends to increase further North particularly at higher altitudes. Moreover, in areas such as Cornwall, the rainfall is considerably greater during the winter than during the summer, whilst in the Midlands the monthly precipitation is fairly constant throughout the year (see Fig. 14.3). A map showing these local statistics is published by the Ordnance

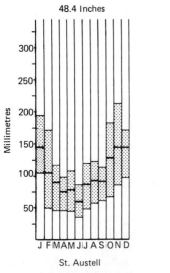

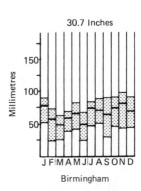

Fig. 14.3. Average annual rainfall 1916–1950 for St Austell (Cornwall) and Birmingham (Midlands). Bar across column shows mean monthly value; upper and lower lines show upper and lower quartiles

Survey. A critical factor often forgotten is evaporation, which of course is dependent upon hours of sunshine. The combined effect for most areas is that the ground becomes waterlogged from November to April, and surplus water runs off the land into drainage ditches and the rivers. During the summer, when evaporation exceeds precipitation, vegetation has to draw upon reserves of water in the soil to satisfy transpiration requirements and a 'moisture deficit' is created. The

Meteorological Office prepares estimates of soil moisture deficits for the use of river authorities and farmers (see Fig. 14.4). Hours of daylight are readily predictable, resulting in the traditional shorter working day during the six weeks before and after the Christmas week (see Fig. 14.5). Frosts are more variable, but statistically usually occur during the months of December to March.

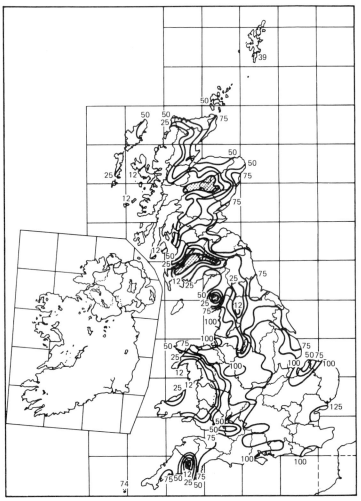

Fig. 14.4. Estimated soil moisture deficit, 0900 GMT 29 July 1970. Figures are mm

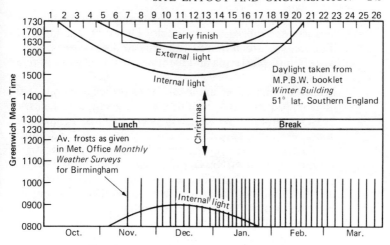

Fig. 14.5. Time lost due to darkness and frost

c. *Protection.* Precautions can be taken to minimise many of the damaging effects of inclement weather upon construction activities, the extent in most cases being determined by financial considerations rather than technical limitations. The key to success is good management, planning well ahead, and organising men and materials for the chosen course of action.

i. Ahead of operations, materials can be covered against the rain, e.g. sand, aggregate and bricks. Ground and works may be cleared of ice and snow by steam jets or flame guns. Early drainage and temporary roads are obvious precautions. The use of weather forecasts to help decide operational tactics has been explored, and has much potential yet to be realised. Specific advance warnings can be obtained from local meteorological stations of strong winds which might menace tower cranes, or heavy frosts which require large concrete pours to be safeguarded.

ii. During construction, men and materials can be provided with shelter, from the use of simple scaffolding and translucent reinforced tarpaulins to complete air-supported structures. Working areas can be warmed by space heaters, fired by either bottled gas or paraffin. Water for concrete and mortar may be heated (max. 80°C) in simple boilers or by electric immersion heaters, and sand can be heated (max. 50°C) by high-pressure steam or gas burners. Artificial light is the easiest remedy to apply, and probably the least expensive aid, and a great variety of both electric and gas appliances are available. Different standards of illumination are required for general access areas, local workpoints, plastering and painting, or skilled work of fine detail.

Proprietary additives are available to protect concrete and mortar, provided that conditions and specifications allow.

Most important however are the steps that may be taken to conserve and protect the more vulnerable and most expensive resource on the site, the operatives. Investigations carried out by Dr. Geoffrey Taylor for the M.P.B.W. (now D.O.E.), have indicated that many building workers had low temperatures (hypothermia) sufficient to impair their efficiency. Yet protective clothing, similar in design and materials to sports wear or walking and climbing equipment, are now available with waterproof qualities combined with warmth and ventilation. Heated cabs or specially designed body muffs are necessary for construction machinery drivers, particularly on tower cranes.

iii. Completed work can be protected against frost by insulating blankets of many kinds, or heated by electrical quilts. Such precautions can avoid longer curing periods which tie up equipment and hinder progess, or damage requiring expensive repair. Buildings can be speedily dried out by dehumidifiers which literally extract the water from preceding wet trades, and so allow painting and floor finishes to continue without risk.

d. *Policy*. In addition to the direct benefits of contract progress and improved productivity, there are a number of indirect reasons for taking advantage of winter building techniques. Redundancy payments, the guaranteed week and guaranteed minimum bonus, the scarcity of skilled labour and the costs of hiring and firing, specific contract requirements and penalties for delay, and escalating inflation, all combine to make continued production a desirable objective despite all the assaults of the weather. It should therefore be company policy to encourage the adoption of all reasonable efforts to maintian optimum production levels throughout the winter period of mid-November to mid-March, whilst leaving the precise extent and methods to be decided by site managements. The effects of winter should be fully taken into account when one is drawing up a contract programme, whilst at the same time determining to take full advantage of the techniques and equipment now available to reduce those effects to the economic minimum. Finally, it must be remembered that bad weather can turn a safe site into a dangerous one in a matter of minutes. Walkways, gangways and vehicle roads can be made treacherous by rain, frost or snow. Rain can loosen the sides of a trench or larger excavation and cause a collapse. High winds can blow objects about, turn weak structures over, or blow a man off a roof when carrying a cladding or formwork sheet. It is, therefore, essential that we always have a lively regard for the weather conditions prevailing.

BIBLIOGRAPHY

Organisation of Building Sites, National Building Studies Special Report No. 29, H.M.S.O., 1959.
The Lighting of Building Sites and Works of Engineering Construction, Technical Report No. 3, The Illuminating Engineering Society.
Materials Handling on Building Sites, Issued by The London Building Productivity Committee.
R. E. Calvert, 'Soil Moisture Deficit and Construction', *The National Builder,* March 1970.
Weather and the Builder, Advisory leaflet No. 40, Department of the Environment.
Site Lighting, Advisory leaflet No. 71.
Bricklaying in Cold Weather, Advisory leaflet No. 8.
The Effect of Adverse Weather on Building Productivity, Report 50, C.I.R.I.A.
Survey of Meteorological Information for Architecture and Building, Current Paper 5/72, Building Research Station.
Winter Building, Department of the Environment, 1971.
Protective Clothing for Workers on Construction Sites, Ministry of Public Building and Works, 1968.
'Cold and scurvy threaten site workers' health', *Contract Journal,* 8 March 1973.
Alan Pink, *Winter Concreting,* Cement and Concrete Association, 1978.
E. M. Baker, *Procedures Prior to Commencing a Contract,* Site Management Information Service No. 60, Institute of Building.
Management of Building Contracts, National Joint Consultative Committee.
Materials Control to Avoid Waste, Building Research Establishment Digest No. 259, H.M.S.O., 1982.
The Practice of Site Management, The Institute of Building, 1976

Chapter 15

Contract Supervision

1. Control

Controlling a construction contract is a continuous activity that begins with a successful tender and ends with a satisfactory final account. Effective control entails a regular comparison of actual progress or performance against the pre-determined intentions or requirements, followed by the initiation of appropriate action to achieve or maintain the desired objectives. The proper direction and speed cannot economically be attained by force, but require the creation of conditions that will encourage self-control, and foster the team spirit that is so essential to a happy and efficient contract.

Planning and organisation provide the strategy and means for subsequent control and co-ordination, and site management like any other executive function makes use of the 'exception' principle. This implies a constant interchange of information, which in turn pre-supposes good communication systems for the effective transmission of ideas, instructions, and details.

a. Supervision. This may take several forms, depending upon the size and nature of the particular project, and the peculiar organisation of the contractor. A small, local job might be controlled centrally, with a general foreman on the site, daily visits from a contracts supervisor and strategic decisions taken by the contracts manager at head office. Alternatively, a large and distant site may be run by the general foreman, directly supervised by his resident agent and project manager. In both instances however, the principles involved are the same, and only superficial details of administration and communication should vary.

A well-documented 'Manual of Company Procedures', detailing responsibilities and administrative conventions, should be available on site for general guidance.

Typical staff organisation charts or 'family trees' are shown in Figs. 15.1 and 15.2, to give an indication of the possible variations in size, complexity, division of responsibilities and delegation of authority.

Under the standard forms of contract the Client also maintains a site supervisory staff, headed by the Architect (Building) or Engineer (Civil Engineering). The Architect/Engineer acts as an interface between design and construction, and as an independent arbiter in contract matters. On building contracts the Architect may only visit the site at intervals, but is represented by a resident Clerk of Works who has limited authority. A professional Quantity Surveyor is responsible for the agreement of monthly valuations, final accounts and contract claims; and the settlement of nominated sub-contractors' accounts.

b. *Roles.* A Contractor's site personnel are grouped into three main categories: technical, clerical and works. But precise titles vary from company to company, and the same name may mean something very different in another organisation. However, the following major roles can be distinguished, although the actual numbers of staff will vary from project to project and at different times of a contract.

i. *Contracts Manager* or Contracts Supervisor is usually based at Head Office, and visits his group of contracts on a regular weekly basis or as the situation demands. His chief concerns are to ensure that progress and the financial outcome are satisfactory, and that time, cost and quality are to the satisfaction of the client. He may or may not be a director of the firm.

ii. *Project Manager,* Site Manager or Agent is the company's senior representative on site. He is the leader and chief executive of the contractor's site organisation, and because of the many day-to-day decisions that have to be taken he is usually given wide discretionary powers. His main duties are to see that the construction is carried out economically and to time, and in accordance with the contract documents. He is usually qualified technically.

iii. *Works Manager* or General Foreman is responsible for the recruitment and deployment of direct labour and plant, with a special responsibility for safety. He maintains site discipline and handles daily negotiations with the unions and their representatives, and co-ordinates sub-contract labour.

iv. *Office Manager* or Cashier is responsible for all of the clerical tasks – timekeeping, payment of wages, checking and storage of materials, and general office functions.

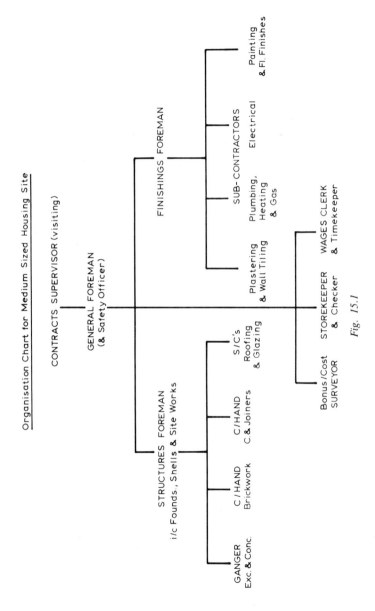

Organisation Chart for Medium Sized Housing Site

CONTRACTS SUPERVISOR (visiting)

GENERAL FOREMAN
(& Safety Officer)

STRUCTURES FOREMAN
i/c Founds., Shells & Site Works

FINISHINGS FOREMAN

GANGER
Exc. & Conc.

C/HAND
Brickwork

C/HAND
C.& Joiners

S/C's
Roofing
& Glazing

Plastering
& Wall Tiling

SUB-CONTRACTORS

Plumbing,
Heating
& Gas

Electrical

Painting
& Fl. Finishes

Bonus/Cost
SURVEYOR

STOREKEEPER
& Checker

WAGES CLERK
& Timekeeper

Fig. 15.1

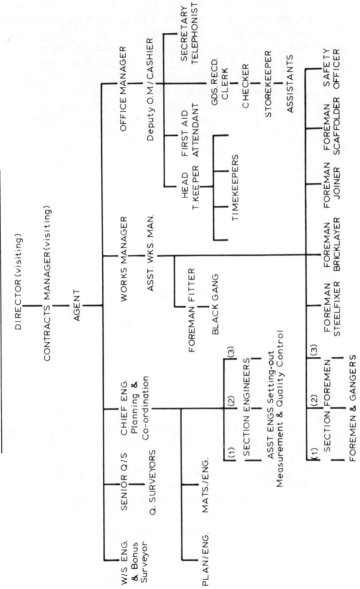

Staff Organisation Chart for Major Industrial Contract

Fig. 15.2

v. *Chief Engineer* is responsible for setting-out the works, measurement and records, and quality control procedures. He also prepares and monitors detailed works programmes and co-ordinates the flow of drawings and other information. It is also his responsibility to take-off and requisition materials, and after the Office Manager has obtained the necessary quotations, to place orders after having checked quality, delivery and price.

vi. *Building Surveyor* or Contractor's Quantity Surveyor is responsible for interim and final measurement of the construction. He handles all legal and financial aspects of the contract, and together with the Client's Quantity Surveyor agrees the valuation of variation orders and dayworks, and the settlement of any claims. It is also his duty to measure and agree all sub-contractors' accounts.

Once again, Figs. 15.1 and 15.2 illustrate the range and variety of roles.

2. Objectives

Each of the individual components that together comprise either a building project or a civil engineering undertaking, must be carefully marshalled and monitored to ensure that adequate quantities, of the proper item, to the correct quality, arrive in the specified place at the required time.

a. *Labour.* Although the general foreman is responsible for the engagement and direction of operatives, it is desirable to have a department at head office which acts as a clearing house and advertises vacancies, etc. It is usual for the architect/engineer to require a daily or weekly statement of labour strength, and this may be used to compile a graph such as is drawn at the bottom of Fig. 13.7. This, however, is only an approximate guide, and a regular comparison with the anticipated requirements of tradesmen, shown in Fig. 13.12, would be more helpful. The maintenance of the requisite labour force must of course be judged in conjunction with the progress record.

b. *Plant.* The method statement and more particularly the plant schedule (Fig. 13.17) prepared during the planning stage should be used to ensure that machines are brought on to the site at the appropriate time. Equally important is the necessity to return equipment as soon as it becomes redundant. Method study techniques may be employed to raise the level of plant utilisation, while instruction in the correct use and insistence on regular maintenance is essential if standing time due to breakdowns is to be avoided.

c. *Materials.* Timed schedules of requirements prepared in conjunction with the contract programme (see Figs. 13.5 and 13.6, and Chapter 13, 8, iii), should ensure that materials are requisitioned and ordered in good time, and assist the chasing of deliveries when suppliers fall down or earlier despatch has to be effected. To check that all components are actually requisitioned, it is helpful to prepare a materials schedule similar to Fig. 15.3 for every drawing, and thus provide a means of supervising the initiation of purchasing. Methods of progressing supplies, including plant replacements, and of controlling waste by reconciliations are described in Chapter 11, 3 (1) and (2).

CONTRACT: General Dairy Ltd.			
DRAWING No: 1001/2	SECTION External Works		
DATE OF ISSUE 3rd. Feb. 1975.	TITLE Drainage Layout		
MATERIALS SCHEDULE	Serial No:		
Description	Requisition		Date of Delivery
	Number	Date	
G.S.W. Pipes & Fittings	1763	7-2-75	14-2-75
C.I. Manhole Covers			
Engineering Bricks	1765	10-2-75	

Fig. 15.3

d. *Information.* A means of providing for outstanding information was given in Chapter 13, 8, i, but it is also necessary to institute a reliable record of site instructions in order to prevent later misunderstandings and disputes. All verbal details and directions given either by the architect or clerk of works should be entered in a book, preferably initialled, and afterwards confirmed by the builder's surveyor if necessary.

e. Sub-contractors. Copies or abstracts of all relevant programmes, drawings, schedules, instructions, ec., must be speedily passed on to the sub-contractors concerned. In turn, their labour strengths and progress achievements should be recorded, and any labour, material or information difficulties noted and followed up. An initial site meeting to settle queries and discuss trade sequences and attendance requirements, can greatly improve co-operation.

With the growth of labour-only sub-contracting, it is important that the tax requirement for the production of forms 714 should be implemented strictly and without delay.

3. Techniques

Gathering together the various ingredients is one half of site management, while the practical application of control techniques for their integration is the other.

a. Progress. Every general foreman and agent should keep a *site diary* in which to record weather observations, work executed, delays experienced, visitors, comments and any noteworthy occurrences. *Physical progress* can be marked on the programme chart by filling or colouring the appropriate bars, and by drawing a line underneath to indicate the period occupied on each operation (see Fig. 13.9). Some form of week indicator, such as a sliding plumb line, should be used to mark the present date so that forecast and achievement are readily comparable. Charts might also incorporate a special column sub-divided into ten, so that the percentage completion of individual items of work may be logged (see Fig. 13.7). Alternatively, plans or elevations may be coloured to indiate the completion of different operations on particular sections of the works, or particularly on repetitive work, a special progress chart may be marked up to record the current stages of trade sequences (see Fig. 15.4). A check should also be kept on *financial progress* by marking interim valuations on a graph such as Fig. 13.8.

b. Variations. It is almost inevitable that the client, site conditions, or other unforeseen circumstances, will produce a number of variations as the contract proceeds. Nevertheless, the practice of introducing alterations right up to the last few weeks of a contract is to be deprecated, and, if possible, a date should be agreed beyond which no extras shall be

<table>
<tr><th colspan="14">PROGRESS CHART
62 Dwellings at Greenfield End</th></tr>
<tr><th>FINISHING TRADES</th><th>INTERNAL PLUMBING</th><th>GAS & ELECT. CARCASSING</th><th>C + J 1ST. FIXINGS</th><th>PARTITIONS & SILLS</th><th>PLASTERBOARD CEILINGS</th><th>PLASTER WALLS & CEILINGS</th><th>C + J 2nd. FIXINGS</th><th>SANITARY FITTINGS</th><th>FLOOR SCREEDS</th><th>DRYING-PERIODS</th><th>PAINTING</th><th>ELECTRICAL FITTINGS</th><th>FLOOR TILING</th></tr>
</table>

BLOCK 'A'													
1	Wk 9	10	11	12	13	14	15	16					
2	Wk 10	11	Wk 12	13	14								
3	Wk 11	12	Wk 13	14									
4	Wk 12	13	Wk 14										
5	Wk 13	14	15										
6	Wk 14	15	16										
7	Wk 15	16											
8	Wk 16												

BLOCK 'B' comprises rows 5–8.

Fig. 15.4

instructed unless the contract period is also extended and the resultant overheads reimbursed. In order both that financial adjustments may be settled amicably, and drains or services, etc., shall be recorded 'as built' for future reference, it is imperative that all changes should be methodically agreed and measured. Original and final site levels, extra depths of excavation or concrete, and all additional construction details must be placed on *record drawings* and submitted for signature. Works not immediately measurable should be recorded in *daywork sheets* on a time and material basis, in accordance with a mutually agreed procedure. When *variation of price* records (such as Fig. 11.2) are required, these should be kept right up-to-date and presented for regular inspection. If grounds for *claims* arise, then these should be notified in writing as quickly as circumstances allow, so that they may be discussed and if possible settled at the next site meeting. The prompt adjustment of variations is advantageous to all parties, and promotes that friendly co-operation so essential to a successful venture.

c. *Quality.* The maintenance of quality is a most important factor in modern construction, and on large works it may justify the full-time appointment of personnel and expensive laboratory facilities. Management must give a clear lead in setting the required standards and seeing that they are attained, particularly when incentive schemes are based on output, or piecework (labour-only) gangs are employed. Quality control includes accurate setting-out and levelling, fair faced brickwork and concrete finishes, as well as the more intricate techniques for concrete and soil stabilisation tests, etc.

On certain projects e.g. a nuclear power station, reliable, high-quality work must not only be achieved but also be demonstrated by adequate records. A system of 'Quality Assurance' (QA) was devised originally for the U.S. space programme and has since been adopted in other industries, but is a new discipline for construction. The contractor writes a quality manual detailing operations, methods and inspection forms, which are approved by the designer. Self-policing is carried out by a team of inspectors who ensure that the check are done and keep the QA records. In turn the designer's staff make sure that QA procedures are being adhered to, by spot checks and inspection of records; and also keep their own independent records. Obviously, this double checking and assembling of documents is costly, but when quality is paramount the benefits of QA are invaluable.

QA practices and systems are being specified at a steadily increasing rate on larger construction contracts; sometimes based upon B.S. 5750 (defence industries) or B.S. 5882 (nuclear power stations).

d. *Co-ordination*. The process of linking together the separate members of the team, and the correlation of their various efforts into a harmonious performance, requires an efficient network of communications both verbal and written. This is generally recognised to be one of the weaker mechanisms in the building industry, although the following procedures are widely known if not always practised.

   i. *Site reports* to the architect's office may be required weekly from the general foreman where there is no clerk of works on site, and a copy of this may also suffice to keep the contractor's head office aware of general progress and any necessary action. Otherwise, a daily or weekly report should be submitted in order that the pulse of the job can be watched, and any assistance provided. A report should include the following information: labour strength including sub-contractors, labour, plant, material, information or sub-contractor shortages, delays incurred with causes, e.g. weather, breakdowns, visitors and instructions received. Works progress may be advised by means of a shuttle copy of the programme chart, or by a statement of percentages for each operation.

ii. *Weekly meetings* of site supervisory, technical and senior clerical staff, together with chosen sub-contractors, under the chairmanship of the agent, are an excellent way of exercising control. Progress can be related to the programme, shortages discussed and means of overcoming them decided, and anticipated problems settled or by-passed. Such a meeting every Friday, to review the past week and survey the week ahead, can do much to lubricate the organisational machinery and weld the individual functions into a synchronised machine. This semi-informal meeting is only one step away from the conscious purpose of short term planning, mentioned in an earlier chapter.

iii. *Site meetings* held at the start of a contract, and thereafter regularly each month, or as required during the progress of the work, are highly desirable, and should be initiated by the contractor if neglected by the architect. Well-organised site meetings maintain the impetus of the job, help to avoid delays, and can resolve differences before they generate friction and lead to misunderstanding. Meetings should be conducted in a formal manner in accordance with good committee practice, with an agenda sent out beforehand and minutes (including an 'action' column) circulated afterwards. A permanent chairman and secretary may be chosen by agreement between the architect and the general contractor, but other members should be restricted to those actually concerned at the particular stage and must be responsible representatives authorised to take decisions. Any procedure for meetings should include the following: a list of persons present; the acceptance of previous minutes; matters arising from the minutes; progress of the works and causes of any delays; labour, plant or material shortages; outstanding information; a review of nominated sub-contractors and suppliers; variations and/or claims for extras; any other business and the date of the next meeting.

iv. *Mechanical and electrical* services can nowadays be a very significant proportion of the contract, and special attention must therefore be given to these particular sub-contracts. In addition to the usual two bars on the master programme, it is essential that detailed programmes be prepared for individual M & E activities to show inter-dependencies with the builder's work, and so that progress may be properly monitored. For example, a modern hospital is a network of multitudinous services, and it may be necessary for the main contractor to employ his own specialist engineer to advise on these aspects and avoid any misunderstandings. Regular progress reports must be submitted by the sub-contractors, and it is likely that separate site meetings will be required to co-ordinate information, progress, variations and any problems arising. Later, it is essential that comprehensive testing and commissioning programmes be agreed because these vital, but often overlooked, operations can occupy a considerable time and may delay internal finishings. Genuine co-operation is required on both sides to ensure that the total project is completed and handed over to the satisfaction of the client.

e. *Wastage.* The storage and handling of materials was referred to in Chapter 14 under 1. Layout, section ii and 3. Winter Building, section *c*; and now we must consider materials control. Some waste of materials is unavoidable on building sites, and this is generally recognised and allowed for by estimators and quantity surveyors when pricing. However, work by the Building Research Establishment has suggested that true wastage is anything up to 100% more than the historical norms assumed, depending upon the quality of site management. Since between 35–45% of the estimated cost of building is in materials, it is essential that cost-effective control procedures be instituted and supervised.

Much can be done to reduce the problem, beginning with a recognition of the causes of waste. Materials may be delivered to the wrong specification, short delivery or damaged. Losses and/or damage may occur during site storage or internal transit. At the workplace wastage can be due to conversion, excess materials supplied, fixing, cutting, learning, wrong use and borrowing by other trades. Other direct losses may be due to pilfering, theft or vandalism. Indirect waste, not necessarily producing a total financial loss, may be caused by substitution e.g. facing bricks for commons, temporary works and negligence, perhaps in overlarge excavation for concrete.

A determination of the size and extent of significant wastage on a site will be produced by regular reconciliations of deliveries, measured work and stocks; and random sampling of chosen items. Better planning, and more effective control by management, must begin by educating site personnel in the value and care of these expensive and limited resources.

f. *Conclusion.* It will be seen that construction control or contract supervision is a matter of checking and cross-checking. If the service departments are properly organised, and the planning has been thoroughly carried out, then all the information should be readily available to support the intuitive assessment of the manager. This sixth sense born of training and experience, is the irreplaceable contribution of the personality in control, for, like the master mariner who is dependent upon the elements, the master builder is also subject to chance, in the form of weather, the type of labour available, and the vagaries of supplies.

4. Project Management

The *traditional method* of managing building contracts is for the client to appoint consultants to act on his behalf, to produce the design and supervise the site construction. The architect usually acts as team leader coordinating the members of the design team, and supervises the builder.

Although many clients amend the documents as they think fit, there are four major forms of contract:

i.   Standard form of Building Contract (JCT 80) issued by the Joint Contracts Tribunal and published by the R.I.B.A.
ii. The G.C./Works/1 – Edition 2 form of contract for government building and civil engineering works, published by H.M.S.O.
iii. The I.C.E. Conditions of Contract 5th Edition for civil engineering works, published by I.C.E.
iv. The F.I.D.I.C. form of contract used internationally for work overseas, published by Fédération International des Ingénieurs – Conseils.

Because of the increasing complexity of buildings, the need for a greater degree of financial planning, and a desire to reduce both design and construction times, there have been numerous attempts to find new ways to plan and control the building process. A *'design-construct'* contract, 'package deal' or 'turnkey' contract is intended to bridge the gap which normally separates design from execution. The contractor is appointed directly by the client and assumes responsibility for the whole process from initial briefing to the production of the completed building. In addition to taking on the role of 'leader of the team', the builder also contributes his own unique experience of construction materials, methods and costs.

The *management contract* has evolved to give unified management responsibility for a project without limiting the advantages of competitive tendering. The management contractor is directly employed by the client as an equal member of the professional team, to provide a purely construction management service in return for a fee. The contractor is responsible for the setting-up of overall site establishment and general back-up services, but does not carry out any of the construction which is let out on a competitive basis to a number of specialist sub-contractors.

The wish of some clients for a fully independent Project Manager has led to a further separation of management roles from the design and construction elements. This separated role has developed into *Project Management,* defined by the CIOB as 'the overall planning, control and co-ordination of a project from inception to completion aimed at meeting a client's requirements and ensuring completion on time, within cost and to required quality standards'. Project management services may vary according to the type of project and the needs of the client. Where the client has in-house resources, the Project Manager may have a non-executive role and be responsible solely for coordination. At the other extreme the Project Manager is fully responsible for the total management of the project, and handles all matters on behalf of the client. In either situation the Project Manager provides only management expertise and no design nor construction service, and has therefore no conflict of interest. The success of project management depends chiefly on the personal qualities of the individual project manager. Since the role is multi-disciplinary no single profession can lay exclusive claim to it, and background is of less importance than management experience and leadership qualities. Since the duties of a Project Manager may include initial brief, feasibility and pre-construction stages, construction and completion, it has become apparent that opportunities for specific education for project management are now essential.

BIBLIOGRAPHY

Civil Engineering Procedure, 2nd edn, The Institution of Civil Engineers, 1971.
A. C. Twort, *Civil Engineering Supervision and Management,* Edward Arnold, 1972.

A. A. Macfarlane, *Site Supervision,* The Architectural Press.

The Practice of Site Management, Volumes 2 and 3, Chartered Institute of Building, 1985.

J. R. Davis and R. Davies, 63. *The Clerk of Works and the Site Management Team,* 1975.

D. P. Wyatt, 75. *The Control of Materials on Housing Sites,* 1978.

Site Management Information Service, The Institute of Building.

247. *Waste of Building Materials,* 1981.

259. *Materials Control to Avoid Waste,* 1982.

Digests by Building Research Establishment, H.M.S.O.

Project Management in Building, The Institute of Building. 1979.

Education for Project Management in Building, The Institute of Building, 1981.

Heathrow Terminal No. 4, supplement to *New Civil Engineer,* 27 September 1984, The Institution of Civil Engineers.

'Tight Tabs Kept on Torness', *New Civil Engineer,* 8 November 1984, The Institution of Civil Engineers.

The Placing and Management of Contracts for Building and Civil Engineering Work (The Banwell Report), H.M.S.O., 1964.

Part III

Management Techniques

Chapter 16

Statistics and Sampling

1. Statistics

Statistics in the plural are measurements or numbers of mass phenomena, systematically arranged so that they signify their interrelationships. In the singular, statistics is the numerical study of a practical problem by means of the analysis and interpretation of measured or estimated data. This branch of applied mathematics may be used in any technical, commercial, or social field in order to provide statistical evidence as a guide to action or decision, in the place of opinions or general impressions. However, it must be remembered that unlike the laws of physical sciences, statistical laws are only held to be true *on the average*.

1. *Collection*. Since the final result of any statistical investigation can only be as accurate as the least accurate of the figures to be analysed, it will be realised that this preliminary stage is of prime importance. The units and their meanings must be clearly defined, observations must be recorded logically and tidily, and information compiled by others, e.g. cost returns from sites, must be carefully criticised. Published facts particularly, require editing to ensure that terms are understood, that factors are unchanged, and that the information provided is complete.

2. *Tabulation*. The first step in an analysis is to classify and tabulate the answers collected, or to re-arrange them into suitable groupings in order to bring out their salient points. This operation of dissecting and summarising the raw data may involve any of the following processes.

   a. When *counting* similar observations it is convenient to place a stroke for each item as follows:

/	//	///	////	////
1st	2nd	3rd	4th	5th

   so that the groups of five stand out, and are easy to total.

b. By *converting* the individual figures to percentages of the total, it is sometimes easier to grasp the significance of a table. Thus in Fig. 16.1 Table A would be replaced by Table B.

It will be noticed that the total number of observations upon which the percentages have been based, has been given since this is essential information.

Table A. Employment in the Constructional Industries, 1959
Operatives (Thousands)

Contractors new housing	Contractors new non-housing	Contractors other work	Public authorities directly	Total
275	445	336	366	1,422

Table B. Percentage Distribution of 1,422 Thousand Operatives Employed in the Constructional Industries, 1959

Contractors new housing	Contractors new non-housing	Contractors other work	Public authorities directly	Total
19·3	31·3	23·6	25·8	100·0

(taken from *Statistics on Construction,* May 1960.)

Fig. 16.1

c. The *classifying* of data is the process of sorting into groupings according to their common characteristics, the four general types of categories being time, place, quality or quantity. In the two latter cases it is usual to arrange the table from left to right in decreasing order of standard or measurement, so that the meaning is obvious. Data grouped according to a numerical characteristic are termed *Groups,* while non-measurable collections are known as *Classes.*

d. Finally, *constructing* the statistical table consists of entering the various items in columns under the appropriate headings. In Fig. 16.2 Table A is an example of 'sample' tabulation, and Tables B and C are examples of 'double' and 'treble' tabulation respectively, or complex tabulations.

3. *Presentation.* Although in certain cases the tabulation itself may present a sufficiently clear picture of the significance of the facts, it is often difficult to appreciate the relationships which may exist because of the mass of information displayed.

Table A

Type	General builders	C.E. and B.& C.E.	Specialist trades	Total
Firms	29,480	3,950	30,330	63,760

Table B

Type	General builders	C.E. and B. & C.E.	Specialist trades	Total
Firms	29,480	3,950	30,330	63,760
Operatives	328,000	406,000	278,000	1,012,000

Table C

Type	General builders		C.E. and B. & C.E.		Specialist trades		Total	
Size of firm	Firms	Th. Ops.	Firms	Th. Ops.	Firms	Th. Ops.	Firms	Th. Ups.
Number of operatives								
1 to 10	21,600	80	1,100	6	25,590	83	48,290	169
11 to 50	6,910	146	1,500	39	4,020	83	12,430	268
51 to 99	660	44	560	40	410	28	1,630	112
100 to 499	300	50	660	136	280	52	1,240	238
500 and over	10	8	130	185	30	32	170	225
Totals	29,480	328	3,950	406	30,330	278	63,760	1,012

(taken from *Statistics on Construction*, May 1960.)

Fig. 16.2. Structure of Contracting Industry, 1959

It therefore becomes necessary to illustrate the mathematical differences between items by the use of charts or drawings, so that the salient features are highlighted and so may be visualised by the reader without a detailed study of the figures. According to the particular problem the methods of portrayal are innumerable and the variations including colour, almost unlimited, but the following basic types have general applications.

a. *Pictorial* representation is a popular method often employed in government pamphlets and public advertisements because they require no training to understand, but they lack the precision necessary for more serious work:

   i. Picturegrams represent the various subjects by sketches and the comparison is made via the size of the unit. But if the ratios are intended to be shown by the heights, then difficulties may arise through confusion with the printed areas or volumetric impressions (see Fig. 16.3a).

ii. Ideographs depict the size of each item by comparing differing groups of pictorial units each of the same size (see Fig. 16.3b).

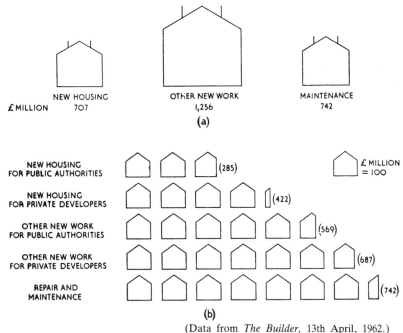

(Data from *The Builder*, 13th April, 1962.)

Fig. 16.3. Value of construction in Great Britain, 1961

iii. Maps may be marked or shaded to represent spatial distributions such as population densities.

b. *Diagrammatic* aids to presentation are particularly valuable in administration and commerce for they display the information, by means of geometrical constructions, in a manner which makes a quick but lasting impression. However, it is important to label any diagram so that details may be easily understood without reference back to the original data.

i. Pie charts or circle diagrams are convenient if the items in the class represent component parts of a whole. The circle is divided into segments so that the areas (or angles subtended at the centre) are proportional to the size of each category (see Fig. 16.4a).

ii. Compound bar diagrams are equally effective for showing the distribution of an aggregate into its parts upon a percentage basis (see Fig. 16.4b). Charts composed of several compound bars, arranged either vertically or horizontally, may also be used to display comparative analysis figures for various subjects or the same subject over a period of time.

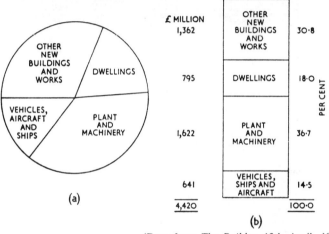

(Data from *The Builder*, 13th April, 1962.)

Fig. 16.4. Fixed capital investment, United Kingdom, 1961

iii. Bar charts are simple to interpret and most suitable when the items are only related by their possession of a common characteristic. Variations include lines, bars and blocks, either vertical or horizontal, and touching each other or spaced at equal intervals, or in a series of groups (see Fig. 16.5). Bars should invariably start from zero otherwise the optical effect will give a false impression. It should be remembered that it is the areas of the rectangular blocks which represent the relative ratios between the various classes, although it is usual to make the widths constant so that the heights are proportional to the areas and hence also to the ratios.

c. *Graphical* methods are used for the treatment of regular and continuous series of data, in order to show the amount

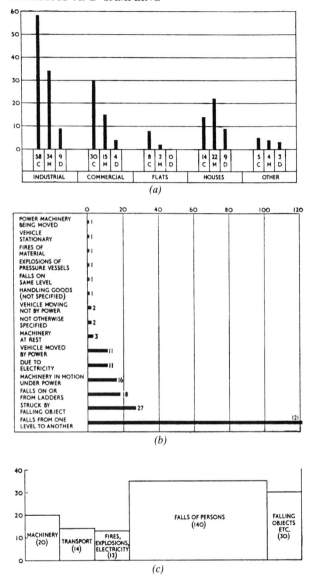

Fig. 16.5. Fatal accidents on building operations 1960

(a) Analysis by type of building and construction (C), maintenance (M) or demolition (D), (b) Analysis by cause, (c) Analysis by group cause

(Data from The National Builder, October, 1961.)

of change between succeeding observations. The rising or falling line connecting the individual points is called a 'continuous curve', and the 'line chart' itself is known as a 'graph'. Since graphs require two measurable variables, statistical classes cannot be shown by this means. Groups and time series, however, are more forcefully illustrated because, in addition to a presentation of the facts, new relationships such as 'trend' and 'correlation' may be suggested which are not apparent from a study of the figures themselves.

i. A simple graph such as Fig. 16.6 consists of two straight lines or axes at right-angles to one another, their intersection being the origin or zero point for both series of measurements. It is customary to mark the independent variable along the horizontal axis and the dependent along the vertical axis; in this example the crushing strength is dependent upon the water/cement ratio. The

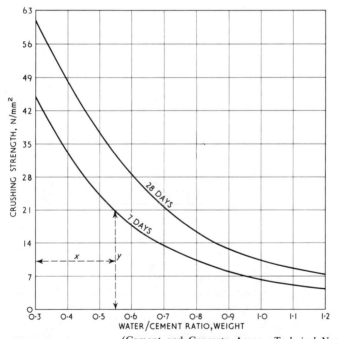

(Cement and Concrete Assoc., *Technical Notes.*)
Fig. 16.6. Relation between crushing strength and water/cement ratio for cubes of fully compacted concrete made with ordinary Portland cement

scales of measurement are chosen for convenience, and there is no necessary connection betwen the two. Rectangular co-ordinates are dimensioned towards the right and upwards for each observation as indicated by distances x and y, and the individual points so plotted are connected to complete the graph. Records such as this which pass from one value to another by immeasurably small gradations, form a 'continuous' series and should be drawn as a smooth curve. A 'discrete' series which rises in a series of jumps with a definite break between each value, should be represented by straight lines joining the locations plotted.

ii. A scatter diagram may be used to indicate the relationship existing between two separate characteristics of a subject. Fig. 16.7 records the respective weights and

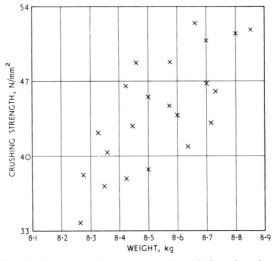

Fig. 16.7. Relation between crushing strength and weight for cubes of concrete tested at 28 days on one site

crushing strengths of a number of concrete test cubes, the crosses being placed to correspond with the two measurements of each cube. Thus the cross in the bottom left-hand corner represents a cube weighing 8.27kg and with a strength of 33.75 N/mm². The manner in which the marks tend to cluster along a line running approximately from the bottom left to the top right, clearly suggests that the heavier cubes are generally stronger, i.e. concrete stength is associated with relative density.

iii. A historigram is the particular graph of a statistical series where the one variable is time, i.e. the various measurements have been taken at intervals over a period of time. This is perhaps the commonest form of business chart with innumerable applications as a control instrument; Fig. 13.8 in the chapter on planning is an example. Two or more variables may be shown on the same graph, e.g. cost of money expended and value of work produced, using coloured or differently drawn lines. Alternatively a total such as cost may be divided into its components of labour, plant and material, in which case the three layered graph would be known as a 'band' or 'strata' chart.

iv. When the rate of change, or the relative movements, are of more interest than the actual movements, then the ratio scale may be used as an alternative to the natural scale on a graph. An absolute series may be converted into a ratio series by plotting the logarithms of the variables instead of the actual values, so that equal vertical distances represent equal propo.tionate movements. For example, the values for concrete crushing strength at 28 days can be scaled from Fig. 16.6, converted by logarithms, and replotted on Fig. 16.8, where the straight line graph shows that the rate of change is directly proportionate to the variation in water/cement ratio.

The ratio scale is also useful when a wide range of magnitudes is to be represented graphically. It would be difficult to show conveniently on a natural scale the 'Structure of the Construction Industry by size of Firms' as indicated in the distribution diagram Fig. 16.9.

4. *Identification.* It is important to quote the source of the statistics used to illustrate a relationship, and even more essential to give the date of their collection. Although the facts shown in Fig. 16.9 are for 1959, nevertheless they adequately illustrate the method of constructing a statistical table. If, however, your interest is in knowing the present-day structure of the contracting industry, then Fig. 16.9 is useless and must be replaced by Fig. 16.10 which gives comparable figures for 1981. The numbers of firms by occupation are

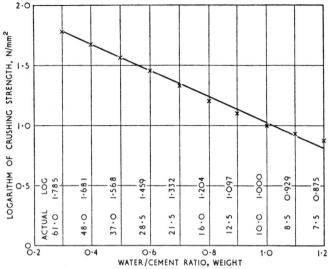

Fig. 16.8. Strength of concrete

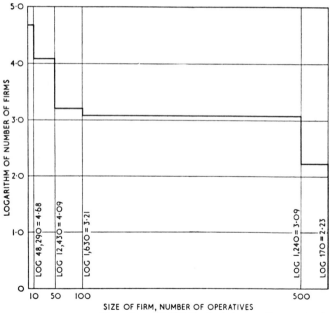

SIZE OF FIRM, NUMBER OF OPERATIVES

(Data from F.C.E.C. *Statistics on Construction.*)

Fig. 16.9. Structure by size of firm at April 1959

readily compared with Table A: General Builders 45 889; Civil Engineering and Building & Civil Engineering 5001; Specialist Trades 64 296; Total 115 186. Thus over 22 years the categories have increased by approximately 50%, 25% and 100% respectively. However, the number of firms by size group cannot be compared precisely, since the size groupings have been altered. A meaningful representation of the changes between 1959 and 1981 could, however, be shown by superimposing the latest figures upon the distribution diagram Fig. 16.9.

Table A. Number of firms by service

General builders	Building/civil engineering	Civil engineering contractors	Specialist trades	Total
45,889	2880	2121	64,296	115,186

Table B. Number of firms by size group

No. of operatives	No. of firms
1 to 7	95,308
8 to 13	9161
14 to 59	8892
60 to 114	944
115 to 599	760
600 and over	121
Total	115,186

(taken from *Housing and Construction Statistics*, 1971–1981, D.O.E. – H.M.S.O.)

Fig. 16.10. Structure of contracting industry 1981

Similarly, Fig. 16.3 fully illustrates the use of picturegrams and ideographs in pictorial representation. The fact that the actual figures are out-dated does not detract from their example. Every year new statistics will supersede those before, and to be useful must be looked up in the appropriate source.

Purely as a matter of interest, I give the comparable figures for 1980 in £ million at 1975 prices:

New housing, public	964
New housing, private	1351
Other new work, public	1906
Other new work, private	2629
Repairs and maintenance	4142
Total	10 992

The apparent increase in the proportion of repairs and maintenance is as much due to the fall in new work as the rise of R and M. These construction output figures for 1971 to 1980 are taken from *Building Technology and Management*, November 1981.

2. Frequency

The manner in which statistical data can be classified according to either measurable or descriptive characteristics, has been described earlier under the heading of tabulation. In addition however, statistical groups of quantitative variables can also be graded according to the relative frequency or number of times that successive values occur, and hence over chosen intervals the frequency distribution may be studied. For example, on the facing page is a table of test cube results for a series of samples taken over a period of 21 days on one site.

These data can be displayed as a simple graph of a discrete series, to demonstrate the variability of concrete strength on one site – Fig. 16.11. However, by an analysis of the frequency distribution (see Fig. 16.12), additional information may be learnt from the figures provided. Although not essential, all the group intervals should preferably be equal in width, and since the values have been taken to the nearest 0.05 N/mm^2 the divisions between grades have been arranged at 0.075 N/mm^2 to secure an even allocation. Cube reference numbers could have been 'arrayed' alongside each grade, but for simplicity the frequencies have been counted as described earlier under tabulation.

It is clear from this distribution table that the number of times each grade occurs increases with the strength until the most usual value is reached, after which the frequency of occurrences falls off again. This tendency can be illustrated graphically either by a 'histogram' (Fig. 16.13) or by a 'frequency polygon' (Fig. 16.14). A

Cube Crushing Strength at 28 days in N/mm²

1	23·80	27	32·90	54	35·00	81	34·65		
2	28·00	28	31·85	55	34·30	82	25·20		
3	25·20	29	26·60	56	23·80	83	26·25		
4	20·30	30	27·65	57	23·80	84	32·90		
5	32·20	31	32·20	58	20·65	85	34·65		
6	23·80	32	34·30	59	25·20	86	29·05		
7	26·95	33	21·35	60	18·20	87	30·10		
8	21·00	34	27·30	61	18·90	88	32·90		
9	26·95	35	19·60	62	23·80	89	40·25		
10	28·00	36	26·60	63	32·55	90	32·90		
11	28·70	37	27·65	64	33·25	91	28·70		
12	28·70	38	26·95	65	32·55	92	44·10		
13	24·85	39	22·40	66	28·00	93	39·55		
14	36·75	40	27·30	67	28·70	94	24·50		
15	41·65	41	38·50	68	31·15	95	20·65		
16	36·40	42	29·40	69	25·20	96	34·65		
17	36·40	43	29·75	70	26·95	97	21·00		
18	39·90	44	29·40	71	17·50	98	16·80		
19	37·80	45	16·45	72	28·35	99	28·35		
20	39·20	46	24·15	73	22·05	100	31·15		
21	36·40	47	25·55	74	31·85	101	29·40		
22	32·90	48	32·20	75	28·00	102	21·35		
23	26·60	49	28·00	76	19·95	103	26·25		
24	29·40	50	24·15	77	30·45	104	24·50		
25	32·20	51	23·45	78	30·80	105	20·65		
26	26·95	52	31·85	79	24·50	106	30·45		
		53	27·65	80	26·25				

(Data scaled from *Building Research Station Digest* 13 (second series).)

histogram, like the block diagram, represents values by proportional area, and must not be confused with the historigram which portrays a time series. The polygon is more suitable for comparative purposes, since two or more may be plotted on the same chart where the lines will be more likely to cross than to overlap.

1. *Distributions.* In theory, provided that the data are alike in relevant aspects, it is assumed that a particular distribution represents a sample taken at random from an indefinitely large 'population' which obeys a regular law, and therefore that any fluctuations are due to the smallness of the sample, which tends to exaggerate the effects of abnormal items. With an indefinitely large number of observations and extremely small intervals, a regular histogram will consequently merge into a smooth 'frequency curve'. A histogram showing regular tendencies may upon this justification be 'smoothed' by drawing a regular curve through the rectangles in such a way that the total area of the final figure is exactly equal to the total area of the original diagram. Smoothing is demonstrated

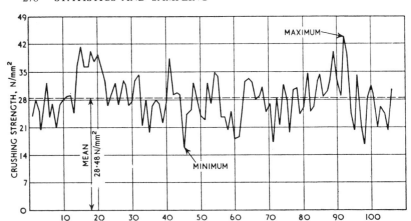

Fig. 16.11. Graph showing variability of concrete strength on one site

FREQUENCY DISTRIBUTION OF CUBE CRUSHING STRENGTHS		
Strength N/mm²	Frequency Array	Total
14·000 to 17·475	11	2
17·500 to 20·975	卌 1111	9
21·000 to 24·475	卌 卌 1111	14
24·500 to 27·975	卌 卌 卌 卌 卌	25
28·000 to 31·475	卌 卌 卌 卌 11	22
31·500 to 34·975	卌 卌 卌 卌 1	21
35·000 to 38·475	卌 1	6
38·500 to 41·975	卌 1	6
42·000 to 45·475	1	1
		106

Fig. 16.12.

by the dotted line on Fig. 16.13 where it should be noted that the peak of the curve rises above the peak of the histogram. Frequency curves are valuable since they enable the properties of distributions to be examined, described and compared in a general way. Although frequency distributions may take many different forms, it is often possible to visualise an underlying approximation to one of the more usual distinctive types of curves.

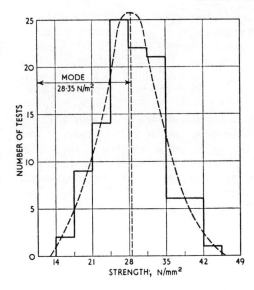

Fig. 16.13. Histogram

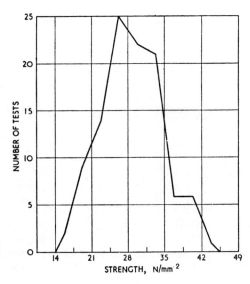

Fig. 16.14. Frequency polygon

  a. Symmetrical or *bell-shaped* curves are usual for measurements of natural phenomena or events involving chance, and this form is therefore known as the normal frequency curve or the probability curve. If a sufficiently large number of common building bricks conforming to B.S. 657 were sampled and measured, then the hypothetical frequency curve might be as shown in Fig. 16.15. The probability that the length of one random sample will be between 5232 mm and 5245 mm will be proportional to the frequency with which these lengths occur, and is the ratio of the shaded area to the total area beneath the limiting curve, i.e. 1 in 6.

  b. Unsymmetrical or *skewed* curves often represent economic or social observations, as for example Fig. 16.16. This illustrates the average rate of replacement required to

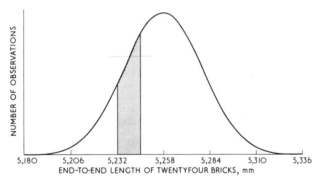

Fig. 16.15. Bell-shaped frequency curve

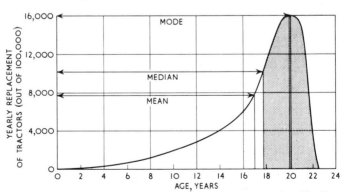

(From "The Cost and Economics of Contractors' Plant," *The National Builder*, Dec. 1959.)

Fig. 16.16. Skewed frequency curve

maintain a contractor's fleet of tractors at full strength as estimated from a survey made by the Building Research Station in 1954.

c. A *J-shaped* curve indicates a distribution with a high degree of asymmetry, being highest near the origin, falling rapidly and then more slowly. An unusual but distinctive curve with a minimum value in the centre and maximum values at either end, is known as a *U-shaped* frequency curve. These two forms of distribution are shown on Fig. 16.17, the former being an analysis of the successful candidates in the Institute of Builders Final Part II examination held in 1961.

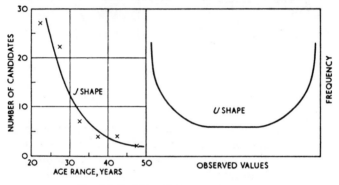

Fig. 16.17. Unusual frequency curves

d. When it is desired to read off the number of observations which are 'more than' or 'less than' a stated value, then a cumulative frequency curve or *ogive* is useful. For example, from Fig. 16.12, by adding each frequency to the total of the previous ones we can obtain the following cumulative totals: 2, 11, 25, 50, 72, 93, 99, 105 and 106, which may then be plotted as in Fig. 16.18.

Two or more frequency curves, either simple or cumulative, may be plotted on the same chart in order to compare frequency distributions, but it is then more effective to reduce the frequencies to a percentage or per mille basis.

2. *Averages.* Although the salient features of statistical data can be represented first by tables, and then more graphically by means of diagrams, the next stage is to formulate a numerical expression which both describes the whole group of figures and provides a quantitative basis for comparison with other groups. The size of the representative item of a group is

indicated by the average, a single figure which summarises the overall characteristics of the whole group. Three different kinds of average are in common use, the choice being dependent upon the particular data and the purpose to be served.

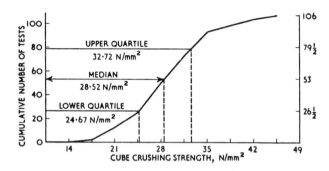

Fig. 16.18. Cumulative frequency curve

a. The arithmetic average or *mean* is the sum of the values of all the items concerned, divided by their total number. Thus from the table on page 277 the mean crushing strength is simple to calculate as 28.48 N/mm² and this is shown as a dotted line upon Fig. 16.11. Since all these values are large, heavy work can be avoided by first subtracting a constant amount, e.g. 15.00, from each of them. The mean of the modified values is then found and the constant of 15.00 added on again. The arithmetic mean is the most usual kind of average, being easy to calculate, but is unduly affected by extremes so that it may be misleading in such circumstances.

b. The most frequent value is known as the *mode,* that is the most fashionable item in the series. Being the most common value, the mode corresponds to the highest point of the frequency curve, and can be located easily on a smoothed histogram (see Fig. 16.13). In the case of a discontinuous variable the mode, unlike the mean, does represent an actual item. The mode is also unaffected by abnormal items, but precise calculation is complicated and it may therefore be difficult to locate exactly. For example, an examination of the distribution table in Fig. 16.12 indicates that the mode is somewhere among the two groups, 24.500 to 27.975, and 28.000 to 31.475. By making the intervals smaller over this area the following table is produced:

24.500/26.225–9; 26.250/27.975–16;
28.000/29.725–15; 29.750/31.475–7.

Consideration of this distribution suggests that the mode lies around the value of 28.000, but any further reduction of the intervals will also make the frequencies smaller and the distribution irregular.

c. The size of the middle item is known as the *median*; this value is such that half the observations are greater than, and half the observations are smaller than the normal. When the number of items is even, it is usual to take the average of the two middle terms. In the case of a continuous frequency distribution the median must be estimated by interpolation from the cumulative figures, and for grouped distributions particularly, the ogive curve is most useful. Reference to Fig. 16.18 shows the position of the median and its approximate value of 28.52 N/mm^2. Again, the median eliminates the effect of extreme values but it cannot be located precisely when the items are grouped.

d. For purposes of comparison the three usual types of average are shown upon Fig. 16.16, and the following geometrical interpretations of these measurements illustrate their different natures. The vertical line at the median value divides the area under the frequency curve into halves. The vertical line at the mode point passes through the peak of the curve, while the vertical line at the mean passes through the centre of gravity of the enclosed figure.

3. *Dispersion.* Another quantitative description of a statistical group is provided by the dispersion, which measures the extent to which the various items within the group vary in size. Mean, mode or median, is a typical representative of the group, but for a more complete description it is also important to measure the variability of the individual members, both between each other and about the average value. If the test cube results depicted in Fig. 16.11 were from concrete specified to be 21.00 N/mm^2, then the mean of 28.48 N/mm^2 would appear to be eminently satisfactory until the minimum strength of 16.45 N/mm^2 prompts further consideration.

a. The simplest measure of dispersion is the difference between the values of the largest and the smallest items, known as the *range*. From Fig. 16.11 the minimum of 16.45 and the maximum of 44.10 gives a range of 27.65 N/mm² but this information does not materially assist the examination of quality since it is entirely dependent upon extreme observations.

b. Another measure of the range of dispersion is the *quartile deviation,* i.e. half the distance or difference between the upper and lower quartiles. Whereas the median divides the group into two equal parts, the quartiles subdivide the distribution into four quarters. The lower quartile is one-quarter the way along, and the upper quartile is three-quarters along the distribution as illustrated on Fig. 16.18, where the quartile deviation equals ½ (32.72–24.67) or 4.025 N/mm². This measure is undisturbed by abnormal items, and is a significant value since the interquartile range itself contains half of the group population.

c. When important items lie beyond the quartiles or it is desirable to know the variation of all the items, then the *mean deviation* may be determined. This is the sum of all the deviations of the group, taken as positive from either the mean, mode or median, divided by their number. From the frequency distribution in Fig. 16.12 and the median of 28.52 N/mm² scaled from Fig. 16.18, the mean deviation of

Mean Deviation of Cube Crushing Strengths

Strength N/mm^2	Number of cubes	Av. deviation from median	No. × deviation
14·0 to 17·5	2	12·77	25·54
17·5 to 21·0	9	9·27	83·43
21·0 to 24·5	14	5·77	80·78
24·5 to 28·0	25	2·27	56·75
28·0 to 31·5	22 { 3·3	0·26	0·858
	18·7	1·49	27·863
31·5 to 35·0	21	4·73	99·33
35·0 to 38·5	6	8·23	49·38
38·5 to 42·0	6	11·73	70·38
42·0 to 45·5	1	15·23	15·23
	106		509·541

Mean deviation = 4·807 N/mm²

Fig. 16.19

the concrete crushing strengths can be calculated as follows in Fig. 16.19. The grouped strengths have been amended to give continuity, and the deviations have been taken from the centre of each group. Since, however, the group 28.0 to 31.5 contains the median it would be erroneous to assume its whole frequency concentrated at the midpoint and they have been approximated in the ratio of 52 : 298 below/above the median. These average deviations are consequently $\frac{1}{2} \times 52$ and $\frac{1}{2} \times 298$ respectively.

Alternatively, by taking the calculated mean of 28.48 N/mm^2 and the original data on page 277 the mean deviation may be arrived at by another way. The 49 values above the mean total 1636.95, and the 57 values below the mean total 1381.80. Hence the mean deviation

$$= \frac{1}{106} \left[(1636.95 - 49 \times 28.48) + (57 \times 28.48 - 1381.80) \right]$$

$$= \frac{1}{106} \left[(1636.95 - 1395.52) + (1623.36 - 1381.80) \right]$$

$$= \frac{1}{106} (241.43 + 241.56) = \frac{482.99}{106} = 4.556 \ \text{N/mm}^2$$

d. In order to emphasise the larger deviations by weighting them more heavily than the smaller ones, the *standard deviation* is the one most commonly used, particularly in sampling. For this purpose the sum of the squares of the individual deviations, usually from the arithmetic mean, is divided by their number, and the square root of the result taken. Thus the standard deviation for the concrete cube results in the previous example can be tabled as Fig. 16.20 below.

The calculated mean of 28.48 N/mm^2 has been used, and the central group assumed to be disposed in the ratio of 48 : 302 below/above the mean. It will be noticed that the root-mean-square or standard deviation is larger than the others, and since the distribution is fairly symmetrical the relationships are approximately:

  i. Quartile deviation = $\frac{2}{3}$ standard deviation.

  ii. Mean deviation (from mean) = $\frac{4}{5}$ standard deviation.

e. When the two groups to be compared differ greatly in average size, then a relative measure or *coefficient of dispersion* is better, found by dividing the measure by its

Standard Deviation of Cube Crushing Strengths

Strength (N/mm²)	Number	Av. deviation	Deviation ²	No. X deviation²
14·0				
17·5	2	12·73	162·053	324·106
21·0	9	9·23	85·193	766·737
24·5	14	5·73	32·833	459·662
28·0	25	2·23	4·973	124·325
31·5	22 { 3 19	0·24 1·51	0·058 2·280	0·174 43·320
35·0	21	4·77	22·753	477·813
38·5	6	8·27	68·393	410·358
42·0	6	11·77	138·533	831·198
45·5	1	15·27	233·173	233·173
	106			3670·866
				$\sqrt{34 \cdot 6308}$

Standard deviation = 5.885 N/mm²

Fig. 16.20

appropriate central value. In particular, the quantity standard deviation ÷ arithmetic mean when expressed as a fraction of 100 is known as the *coefficient of variation*. In the previous example the C.V.

$$\frac{5.885}{28.48} \times 100 = 20.6\%.$$

An excellent example of the practical application of mean, standard deviation, and coefficient of variation to the problem of quality control, is given in *The Construction of a Hard Runway at the Coventry Aerodrome in Soil-Cement* by H. D. Bannister (Paper No. 6560. Institution of Civil Engineers).

4. *Skewness.* A third factor in assessing the properties of a statistical group is the tendency to depart from symmetry, i.e. its lopsidedness or skewness. Figure 16.15 is perfectly symmetrical and hence the mean, mode and median coincide; Fig. 16.13 is slightly skewed, Fig. 16.16 is moderately skewed and Fig. 16.17 ('J'-shaped) is highly skewed. Skewness, like dispersion, may be measured in either absolute or relative terms.

 a. The *standard method* makes use of the effect of skewness to separate mean and median from the mode, by defining skewness as the difference between mean and mode. Thus, when the mean and the 'tail' of the distribution is to the right of the mode, then the skew is said to be positive; conversely when the mean and the tail is to the left of the mode, the skew is negative. For example, Fig. 16.16 is negatively skewed and Fig. 16.17 ('J'-shaped) is positively skewed. In Fig. 16.13, skew = 28.48–28.35 = + 0.13 N/mm^2. The *first coefficient* is defined as: mean minus mode, divided by the standard (or mean) deviation.

b. Another entirely different method, known as the *quartile measure,* depends upon the fact that in a skewed distribution the median is not exactly half-way between the two quartiles, and expresses skewness as the sum of the quartiles minus twice the median. In Fig. 16.18,

Skew = (32.72 + 24.67) − 2(28.52) = 57.39 − 57.04
     = + 0.35 N/mm^2

The *second coefficient* is obtained by dividing the quartile measure by the quartile deviation.

3. Time Series

Statistical methods may be used to analyse either a group of data which describes a static state of affairs existing at a particular moment, or a series of successive observations which measures the changing phenomena over a period. In both cases it may be necessary to measure the various aspects of frequency distribution, but in addition, the introduction of time calls for consideration of the peculiar changes taking place between those items which have gone before, and those which follow.

1. *Accumulative variation.* For control purposes the 'Z' chart, so-called on account of its characteristic shape, is most useful

Monthly Turnover (£1,000)

Month	Jan	Feb	Mar	Apr	May	Jun	Jul	Aug	Sep	Oct	Nov	Dec
1970	40	30	40	45	55	60	65	60	45	50	45	40
Cum.	40	70	110	155	210	270	335	395	440	490	535	575
1970	50	45	40	45	60	65	60	70	60	55	45	35
Cum.	50	95	135	180	240	305	365	435	495	550	595	630
Diff.	+10	+15	0	0	+5	+5	−5	+10	+15	+5	0	−5
Total	585	600	600	600	605	610	605	615	630	635	635	630

Fig. 16.21

for recording financial or sales data, etc. It records three vital statistics – the result of the current period, the cumulative total for the year to date, and the moving total showing the result of the previous 12 months. The moving annual total (M.A.T.) for the current month = M.A.T. for previous month + difference between the current month and the corresponding month of the previous year. Assuming that the values tabulated in Fig. 16.21 are a builder's record of his total monthly valuations or turnover, then the chart shown in Fig. 16.22 can be drawn from the results. If desired, the graph of the current period may be magnified by making its scale, say, five times that of the cumulative. The advantage of the cumulative curve is that it smoothes out abnormal fluctuations, and by comparison with the previous year makes possible a forecast for this year's result. Similarly the M.A.T. curve eliminates seasonal variations, and also indicates the trend of events.

2. *Secular variation.* The path that would be taken by the curve of a time series in the absence of disturbing factors, is known as the trend or secular variation. In practice, the general tendency of an economic series is usually obscured by any or all of the following movements:
   i.   seasonal variations associated with the weather, or other annual phenomena.
   ii. cyclical variations corresponding with the fluctuations of the trade cycle, which is supposed to operate every 7 to 10 years.
   iii. special variations caused by unusual or occasional events.
   Figure 16.23 gives the annual rates for softwood consumption, and from these statistics the graph in Fig. 16.24 has been constructed to show these various elements.

An examination of the bar chart depicting the quarterly figures discloses the obvious seasonal movement, with high activity in the July to September periods and a slack time in the winter months. The catastrophic effect of the World War is also noticeable after the 1939 to 1946 recess.

In order to detect clearly the general trend of a series it becomes necessary to eliminate the secondary variations. Monthly or quarterly fluctuations are easily eradicated by taking annual averages as can be seen from the graph. Cyclical variations can be removed by the method of moving averages as employed for the 'Z' chart. The period of the cycle must be estimated from the historigram, but may be

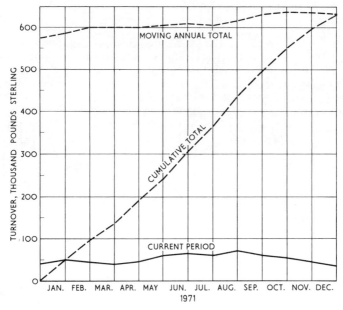

Fig. 16.22. 'Z' chart

Annual Rates of Softwood Consumption (Thousand Standards) (4672m³)

Year	1919	1920	1921	1922	1923	1924	1925	1926	1927
Rate	1384	1307	695	1328	1547	1709	1683	1629	2034

Year	1928	1929	1930	1931	1932	1933	1934	1935	1936
Rate	1574	1771	1658	1471	1454	1930	2190	1972	2371

Year	1937	1938	1939						
Rate	2392	1778	1561						

Year	1946	1947	1948	1949	1950	1951	1952	1953	1954
Rate	1082	979	1111	1150	1030	1142	1093	1300	1537

Year	1955	1956	1957	1958	1959	1960	1961		
Rate	1598	1506	1505	1412	1591	1686	1725		

| Year | 1960 | 1960 | 1960 | 1960 | 1961 | 1961 | 1961 | 1961 | 1962 |
Qtr	1st	2nd	3rd	4th	1st	2nd	3rd	4th	1st
Rate	1510	1732	1860	1634	1695	1738	1817	1651	1429

(Data from *The Times Review of Industry* (London & Cambridge Bulletin).)

Fig. 16.23

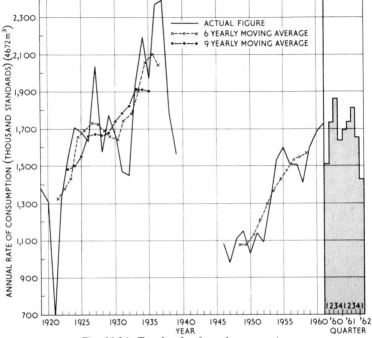

Fig. 16.24. Trends of softwood consumption

increased if the first attempt does not produce a sufficiently smooth curve. Moving averages are calculated from the original data as demonstrated in Fig. 16.25 based upon a 6-year cycle which produces a satisfactory trend curve for the post-war years. It will be noticed that since this is an even-numbered cycle the average is located between the third and fourth years.

However, for the prewar years there are still signs of a cyclic variation, so that a new moving average based upon a 9-year cycle has been calculated in Fig. 16.26, which is better but still not perfect and perhaps an 11-year cycle might be more even. With this odd-numbered cycle the average is positioned in the fifth year.

3. *Relative variation.* When it is necessary to show the movements of several related items, it is very convenient to use *index numbers* or combined percentages in order to sum up the constituent variations in a single expression. An index number is a device for estimating relative movements over a

Annual Rates of Softwood Consumption (Thousand Standards) (4672m³)

	1919	1920	1921	1922	1923	1924	1925	1926	
Year	1919	1920	1921	1922	1923	1924	1925	1926	
Rate	1384	1307	695	1328	1547	1709	1683	1629	
Diff.							+299	+322	
6 yr Cum.	1384	2691	3386	4714	6261	7970	8269	8591	
Av.				1328	1378	1432	1655	1696	1733

	1927	1928	1929	1930	1931	1932	1933	1934
Year	1927	1928	1929	1930	1931	1932	1933	1934
Rate	2034	1574	1771	1658	1471	1454	1930	2190
Diff.	+1339	+246	+224	−51	−212	−175	−104	+616
6 yr Cum.	9930	10,176	10,400	10,349	10,137	9962	9858	10,474
Av.	1725	1689	1660	1643	1746	1779	1898	2051

	1935	1936	1937	1938	1939
Year	1935	1936	1937	1938	1939
Rate	1972	2371	2392	1778	1561
Diff.	+201	+713	+921	+324	−369
6 yr Cum.	10,675	11,388	12,309	12,633	12,264
Av.	2105	2044			

	1946	1947	1948	1949	1950	1951	1952	1953
Year	1946	1947	1948	1949	1950	1951	1952	1953
Rate	1082	979	1111	1150	1030	1142	1093	1300
Diff.							+11	+321
6 yr Cum.	1082	2061	3172	4322	5352	6494	6505	6826
Av.			1082	1084	1138	1209	1283	1363

	1954	1955	1956	1957	1958	1959	1960	1961
Year	1954	1955	1956	1957	1958	1959	1960	1961
Rate	1537	1598	1506	1505	1412	1591	1686	1725
Diff.	+426	+448	+476	+363	+319	+219	+149	+127
6 yr Cum.	7252	7700	8176	8539	8858	9149	9298	9425
Av.	1423	1476	1525	1550	1571			

Fig. 16.25

period of time, in cases where direct measurement of the actual items is impracticable, e.g. business prosperity; or when the direct comparison of items is inconvenient due to the unstable composition of the variates, e.g. 'the cost of living'. This method of standardisation by means of arbitrary averages is widely used for the study of economic activity. The construction of an index number depends upon the following considerations.

a. *Relatives* are the ratios between the values of succeeding years and that of a standard year, expressed as a percentage of the latter. A relative series is formed by multiplying the corresponding absolute series by a constant factor, as illustrated in Fig. 16.27.

292 STATISTICS AND SAMPLING

Annual Rates of Softwood Consumption (Thousand Standards) (4672m³)

Year	1919	1920	1921	1922	1923	1924	1925	1926
Rate	1,384	1,307	695	1,328	1,547	1,709	1,683	1,629
Diff.								
9 yr Cum.	1,384	2,691	3,386	4,714	6,261	7,970	9,653	11,282
Av.					1,480	1,501	1,552	1,659

Year	1927	1928	1929	1930	1931	1932	1933	1934
Rate	2,034	1,574	1,771	1,658	1,471	1,454	1,930	2,190
Diff.		+190	+464	+963	+143	−93	+221	+507
9 yr Cum.	13,316	13,506	13,970	14,933	15,076	14,983	15,204	15,711
Av.	1,675	1,665	1,678	1,746	1,784	1,821	1,912	1,913

Year	1935	1936	1937	1938	1939
Rate	1,972	2,371	2,392	1,778	1,561
Diff.	+343	+337	+818	+7	−97
9 yr Cum.	16,054	16,391	17,209	17,216	17,119
Av.	1,902				

Fig. 16.26

Weekly Earnings of Operatives

Year at October	Actual earnings		Index of earnings	
	Building	Civil engineering	Building	Civil engineering
	s d	s d	(Relatives)	
1948	128 4	139 10	100	100
1949	134 9	147 6	105	105
1950	141 8	159 3	110	114
1951	157 5	176 3	123	126
1952	170 10	191 2	133	137
1953	180 6	197 9	141	141
1954	193 8	220 8	151	158
1955	210 10	235 7	164	168
1956	229 3	257 5	179	184
1957	233 11	270 1	182	193
1958	241 4	281 11	188	202
1959	251 9	289 4	196	207

(Data from F.C.E.C. *Statistics on Construction*.)

Fig. 16.27

b. The *base* is the figure used for comparisons, and the standard year is known as the base year – 100 and 1948 respectively in the previous example. In this instance 1948 has been chosen as a fixed base and adhered to for an indefinite period. However, it may be that because of changed conditions new items should be introduced or old

STATISTICS AND SAMPLING   293

ones deleted, or that comparisons with the immediate past are more important than those with a distant period, for which reasons the chain base method might be used. The values are calculated using each preceding year as base, and the results chained together as shown in Fig. 16.28.

Hourly (London) Rates for Craftsmen

Year at February	s	d	Fixed base		Chain base	
1954	3	9		100		100
1955	3	11	47 × 100/45	104	47 × 100/45	104
1956	4	2½	50½× 100/45	112	50½× 100/47	108
1957	4	6	54 × 100/45	120	54 × 100/50½	107
1958	4	8½	56½× 100/45	126	56½× 100/54	105
1959	4	10½	58½× 100/45	130	58½× 100/56½	104

(Data from *The Builder* "Cost of Building.")

Fig. 16.28

c. The *items* selected must be representative of the field of inquiry, easily identifiable and clearly described as to quality or grade. For this reason raw materials are more widely used than manufactured articles, and hence index numbers usually relate to producers rather than consumers, or to the less sophisticated groups of the community. For example, an index of the cost of construction work might include basic wage rates for craftsmen and labourers, together with indices of the main materials such as bricks, concrete aggregates, cement and mild steel reinforcement.

d. A *weighting* system is usually required in order to differentiate between the relative importance of constituent elements either by volume or value. Weights are decided arbitrarily, as far as possible in convenient numbers since it is not necessary to seek a high degree of accuracy in this respect. A typical weighting is shown in Fig. 16.29, but it should be noted that the total weight has been adjusted (for net interest paid).

e. The *average* employed is either the arithmetic mean or the geometric mean, depending upon the information required. The former is simpler but tends to exaggerate the effect of increases and extreme items, and for these reasons the geometric mean is often used, particularly if the number of items is small. Both forms of average are calculated in Fig. 16.30 below, from the data tabled in Fig. 16.29, although neither result is exactly the same as the official index because of the adjustment mentioned previously.

Real National Product

	Weights	1958	1959	1960	1961
Agriculture	44	100	103	112	117
Industrial production	476	100	105	112	114
Transport	80	100	104	100	110
Distribution	126	100	105	110	112
Other services	300	100	104	107	109
Total	1,000	100	104·5	109·8	111·5

(Data from *The Times Review of Industry* (London & Cambridge Bulletin).)

Fig. 16.29

Real National Product 1961

$$117 \times 44 = 5,148$$
$$114 \times 476 = 54,264$$
$$110 \times 80 = 8,800$$
$$112 \times 126 = 14,112$$
$$109 \times 300 = 32,700$$

1,026   115,024

112·10 **Arithmetic Mean**

$$\log. 117^{44} = 2·06819 \times 44 = 91·00036$$
$$\log. 114^{476} = 2·05690 \times 476 = 980·08440$$
$$\log. 110^{80} = 2·04139 \times 80 = 163·31120$$
$$\log. 112^{126} = 2·04922 \times 126 = 258·20172$$
$$\log. 109^{300} = 2·03743 \times 300 = 611·22900$$

1,026   2,103·82668

2·05051

ant. 2·05051 = 112·33 **Geometric Mean**

Fig. 16.30

4. Sampling

A complete investigation of a statistical problem would be expensive both of time and money, so that it is usual to study only a proportion of the subject matter and then apply the results to the whole field of enquiry. Statistical induction, i.e. the inferring of general law from particular instances, is governed by two general laws.

   a. The law of statistical regularity asserts that a small group (sample) of items chosen at random from a larger group (population) will tend to possess the same characteristics as the larger group.

   b. The law of inertia of large numbers states that the movements of the separate parts of an aggregate will tend to compensate one another, and that consequently larger aggregates are relatively more stable than smaller ones.

However, it is essential that the sample shall be

i   chosen at random,

ii. sufficiently representative, and

iii. sufficiently large a proportion of the whole.

Every item in the population must have an equal chance of inclusion, and the safest method of securing a perfect random selection is to draw lots or use Tables of Random Numbers. Devices to ensure a sample contains examples of all the types in the whole group may be found in many British Standards, e.g. B.S. 882 for Concrete Aggregates. Since the compensating effect will be more complete in a larger sample, it follows that the required size will 'depend in some way upon the accuracy demanded.

1. *Errors.* Despite every precaution it is unlikely that any sample will be perfectly representative, and due to chance or human bias slight variations must emerge, which raise questions concerning the reliability of the results obtained. The likelihood and magnitude of such fluctuations of sampling can be estimated by means of the mathematical theory of probability. The expectation that an event will (or will not) happen, can be expressed as a proportion of the total alternatives that are possible. If a coin is spun, the chance of a head turning up is 1 in 2; the possibility of a thrown dice showing six, is 1 in 6; and the probability of a telephone number, chosen at random from the directory, ending in nought is 1 in 10. When these experiments are tried, say twenty times as a sample, then the results may not be precisely in the expected proportions of 1/2; 1/6; or 1/10. However, if the samples are repeated a sufficient number of times, and the results recorded as frequency distributions, then the averages will tend towards the anticipated proportions of (0.5 : 0.5); (0.167 : 0.833) and (0.1 : 0.9). Provided that the results are determined solely by

chance (or luck), then the frequency distributions will approximate to the normal frequency curve considered earlier (see Fig. 16.15). Also known as the probability (or Gaussian) curve, the series follows the law of the binomial theorem and is given by the expansion of $(q + p)^n$, where n is the number in the sample and p and q are the odds whose sum is unity,

e.g. $(0.9 + 0.1)^{20} = (0.9)^{20} + \dfrac{20}{1}(0.9)^{19}(0.1) + \dfrac{20 \times 19}{1 \times 2}(0.9)^{18}(0.1)^2$

+ etc. These terms of the binomial series $1{,}000\,(q + p)^{20}$ are tabled in Fig. 16.31, for both the coin and the telephone number, and the resulting curves are shown in Fig. 16.32. In both distributions the mean is given by pn, and the standard deviation by $\sqrt{pqn}$. Now since the means of random samples from a normal population are normally distributed with standard error, then the *number* of successes that may be expected in a random sample of n can be equated as $pn \pm \sqrt{pqn}$, and dividing through by n gives the expected

proportion of successes as $p \pm \sqrt{\dfrac{pq}{n}}.$

Thus for a qualitative variate, i.e. one whose characteristic is not measurable, the proportion of the population possessing that characteristic can be determined from a random sample

within an error of $\pm \sqrt{\dfrac{pq}{n}}.$

The standard error of a quantitative variate, i.e. one whose characteristic is measurable, can be shown to be equal to the standard deviation divided by the square root of the sample size. Therefore the arithmetic mean of the population can be estimated from a random sample within an error of

$\pm \dfrac{Std.\ Devn}{n}.$

Any normal frequency curve is uniquely determined by its arithmetic mean and standard deviation as illustrated in Fig. 16.33. These limits can be used to calculate the reliability of an answer computed from a sample, when it is grossed up to apply to the total population. There is one chance in three that the estimate will differ from the truth by as much as one standard deviation, one chance in twenty-two that it will differ

Samples of Twenty, Repeated One Thousand Times

A coin turning up "heads"			A 'phone number ending with "0"		
Successes	Frequency	Totals	Successes	Frequency	Totals
0	—	—	0	122	—
1	—	—	1	270	270
2	—	—	2	285	570
3	1	3	3	190	570
4	5	20	4	90	360
5	15	75	5	32	160
6	37	222	6	9	54
7	74	518	7	2	14
8	120	960	8	—	—
9	160	1,440	9	—	—
10	176	1,760	10	—	—
11	160	1,760	11	—	—
12	120	1,440	12	—	—
13	74	962	13	—	—
14	37	518	14	—	—
15	15	225	15	—	—
16	5	80	16	—	—
17	1	17	17	—	—
18	—	—	18	—	—
19	—	—	19	—	—
20	—	—	20	—	—
Mean = 10	1,000 Times	10,000 Heads	**Mean = 2**	1,000 Times	1,998 "O"

Heads		Av. deviation		Products	Noughts		Av. deviation		Products $d^2 \times F$
No.	Freqy.	d	d^2	$d^2 \times F$	No.	Freqy.	d	d^2	
3	1	−7	49	49	0	122	−2	4	488
4	5	−6	36	180	1	270	−1	1	270
5	15	−5	25	375	2	285	0	0	0
6	37	−4	16	592	3	190	+1	1	190
7	74	−3	9	666	4	90	+2	4	360
8	120	−2	4	480	5	32	+3	9	288
9	160	−1	1	160	6	9	+4	16	144
10	176	0	0	0	7	2	+5	25	50
11	160	+1	1	160					
12	120	+2	4	480					
13	74	+3	9	666					
14	37	+4	16	592					
15	15	+5	25	375					
16	5	+6	36	180					
17	1	+7	49	49					
	1,000			5,004		1,000			1,790
Std. deviation = 2·24				$\sqrt{5\cdot004}$	**Std. deviation = 1·33**				$\sqrt{1\cdot790}$

Fig. 16.31

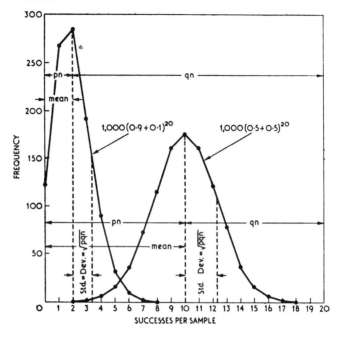

Fig. 16.32. Probability curves for coin and phone number experiments

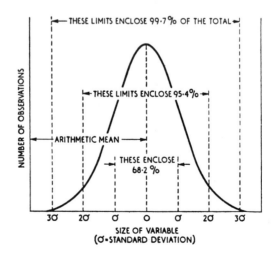

Fig. 16.33. Normal frequency curve

by twice the standard deviation, and only three chances in a thousand that it will differ by three times the standard deviation.

2. *Quality control.* Statistical sampling forms the background to both activity sampling, which is described more particularly in the chapter on work study, and to industrial quality control which aims at monitoring production processes in order to detect faulty operations or components in time for remedial action to be taken. Individual testing would be impracticable and unnecessary, but inspection by sample with statistical controls ensures that the proportion of defectives produced does not exceed a predetermined and acceptable limit. If a production process is stable, i.e. running satisfactorily, then the statistical characteristics of samples taken at intervals will be distributed within the limits of the normal frequency curve as indicated on Fig. 16.33. By measuring the grand mean and the mean range of a series of equal sized samples, taken over an initial trial period when work is proceeding smoothly, control charts are prepared upon which future results can be plotted so that any tendency to 'get out of control' will be recognised immediately.

Use is made of the fact that the ratio of standard deviation to sample range is the same for all normal distributions, dependent only on the sample size n. The typical curves illustrated in Fig. 16.34 indicate the different ranges, and since the standard deviation varies as the square root of the sample size (see Fig. 16.32), the approximate values of the ratios can also be seen. To avoid the inconvenience of

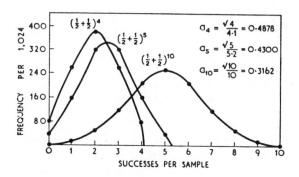

Fig. 16.34. Relationship between range and sample size

working from first principles, tables of constants are used for obtaining the various control limits which may vary with the degree of control necessary. A table of constants for the conventional limits of 1/1,000 for mean, and 5/1,000 for range is given in Fig. 16.35 below.

Statistical Quality Control Constants

No. in sample	Standard deviation ÷ range$_n$	Mean (99·9%)	Range (99·5%)	Tolerance (Range)	Tolerance (Mean)
2	0·8862	1·94	3·52	0·18	0·80
3	0·5908	1·05	2·58	0·27	0·77
4	0·4857	0·75	2·26	0·33	0·75
5	0·4299	0·59	2·08	0·37	0·73
6	0·3946	0·50	1·97	0·41	0·72
7	0·3698	0·43	1·90	0·44	0·71
8	0·3512	0·38	1·84	0·46	0·70
9	0·3367	0·35	1·79	0·48	0·69
10	0·3249	0·32	1·75	0·50	0·69
n	a_n	A	D	L	M

(From *Elements of Mathematical Statistics.*)

Fig. 16.35

Since in a normal distribution 3.09 Standard Deviations include 99.9 per cent of the population,

$$A = \frac{3.09a_n}{\sqrt{n}}, \; L = \frac{1}{6.18a_n} \text{ and } M = 3.09a_n - A.$$

The constant $D = a_n$ multiplied by the value for 99.5 per cent taken from a cumulative percentage frequency table for Range$_n$ ÷ Std. Deviation.

The routine for installing a quality control system can be followed from this example, using the concrete test cube results previously listed on page 277, and assuming the arbitrary tolerance limits of 17.5 and 45.5 N/mm². By taking a sample size of 5 cubes per day, and treating the first 5 days as a trial run, figures are obtained for the grand mean and mean range of 30.56 N/mm² and 9.80 N/mm² respectively (see Fig. 16.36).

Day 1	Day 2	Day 3	Day 4	Day 5	
23·80	23·80	28·70	36·40	36·40+	25·90
28·00	26·95	28·70	36·40−	32·90	25·34
25·20	21·00−	24·85−	39·90+	26·60−	32·13
20·30−	26·95	36·75	37·80	29·40	37·94
32·20+	28·00+	41·65+	39·20	32·20	31·50
5) 129·50	5) 126·70	5) 160·65	5) 189·70	5) 157·50	5) 152·81
Mean 25·90	25·34	32·13	37·94	31·50	30·56
Range 11·90	7·00	16·80	3·50	9·80	5) 49·00
					9·80

Fig. 16.36

i. Maximum permitted mean range = L (tolerence limits)
    $= 0.37 (45.5 − 17.5) = \underline{10.36}$ which is more than 9.80

ii. Allowable width of control limits are at distances M (mean range) inside the tolerance limits.
    M (mean range) $= 0.73 \times 9.80 = 7.15$.
    ∴ Upper limit $= 45.50 − 7.15 = \underline{38.35}$.

    Lower limit $= 17.50 + 7.15 = \underline{24.65}$.

iii. Control limits for means are grand mean $\pm A$ (mean range)
    $= 30.56 \pm (0.59 \times 9.80)$
    $= 30.56 \pm 5.78 = \underline{36.34}$ and $\underline{24.78.}$

    Both are within the allowable control limits.

iv. Control limit for Ranges = D (mean range)
    $= 2.08 \times 9.80 = \underline{20.38.}$

The control charts prepared from these values are shown in Fig. 16.37 with the subsequent sample means and ranges plotted for the remaining series Nos. 27 to 106. The low mean of sample No. 7 shows that the concrete strength was 'out of control', and the range of sample No. 14 which is off the chart indicates at least a loosening of control.

3. *Conclusion.* The importance of the preparation and presentation of statistics was emphasised by the National Consultative Council of the Building and Civil Engineering Industries,

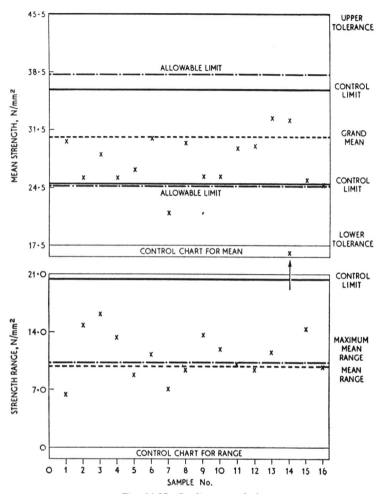

Fig. 16.37. Quality control charts

when it met in October 1962 to consider the Emmerson Report. Indeed, the proper use by management of scientifically prepared figures is vital to any business that wishes to know where it stands and where it is going. However, the statistics must be fully understood by all concerned, they must be made available in time for effective action, and the costs of preparation must be compared with the resulting gains in productivity.

BIBLIOGRAPHY

Samuel Hays, *An Outline of Statistics*, Longmans.
L. R. Connor, *Statistics in Theory and Practice*, Pitman.
M. J. Moroney, *Facts from Figures*, Penguin Books.
P. G. Moore, *Principles of Statistical Techniques*, Cambridge University Press.
T. G. Rose, *Business Charts*, Pitman.
J. F. Ratcliffe, *Elements of Mathematical Statistics*, Oxford University Press.
Directory of Construction Statistics, prepared by Ministry of Public Building & Works, H.M.S.O., 1968.
Construction: Key Facts, produced by B. A. S., National Builder, House Builder & Estate Developer; Federated Employers Press Ltd., 1975.

Chapter 17

Work Study

1. Productivity

Productivity is defined as the ratio between output and input, and industrial productivity is the arithmetical ratio between the work produced and the total resources used. A building productivity ratio can thus be equated as the measured value of construction, divided by the total cost of labour, plant and materials.

With the example of the 1962–3 National Productivity Year, and the appointment of the Director-General of Research and Development in the (then) Ministry of Public Buildings and Works, it may be assumed that the vital need for increased productivity in the building and civil engineering industries is both widely known and understood. Only higher productivity can enable the construction industries to provide the additional houses and roads required by the nation, can assist the contracting companies to meet the ever-increasing competition, and will improve the working conditions of the operatives. Higher productivity means, for the nation, that more is produced with the same expenditure of resources, and, to the builder, that the same amount is produced at less cost, but good human relations are essential in order to obtain the goodwill of the workers. The co-operation of employees is important, and they must be assured that rising productivity will not lead to redundancy but to higher real earnings.

1. *Construction time.* The four basic resources of production are land, materials, machines and manpower. Although land is a key factor in speculative development, it is generally the sphere of the designer rather than the builder proper. Construction resources can be grouped as time and materials, each contributing approximately half of the total cost of a project. The effective utilisation of materials is primarily the concern of design, while the prevention of waste has already been discussed under Purchasing, but other savings may be

304

effected, directly or indirectly, by proper storage, handling and processing during the operation stage. Since the cost of both labour and plant are proportional to the time expended, it is helpful to consider the make-up of construction time.

The basic work content of the operation is the irreducible minimum time required under perfect conditions. In practice, however, the work content is increased, either by defects in design or specification or by inefficient methods of construction. Examples of unnecessary work added by bad design include: units which need to be held by a crane while being secured, too many varieties of reinforced concrete column or beam sections, unnecesary fair face work, and the removal of excess excavation to provide working space. Wrong methods of operation may mean using a dragline to dig a narrow trench, double handling of spoil or materials, using a metallic sanding disc for rubbing-up concrete instead of one based on silica, placing the concrete mixer too far from the hoist, or faulty formwork which necessitates touching-up.

The duration of an operation may be further extended by interruptions or ineffective time, due to shortcomings on the part of the management or for reasons within the control of the workmen. Ineffective time is also caused by the excessive variety of design and lack of standardisation which results in the 'one off' nature of building, and design changes after work has commenced.

Management can contribute to idle time by bad planning which may result in discontinuity due to unbalanced gangs or shortage of materials, plant breakdowns or reduced output caused by lack of maintenance, or bad working conditions leading to fatigue and accidents. The workers themselves can add to the total time by absence, lateness, idleness or restrictive practices, bad workmanship, and accidents caused by carelessness or malpractice.

In order to tackle these problems of unnecessary work and ineffective time, certain management techniques have been evolved which were earlier known as 'time and motion study' but are now generally termed work study.

2. *Work Study*. The term work study embraces the parallel techniques of method study and work measurement, which, by a systematic procedure of investigation and improvement, endeavour to obtain the best possible use of human and material resources. Work study is potentially one of the most useful tools of management, and by its continuous use

ordinary men can achieve exceptional results by eliminating wasted effort and time, and setting proper standards of performance.

2. Method Study

The object of method study is to examine the ways of doing work in order to develop easier and more effective methods of production. Although the detailed analysis may become very complex, the basic procedure is the same for every investigation and strict adherence to this is essential for success.

i. Select the work to be studied.
ii. Record the observed facts of the present or proposed method.
iii. Examine the facts critically to determine their true purpose and seek possible alternatives.
iv. Develop the most practical, economical and efficient method, with due regard to all the relevant circumstances.
v. Install the improved method as standard practice.
vi. Maintain the new method by regular inspections.

1. *Selection.* The first choice should be the job most likely to affect the overall productivity of the total enterprise. Factors to be considered may be economic, technical or human. Economic considerations include 'bottlenecks' which are holding up other activities, e.g. form work on R.C. framed buildings; operations which involve a lot of labour/plant or the transport of material over long distances such as bulk excavation with long hauls; and repetitive work like house building. Technical problems are usually obvious, but they must be solved upon the advice of specialists.

Human reactions to change are notoriously difficult to anticipate, but studies likely to lead to unrest no matter how promising from other points of view, should be left alone. Everyone should be instructed in the general principles of method study, and if dirty, heavy, or otherwise unpopular tasks are tackled first, the climate of opinion will possibly become more favourable.

2. *Records.* In order that the method of work concerned may be subjected to a critical analysis it is necessary to prepare a factual record of the activities involved, and this also allows a 'before and after' comparison to be made when the improved procedure has been installed.

The facts required may be obtained by visual observation or by means of a photographic technique in the case of existing methods, and by calculation or synthesis for proposed processes. Depending upon the nature of the activity being studied, and the purpose for which the information is required, the record may take the form of a chart for process and time sequences, or diagrams for representations of movement routes.

Standard symbols have been developed to represent the various types of activity in a procedure or process, and these are shown in Fig. 17.1 below.

Symbol	Activity	Explanation and Example
○	OPERATION	A positive step towards completion, e.g. assembly, preparation, or alteration
□	INSPECTION	Verification of quality and / or quantity, e.g. comparison or measurement
⇨	TRANSPORT	Deliberate movement or handling, e.g. lift or carry
▽	STORAGE	Protective custody, e.g. on a file or in stock
D	DELAY	Temporary or unnecessary condition, e.g. waiting or temporary storage

Fig. 17.1. Method study symbols

Symbols may be combined to indicate activities being performed at the same time. In addition the following information should be provided to ensure that the record is properly understood:

i. A description of each activity entailed in the process.
ii. Whether the existing or improved method is shown.
iii. A specification of where activities begin and end.
iv. Any time or distance scales used.
v. An explanation of any abbreviations, etc.
vi. The date of preparation of the record.
a. An *outline process chart* provides a preliminary picture of a procedure, and only shows the operations and inspections involved and the points at which materials are introduced. Also known as an operation process chart, it can be used for deciding whether a more detailed study is worthwhile, and is very useful in the design stage. The major process is

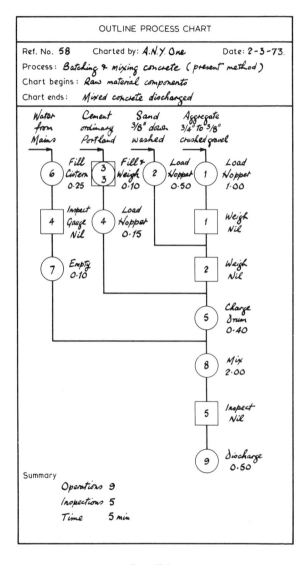

Fig. 17.2

drawn down the right-hand side of the chart and sub-
sidiaries are shown to its left, joining each other and the
main trunk at points of material entry or assembly stages.
Fig. 17.2 is a hypothetical example of this type of graphic
representation, outlining the sequence of all the principal
operations involved in operating a rotary drum concrete
mixer with built-in weigher, drag shovel and cement silo.

b. For greater detail a *flow process chart* may be constructed
to record all of the events under review, including
'transports', 'delays' and 'storages'. The flow of work may
be expressed in terms of the activities of either the man,
material or equipment concerned, but any one chart can
only refer to a single subject. When two or more subjects
are interdependent, this may be indicated by recording the
relevant flow process charts alongside each other. Movement in any particular direction may be shown by facing the
'transport' symbol in the appropriate way, and it is usual to
record time and distance on the left of the 'operation' or
'transport' symbol observed. In Chapter 10, Fig. 10.1 is a
type of flow process chart where the subject is an official
order form. Preprinted process chart blanks simplify the
work of compilation, standardise the order of recording,
and ensure that no essential information is omitted.
The example in Fig. 17.3 illustrates a design suitable for
either outline or flow process charting, in this instance
setting out the sequence of the flow of work associated with
reinforcement steel in a precast concrete yard.

c. The *multiple activity process chart* is used to record the
activities of two or more subjects in relation to one another.
Their activities are recorded either as working time or idle
time, and by representing each operator and/or machine
against a common time scale, it is possible to show up
periods of ineffective time within the process. This type of
chart is therefore particularly useful for organising maintenance work so that expensive machinery is out of commission for the minimum time, and also for co-ordinating team
work in order to reduce waiting time and improve
continuity. As an example Fig. 17.4 shows the sequence of
laying a monolithic grano floor, where in the original
method eight operatives completed two bays each day. The
better balanced team of ten operatives by the improved
method achieve four bays in the same time, an increased
output per man of 60 per cent.

REF. No. 91 CHARTED BY: A. N. Observer DATE: 25/1/85									
TASK: Preparation of steel reinforcement for lintels									
~~MAN~~/MATERIAL/~~EQUIPMENT~~ M. S. Bars PRESENT/~~PROPOSED~~ METHOD									
CHART BEGINS: Delivery by road									
CHART ENDS: Ready for concrete to be poured									

DESCRIPTION	QUANTITY	DISTANCE	TIME	OPERATION	INSPECTION	TRANSPORT	STORAGE	DELAY	REMARKS
Random lengths delivered				O	□	⇨	▽	D	By road
Unloaded and sorted				O	□	⇨	▽	D	By hand
Taken to store		30		O	□	⇨	▽	D	By hand
In storage racks				O	□	⇨	▽	D	
To cutting bench		20		O	□	⇨	▽	D	By hand
Awaiting cutting				O	□	⇨	▽	D	
Cut to length				O	□	⇨	▽	D	Labourers
Awaiting bundling				O	□	⇨	▽	D	
To bending bench		80		O	□	⇨	▽	D	By hand
Awaiting bending				O	□	⇨	▽	D	
Bent and hooked				O	□	⇨	▽	D	Steelfixer
Carried to bench		30		O	□	⇨	▽	D	Labourer
Awaiting fabrication				O	□	⇨	▽	D	
Made-up into cages				O	□	⇨	▽	D	Steelfixer
Awaiting collection				O	□	⇨	▽	D	
Taken into beam shop		80		O	□	⇨	▽	D	Hand trolley
Awaiting use				O	□	⇨	▽	D	
Placed inside mould				O	□	⇨	▽	D	Concreter
Ready for concrete				O	□	⇨	▽	D	
Final inspection before				O	□	⇨	▽	D	Foreman
concrete is poured				O	□	⇨	▽	D	
				O	□	⇨	▽	D	
				O	□	⇨	▽	D	
				O	□	⇨	▽	D	
				O	□	⇨	▽	D	
				O	□	⇨	▽	D	
				O	□	⇨	▽	D	
				O	□	⇨	▽	D	
				O	□	⇨	▽	D	
				O	□	⇨	▽	D	
SUMMARY. Present		240		5	1	6	1	7	
Proposed									
Saving									

Fig. 17.3. Flow process chart

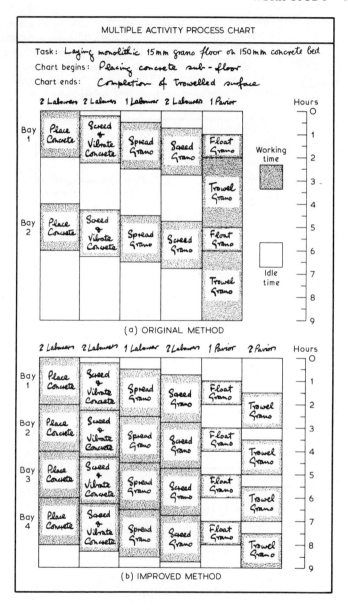

Fig. 17.4

d. A *flow diagram* is used to supplement the flow process chart with which it is usually associated. Upon a scale plan of the working areas are superimposed the numbered symbols to show the location of the various activities, but without the descriptions. The paths of the subject's movements are represented by a line joining the symbols in

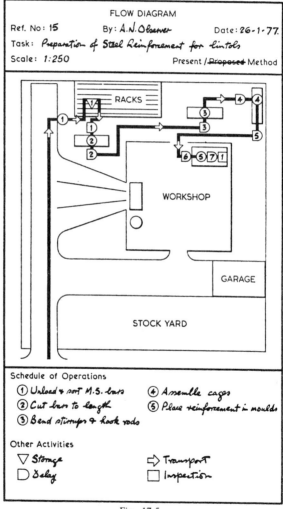

Fig. 17.5

sequence, and the directions are shown by the 'transport' symbols. Fig. 17.5 is a record of the material flow described in the earlier chart, Fig. 17.3. This type of record indicates clearly any undesirable features such as backtracking, congestion or unnecessarily long movements, and is therefore particularly suitable for investigating problems associated with layout in workshops, stores, material compounds and site plant. When vertical movement is involved a flow diagram can be drawn upon the relevant elevation, and if several floor levels are occupied by the process then a three-dimensional flow diagram is a useful variation.

e. In order to study the frequency of irregular movements between various points, a *string diagram* can be used to plot the sequence and distance of alternative routes within a limited area for a given period of time. All the relevant

MOVEMENT STUDY SHEET				
Ref. No. 133 By: A. N. Observer Date: 14-9-77.				
Task: Normal working in Joiners Shop				
Cross Ref.: String diagram No. 27 Operator: J. I. M.				
1 Time Dep.	2 Time Arr.	3 Time Taken	4 Move to Destination	5 Notes
	8·05		Machine A	
8·10	8·13	3	A to m/c N	
8·18	8·19	1	N to m/c I	
8·21	8·22	1	I to bench F	
8·29	8·30	1	F to m/c E	

Fig. 17.6

facts are first observed and methodically recorded on a *movement study sheet* (see Fig. 17.6), to identify the path and timing of each succeeding journey. A scale drawing of the working area is then prepared, including building features, plant and equipment and any items in the vicinity that might affect movement. This plan is then mounted on a board, and pins are driven into it at every stopping point and change of direction, the heads being allowed to stand about 15 mm clear of the surface. A length of thread is then tied to the pin at the starting point, and led around the other points of call in the sequence in which they were visited according to the movement study. In this way the frequency of particular paths can be determined, and their total distance calculated by measuring the length of string used. The paths of several subjects can be traced by using different coloured threads to distinguish them. The result is to give a picture of the various movements involved in a

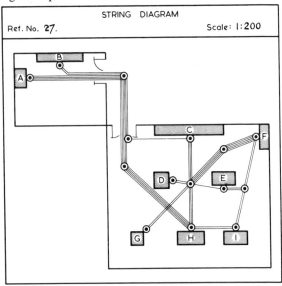

STRING DIAGRAM

Ref. No. 27.   Scale: 1:200

Fig. 17.7

process, those which are most frequently undertaken being covered by the greatest number of strings. This effect can be seen in Fig. 17.7 which records the paths traversed in a small joiner's shop during the normal morning's work. Ideally the most frequent journeys should be as short as possible, leaving the longer trips to be followed infrequently so that the overall distance travelled is a minimum. Improved lay-outs can be investigated by preparing cardboard templates to represent the various machines and workbenches, and re-stringing and measuring alternative arrangements until the most satisfactory scheme has been found. The string diagram technique has many applications within the building industry and is one of the most useful tools of method study.

3. *Examination.* Now, the recorded facts concerning the work under investigation must be exhaustively examined, in an ordered sequence and objective manner. This is the crux of the method study, and to ensure an impartial judgement it is sometimes valuable for two people to collaborate at this stage; while full use must be made of all available technical information. A detailed and critical review is made of every separate activity, with the object of eliminating any unneces-sary jobs and of simplifying the essential tasks, in order to discover a more effective method. Since only operations actually forward the process of production, it follows that the activities of inspection, transport, storage and, of course, delay are the first links to be attacked.

Each step in the process is logically and impartially challenged by means of the questioning technique, firstly to determine the basic facts and their underlying reasons, and secondly to consider the advantages and disadvantages of possible alternatives and so to select the most appropriate. All aspects of the activity must be probed to ascertain the true purpose, the actual place, the sequence or timing, the person involved

The Questioning Technique

What?	*Why?*	*Could it be?*	*It should be?*
PURPOSE is achieved	**IS THAT** necessary	**WHAT** else	**WHAT**
PLACE is occupied	**THAT** place	**WHERE** else	**WHERE**
SEQUENCE is followed	**THAT** time	**WHEN** else	**WHEN**
PERSON is involved	**THAT** person	**WHO** else	**WHO**
MEANS is used	**THAT** way	**HOW** else	**HOW**

Fig. 17.8

and the means used to achieve the result. This systematic approach summarised in the above table (Fig. 17.8) should be memorised, for its rigid sequence ensures that no point is overlooked.

4. *Development.* As a result of the above examination the investigator will now have a comprehensive statement of the existing method together with clear indications of possible improvements. The most effective method must now be developed, using the essential operations and inspections as a

framework. Opportunities for increased efficiency may be found in any of the following main directions:

i.   Layout may be redesigned to remove restrictions or reduce ineffective movement, and the use of templates or scale models are especially valuable for siting erection cranes or deciding the arrangement of a concrete casting yard.

ii. Working procedures may require to be changed, particularly if 'the original reason for a particular practice has been forgotten'. For example, the laborious copying of an Advice Note on to a Checker's Note may be entirely unnecessary.

iii. Utilisation of labour, plant or material may be increased by the reduction of waste or the elimination of delays. The introduction of further mechanisation or a better balancing of operations may release expensive labour or prevent under-employment within a team. The replacement of flag men by automatic traffic signals, and the proper phasing of finishing trades on housing are obvious examples.

iv. Environment has a direct effect upon productvity both on the site or in the office, and the arrangements for tea-breaks or the provision of polythene tents for winter working are potential fields for attention.

v.   Specification changes may be suggested, and quite minor amendments in design or material standardisation may bring great rewards. On multi-storey buildings it may be possible to pre-cast flights of steps so that direct access to floors can be speeded, or the variety of concrete aggregate sizes might be curtailed with consequent economies at the mixer. When the improved method has been fully synthesised it should be recorded on a flow process chart, with a summary of the total numbers of activities, so that the savings in time and/or distance may be compared. This summary in turn must be subjected to the same searching analysis to ensure that the proposed method is logical and practical.

5. *Installation.* Acceptance of the proposed changes by the departmental supervisor should first be gained by discussion, and then the proposals must be submitted to the management for approval. This should be in the form of a written report showing the relative costs of the two methods and expected savings, the anticipated cost of installing the new method, and the administrative requirements of implementing the improved process. A written Standard Practice should also be

prepared, defining the new method for reference purposes, and as an aid to operatives. Finally the co-operation of the employees concerned must be sought by explanation and the operators retrained in the revised procedure. The intitial running-in is a critical period requiring close supervision, tact and restraint.

6. *Maintenance.* Once installed, it is important that the specified method should be maintained by regular routine checks, to prevent any drift from the authorised practice. However, current practice must be reviewed at suitable intervals to incorporate any valid amendments and suggestions, and to ensure that operating instructions remain 'live' documents.

3. Work Measurement

Method study requires the complementary technique of work measurement in order to derive the maximum benefits from a systematic study of work. While the former is associated with the manner in which work is executed, the latter is concerned with the human effort involved or the 'work content' of the job. Although distinct, the two procedures are, however, interdependent, and in practice cannot be completely separated from each other.

Although the mental aproach to method study is primarily the ordered application of common sense, assessment of the time required to perform a specified task by work measurement, because of the special techniques employed, is mainly the field of the trained and experienced expert. Nevertheless a building manager must have an adequate understanding of the principles involved, if he is to employ the tools of work study successfully.

Since work measurement is likely to reveal the shortcomings of management and to show up the behaviour of workmen, it is apt to meet with resistance, so that an understanding of the human factors involved is always especially important. It must be realised that a time study is a record of a particular operation, and not a check on any individual's performance.

The general procedure of work measurement is:

i.   Select the work to be measured.

ii. Define the method being used and the job elements.

iii. Measure the quantity of work and assess the rating.

iv. Calculate the standard time including allowances.

v.   Compile and issue the allowed time with a job specification.

1. *Selection.* Work measurement is the determination of the time required for the average worker to carry out a particular task in

accordance with a specified method and standard of performance. The study may be either the preliminary to making a
method study or the consequence of such an investigation, but
there is usually a strong reason for choosing a certain job for
attention. Possible reasons include: the introduction of a new
operation or a change in method for an existing activity; a
'bottleneck' within a process or the appearance of excessive
production costs; a desire to compare the relative efficiency of
alternative methods; or a means of equating the work of
members within a team or deciding the economic manning of
plant and equipment. Time standards may be required for
estimating or planning purposes, either to decide the labour
strength necessary to produce a required output, or to forecast
the possible output from the labour force available. The same
information can also be used as a basis for incentive schemes or
to set targets of machine utilisation; and since time is a measure
of cost the standards will enable cost controls to be set up.
When selecting a job for work measurement it should be
remembered that the causes of ineffective time within the
influence of management are much more numerous than those
over which the workers have direct control. Furthermore, the
purpose for which work measurement is being undertaken
must always be made perfectly clear to everyone likely to be
concerned.

2. *Definition*. Before measurements are taken it is necessary to
   record all the relevant information about the job, and to
   prepare a complete description of the operation by identifying
   its component elements.

   a. Full *information* concerning the operation, the operator and
      the prevailing conditions must be obtained by direct
      observation, and recorded, usually at the top of the sudy
      sheet. The following groups of information are normally
      required to facilitate quick and accurate reference later:
      i.   Study reference number, sheet number, date, and name
           of observer,
      ii. Details of drawings, materials or quality requirements
           when applicable,
      iii. Title of contract, operation and location, plant and
           equipment used and sketch of the layout,
      iv. The operatives concerned, usually by trade only,
      v.   The start and finish times, elapsed (duration) time of the
           study, and weather or working conditions.

b. A complete *description* of the specified method must be recorded by breaking down the operation into its distinct constituent parts or elements, chosen for convenience of observation and measurement. A complete sequence of elements comprising an operation is known as the work cycle, starting at the beginning of the first element, and ending at the beginning of the first element of the following cycle. Elements are separated by decisive break points which occur at the start or finish of a natural basic movement such as 'fetch', 'take-off' or 'cut', and should be easily recognisable either by eye or ear, e.g. putting down a tool. This detailed breakdown into small parts or elements is necessary in order to separate effective time from ineffective time, to isolate periods of fatigue, to establish standard values for recurring actions, and to facilitate the assessment of rates of performance when the pace varies throughout the cycle. Elements written into a job specification also enable standards to be checked, since additions or omissions can easily be detected.

Elements should be as short as possible, but although 20 seconds is common for manufacturing processes, building site activities are more likely to be from 1 to 3 minutes. Different types of elements should be kept separate, and hand time should be distinguished from machine time. Repetitive elements recur in every cycle while occasional elements occur at intervals; constant elements are identical but the duration of variable elements varies with some physical characteristic; foreign elements are unnecessary motions. Elements should be observed throughout a number of cycles as a check, and written down on the study sheet before measuring begins.

3. *Measurement.* Although work measurement can be carried out by more advanced methods, time study is the basic technique; synthetics, analytical estimating and activity sampling are referred to later in section 4.

    a. Timing is usually performed with a watch, unless extremely accurate measurements are required, when devices such as the ciné camera or portable paper tape machine may be used. The watch can be a good wrist or pocket type with a seconds hand, but a stopwatch is better and more convenient. Stopwatch dials are graduated either by intervals of ⅕th of a second, by ¹⁄₁₀₀th of a minute (the decimal minute) or by ¹⁄₁₀,₀₀₀ths of an hour. Movement may be controlled by means of a stop and start slide, and pressure on the winding-knob to return the hands to zero (fly-back type); or solely by pressures on the winding-knob – the first starts, the second stops, and the third returns the hands to zero. The decimal-minute stopwatch fly-back type (see Fig. 17.9)

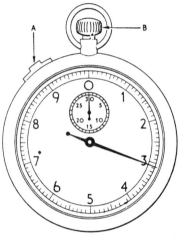

Fig. 17.9. Decimal-minute stopwatch, flyback
type.
(A) Slide for starting and stopping the movement.
(B) Winding knob which also returns the
hands to zero.

is in most general use by work study engineers, since it is easier to read and simplifies calculations.

The only other specialised equipment necessary is a study board to which the record forms can be fastened by means of a spring clip. Purpose-made boards often have a fitting to hold the stopwatch so that the observer's hands are left free.

There are two methods of using the stopwatch, either continuous or repetitive timing. In continuous or cumulative timing the watch is started at the beginning of the first element and is not stopped until the whole study is completed. Watch readings are taken at the end of each element and individual times are found by successive subtractions afterwards. This method is more accurate and is therefore generally recommended particularly for gang operations (see Fig. 17.10).

In repetitive timing the watch is simultaneously read and snapped back to zero at the end of each element, although the movement of the watch is never stopped. A slight delay

CONTRACT: Plastics Ltd. Office Block	STUDY No. 1096
OPERATION: Erect 2m × 1m stove enamelled	DATE: 21ST July '78
facing panels below first floor windows	TIME START: 2·30 pm
Ground to 1st. floor 3m	TIME FINISH: 3·09 pm
Stack to building 15m	ELAPSED TIME: 39 min
OPERATIVES: 2 joiners + 2 labourers	OBSERVED TIME:
PLANT/EQUIPT.: Block and tackle	DIFFERENCE:
CONDITIONS: Cool. Access uneven	OBSERVER: A. B. Count

ELEMENT	R.	W.R.	O.T.	B.T.	ELEMENT	R.	W.R.	O.T.	B.T.
Start watch 2·30 pm		0·00			J₁ waiting	I.T.	11·55	(·35)	
Check time					J₂ as before	100		·35	·35
		2·55			L₁L₂ fit sling	120		·70	·84
J₁J₂ L₁L₂ collect	85	10·0	8·5				12·30		
block + tackle, slings,					L₁L₂ hoist panel	120		2·40	2·88
ladder + clips from					J₁J₂ guide panel	120		2·40	2·88
store and walk							13·50		
25 yds to building					L₁L₂ hold panel	80		1·30	1·04
		5·05			J₁J₂ engage clips	80		1·30	1·04
J₁ climbs ladder to	90	2·05	1·85				14·15		
1st. floor and suspends					J₁J₂ adjust + tighten	100		1·80	1·80
block + tackle.					L₁L₂ collect panel	100		1·80	1·80
J₂ assists + repositions	90	2·05	1·85				15·05		
ladder on inside.					J₁ transfers tackle	90		1·15	1·03
L₁L₂ collect panel	100	4·10	4·10		J₂ tightens clips	100		1·15	1·15
		7·10			L₁L₂ as before	100		2·30	2·30
J₁J₂ as before	90	·90	·81				16·20		
L₁L₂ fit sling	100	·90	·90		J₁ waits	I.T.		(·55)	
		7·55			J₂ as before	100		·55	·55
L₁L₂ hoist up panel	110	2·70	2·97		L₁L₂ fit sling	80		1·10	·88
J₁J₂ guide panel	110	2·70	2·97				16·75		
into position					L₁L₂ hoist panel	85		3·10	2·63
		8·90			J₁J₂ guide panel	85		3·10	2·63
L₁L₂ hold panel	90	1·20	1·08				18·30		
J₁ engages top 2 clips	90	·60	·54		L₁L₂ hold panel	115		1·00	1·15
J₂ from ladder	90	·60	·54		J₁J₂ engage clips	115		1·00	1·15
engages bottom 2 clips							18·80		
		9·50			J₁J₂ L₁L₂ relax	I.T.		(·80)	
J₁J₂ adjust panel +	100	2·20	2·20				20·50		
tighten clips									
L₁L₂ collect panel	100	2·20	2·20		J₁J₂ adjust + tighten	90		2·20	1·98
		10·60			L₁L₂ collect panel	90		2·20	1·98
J₁ Transfer tackle	110	·95	1·04				21·60		
J₂ as before	100	·95	·95		(Continued)				
L₁L₂ as before	100	1·90	1·90						

| R.=Rating | W.R.=Watch reading | O.T.=Observed time | B.T.=Basic time |

Fig. 17.10. Time study record (continuous timing)

CONTRACT:	Parkfields Estate (Phase II)			STUDY No.	1075
OPERATION:	Loading out scaffold at chamber joist level of pair of houses type S.D/2A. Stack to ladder 10 m			DATE:	20th June '78.
				TIME START:	10.30 am.
				TIME FINISH:	11.01 am
				ELAPSED TIME:	31 mins
OPERATIVES:	1 Bricklayers' Labourer			OBSERVED TIME:	30.55
PLANT/EQUIPT.:	—			DIFFERENCE:	1.5%
CONDITIONS:	V. Warm. Access clear + level			OBSERVER:	A.B. Count

ELEMENT	R.	W.R.	O.T.	N.T.	ELEMENT	R.	W.R.	O.T.	N.T.
Check time			2.21		7	105	.29		
1. Load hod with 10 bricks	90		.80	.72	8	110	.40		
2. Hoist hod onto shoulder	100		.14	.14	9	95	.24		
3. Walk to ladder	80		.25	.20	1	90	.80		
4. Climb ladder onto scaffold	110		.60	.66	2	100	.15		
5. Walk to position and rest hod	95		.46	.44	3	90	.24		
6. Unload bricks and shoulder hod	105		.33	.35	4	95	.71		
7. Walk back to ladder	90		.33	.30	5	90	.50		
8. Descend ladder	85		.50	.43	6	105	.32		
9. Walk back to stock pile and rest hod	90		.24	.22	7	90	.34		
1	85		.88	.75	8	85	.54		
2	90		.17	.15	9	80	.31		
3	100		.21	.21	1	80	.90		
4	80		.88	.70	2	85	.19		
5	90		.48	.43	3	80	.30		
6	100		.37	.37	4	80	.85		
7	80		.35	.28	5	85	.54		
8	75		.64	.48	6	90	.40		
9	110		.19	.21	Admire scenery	I.T.	(2.08)		
Light cigarette	I.T.		(1.66)		7	90	.33		
1	95		.81	.77	8	80	.56		
2	100		.14	.14	9	80	.30		
3	85		.26	.22	1	90	.89		
4	95		.72	.68	2	95	.17		
5	90		.51	.46	3	100	.23		
6	80		.50	.40	4	105	.67		
					5	110	.44		
					6	100	.39		
					7	105	.30		
					8	100	.46		
					9	105	.22		
					Check time		.86		
							30.55		

R.= Rating	W.R.= Watch reading	O.T.= Observed time	N.T.= Normal time

Fig. 17.11. Time study record (repetitive timing)

occurs when the hand is returned to zero, and this leads to errors particularly with short-element short-cycle jobs. This procedure also requires check time periods to be included both at the start and finish of the study in order to synchronise the stopwatch with the master clock (see Fig. 17.11).

With either method, however, it is usual to make an independent check of the overall or elapsed time using another watch or clock. The total recorded or observed time must be reconciled with the elapsed time, and the element times adjusted proportionately, but any difference greater than ± 2 per cent should be suspect.

b. *Rating* of the operative's performance must also be assessed, and recorded before the watch reading.

Since the 'average' man does not exist except as an idea, it is necessary to judge the effective speed of the workman under observation, in order that the recorded element times can be related to the equivalent periods that would be expected from someone working at the theoretical standard pace. In this country the generally accepted rate of activity which is considered to be average or 'normal', can be compared to the skill, physical effort and mental concentration that is exhibited by a man of average physique when walking unladen, in a straight line, on level ground, at a speed of three miles per hour. Another standard of comparison is to the dexterity, muscular energy and mental application required in order to deal a pack of 52 playing cards in 30 seconds. This pace appears deliberate and slow, but can be maintained over a long period without undue physical fatigue or mental strain, and is therefore taken to be the normal performance for work carried out under proper supervision in return for the basic wage or hourly rate. The performance levels of a group of workers engaged on identical tasks would vary greatly, due to a number of factors such as their comparative physique, intelligence, training, experience and general attitude of mind. Under normal conditions the figures would show a distribution conforming to the normal frequency curve (see Fig. 16.15). Moreover, the individual workman does not in practice sustain a uniform exertion for long, since his effectiveness fluctuates according to the surrounding conditions, his powers of concentration, the effects of fatigue, and deliberate or unconscious ineffective movements and activities. Hence the technique of rating is an alternative to the taking of numerous studies of different operatives, in order to provide an adequate sample for the determination of an average. The procedure is not an exact science but a matter of skilled judgement, and confidence can only be acquired by long experience and constant practice. Nevertheless it is possible for a qualified time study man to assess relative rates well within the practical requirements.

There were several scales of rating in early use, including the 'point' scale which represented normal performance as 60, one with a normal of 75, and the 'percentage' scale of 100-normal which was often used here and favoured on the continent. Examples of these three scales are shown for comparison in Fig. 17.12, but the British Standards Institution recommends the 0/100 scale where a standard

Comparison of Principal Rating Scales

Rating			Description	*Walking speed km/h*
60/80 N = 60	75/100 N = 75	100/133 N = 100		
60	75	100	Average hourly rate (normal)	4·8
80	100	133	Incentive bonus rate (B.S.S. "standard")	6·4
100	125	167	Expert piecework rate	8·0

Fig. 17.12

rating of 100 corresponds to the performance from a motivated worker. It is the usual practice to estimate ratings to the nearest five points on any scale.

Any idle or ineffective time, including relaxation periods, should be recorded as such in the rating column.

4. *Calculation.* Having completed the time study over a sufficient number of cycles at the place of work it is now possible to work up the results in the office and arrive at the standard time for the job. The normal allowed time for the operation is compiled step-by-step in the following fashion:

   i. If the method of repetitive timing has been used then the complete series of observed times, together with the start and finish check times, must be totalled, compared with the elapsed time shown on the master clock, and any necessary adjustments made to the element times.

ii. In the case of continuous timing, the successive watch readings must be subtracted and the individual observed times entered against each element.

iii. With the exception of periods of ineffective time, every element time is now 'normalised', i.e. converted to a normal time, by multiplying it by the appropriate rating:

$$\text{Observed time} \times \frac{\text{rating assessment}}{\text{normal}} = \text{normal time}$$

When using the British Standard Scale the observed time is similarly extended to basic time:

$$\text{Observed time} \times \frac{\text{observed rating}}{\text{standard rating}} = \text{basic time}$$

These 'normal' or 'basic' times are entered in the relevant column, perhaps in a distinctive colour for clarity.

iv. In theory, the basic times computed for any particular element should be constant throughout the series of cycles, but due to inaccuracies and approximations this is rarely so in practice. Therefore, the basic times recorded for successive repetitions of each separate element must be abstracted and examined. Unless there are values that are obviously faulty, in which case the operation should be re-timed, the representative time for each element is found by taking the simple arithmetical average. (See Fig. 17.13.)

Alternatively, the arithmetical mean of all the observed times may be multiplied by the arithmetical average of all the ratings for that element.

v. Since all idle time and relaxation periods observed during the study have been excluded, it is necessary to add back certain allowances in order to produce a realistic standard for the proper performance of the work. Once again accurate assessment requires judgement and experience, but tables of suggested figures for the usual factors are published in text books.

A process allowance may be necessary to make provision for enforced idleness such as unavoidable waiting time, or an indirect activity, e.g. cleaning a concrete mixer at the end of the day. Such compensation is particularly essential when the standard time is to be used as the basis for an incentive scheme.

ELEMENT	1	2	3	4	5	6	7	8	9	
	72	14	20	66	44	35	30	43	22	
	75	15	21	70	43	37	28	48	21	
	77	14	22	68	46	40	30	44	23	
	72	15	22	67	45	34	31	46	25	
	72	16	24	68	46	36	30	45	24	
	80	16	23	70	48	39	32	46	23	
TOTALS	4·48	0·90	1·32	4·09	2·72	2·21	1·81	2·72	1·38	
FREQUENCY	6	6	6	6	6	6	6	6	6	
NORMAL TIMES	0·75	0·15	0·22	0·68	0·45	0·37	0·30	0·45	0·23	min

STUDY No. 1075

(a)

ELEMENT	BASIC TIMES						TOTAL	FREQ?	UNIT TIME
Collect tools, prepare, and clear away	8·50	1·85	1·85	0·81	1·40	10·0			
							24·41	1	24·41/shift
Collect panels	4·10	2·20	1·90	1·80	2·30	1·98			
	1·80	1·80	1·98	2·09	2·31				
							24·26	6	4·04/panel
Fit sling	0·90	0·84	0·88	0·88	0·95	0·90			
							5·35	6	0·89/panel
Hoist and guide panels	2·97	2·97	2·88	2·88	2·63	2·63			
	2·80	2·80	2·70	2·70	2·75	2·75			
							33·46	6	5·58/panel
Hold panels and engage clips	1·08	0·54	0·54	1·04	1·04	1·15			
	1·15	1·10	1·10	1·15	1·15	1·08			
	1·08						13·20	6	2·20/panel
Adjust panels and tighten clips	2·20	0·95	0·35	1·80	1·15	0·55			
	1·98	0·90	0·36	1·80	0·99	0·45			
	2·09	1·15	0·50	2·10	1·40		20·72	6	3·45/panel
Transfer tackle	1·04	1·03	1·05	1·04	1·05				
							5·21	5	1·04/panel

STUDY No. 1096

(b)

Fig. 17.13. *Time study analyses*

The major addition to the basic time is the rest or relaxation allowance, which is intended to provide the worker with an opportunity to attend to his personal needs and recover from the effects of physical or mental weariness. A variable allowance may also be necessary to combat the effects of fatigue due to the peculiar demands of the job itself, or to the particular factors of the working conditions (see Fig. 17.14).

Factors Taken into Account when Assessing Rest Allowances

Personal Constants

Personal Needs	5/6%	Relaxation	0/4%

Variable Conditions

Body Position	Sitting	0	Very Cramped	10%
Muscular Effort	Lifting 7 kg.	2%	Maximum	50%
Heat and Humidity			Extreme cases	100%
Bad Light		0/5%		
Background Noise		0/5%		
Concentration or Mental Strain		0/10%		
Monotony or Tediousness		0/10%		

N.B.—These values are typical only, to illustrate the ranges.

Fig. 17.14

It is usual to draw up a composite allowance expressed as a percentage of the basic time (see Fig. 17.15).

Special allowances can also be made for periodic activities such as the sharpening of tools, interference by other trades, or contingencies including normal plant break-downs and organisation difficulties.

The result of this empirical procedure is to produce the standard time for each element.

Basic time + allowances = standard time.

In certain circumstances a further policy allowance may be added, to make up the bonus level or to take account of temporary conditions such as poor quality material or abnormal weather. This allowance, if any, is given at the discretion of the management, and does not form part of the basic standard time; it is used to modify the allowed time only in exceptional circumstances.

5. *Compilation.* With the completion of a summary (see Fig. 17.16), the work measurement is finished and the allowed time for the operation can be issued for use. It is usual also to quote the number of items per hour expected, either at normal time or the standard incentive performance. The task value of the work can be expressed either as a time in-

| CONTRACT: Parkfields Estate (Phase II) | | | | | | | DATE: 20th June '78. | | |
| OPERATION: Loading out scaffold for bricklayers at C.J. level | | | | | | | STUDY No. 1075 | | |

No.	DESCRIPTION	PERSONAL CONSTANT	BODY POSITION	MUSCULAR EFFORT	BAD LIGHT	HEAT AND HUMIDITY	NOISE LEVEL	CONCENTRATE OR STRAIN	MONOTONY TEDIOUSNESS	TOTAL %
1	Load hod	8	3	5		5		0	0	21
2	Shoulder hod	8	2	10		5		0	0	25
3	Walk to ladder	8	2	15		5		0	0	30
4	Climb ladder	8	2	30		5		2	0	47
5	Walk to position	8	2	15		5		1	0	31
6	Unload bricks	8	5	10		5		0	0	28
7	Return to ladder	8	2	5		5		0	1	21
8	Descend ladder	8	2	5		5		0	2	22
9	Return to stockpile	8	2	5		5		0	1	21

(a)

| CONTRACT: Plastics Ltd. Office Block | | | | | | | DATE: 21st July '78. | | |
| OPERATION: Erect facing panels at first floor level | | | | | | | STUDY No. 1096 | | |

No.	DESCRIPTION	PERSONAL CONSTANT	BODY POSITION	MUSCULAR EFFORT	BAD LIGHT	HEAT AND HUMIDITY	NOISE LEVEL	CONCENTRATE OR STRAIN	MONOTONY TEDIOUSNESS	TOTAL %
1	Collect tools + clear	8	2	5		4		0	0	19
2	Carry panels	8	3	15		4		0	1	31
3	Fit sling	8	2	2		4		0	0	16
4	Hoist panels	8	5	25		4		0	0	42
5	Engage clips	8	3	2		4		1	0	18
6	Tighten clips	8	4	10		4		2	0	28
7	Transfer tackle	8	2	5		4		0	0	19

(b)

Fig. 17.15. Time study allowances

ELEMENT No.	NORMAL TIME	% REST ALLOWANCE	FREQUENCY PER CYCLE	STANDARD TIME
1	0·75	21	1	0·91
2	0·15	25	1	0·19
3	0·22	30	1	0·29
4	0·68	47	1	1·00
5	0·45	31	1	0·59
6	0·37	28	1	0·47
7	0·30	21	1	0·36
8	0·45	22	1	0·55
9	0·23	21	1	0·28
				4·64

CONTRACT: Parkfields Estate (Phase II)   DATE: 20th. June '78.
OPERATION: Loading out scaffold for bricklayers at chamber joist level   STUDY No. 1075

OTHER ALLOWANCES: Contingency 8%   0·37
ALLOWED TIME PER: Cycle   5·00 Std. Min
1 man /PER HOUR AT 100 (METRIC)   120 Bricks

(a)

CONTRACT: Plastics Ltd. Office Block   DATE: 21st. July '78.
OPERATION: Erect facing panels at first floor level   STUDY No. 1096

ELEMENT No.	BASIC TIME	% REST ALLOWANCE	FREQUENCY PER CYCLE	STANDARD TIME
1	24·41	19	1/6	4·84
2	4·04	31	1	5·29
3	0·89	16	1	1·03
4	5·58	42	1	7·94
5	2·20	18	1	2·60
6	3·45	28	1	4·42
7	1·04	19	1	1·24
				27·36

OTHER ALLOWANCES: Contingency 6%   1·64
ALLOWED TIME PER: Panel   29·00 Std. Min
4 men /PER HOUR AT 100 (B.S.S.)   8 panels

(b)

Fig. 17.16. Time study summaries

standard minutes or as a number of work units. It should be noted that, in the examples given, the continental rating scale of 100/133 has been used for Study No. 1075, while the British Standard scale of 0/100 has been employed on Study No. 1096. Hence the bricklayer's labourer, in performing an average over the day of one cycle every five minutes, is only working at a rate equivalent to 4.8 km/h, while the gang of joiners in fixing panels on average one every seven and a quarter minutes are working at the equivalent rate of 6.4 km/h. This difference must be remembered when the allowed time is used for planning or estimating purposes, or as the basis for an incentive scheme.

For convenience it is usual to adopt 100 work units per hour as standard performance, which represents the daily average speed of movement for a qualified workman who is motivated by suitable incentives. On this comparative basis the work content of 120 bricks can be expressed as 75 work units, and 8 panels as 400 work units, since the former was quoted at normal (hourly rate) time and the latter at standard (bonus rate) peformance.

Once the allowed time has been compiled it is necessary to prepare a job specification, in order to record the method, materials and machines used, and the operating conditions experienced. These details should be brief, but sufficient to enable the effect of any later changes upon the work content to be detected. All the relevant time study data, i.e. record, analysis, allowance and summary sheets should be attached.

4. Applications

The objective of work study is to obtain optimum productivity from the available manpower and materials, and since it is management's responsibility to see that the best use is made of an organisation's resources, it is, therefore, building managers who must be convinced of the value of work study applications to building operations. Process study can be said to be employed, since this covers such technical decisions as the system of building and the kind of materials to be used at the design stage, or the type of plant to be utilised during construction. By and large, however, the advantages to be gained from method study or work measurement techniques are insufficiently appreciated by contracting firms. To be effective, a work study department must have solid backing from the top, but when given full support and employed with discretion and common sense, it can give practical assistance to every management process.

1. *Forecasting.* Accurate labour costs based upon the allowed times obtained by direct work measurement, are invaluable in estimating for tendering purposes and produce economic prices that can be relied upon when profit margins must be cut. Over the years a library of standard data can be accumulated from which new time standards may be synthesised.

   a. *Synthetics* or synthesised time standards are built up with individual element times extracted from previous time study records. In this manner the labour content of new operations can be estimated beforehand by utilising similar elements taken from the histories of past experience. Such elements as tightening nuts, driving nails or sawing timber may be common to many different operations, and data compiled from a large number of studies are thus more reliable than a single observation. A synthetics library requires careful organisation and constant revision, but its use may sometimes eliminate the need for prolonged studies. Whenever possible it is usual to check a synthetic time by making a short production study to ensure that no activity has been overlooked. These check studies are similar to normal time studies except that their element breakdown is not so detailed, but they must cover a complete working shift.

   b. *Analytical estimating* can be used to assess time standards for non-repetitive work where work measurement by time study is uneconomic or impossible. Estimators must be thoroughly trained and experienced in work study, and time-study data or synthetic times should be used wherever possible. The technique involves analysing the job into its elements and estimating standard performance times on the basis of personal experience, followed by the addition of rest allowances and the compilation of an allowed time as before. Although simple in theory, analytical estimating needs to be applied by an expert, but within the obvious limits of their accuracy the results are of special value in jobbing or repair work and planned maintenance of plant.

2. *Planning.* Contract planning depends for its success upon the provision of accurate information, in order that the flow of work shall be continuous and labour and plant be fully utilised. Flow charts and string diagrams can be used to plan site

layouts, and the basic data supplied as a result of method study or work measurement is ideal for drawing up a production programme, or for comparing the relative costs of alternative methods of construction. Only upon a foundation of directly observed facts can working methods be really improved, gangs or related items of plant be properly balanced, and reliable completion periods be calculated. Operational research techniques such as queue theory and simulation also have applications to production planning, but these also rely upon accurate data such as only work study can supply.

3. *Organising.* Organising the most effective utilisation of labour and plant implies a full consideration of all the technical and economic factors involved, in order to ensure the optimum return from all resources. Devising the most efficient relationships between labour and plant involves the use of method study, while to check the overall economy of production it is necessary to employ work measurement. The use of work study principles in the office to achieve savings in clerical costs is now well established under the more usual term of organisation and methods – see Chapter 10. On civil engineering projects such as opencast coal sites, where expensive machines like mechanical shovels or large draglines are used for long periods on continuous operations, method study can achieve significant increases in output. Similarly, the precise standards of work measurement are necessary for the calculation of wages incentive schemes when productivity is so dependent upon the plant utilisation. The application of work study to local authority problems has been well described by the Borough Engineer and Surveyor of Walsall in a paper to the Institution of Civil Engineers.

4. *Motivating.* The motivation of human behaviour is influenced by a variety of considerations, including the desires for money or power, the forces of fear, uncertainty or custom, the satisfaction of self expression, social relationships and a sense of common purpose. However, while it must be recognised that industrial effort is partly dependent upon deeper values than pure cash rewards, financial incentives can play an important role in the achievement of higher productivity.

    a. Financial incentive schemes are intended to remove substandard performance, and encourage increased output by the payment of bonus money related to the level of production. They are broadly based upon the theoretical assumption (not borne out in practice) that the normal performance of an average workman under proper supervision is unhurried wihout being intentionally time wasting, but well within his potential capability, i.e. a fair day's work for the basic union rate of pay. The same workman under the stimulus of financial rewards can achieve and maintain a pace of work up to 33⅓ per cent above his normal, without loss of quality or personal strain.

Estimates published in the *Ministry of Labour Gazette* 1961 showed that the overall percentage of manual workers being paid under some form of output bonus system had risen from 31 to 33 per cent in four years, although in construction it was only 14 per cent. Besides promoting higher output, such schemes should also lower unit costs because of the reduced incidence of overheads, and at the same time increase the workers' earnings.

On an individual basis the most common form of incentive payment system is straight piece-work, which pays a uniform price per unit of production so that the labour cost per unit is constant. Labour only brickwork or joinery sub-contracts are current building trade examples of money piece-work. In time piece-work a time is allowed for each operation or unit and the worker is paid at his basic rate per hour for the time allowed, so that he gains the value of any time saved. The work units procedure, referred to earlier under 3, (5), *Compilation,* is embodied in point-rating schemes as a means of calculating the allowed time. The premium bonus system is similar to time piece-work except that the time allowed is paid for at the basic rate plus a premium. The much maligned Bedaux system paid three-quarters of the premium payment to direct workers and the remaining quarter to the foreman.

Differential piece-rate systems have been devised in which the labour cost per unit is adjusted in relation to output. The Taylor two-price system increased the piece-work price when the normal had been exceeded, with the object of reducing heavy overhead costs. Other well known systems like the Halsey (or Weir) and the Rowan were based upon standard time allowances, but the labour cost per unit falls as output increases while the worker's hourly rate increases but at a reduced proportion. A comparison between these different systems is shown diagrammatically in Fig. 17.17.

In manufacturing industry these incentive payment methods have been an integral part of scientific management for

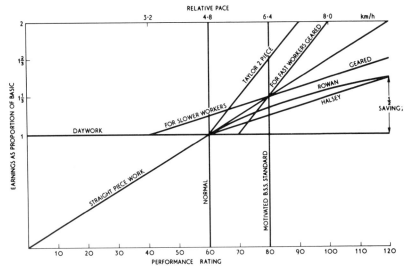

Fig. 17.17. Comparison of incentive payment systems

nearly three quarters of a century, but during the last twenty-five years there has been a movement away from mechanistic appraisals of work towards decentralised management. Traditional time standards have been replaced by output norms established by each individual worker in conjunction with his foreman. However, at the present stage of development in the building and civil engineering industries, there is great scope for the further spread of payment by results.

b. *Payment by results* was introduced in the building and civil engineering industries by the Ministry of Works in 1941, and was applied to all sites scheduled under the war-time Essential Work Order. Schedules of output targets per man hour were laid down for most operations, together with bonus rates for production in excess of the basic calculated as two-thirds of the cost saved. Bonuses were paid by gangs and distributed according to specified shares, i.e. charge hands 5, tradesmen 4, and labourers 3, each. When the emergency works programme was completed in March 1947, the scheme came to an end, although bonusing had been permissible in the civil engineering industry since the original 1921 Agreement. In October 1947 the National

Joint Council for the Building Industry reached an agreement which enabled bonus schemes to be applied 'giving an operative of average ability and capacity a reasonable opportunity to achieve . . . earnings 20 per cent higher than those yielded by the normal prescribed rate'. Despite this opportunity there has been a widespread reluctance to introduce bona-fide incentive schemes, and due to difficulties and doubts on the part of both employers and operatives, plus rates or guaranteed bonus, and payments based upon the foreman's judgement, are common expedients. A Ministry of Labour survey in 1955 revealed that only an estimated 16 per cent of the building labour force worked under incentive schemes linked to measured productivity, and the National Federation of Building Trades Employers expressed their intention to publish further guidance on this subject as a contribution to National Productivity Year 1962/1963. 'General principles concerning incentive schemes and productivity agreements' have since been included in the National Working Rules.

Financial incentive schemes are not likely to be effective where a machine determines the pace of work, or where the flow of production is spasmodic, so that the response of labour is contingent upon the management first putting its own house in order. Basic requirements are a feasible programme, properly defined methods and procedures including quality controls, carefully organised deliveries of materials and components, well maintained plant and equipment, facilities for accurate labour allocations, and factual performance standards. A satisfactory system of incentive payments should be:

i.   Fair and equitable to both employer and operatives,
ii. Clearly defined in order to avoid disputes,
iii. Simple and inexpensive to operate,
iv. Readily understood so that a worker may check his bonus,
v.   Quick to calculate so that operatives may know as quickly as possible what they have earned, and
vi. Capable of regular weekly payment.

The two types of target widely used in the building industry are:

i.   Stage or operation in which a target of man hours or money value is set for a specific task or section or work, e.g. brickwork 'topping out', and the bonus paid is a proportion of the time or wages saved. This necessitates preparatory work to determine the work content or value of the task before the start of a job, but is very suitable for repetitive operations such as house building.

ii. Unit rate by which predetermined rates of output are specified, e.g. square metres of formwork per man hour. The work performed is measured and the actual labour cost then compared with the calculated target. Again a proportion of the saving is paid as bonus in addition to the plain time rates. This form of target is useful when a variety of operations and non-repetitive work is involved or where the quantity is unknown beforehand, e.g. excavations, but requires regular measurement as construction proceeds. Both general rules and suggested targets were given by the Amalgamated Union of Building Trade Workers in their *Guide to Incentives*, but these are considered to be 'too low in present-day circumstances' by the National Federation of Building Trades Employers, who also repudiate any national schedule of bonus targets which disregards the varying quality and methods peculiar to each contract.

Opinions differ as to the proportion of savings to be disbursed as bonus, varying from the 50 per cent suggested by the N.F.B.T.E.* to the 100 per cent proposed by the A.U.B.T.W. There are valid arguments in favour of less than 100 per cent of the savings being returned, i.e. administration costs, allowances for substandard performance and remedial work, uncertain targets, a desire to reduce costs, and a share in the fruits of well organised conditions that made the increased production possible; these, however, are all outweighed by the psychological effect of complete distribution to the operatives, and the incidental reduction of overheads. These considerations do underline the absolute necessity of accurate and dependable performance figures such as only work study can provide, in place of the empirical or rule of thumb standards often used at present. Moreover, since the two variables of target and percentage paid are interdependent, they should be considered together when preparing a bonus scheme. 'Geared' bonus systems

* Higher calculation factors are recommended in *The Principles of Incentives for the Construction Industries*.

exist in which the proportion of the saving paid varies with the level of output, either to encourage the faster workers to attain very high performances or to encourage the slower workers to attempt inprovements (see Fig. 17.17). Both of these systems are difficult to operate and run the risk of being misunderstood by the operatives. Since most payment by result schemes are calculated on a gang basis, the distribution of bonus between the operatives presents another possible variable Although individual incentive rewards are theoretically the ideal, the majority of construction work is team effort so that in practice bonus is paid to gangs or trades. The share of the total bonus paid to each member is invariably calculated in proportion to the hours worked by him, and possibly is also modified according to his comparitive hourly rate or actual wages. Alternatively, both craftsmen and labourers may be paid equal shares per hour, or allocated varying shares as between chargehands, craftsmen, labourers and apprentices – see Fig. 17.18 for a typical bonus sheet. Staff general foremen are usually excluded from these schemes, but trades foremen on the timebook may be paid bonus on productive work and an allowance given for supervisory time.

The level of bonus payments may vary considerably with trade, site, firm or district, but the 33⅓ per cent recommended by BAS (19) is still technically correct, although 100% or more is common today. Because operatives are paid the minimum basic hourly rates even when targets are not reached, the problem of 'gains' and 'losses' is associated with this wide variability of performance, since each week's work is judged by itself. Again the only real answer is accurate targets produced by work measurement, but in practice the week's work is often averaged out so that ups and downs are balanced in a nett result.

c. *Other collective systems* of incentive payments have particular or partial applications with varied records of success. A task system of payment exists in the mastic asphalt laying industry, where an agreement made by the National Joint Council stipulates hourly rates of pay and also determines the amount of work expected to be performed in a normal day by a gang of usual size.

WEEKLY BONUS SHEET

TRADE		HOURS	SHARE	£	p	RATE	
C/Hand	5	42	210	52	20	1.24	CONTRACT: Merit Assurance
B/Layer	4	146	584	145	15	0.99½	GANG: Jackson
B/L Lab.	3	82	246	61	15	0.74½	
							WEEK ENDING: 3rd. March 1975
			1040	258	50		

CHECK No.	TRADE	NAME	HOURS	RATE	£	p
517	C/Hand	A.G. Jackson	42	1.24	52	20
2025	B/Layer	T. Smith	44	0.99½	43	78
2026	B/Layer	A. James	38	,,	37	81
2027	B/Layer	C.W. Tootal	20	,,	19	90
2029	B/Layer	O. Jenkins	44	,,	43	78
2050	B/L Lab	M. Black	44	0.74½	32	78
2052	B/L Lab	W. Crains	38	,,	28	31
			270		258	56

HOURS	DESCRIPTION OF WORK	MEASURE	TARGET	UP	RATE	£	p
60	115mm Brickwork	80 m²	60 m²	20	3.75	75	00
120	230mm Brickwork	90 m²	75 m²	15	6.00	90	00
60	Weather pointing	90 m²	60 m²	30	2.75	82	50
30	75mm Breeze partition	50½ m²	45 m²	5½	2.00	11	00
270						258	50

Fig. 17.18

The question of incentives for indirect labour, such as maintenance fitters, is a problem, although their contribution is essential to the output of other workers, for payment by results cannot be directly applied. Where the work is itself measurable as in the case of unloading gangs, payment may be ordinary piece-work, but these ancillary operatives must receive some additional monetary award associated either with a particular or general output of the site or with the bonuses of direct workers.

Profit-sharing schemes are operated by certain building employers, under which operatives receive a bonus depending upon the company profit over a period – usually at Christmas for the previous year.

Co-partnership schemes have been developed in other industries, by which shares are issued usually to long serving employees and dividends are paid periodically from the profits of the firm. The two latter systems are only suitable for regular staff, and in any case a little too remote to affect collective productivity. However, like other composite schemes of merit payment they can encourage good workmanship, while the contrary is the usual objection to direct output incentives.

5. *Controlling.* Good management control depends upon the laying down of standards of performance against which actual results can be judged. The accurate standards established by work measurement provide an effective means of controlling machine utilisation and labour costs based on allowed times. They are certainly the best basis for budgetary control, and in particular for standard costing.

   a. The work study technique of *activity sampling* is a useful and economical means of checking on site supervision and planning, by estimating group activity or productivity from a statistical analysis of random sample observations. In theory the percentage *number* of observations recording either activity or delay is a reliable estimate of the percentage *time* that the operation is in either state, provided that sufficient observations are taken and the rules of random selection are observed. As in the Statistical Sampling described in Chapter 16, the method consists of selecting a sufficient number of samples from a large group and from them making a prediction for the whole; it is therefore not applicable to individual workmen. Two variations of the system are possible, either to measure the overall activity of

REF. No. **113** OBSERVER: *J. C. Awle* DATE: 10th *July* 1978

SERIES No.	TIME	1	2	3	4	5	6	7	A	B	C	D	E	F	G	No.
①	9.50	✓								✓						1
			✓								✓					2
				✓								✓				3
					✓									✓		4
						✓			✓							5
							✓			✓						6
								✓				✓				7
②	10.00	✓								✓						8
			✓								✓					9
				✓								✓				10
					✓										✓	11
						✓				✓						12
							✓							✓		13
								✓				✓				14
③	10.06	✓								✓						15
			✓									✓				16

Fig. 17.19. *Random observation study*

REF. No. **113/A**   SUMMARY   DATE: 21st *July* 1978

Level of confidence 95%. Accuracy required ± 2¼%
Estimated max. %age per activity 40%

$$\text{Required no. of observations} = \frac{4 \times 40 \times 60}{5 \cdot 06} = \frac{1900}{\text{say } 27} \text{ i.e. } 7 \times 272 \text{ times for 10 days}$$

$$\text{Limits of max. \%age for activity G} = 2\sqrt{\frac{33 \cdot 1 \times 66 \cdot 9}{1890}} = \underline{2 \cdot 16}$$

	OBSERVATIONS			% OF TOTAL TIME	
ACTIVITY	NUMBER	% OF TOTAL	LIMITS	MIN.	MAX.
A	368	19·5	± 1·8	17·7	21·3
B	420	22·2	± 1·9	20·3	24·1
C	57	3·0	± 0·8	2·2	3·8
D	175	9·2	± 1·3	7·9	10·5
E	185	9·8	± 1·4	8·4	11·2
F	60	3·2	± 0·8	2·4	4·0
G	625	33·1	± 2·2	30·9	35·3
TOTAL	1890	100·0	OBSERVER: *J. C. Awle*		

Fig. 17.20. *Random observation study summary*

a contract over a period of time, or to determine the effectiveness of a team working on a particular operation.

b. A *field activity count* will show how fully the operatives are employed, and since a high level of activity is a prerequisite of good productivity, the results indicate management efficiency. The procedure is to use two mechanical counters, held one in each hand, and during a tour of the complete site to record all the personnel observed, either as active on one counter, or inactive on the other. Counts are usually made twice daily, in the morning and afternoon at random times and by varying routes. The total number of men observed should be reconciled with the time book – between 75 and 80 per cent is valid – and the activity rating calculated as a percentage:

$$\text{Activity rating} = \frac{\text{No. observed active} \times 100 \text{ per cent}}{\text{Total No. observed}}$$

The results of such counts may be used to draw graphs showing the varying pattern of activity over the week, or if more frequent studies are taken to illustrate the rise and fall during the day.

c. A *random observation study* may be used to determine the amount and nature of ineffective time present in a particular operation, and for this reason the method is sometimes known as a *ratio-delay study*. The operation is first broken down into its constituent elements as for a time study, and a coding system is devised for ease of recording. Over a period of perhaps two to four hours the gang is observed at random intervals, and at each instant of observation the precise activity of each member is recorded (see Fig. 17.19). Productive and non-productive observations are then compared and the delay percentage calculated:

Delay (or ineffective time)

$$= \frac{\text{No. of non-productive observations} \times 100 \text{ per cent}}{\text{Total No. of observations}}$$

Individual activities as coded may also be expressed as percentages of the total observations and presented on suitable charts (see Fig. 17.20).

    d. Precautions are necessary to ensure that the conditions of sufficient and random samples are observed. The size of sample necessary can be estimated as follows:

$$\text{No. of observations required} = \frac{KP\,(100 - P)}{L^2}$$

where P is the anticipated percentage activity
    L is the allowed limit of error ($\pm$ per cent)
    K depends upon the measure of confidence required.

Std. deviations	Assurance %	Level of confidence	K
1	68	Moderate	1
2	95.5	High	4
3	99.7	Very high	9

The limits of ± 2.5 per cent variation have been generally accepted for practical purposes, so that the 95 per cent guarantee given by a K of 4 is usually sufficient. After completing a study the actual size of the sampling variations should be obtained as follows:

Limits of error with 95 per cent confidence

$$= \pm\, 2\, \frac{P\,(100 - P)}{N}$$

where P is the approximate percentage calculated from the results; N is the total number of observations taken.
Hence the true percentage = P per cent $\pm$ the percentage error.

The random nature may be assured by using published tables of random numbers, although for approximate studies it might be sufficient to draw numbers from out of a hat. Finally it should be remembered that although field activity counts can be carried out by untrained staff, the conclusions to be drawn from random observation studies require the skill and experience of a trained work study officer.

BIBLIOGRAPHY

Introduction to Work Study, The International Labour Office.
Outline of Work Study, Part 1 – Introduction, Part 2 – Method Study, Part 3 – Work measurement, The British Institute of Management.

R. Geary, *Work Study Applied to Building*, The Builder Ltd.

Glossary of Terms in Work Study, B.S. 3138 : 1979, British Standards Institution.

F. Russon, *Bonusing for Builders*, Norman Tiptaft.

Memorandum on Payment by Results, H.M.S.O.

Incentives in the Building Industry, National Building Studies Special Report No. 28, H.M.S.O.

Guide to Incentives, Amalgamated Union of Building Trade Workers.

The Principles of Incentives for the Construction Industries, Advisory Service for the Building Industry.

Chapter 18

Operational Research

1. Introduction

In February 1963, a meeting held in Oslo under the auspices of the International Council for Building Research Studies and Documentation, agreed that Operational Research could be described as 'the application of scientific methods to complex situations in order to find optimum solutions to problems of decision making and control'.

The O.R. approach to a problem is based upon the essence of scientific method, i.e. the development of a viable hypothesis followed by repeated tests, to eliminate other explanations and to prove the particular one finally put forward as the solution. This distinctive process of studying a problem usually follows a well defined pattern:

1. *Formulate the problem.* A clear recognition of the true problem is of prime importance. Attacking a *symptom* does not necessarily improve the overall efficiency since it may result in a worsening of some other sector's performance.
2. *Collect available data.* Enlightened management decisions should be founded upon quantitative evidence rather than upon intuition.
3. *Construct a model.* As it is not usually feasible to experiment with the real life situation under study, some form of mathematical 'model' must represent the 'system'.
4. *Test the model.* Apply data, and define the parameters – which may be conflicting.
5. *Derive an optimum solution.* Consider alternative solutions to the criteria previously decided upon, and modify if necessary.
6. *Report the proposals* arising from the investigation, for consideration and decision by line management.
7. *Implement the chosen solution.* In addition establish controls to measure the effectiveness of the improvements anticipated. Since in the majority of cases the solution is a compromise

344

between a number of alternatives which are optimal with respect to different criteria, feedback is essential in order that modifications may be made in the light of actual results.

Operational research is generally recognised to have emerged as a separate branch of science during the 1939–45 world war. Professor P.M.S. Blackett was probably responsible for the first O.R. study, when the British military approached him for help with their Radar problems. The results of his team's work were so impressive that the military staff set up groups in the three arms of the services to carry out similar research, and when this new staff activity was assigned to G-3 (Operations) it gained its name of Operational Research.

O.R. scientists are drawn from all disciplines, and most O.R. teams include members of several different sciences. This interdisciplinary composition is an essential feature, for by training and working together each is encouraged to appreciate the insufficiency of his own discipline and thus to develop a greater all-round ability.

Case histories have shown that in many diverse industries, executives are confronted by any of eight basic categories of problem. Common problem areas are:

1. *Inventory or stock control problems*. These include size of stock holdings and frequency and quantity of re-order levels.
2. *Allocation or resource problems*. For example, whether to hire or buy plant and the optimisation of cut and fill costs on a motorway.
3. *Queuing problems*. These arise in transport systems.
4. *Sequencing or priority problems*. These are frequent in construction planning.
5. *Routeing*. The basic problem for goods deliveries.
6. *Replacement and maintenance problems*. These concern both light and heavy plant operators.
7. *Competition*. This is a factor in tendering and advertising.
8. *Search problems*. These include accountancy and quality control procedures.

Techniques used to solve the particular problems vary with the circumstances, but they include such mathematical tools as calculus, matrix algebra, simulation, linear programming, network analysis and probability theory. Therefore, managers with an understanding of mathematics will have a marked advantage over those lacking such knowledge.

Although the original breakthrough was made in Britain, where the profession is organised by the Operational Research Society Limited, it would appear that the merits of this analytical approach to management are now more widely appreciated in America. Certainly, a timely review of operational research within the construction industry, produced by a working party consisting of engineers and O.R. scientists, showed that O.R. applications in construction were thinly spread and that nothing like full advantage had been taken of their potential value.*

Yet those who realise that managerial efficiency is even more important than labour productivity, must see that operational research has a great contribution to make to the future development of building and civil engineering. The most successful managements are those which succeed in concentrating their efforts where they have the most telling effect, so that whereas in the past O.R. has been applied largely to the tactical areas of production and control, it is likely that it has the greatest potential in the studies of strategy, planning and decision-making.

2. Network Analysis

One O.R. technique, that has become firmly established in the Building and Civil Engineering industries since about 1965, is network analysis. Known confusingly either as Critical Path Method or Programme Evaluation and Review Technique, the method has increasingly been used for planning and control of construction work, both in the United States and Great Britain.

Originally developed more-or-less in parallel, the fundamentals of both C.P.M. and P.E.R.T. are the same although there were minor differences in theory and application. In 1957 the Du Pont Chemical Company applied C.P.M. to their Refinery Renovation Project, as a tool for the planning, scheduling and control of construction work, with the emphasis on activities. At about the same time the U.S. Navy Department produced P.E.R.T. as a means of planning and evaluating progress on the Polaris Project – a large scale research and development programme, with attention focused on events or milestones. The major difference was that P.E.R.T., designed to cope with uncertainty by use of statistical methods, required three time estimates for each activity – optimistic, most likely, and pessimistic – and applied a probability

* *Building*, February 16, 1968.

distribution to obtain the expected time. Nowadays the statistical approach is rarely used, and network flow techniques combine elements of both systems. The C.P.M. system is clearly more suitable for construction projects, although P.E.R.T. is often used for computer adaptations and developments, loosely as a generic term, and as a synonym for C.P.M.

Network analysis has not made the Gantt chart obsolete, but the method has certain advantages over the normal bar-line programme:

1. It imposes a more rigid discipline during the early thinking about a job, since it is necessary to list the complete sequence of operations.
2. The relationships between preceding and following operations must be precisely decided, and then permanently recorded.

3. Principles of Critical Path Method

1. *Constructing the critical path.* The method involves the graphical representation of a planned programme by a logical network or arrow diagram, depicting the complete series of operations, from the proposed beginning of the project to the target completion date. This is achieved step-by-step in distinct stages, which is a significant advantage for large or complex projects.
   Stage 1. The project is broken down into its constituent operations and these are listed in approximate order of performance. For example: excavate foundation trench; concrete strip footing; build brick wall; lay precast capping.
   Stage 2. A network is then drawn to show the precise sequence in which the operations must be performed. Each *activity*, item of work or job is represented by an arrow, and the *start* and *finish event* of each activity is represented by a circle or node. An identifying number is also given to each event (see Fig. 18.1).
   Stage 3. Time estimates in any suitable unit are now added to the network to indicate the *duration* of each activity (see Fig. 18.2).
   Stage 4. Starting from the beginning, the durations are added together consecutively in order to determine the *earliest possible time* for each event (see Fig. 18.3).

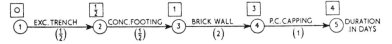

Fig. 18.1. Activities leading to events

① —EXC. TRENCH→ ② CONC. FOOTING→ ③ —BRICK WALL→ ④ —P.C. CAPPING→ ⑤ DURATION
   (½)   (½)   (2)   (1)   IN DAYS

Fig. 18.2. Showing durations of activities

☐0   ☐½   ☐1   ☐3   ☐4

① —EXC. TRENCH→ ② CONC. FOOTING→ ③ —BRICK WALL→ ④ —P.C. CAPPING→ ⑤ DURATION
   (½)   (½)   (2)   (1)   IN DAYS

Fig. 18.3. Showing earliest possible event times

Stage 5. In practice it is usual for networks to be much more complicated, with activities or series of activities proceeding in parallel, i.e. simultaneously (see Fig. 18.4). When there are alternative routes to an event, e.g. **7 → 8 → 10** and **7 → 9 → 10**, each must be calculated, and the *longest* time path will determine the *earliest moment* of achievement.

Stage 6. Starting at the last event, the durations are then subtracted consecutively so that the *latest time* for each event is decided (see Fig. 18.5). In the example shown, event **12** is the last in the chain, and therefore latest time = earliest time, in this case 4 days. Where there are alternative routes, the *lowest* will determine the *latest* possible event time. For example the latest time for event **9** is either $2 - \frac{1}{2} = 1\frac{1}{2}$ days (**10 → 9**) or $3 - 1 = 2$ days (**11 → 9**). Obviously the lower figure ($1\frac{1}{2}$ days) gives the latest time, otherwise event **10** is delayed.

Stage 7. Comparison of the three alternative routes from start to finish in Fig. 18.5, gives three different total durations, viz.:

> **7 → 8 → 10 → 12** requires $1 + 1 + 2 = 4$ days.
> **7 → 9 → 10 → 12** requires $1 + \frac{1}{2} + 2 = 3\frac{1}{2}$ days.
> **7 → 9 → 11 → 12** requires $1 + 1 + 1 = 3$ days.

Route **7 → 8 → 10 → 12**, being the longest, is therefore the Critical Path, and has been distinguished with a thick line. It should be noted that along the Critical path the *earliest* and *latest* times for each event are *identical*.

Stage 8. Events **9** and **11,** not being on the critical path have *slack*, whilst the *activities* leading to these events have *float*. The total float for an activity can be calculated from *latest finish/start – earliest finish/start,* as shown in Fig. 18.6.

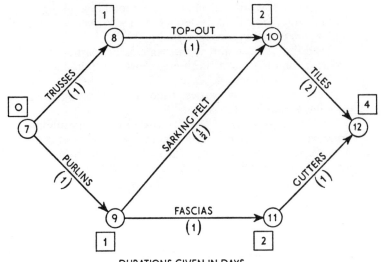

DURATIONS GIVEN IN DAYS

Fig. 18.4. Showing parallel activities

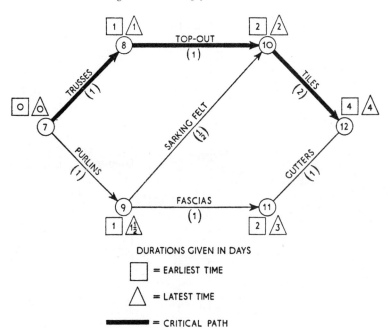

DURATIONS GIVEN IN DAYS

☐ = EARLIEST TIME

△ = LATEST TIME

▬ = CRITICAL PATH

Fig. 18.5. Showing latest possible event times

Fig. 18.7 shows the calculation of the total float in Fig. 18.5. In this table, an activity is defined by a *start event number (i)* and a *finish event number (j)*.

Since the earliest start is the same as the earliest time for event (*i*) and the latest finish is identical with the latest time for event (*j*), then,

earliest finish = earliest time (*i*) + duration, and,

latest start = latest time (*j*) − duration.

The total float for an activity is the maximum amount of time which can be taken up in an emergency without delaying the overall completion time. The term is also used for the sum of floats in an activity chain, e.g. **9 → 12**.

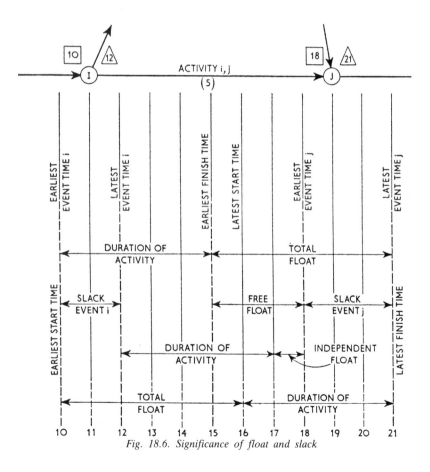

Fig. 18.6. Significance of float and slack

For planning purposes, other types of float can also be envisaged as follows, see also Fig. 18.6:

Independent float: The amount of leeway available when an activity begins at the latest event time without delaying the start of any subsequent activity.

Free float: The amount of leeway available when an activity begins at the earliest event time, again without affecting any following activity.

Interfering float: The overlap in time between the latest finish time of an activity and the earliest start time of the following activity, i.e. the slack of event j.

Activity	Event i	Event j	Duration	Start Earliest	Start Latest	Finish Earliest	Finish Latest	Total Float
Trusses	7	8	1	0	0	1	1	0
Purlins	7	9	1	0	½	1	1½	½
Top-out	8	10	1	1	1	2	2	0
Sarking	9	10	½	1	1½	1½	2	½
Fascias	9	11	1	1	2	2	3	1
Tiles	10	12	2	2	2	4	4	0
Gutters	11	12	1	2	3	3	4	1

Fig. 18.7. Calculation of total float

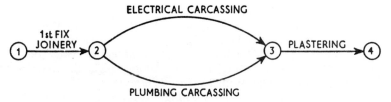

Fig. 18.8. Parallel activities

Fig. 18.9. Parallel activities linked by a dummy

2. *Parallel and overlapping activities.* When two activities have the same start and finish events, they are said to be in parallel, see Fig. 18.8. For some computer programs, each activity requires a unique reference number, which can be obtained by the introduction of a *dummy activity*.

The dummy activity *i3 → j4,* inserted into Fig. 18.9 has created unique event numbers for each activity. Because dummy activities have a *nil duration* they are shown by dotted lines. Such dummies are also useful where a parallel series of activities have a common restraint, as in Fig. 18.10.

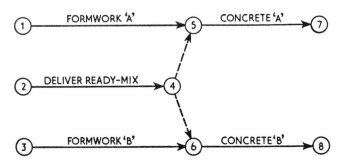

Fig. 18.10. Dummy activities due to common restraint

In building operations, many activities may overlap in time. Fig. 18.11 shows how this situation can be represented on an arrow diagram. Such a diagram shows the true relationship between the sections of overlapping activities. However, for a complex system this form of *incrementing* rapidly becomes cluttered, and a simpler representation, which still gives the correct event times is the *ladder diagram*. Fig. 18.12 shows the ladder diagram equivalent to Fig. 18.11. The reader should study these together to understand their relationship. In the ladder diagram, the *lead times* refer to those portions of activities which must be done before following activities can start; the *lag times* represent those portions of activities which cannot begin until the preceding activities have finished. The rungs of the ladder show the total activity durations. Thus, plastering has a duration of 6 hours, with a lead time of $1\frac{1}{2}$ hours ($\mathbf{3 \to 5}$), and a lag time of $1\frac{1}{2}$ hours ($\mathbf{2 \to 4}$). In the ladder diagram, by convention the events at the heads of arrows are represented by square nodes.

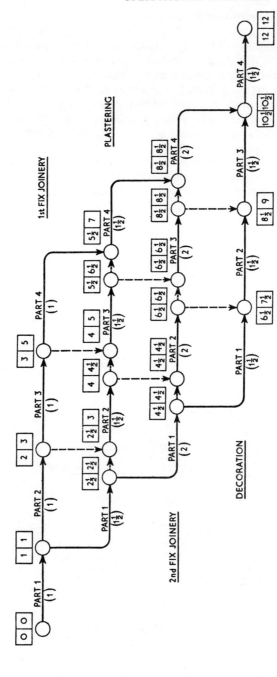

Fig. 18.11. Overlapping activities – incrementing

4. Recommended Procedure

Having described step-by-step the planning and scheduling phases of C.P.M., there remain certain practical recommendations for representing a construction project by network. It is advisable to draw arrow diagrams from left to right so far as possible, although activities may be arranged diagonally if it is required to save space (see Fig. 18.13). When establishing the logical sequence of activities, it is necessary to ask the following three simple questions:

a. Which activities must be completed before a particular operation can proceed?

b. Which other activities can be carried out at the same time as the particular operation?

c. Which activities can begin as soon as the particular operation has been completed?

The extent of detail necessary cannot be specified in a hard-and-fast formula, but a useful rule-of-thumb for an overall master programme would be to include as a minimum every item of

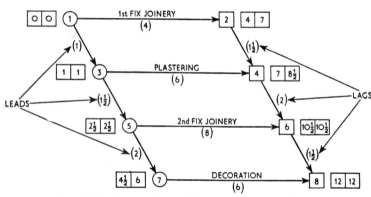

Fig. 18.12. Overlapping activities – ladder convention

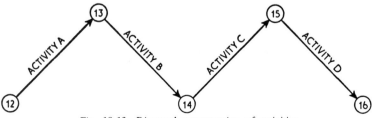

Fig. 18.13. Diagonal representaion of activities

work requiring one per cent of the project period, or comprising one per cent of the project value, i.e. a two-year project should be broken down to activities requiring one week or longer for fulfilment.

Areas of a network may need to be expanded separately, but greater detail should be avoided unless it does effectively contribute to the planning or control of the project.

Ideally events should be numbered so that the i number at the tail of an arrow is smaller than the j number at its head. This sequential numbering is essential for certain computer programs, and it is always good practice for it acts as a check on unintentional 'loops'. To allow for subsequent revisions and additions it is helpful to leave gaps in the numbering, e.g. omit 10, 20, 30 etc.

When assigning durations to the network, the time estimates may be made in a variety of ways. Work may be measured by work study engineers, times may be synthethised from past study data, estimated from standards based upon historical experience, derived from personal experience or merely 'guesstimated' as the most likely time – somewhere between the optimistic and the pessimistic. All estimates must of course bear some relationship to the resources likely to be available, for work load, time and output are interdependent. For example,

$$\text{number of men} = \frac{\text{quantity of work}}{\text{time} \times \text{output per man}}$$

or conversely,

$$\text{time} = \frac{\text{quantity of work}}{\text{no. of men} \times \text{output per man}}.$$

The outputs assumed and resources allocated, e.g. type and number of machines, should be recorded for reference.

Before proceeding with the analysis of a network the following checks should be made for errors. Logic should be reviewed and revised if faulty, to confirm that the network is a true representation of the facts. A check must be made to ensure that no event number has been duplicated. If an effort has been made to ensure that every event number at the head of an arrow is larger than the event number at the tail, it should be easy to make certain that there are no *loops*. Such a logical impossibility is shown in Fig. 18.14. A more common mistake is the unintentional *dangle* seen in Fig. 18.15. Every activity must rejoin the network at a suitable point, continue to the final event, or be terminated with a scheduled date, with a dummy to the final event.

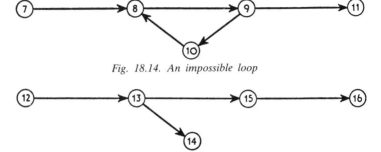

Fig. 18.14. An impossible loop

Fig. 18.15. An unintentional dangle

Two frequent errors of logic involving unnecessary restraints, will be readily uncovered if every event with two or more arrows both entering and leaving is carefully reconsidered. The first type called a *cartwheel,* is illustrated in Fig. 18.16. In this example of road construction, it is true that both erection of kerb formwork and trimming and rolling, are dependent upon formation excavation. It is also true that formwork must be fabricated before it may be erected, but trim and roll are not dependent at all upon formwork fabrication. The correct solution is to add a dummy as shown in Fig. 18.17. The second type of error is very similar, but is disguised as a *waterfall* (see Fig. 18.18). Here, the logic at events **19** and **21** is correct, but a false restraint has been built in at event **20**. Shutter part 3 is dependent upon both Shutter part 2 and Excavate part 3, and similarly Concrete part 2 is dependent upon

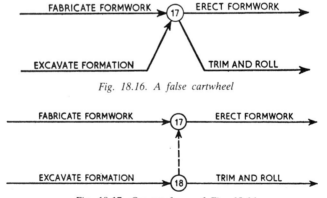

Fig. 18.16. A false cartwheel

Fig. 18.17. Correct form of Fig. 18.16

both Shutter part 2 and Concrete part 1. However, Concrete part 2 is not meant to be dependent upon Excavate part 3 and a dummy must be inserted as shown in Fig. 18.19.

Having made certain that the network is correct, it is now safe to continue with the scheduling process. Analysis of earliest and latest event times will identify the critical path, but it must be realised that

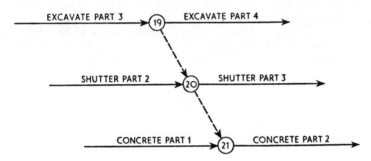

Fig. 18.18. A false waterfall

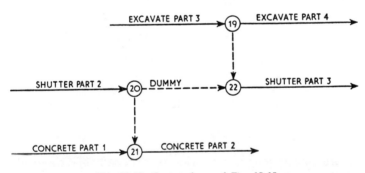

Fig. 18.19. Correct form of Fig. 18.18

there may be more than one critical route as well as other paths very nearly critical. If the overall time is longer than desired or allowed, then an attempt must be made to shorten the period by modifying the critical path. This may be achieved in one of the following ways, or by a combination of them:

  a. Remove dependencies so that activities may begin earlier than previously allowed. This is in effect a modification of the work plan, either by changing the method or where possible persuading someone to relax too stringent conditions. Taking a reinforced concrete building as an example, Fig. 18.20 represents the situation where construction of the walls cannot begin until the floor has attained a minimum strength to be self-supporting. By propping the floors, the walls are no longer dependent upon the curing period so that in Fig. 18.21 the overall time has been effectively reduced.

b. Activities such as finishing trades may be overlapped so that the time period required in Fig. 18.22 is halved when work is rearranged as shown in Fig. 18.12.

c. The original durations may be reduced in a straightforward manner, either by using additional labour or more powerful plant.

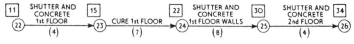

Fig. 18.20. Original work plan

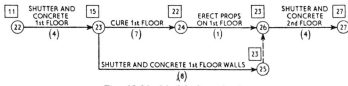

Fig. 18.21. Modified work plan

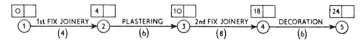

Fig. 18.22. A series of trades

Shortening the length of the critical path or paths may cause other paths to become critical also, and if the project time still requires reduction then each such path must be speeded up until the required end date has been achieved. A final analysis of earliest and latest event times will check the overall project period, and distinguish the resulting critical path(s). This is the appropriate time to add secondary activities such as preparation of drawings and material deliveries, where these have not been so crucial as to have been included in the initial network.

Proceeding with the scheduling stage, the calculated earliest/ latest start and finish times can be converted from working days to calender dates. To do this it is necessary to know whether a 5, 6, or

7 day week is being operated, and what holidays will be observed by the site. It is also possible, if desired, to make some allowance for anticipated inclement weather by arbitrarily setting aside perhaps one day per week, during the nominal winter period. This translation is most easily achieved by means of some form of calendar with the effective working days superimposed, see Fig. 18.23.

To complete the analysis, the information derived from the foregoing operations can be assembled for use in tabular form. The order in which activities are arranged can be varied to suit the specific purpose for which the schedule is intended. The most usual sorting orders are:

    a. By event numbers; see Fig. 18.7. This is easy to follow in conjunction with an arrow diagram.

DECEMBER 1974

S	M	T	W	T	F	S
1 –	2 173	3 174	4 175	5 176	6 177	7 –
8 –	9 178	10 179	11 180	12 181	13 182	14 –
15 –	16 183	17 184	18 185	19 186	20 187	21 –
22 –	23 –	24 –	25 –	26 –	27 –	28 –
29 –	30 188	31 189				

Fig. 18.23. A scheduling day calendar

Activity	Event i	Event j	Duration	Earliest Start	Earliest Finish	Latest Start	Latest Finish	Total Float
Clear Site	2	3	6	6	12	7	13	1
Deliver steel	2	5	24	6	30	6	30	0
Site strip	3	6	7	12	19	18	25	6
Exc. bases	3	4	10	12	22	13	23	1
U/F drains	6	7	4	19	23	25	29	6
Ext. drains	6	10	6	19	25	67	73	48
Conc. bases	4	5	7	22	29	23	30	1
Hardcore	7	8	7	23	30	29	36	6
Access roads	10	14	14	25	39	86	100	61
Conc. slab	8	9	14	30	44	36	50	6
Erect steel	5	9	20	30	50	30	50	0
Cladding	9	11	12	50	62	50	62	0
Partitions	11	12	11	62	73	62	73	0
Services	12	13	15	73	88	73	88	0
Int. finishes	13	14	12	88	100	88	100	0

Fig. 18.24. Sort by earliest start dates

b. By earliest start dates; see Fig. 18.24. This is useful when comparing progress against programme.

c. By minimum float; see Fig. 18.25. This shows up those critical and near critical operations upon which efforts must be concentrated.

d. By responsibility, and, within responsibility, by earliest start dates. This allows comparison of progress with programme within trades, or within individual areas of responsibility e.g. design, procurement, or construction.

Activity	Event i	Event j	Duration	Earliest Start 1980	Earliest Finish 1980	Latest Start 1980	Latest Finish 1980	Total float
Deliver steel	2	5	24	13 Jan.	14 Feb.	13 Jan.	14 Feb.	0
Erect steel	5	9	20	14 Feb.	13 Mar.	14 Feb.	13 Mar.	0
Cladding	9	11	12	13 Mar.	31 Mar.	13 Mar.	31 Mar.	0
Partitions	11	12	11	31 Mar.	15 Apr.	31 Mar.	15 Apr.	0
Services	12	13	15	15 Apr.	6 May	15 Apr.	6 May	0
Int. finishes	13	14	12	6 May	22 May	6 May	22 May	0
Clear site	2	3	6	13 Jan.	21 Jan.	14 Jan.	22 Jan.	1
Exc. bases	3	4	10	21 Jan.	4 Feb.	22 Jan.	5 Feb.	1
Conc. bases	4	5	7	4 Feb.	13 Feb.	5 Feb.	14 Feb.	1

Fig. 18.25. Sort by minimum float

5. Forms of Presentation

The network is an ideal vehicle for mathematical analysis, but is not always such a useful communications document. To the engineer, the logic and information contained in the typical arrow diagram (see Fig. 18.26) may be patently clear, but to the less academic and more practical mind of a site foreman the message may be rather difficult to decipher. One of several alternative forms of presentation may therefore be usefully employed to make interpretation more easy. The *time bar diagram* (Fig. 18.27) contains precisely the same information as the previous arrow diagram, but the display is readily understood by anyone familiar with the conventional bar or Gantt chart. In this form, the concept of float is particularly well illustrated – in this example by the dotted bars. It should be made clear here, that when we talk of an activity starting on a particular day, we must be clear which moment of time we intend since it must be remembered that an event is only an instant. The start of the working day is usually intended e.g. 8.0 a.m., but the end of the day could equally be used provided that this is specified clearly. In Fig. 18.26 the

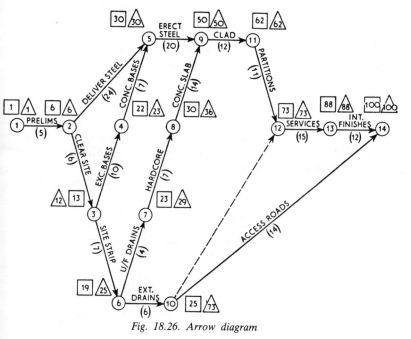

Fig. 18.26. Arrow diagram

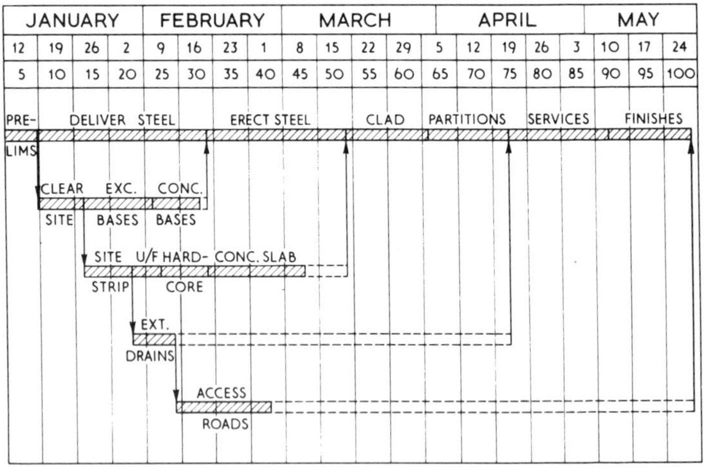

Fig. 18.27. Time bar diagram from Fig. 18.20

operation Erect Steel must be completed by day 50, and in Fig. 18.27 this is shown as the start of the fiftieth day.

When networks become so large that they must for convenience be drawn on more than one drawing sheet, it becomes necessary to employ *interfaces* for the common connection points. These linking events are demonstrated in Figs. 18.28 and 18.29, e.g. events **38, 39, 40, 41** are interface events in the B.S.I. chain of activities. Both diagrams are component parts (or sub nets) of one network – taken from the *Change to Metric in the Construction Industry* document PD 6421 prepared by the National Building Agency. These two figures also illustrate a network which has been laid out in such a manner as to indicate the different fields of responsibility for the overall exercise, i.e. British Standards Institution, manufacturers and contractors. Once again this is an attempt to make an arrow diagram into a more useful communications document, in this instance by dividing it into horizontal divisions of responsibility.

Similarly a network may be divided into vertical divisions as in Fig. 18.30, in this case to indicate the geographical location of the various areas of a building project.

6. The Progressing Phase

Effective planning must of course be a lively operation, a continuing activity throughout the progress of a construction

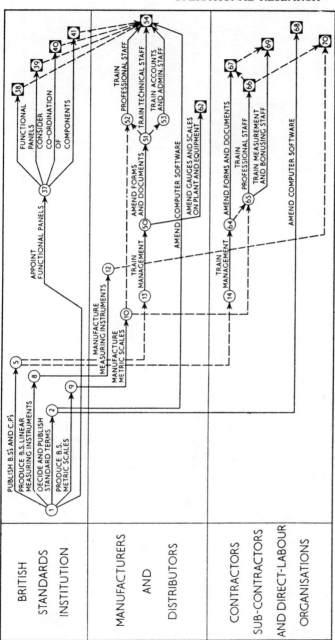

Fig. 18.28. Sub networks showing use of interfaces

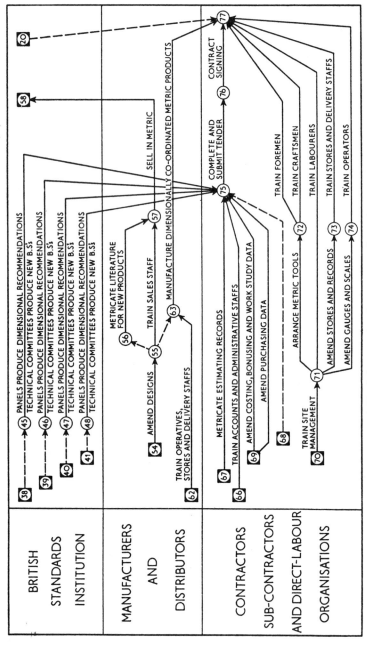

Fig. 18.29. Sub networks showing use of interfaces

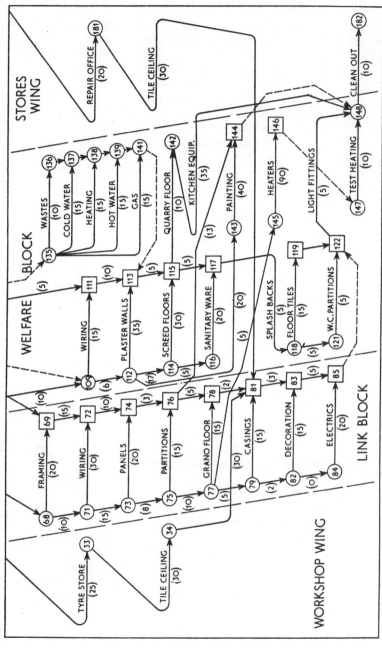

Fig. 18.30. Network divided into vertical divisions to show locations

project, as evidenced by the original title P.E.R.T. (programme evaluation and review technique). So the programming phase leads into the control phase, with regular monitoring of progress, up-dating of the programme and re-scheduling so that the appropriate action may be taken where indicated. At any time '*Now*' activities may be reported as completed or x per cent performed, and start dates or durations may be amended in the light of up-to-date knowledge and more complete information. When a network has been so revised, i.e. up-dated, the mathematical analysis must be performed anew and the scheduling process repeated. The critical path may now be quite different, so that the emphasis of supervision may need to be focused on entirely separate activities. Used in this manner, network analysis is a very potent management tool since it facilitates 'management by exception', highlighting those areas most in need of assistance or correction.

It is at this stage that the value of computer assistance is most likely to become apparent. If the network is extensive, the reviews become frequent, or the revised programmes/schedules are required in a hurry, then the use of a computer is indicated. With unlimited time, the longest and most complicated networks can be analysed manually, but whenever fundamentally the same data has to be reprocessed repeatedly, recourse to a computer program is recommended. Each computer manufacturer has a variety of standard programs available, and other organisations have written their own for their particular needs. Choice may be made on cost, service or personal recommendation, and the current *User Report No. 5* prepared by the University of Loughborough Civil Engineering Department was a particular guide. The Design Office Consortium Evaluation Report No. 9 is more general but up to date (1980).

Every program has its own characteristics and the details may vary considerably, but the procedure is generally the same. Having drawn the arrow diagram and added the durations together with any scheduled dates etc., this information must be written out on a standard pro-forma or data sheet provided for the purpose. A typical data sheet is shown in Fig. 18.31, with part of the arrow diagram from Fig. 18.32 entered up. Most manufacturers also supply a user's handbook for the guidance of customers, or will give advice and assistance if required. This data is then transferred by the computer bureau staff on to punched cards or tape. In this form the information is fed into the computer and to the instructions of the program being used, is processed and the

CLASS	PROJECT CODE	SUB-PROJECT CODE	EVENT NUMBER OR PREC. EVENT			SUCC. EVENT			IDENTIFIER	TIME		TYPE	DESCRIPTION																							DES. S	CARD NUM.
1	2	3	4 5 6 7 8	9	10	1 2 3	4	5 6 7 8	9 20	1 2 3 4 5 6 7 8 9 30 1 2 3																											9 80
A	B	M		1			2		5	P R E L I M S																										S
A	B	M		2			3		6	C L E A R S I T E																										S
A	B	M		2			5		2 4	D E L I V E R S T E E L																										S
A	B	M		3			4		1 0	E X C B A S E S																										S
A	B	M		4			5		7	C O N C . B A S E S																										S
A	B	M		3			6		7	S I T E S T R I P																										S
A	B	M		5			9		2 0	E R E C T S T E E L																										S
A	B	M		6			7		4	U / F D R A I N S																										S
A	B	M		7			8		7	H A R D C O R E																										S
A	B	M		8			9		1 4	C O N C . S L A B																										S
A	B	M		6		1 0			6	E X T . D R A I N S																										S
A	B	M		9		1 1			1 2	C L A D																										S
A	B	M	1 0			1 2				D U M M Y																										S
A	B	M	1 1			1 2			1 1	P A R T I T I O N S																										S
A	B	M	1 2			1 3			1 5	S E R V I C E S																										S

Column-group headers (wide form): I.C.T. 1900 SERIES PERT | ACTIVITY/EVENT CARD (STANDARD) S — RESOURCES: RES. CAT. | QUANTITY | RES. CAT. | QNTY | RES. CAT. | QNTY (columns 40 1 2 3 4 5 6 7 ; 3 4 5 6 7 8 9 70 1 2 3 4 5 6 7 8 9 80)

Fig. 18.31. Data sheet corresponding to part of Fig. 18.26

resultant printed out on continuous sheets, usually in the form of a schedule similar to Figs. 18.24 and 18.25.

The print-out may be used in its schedule form as a communications document, but its value on site may be limited by lack of understanding. However, it is a very simple operation to convert such a print-out (see Fig. 18.32) into a conventional bar chart such as Fig. 18.33, and thus regular up-dating by means of a computer is

ENGINEERING DEPOT.   02/06/67

ALL ACTIVITES IN EARLIEST START ORDER.   TIME NOW 31 MAY 67

PREC EVENT	SUCC EVENT	REPORT CODE	DESCRIPTION	DUR	EARLIEST START	EARLIEST FINISH	LATEST START	LATEST FINISH	TOT FLOAT
071	072	WELFARE BK	CEILING WIRING	0.1	31MAY67	1JUN67	20SEP67	21SEP67	15.4
073	074		CEILING PANELS	1.0	31MAY67	7JUN67	20SEP67	27SEP67	15.4
075	076		DRY PARTITIONS	1.3	31MAY67	12JUN67	21SEP67	30OCT67	16.0
079	081		CASINGS AND DOORS	3.0	31MAY67	21JUN67	19SEP67	10OCT67	15.3
109	111		WIRING ON WALLS	1.3	31MAY67	12JUN67	14AUG67	24AUG67	10.3
112	113		PLASTER ON WALLS	7.0	31MAY67	19JUL67	20JUL67	8SEP67	7.1
135	136		WASTES IN CEILING	0.1	31MAY67	1JUN67	7SEP67	8SEP67	14.0
084	085		ELECTRICAL EQPT	4.0	2JUN67	30JUN67	22SEP67	20OCT67	15.9
145	146		HEATERS PIPEWORK	18.0	7JUN67	12OCT67	29JUN67	3NOV67	3.1
114	115		SCREED FLOORS	4.0	23JUN67	21JUL67	17AUG67	15SEP67	7.4
143	144		PAINTING	8.0	28JUN67	23AUG67	24AUG67	20OCT67	8.1
082	083		FURNITURE ETC	3.0	28JUN67	19JUL67	22SEP67	13OCT67	12.1
116	117		SANITARYWARE	4.0	30JUN67	28JUL67	13SEP67	11OCT67	10.2

Fig. 18.32. Computer print-out corresponding to part of Fig. 18.30

a most convenient way of producing short term programmes. If the print-out lists activities by earliest start dates, it is only necessary perhaps to draw the section of work for five or six weeks ahead. A month later this bar chart itself is up-dated, the additional information only advised to the Bureau, and a new chart produced from the revised print-out. There are of course, numerous rules to be followed and many varieties of coding etc. possible when putting a network on to a computer, but these must be learnt at the time for they differ with each program.

7. Resources and Costs

The work content of a particular task or operation may be expressed as so many man-hours or machine-days, so that the time required for its execution and the resource level necessary for its performance vary inversely to one another. It is usual to resolve this quandary by making initial time estimates for individual

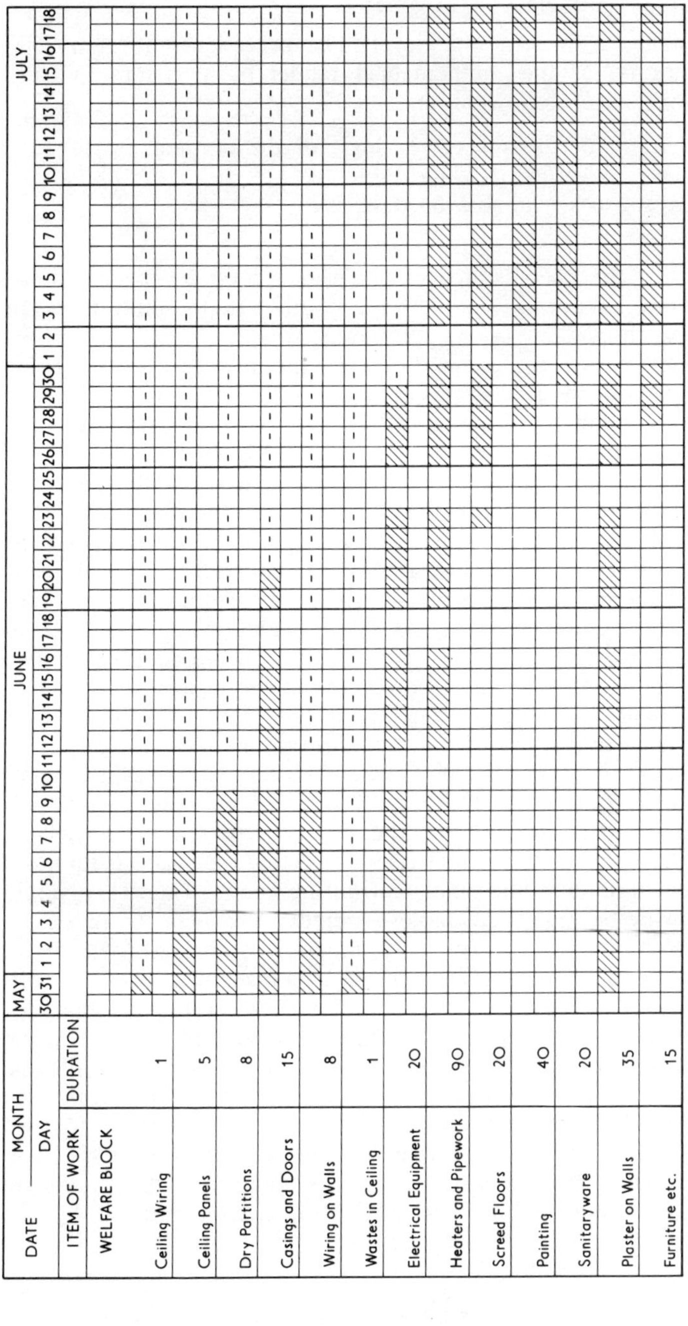
DATE
MONTH
DAY
MAY
JUNE
JULY
ITEM OF WORK
DURATION
WELFARE BLOCK
Ceiling Wiring 1
Ceiling Panels 5
Dry Partitions 8
Casings and Doors 15
Wiring on Walls 8
Wastes in Ceiling 1
Electrical Equipment 20
Heaters and Pipework 90
Screed Floors 20
Painting 40
Sanitaryware 20
Plaster on Walls 35
Furniture etc. 15

Fig. 18.33. Bar chart made from Fig. 18.32

activities on the assumption that sufficient resources will be available at an economic level. The precedence for imposing limitations on the mathematical model of a system i.e. the network, is as follows:

a. Nature of the project or logic of the method employed
b. Time allowed or usual
c. Resources available or desirable
d. Cost.

In this context, resources include manpower by specific skills, machines, materials, money or any other items likely to be in limited supply.

When in turn the demand on certain critical resources is to be investigated, the first step is to carry out a *resource aggregation* to determine the requirements of each resource during each time period. This is achieved by allocating the particular category of asset to a bar chart derived from the analysis of the network, proportioning these along the time scale, and totalling the number for each unit of time. It is usual to begin with activities at their earliest start times (see Fig. 18.34). The demand on the particular resource – in our example some key trade – can now be displayed on a histogram (see Fig. 18.35). Fluctuations in the level of demand can be seen quite clearly, and to avoid standing or idle time it is desirable to smooth any obvious peaks. Resource smoothing is achieved by moving the activities within the limits of their total floats, in order to minimise the peaks and troughs. In the example, activities **I, K, L, M** and **N** can here be scheduled as shown on the upper half of Fig. 18.37, and the revised histogram is given in Fig. 18.36. Although the resource requirements have been considerably rationalised, without affecting the project duration, there still remains one small peak during weeks 10 and 11. It would obviously be highly desirable to remove the need for two extra men for this short period only, unless it is decided to resort to overtime as a temporary expedient. If a maximum level has been predetermined, or if it is decided to restrict the resource for practical reasons, then the schedule of activities must be re-arranged so that the resource level is not exceeded, while the project duration is minimised. Task **I** may be performed by four men over three weeks instead of by six men working for two weeks. The revised programme is shown on the lower half of Fig. 18.37, where the effect of limiting the labour force to a maximum of twelve men has been to extend the overall duration by one additional week.

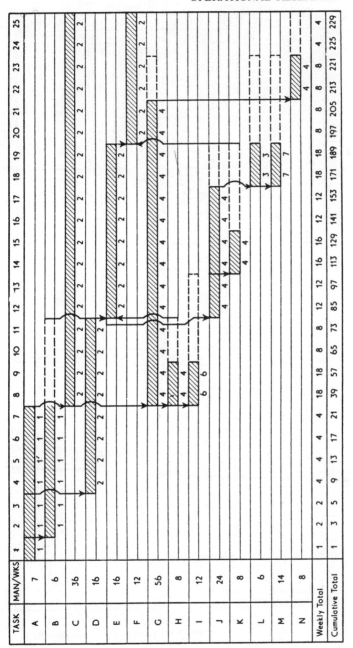

Fig. 18.34. Time bar diagram with earliest starts

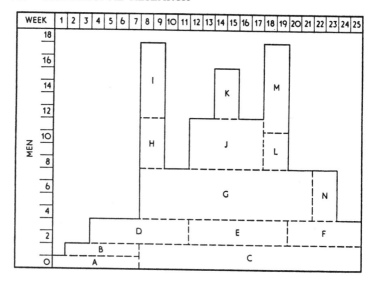

Fig. 18.35. Histogram showing demand using earliest starts

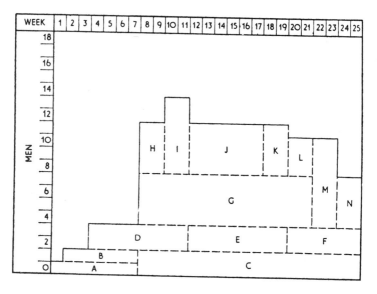

Fig. 18.36. Histogram showing demand after smoothing

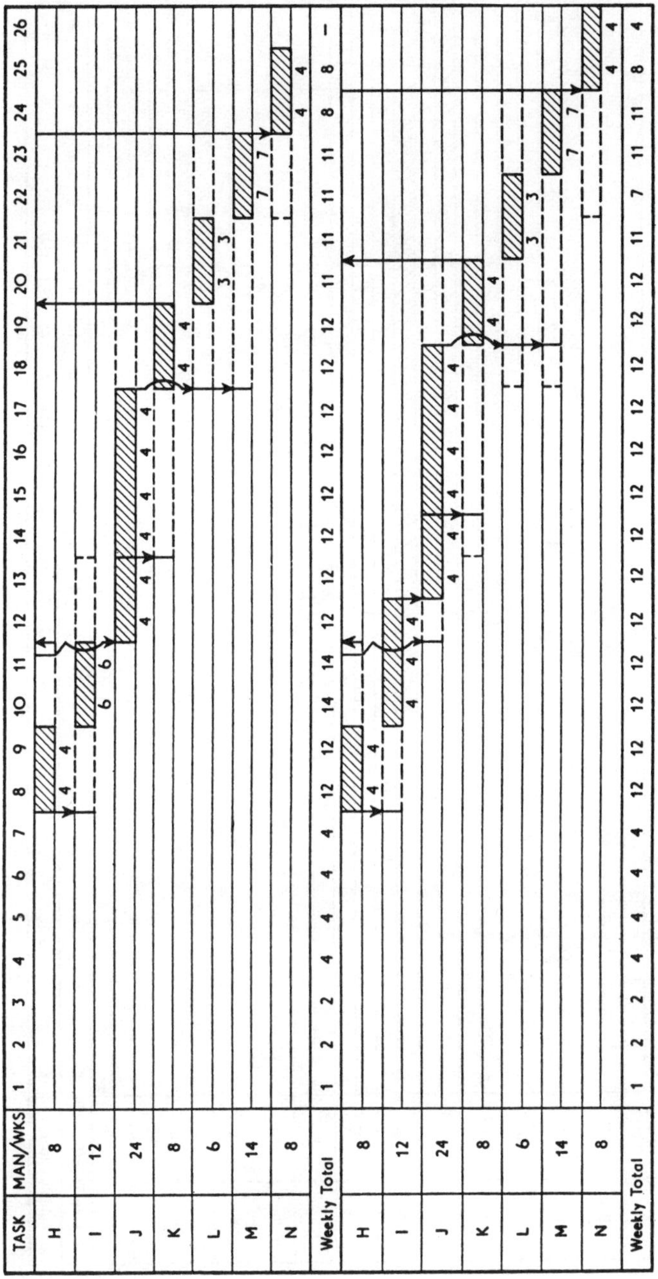

Fig. 18.37. Time bar diagram after smoothing and levelling

TASK	MAN/WKS	1	2	3	4	5	6	7	8	9	10	11	12	13	14	15	16	17	18	19	20	21	22	23	24	25
A	7	1	1	1	1	1	1	1																		
B	6			1	1	1	1	1	1																	
C	36								2	2	2	2	2	2	2	2	2	2	2	2	2	2	2	2	2	2
D	16				2	2	2	2	2	2	2	2														
E	16												2	2	2	2	2	2	2	2						
F	12																				2	2	2	2	2	2
G	56										4	4	4	4	4	4	4	4	4	4	4	4	4	4		
H	8										4	4														
I	12												6	6												
J	24													4	4	4	4	4	4							
K	8																		4	4						
L	6																						3	3		
M	14																						7	7		
N	8																								4	4
Weekly Total		1	3	3	3	3	4	4	5	5	13	13	14	12	12	12	12	12	16	16	8	8	18	18	8	4
Cumulative Total		1	3	6	9	13	17	22	27	40	53	67	81	93	105	117	129	145	161	169	177	195	213	221	229	

Fig. 18.38. Time bar diagram with latest starts

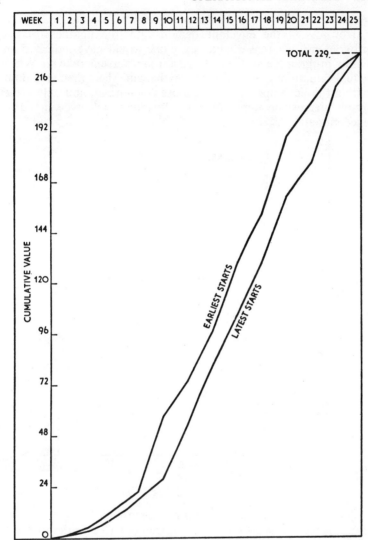

Fig. 18.39. 'Envelope' valuation graph

When the resource is money, either expenditure or income, the summation can be performed like any other resource aggregation, but it is more usual to display the information as a cumulative graph. If this is calculated for the activities at both earliest and latest starts, as shown on Figs. 18.34 and 18.38, then a double graph or 'envelope' may be drawn as illustrated on Fig. 18.39. The narrowness of the envelope demonstrates the tightness of the programme, whereas a wider envelope would have indicated an easier programme with much more room for manoeuvre. When actual valuations are recorded upon the same sheet then variations within the envelope will be diagnosed as normal, and only if the graph pierces the upper or lower boundary will it be noted as exceptional.

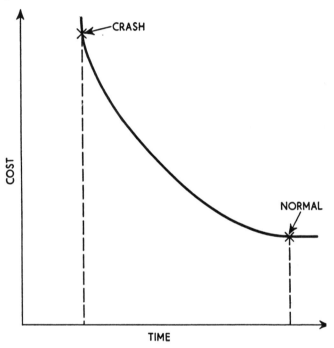

Fig. 18.40. Cost-time relationship showing 'crash point'

Although cost is fundamentally the most important factor in most projects, it is also the most difficult one to consider directly. The time/cost relationship of an activity is not usually a straight line curve, and the manipulation of more than a few key operations thus becomes such a complex and sophisticated exercise that it is not really practicable without the aid of one of the cost expediting programs offered by some of the computer firms. However, an understanding of the basic principles is good background knowledge for cost-conscious constructors.

The cost/time relationship for a typical activity is probably a curve, increasing as the time is reduced below the normal duration, until at the crash point it escalates so rapidly as to be impracticable to pursue further (see Fig. 18.40). For practical purposes it is usual to assume that the curve approximates to one or more straight line relationships, so that the slope of each segment may be expressed as so many pounds (£) per day or week (see Fig. 18.41). If the cost of foreshortening the duration of each activity is estimated in this manner, and the information added to a

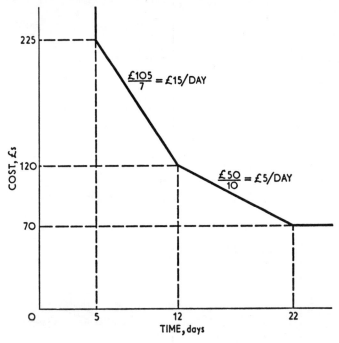

Fig. 18.41. Cost-time relationship as series of straight lines

time bar diagram as in Fig. 18.42, then we may begin to determine the project schedule that incurs the least total project cost. Attacking the critical path here, events **4, 5, 6,** and **7,** it is evident that activity **6 → 7** is the cheapest to expedite. We can reduce the duration of activity **6 → 7** for a cost of £10 per day until activity **5 → 7** becomes critical. To reduce the overall project time still further it is possible to expedite activity **4 → 5** for an additional cost of £20 per day until in turn activity **4 → 6** becomes critical.

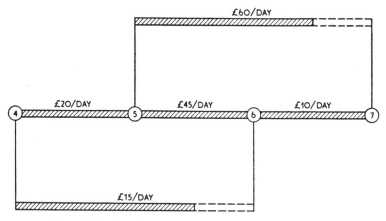

Fig. 18.42. Time bar diagram with expediting costs added

Thus the direct costs for expediting the project period can be evaluated, and may be plotted on a time/cost graph as in Fig. 18.43. If the indirect costs for the contract, i.e. the site overheads etc., are also plotted, then by adding the direct and indirect costs together, the total project cost is found. This total cost will be at its lowest point where the direct and indirect curves intersect, and this will indicate both the least project cost and the least cost scheduled time.

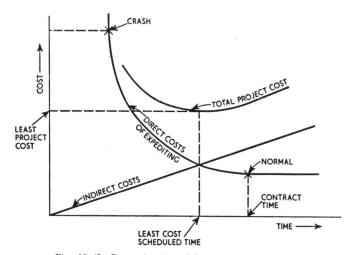

Fig. 18.43. Determination of least cost scheduled time

8. Precedence Diagrams

An alternative form of network, in which the activities are denoted by circles, and the connecting lines or arrows show the sequence of performance and dependencies, is known by a variety of names including *Circle and Link, Activity on Node, Flow Chart* or *Precedence Diagram*. The procedure was developed in France, where it is known as the (MPM) *Metra-Potential Method*. Although this is a complete reversal of the method of representation, the calculation procedure involves principles identical to those used for arrow diagrams, and many of the commercial computer programs can accept either system. Advocates of this method claim that it is easier and quicker in practice than the more popular arrow diagram, largely because of the simplification due to the absence of dummies. It is also claimed that precedence diagrams are easier to modify and that overlapping activities are more easily represented; but in general the choice between arrow or node seems largely to be a matter of personal preference.

However, there are distinct advantages in the precedence diagram when it comes to resource scheduling for repetitive operations such as house building. Part of a simple arrow diagram is shown in Fig. 18.44, and its equivalent precedence diagram is

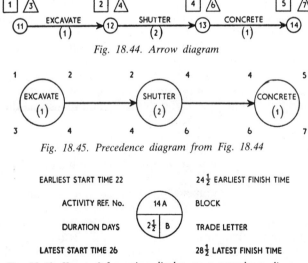

Fig. 18.44. Arrow diagram

Fig. 18.45. Precedence diagram from Fig. 18.44

EARLIEST START TIME 22   24½ EARLIEST FINISH TIME

ACTIVITY REF. No.   14 A   BLOCK

DURATION DAYS   2½ | B   TRADE LETTER

LATEST START TIME 26   28½ LATEST FINISH TIME

Fig. 18.46. Key to information display on a precedence diagram

demonstrated in Fig. 18.45, while Fig. 18.46 indicates how additional information such as earliest and latest start/finish times etc. may be included on the representation.

B.S. 4335 recommends that activity data (at a node) should be recorded like this:

Earliest Start Time	Duration	Earliest Finish Time
ACTIVITY NUMBER		
ACTIVITY DESCRIPTION		
Latest Start Time	Free Float	Latest Finish Time

Fig. 18.47

Extra information (such as resource details and cost code) may be added, preferably within the box for activity number and description.

Assume that the sequence of operations involved in building a typical pair of semi-detached houses on an estate is represented by the precedence diagram depicted on the top row of Fig. 18.48. The schedule of activities, durations and trades are those given in Fig. 18.49. It will be noted that dummy activities **3, 5, 8,** and **11,** each of 1 days duration, have been interposed between each different trade. This is because the durations assigned to each activity are average times, and the pauses will act as buffers to absorb overruns which are inevitable in practice. In this way, following trades are not forced to stand idle when the preceding operations take longer than the average expected. Moreover, it has been observed on repetitive housing sites that such breathing spaces are necessary to allow site supervision to inspect and confirm that one trade has finished in a particular dwelling, and to instruct the next trade to move in. The uncontrolled growth of these minimum inter-trade gaps into 2 or 3 days or more, is the most likely explanation for the extraordinary time of 12 months or more reported to be the national average time for building a council house in this country.

If the completion and hand-over rate required is eight dwellings per week, then it is necessary to begin the construction of four pairs every week. So far as is possible, it is desirable to stagger the start of each block in order to arrange continuity of work, at least for the major trades such as joiners and bricklayers. The following method is based on the second alternative for resource scheduling

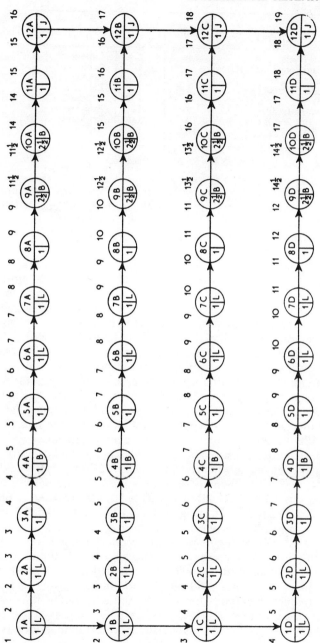

Fig. 18.48. *Precedence diagram for construction of 4 pairs of semi-detached houses*

Activity	Reference number	Duration (days)	Trade	Letter
Reduce levels	1	1	Labourer	L
Exc. and conc. foundations	2	1	Labourer	L
Footings	4	1	Bricklayer	B
Oversite concrete	6	1	Labourer	L
Drains	7	1	Labourer	L
Brickwork 1st lift	9	2½	Bricklayer	B
Brickwork 2nd lift	10	2½	Bricklayer	B
First floor joists	12	1	Joiner	J

Fig. 18.49. Schedule of activities

described in the *Building Research Current Papers, Construction Series* 25. As shown in Fig. 18.48 the sub-net is repeated to represent the four blocks, A, B, C, and D, and links are then added to connect the first and last activities only. Earliest starts and finishes are then calculated for the whole network, followed similarly by latest starts and finishes. In the example, because the durations of first and last activities are identical, earliest times coincide, but this is not necessarily so. If this information is now transferred to a bar chart as in Fig. 18.50, the overlapping or gaps between the various operations performed by any one trade are clearly demonstrated. The flow chart may now be modified to improve continuity and avoid duplication of gangs, taking one trade at a time in a predetermined order of priority.

Taking the joiners as first priority, it is seen that no rearrangement is necessary here. Assuming that the bricklayers are the next most critical resource, activities **4A, 4B, 4C** and **4D** can immediately be connected and then **4D** linked to **9A**. If one tried to link **10A** to **9B**, **10B** to **9C** and **10C** to **9D,** the overall project duration would be extended considerably, so perhaps one should compromise with two gangs and instead join **10A** to **9C** and **10B** to **9D**. Similarly, the deployment of labourers may be rationalised by linking in series **2A** to **1B, 2B** to **1C, 2C** to **1D, 2D** to **6A, 7A** to **6B, 7B** to **6C** and **7C** to **6D**. The original links **1A** to **1B** to **1C** to **1D** are of course removed. The net result of much of this rearrangement of logic is naturally to lengthen the project duration, and resource scheduling in this manner is limited by the additional time acceptable or practicable. Finally the modified network must be re-calculated for earliest and latest start/finish times as in Fig. 18.51. Complete continuity for the labourers and a reduction from four to two gangs for the bricklayers, have been achieved for the price of an extra seven days in the overall project time. A new bar

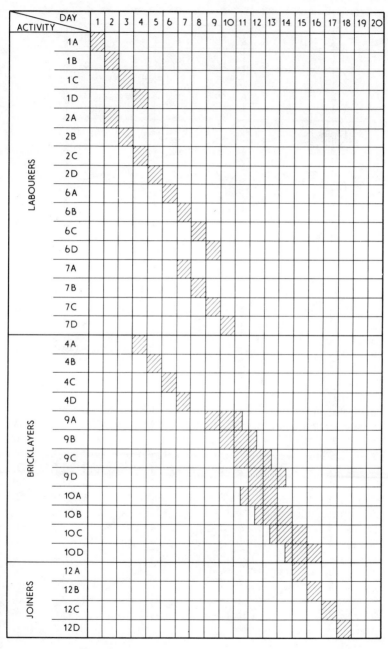

Fig. 18.50. Bar chart representation of Fig. 18.48

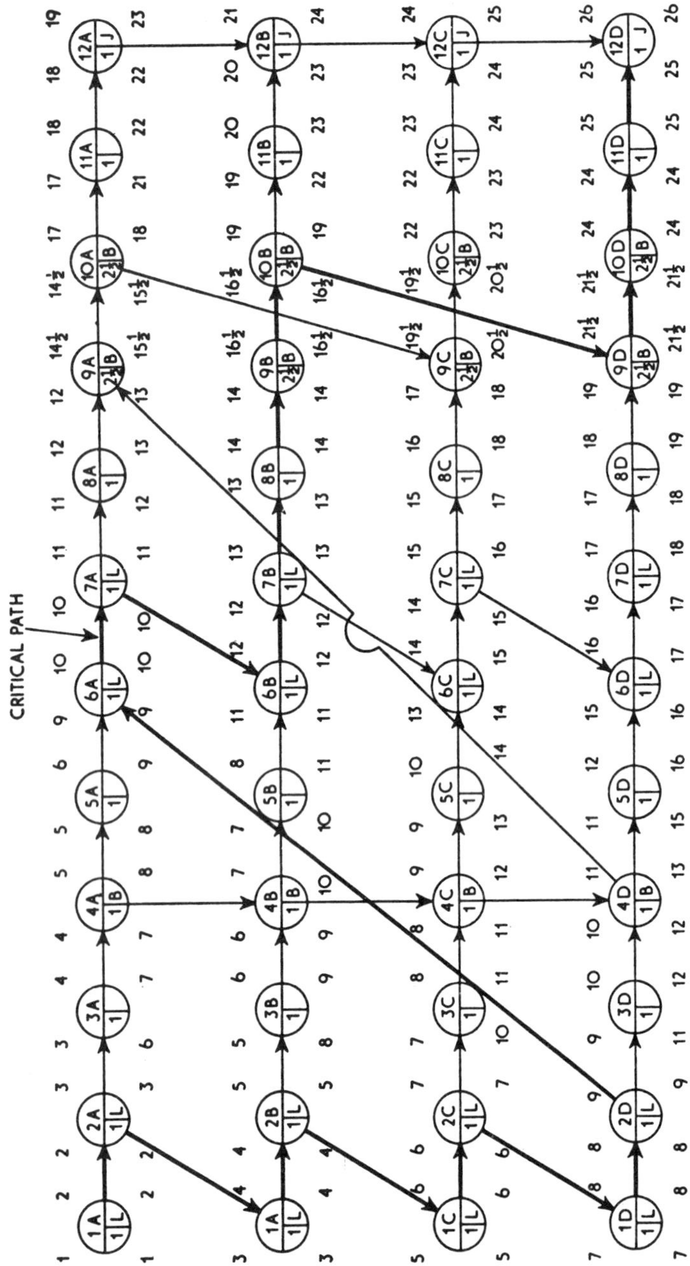

Fig. 18.51. Modified precedence diagram

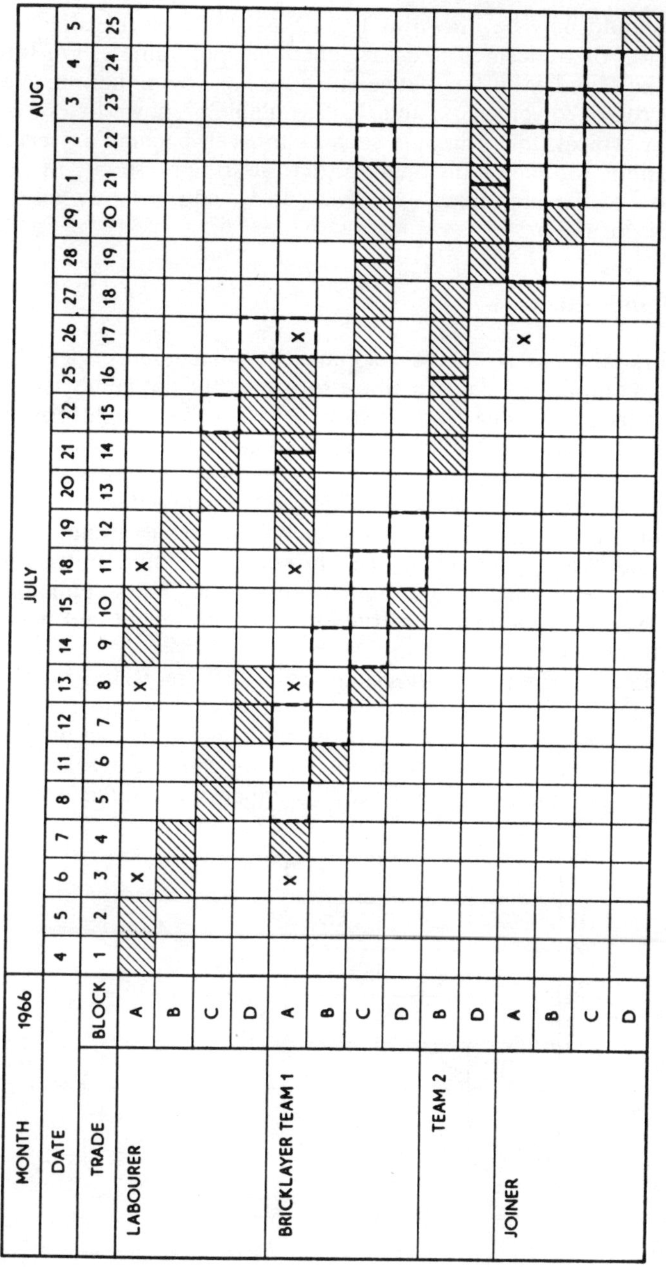

Fig. 18.52. Modified bar chart

chart should now be drawn as Fig. 18.52, to show the effective utilisation of tradesmen and the scheduled programme. On this chart the one day buffers between trades have been indicated by small crosses for block A, and float available is shown by dotted bars. A typical time schedule such as this can become a precise programme for each individual group of four pairs, simply by the addition of the appropriate calendar dates, and is thus a useful control document.

9. Line of Balance

Network analysis is a highly sophisticated technique, ideal for solving complicated construction problems, but too cumbersome even in its precedence diagram form for basically straightforward repetitive processes. A much simpler and more effective technique for analysing such repetitive production programmes as house building is the *Line of Balance*. This was originally developed for planning and controlling mass-production processes in manufacturing industries, but has been used by several building contractors for many years on housing, and by others has been applied to other types of repetitive construction and both taught and publicised by the National Building Agency.

When programming a housing project, there is the task of erecting a certain number of units within an overall contract time of so many weeks. By subtracting the estimated construction time for one house from the total number of working weeks, and dividing the remainder into the total number of units, the rate can

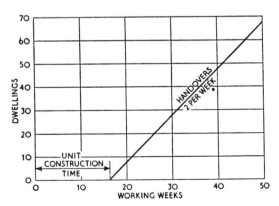

Fig. 18.53. Rate of production – handovers per week

be determined at which dwellings must be completed and handed over each week. For example, if 68 dwellings have to be completed within a contract time of 1 year, then subtracting say 16 weeks from 50 working weeks (i.e. excluding holidays), then 34 divided into 68 gives 2 handovers per week (see Fig. 18.53). This *rate of production* is vital to a housing programme, since it dictates both the delivery rate of materials and components, and the required labour strength for all trades. Thus, if it is estimated that a pair of joiners can perform all the carpentry and joinery work in one house within 2 weeks, then a project where 2 dwellings must be handed over per week, will require 8 joiners on site during the major portion of the time. Similarly, the average total labour force required may be estimated, so that adequate welfare provisions may be planned and also the actual work force build-up be checked. If a representative house requires a total of 1,200 man-hours to construct, then this is equivalent to 30 man-weeks of 40 hours each, and in order to maintain the production of 2 completed dwellings every week, then approximately 60 men will be on site during the peak period. The average overall time taken to build each individual house will not affect the size of labour force, but the longer this period then the more units will be in the pipeline at any moment. In the previous example, houses built in 15 weeks will involve 30 units under construction at any one time, but if they take 30 weeks each then 60 units will be involved.

To produce a given number of houses handed over each week, requires a lengthy queue of alternating trades proceeding in a set sequence at the same average rate of production. Trades such as glazing may operate intermittently. For example, 8 houses every fourth week instead of 2 each week, and superstructures may push ahead at the rate of 4 per week during the summer so as to compensate for a reduced flow during the winter; but the general principle of co-ordinated output must apply.

A flow of trades such as that in Fig. 18.48 can be represented by lines such as those in Fig. 18.54, here shown proceeding at the rate of 2 houses per week. In effect, each line represents a series of events, that is the start and/or finish of a particular activity. This example depicts operations following in parallel, but as explained in the previous paragraph, this is not essential.

In practice it is not possible to recruit a maximum work force immediately, and some form of build-up period is necessary, and possibly a tail-off too. This can be simulated by adding curves to the lines of balance as suggested in Fig. 18.55. The first curve shows a cumulative build-up of 1, 2, 3, 4 and 5, while the other

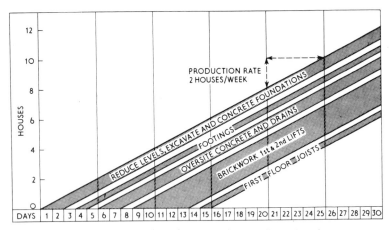

Fig. 18.54. Rate of production – showing flow of trades

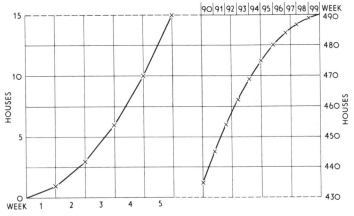

Fig. 18.55. Rate of production – showing build-up and tail-off curves

curve demonstrates a progressive tail-off from 10 to 1 houses per week. Although this progression may be recommended as a practical solution, the choice is purely one of personal decision or experience.

A completed line of balance chart is illustrated in Fig. 18.56, with build-up and tail-off, and due allowances made for holidays. For the sake of clarity only major stages have been shown, i.e. start foundations, start superstructures (= finish foundations), start finishes (= finish superstructures), and complete handovers.

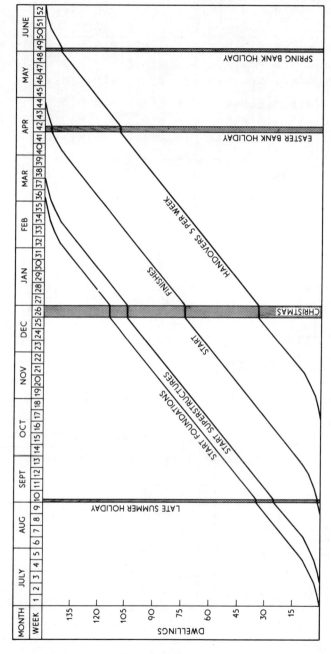

Fig. 18.56. Line of balance chart

MONTH 1968	JULY				AUG					SEPT				OCT					NOV				DEC				
W/E SUNDAY	7	14	21	28	4	11	18	25	1	8	15	22	29	6	13	20	27	3	10	17	24	1	8	15	22	29	5
ACTIVITY	1	2	3	4	5	6	7	8	9	10	11	12	13	14	15	16	17	18	19	20	21	22	23	24	25	26	27
Reduce Levels	1	3	6	10	15	21	28	36	44	50	58	66	74	82	90	98	106	114	122	130	138	146	154	162	170	170	178
Exc. and Conc. Foundations		1	3	6	10	15	21	28	36	44	50	58	66	74	82	90	98	106	114	122	130	138	146	154	162	170	170
Brick Footings			1	3	6	10	15	21	28	36	44	50	58	66	74	82	90	98	106	114	122	130	138	146	154	162	170
Oversite Concrete				1	3	6	10	15	21	28	36	44	50	58	66	74	82	90	98	106	114	122	130	138	146	154	162
Drains					1	3	6	10	15	21	28	36	44	50	58	66	74	82	90	98	106	114	122	130	138	146	154
Brickwork 1st Lift						1	3	6	10	15	21	28	36	44	50	58	66	74	82	90	98	106	114	122	130	138	146
Brickwork 2nd Lift							1	3	6	10	15	21	28	36	44	50	58	66	74	82	90	98	106	114	122	130	138
First Floor Joists								1	3	6	10	15	21	28	36	44	50	58	66	74	82	90	98	106	114	122	130
Brickwork 3rd Lift									1	3	6	10	15	21	28	36	44	50	58	66	74	82	90	98	106	114	122
Brickwork 4th Lift										1	3	6	10	15	21	28	36	44	50	58	66	74	82	90	98	106	114

Fig. 18.57. Line of balance progress schedule

Actual progress may be recorded by superimposing coloured lines, but on a detailed chart this can become complicated if achievements fall behind. Alternatively, each event locus may be drawn as a close double line, and filled in up to the appropriate mark to record progess, rather like a thermometer column. The line of balance chart itself is an excellent planning tool, but for precise control during the course of construction it is better to translate the same information into a progress schedule (see Fig. 18.57). This example shows a progressive build-up to a peak output of 8 dwellings per week, with appropriate reductions for the late summer Bank Holiday (week 10) and the Christmas week (week 26). Scheduled weekly figures and cumulative totals are shown, with spaces left alongside for actual achievements to be recorded for comparison. A progress schedule after this pattern is an excellent control document for week by week reporting, since it immediately pinpoints any divergence from the programme, and indicates the future effects. If desired, the delivery of materials and components may be easily incorporated to complete the picture.

10. Speed Diagrams

The line of balance diagram is essentially a *Speed Diagram* (a graph of time against distance) except that quantity (numbers) has been substituted for distance, so that the slope of the curve represents rate of production instead of speed. But a true speed diagram is a very useful way of expressing a programme for the construction of a motorway or similar roadworks project. The value of these diagrams is greatly enhanced by depicting in block form the cut and fill (excavate in open cut and form embankment) quantities, as shown in Fig. 18.58 for motorway construction. Further information, such as structures (bridges and retaining walls) and drainage can be added as desired.

11. Conclusions

There are of course variations on the foregoing themes, such as the German (BKN) *building box network* which is a combination of precedence diagram and line of balance. An even more involved method is the Russian *arrow cyclogram,* which combines the arrow diagram and a type of line of balance (the cyclogram) for planning

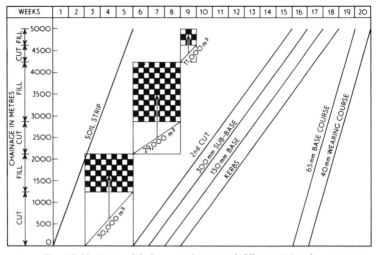

Fig. 18.58. Line of balance with cut and fill quantities shown

flow line production work. But it is a cardinal principle to keep planning and progressing techniques as simple as possible, and for many applications the bar chart is still ideal. For particular allocation problems, such as motorway cut and fill, such linear programming techniques as the *edge cost* method could be used; and *queue theory* and *simulation techniques* have been applied to housebuilding by the Building Research Station. The practical application, however, of these intricate theories is very limited.

As with any type of planning, the resulting solution will be as good as the quality of information upon which it is based – or, as the Americans say, 'Garbage in, garbage out' Despite the B.S. *Glossary of Terms,* many symbols and conventions used in project network analysis are neither standardised nor universally understood, so that any diagram should include a key explaining what is meant by the images used.

Certainly, extra benefits can be expected from extra efforts, but the degree of detail should not exceed what can usefully be applied in practice. In particular, it is essential that those people who will ultimately be responsible for the execution of the construction work, should be personally involved in the decisions taken at the planning stage. It is very easy and only too human to become quickly discouraged when another's plans go awry, whereas we tend to ensure that our own programmes are adhered to through thick and thin.

More and more clients are demanding operational research techniques for the planning and control of building and civil engineering projects, and if used properly they can result in better management control. However, it must be remembered that they are only management tools, and can replace neither management decisions nor actions. They require the full support of executive management, as well as the understanding and co-operation of supervisors if the extra time and money necessarily involved in their use is not to be wasted. Experience over the last fifteen years has shown that the intelligent application of sequencing theory to production planning and control in the construction industry, is both practical and profitable.

12. Systems Management

There are other mathematical tools of Operational Research e.g. Dynamic Programming and Optimisation Theory, which I have not described because of their few direct applications to construction management. However, an alternative insight into the whole process of management which uses many of the O.R. concepts is Systems Management.

A System is a group of related elements organised for a joint purpose; and the nature of systems is studied by the science of Cybernetics and by General Systems Theory. General Systems Theory (GST) is a general theory of organisation and wholeness, and is generally agreed to have been founded by Ludwig von Bertalanffy, who dated its inception from 1940. The theory is that differing types of systems such as molecular, biological and social, have certain common properties which can be applied to organisation structures.

GST has objectives identical with those expressed in 1947 by the founders of Cybernetics, Norbert Wiener and Arturo Rosenbleuth. Defined then as 'the science of control and communication in the animal and the machine', this suggested (i) that a state of 'being in control' depends upon a flow of information, and (ii) that the laws governing control are the same for organic and inorganic systems. Today, the more general definition of cybernetics as 'the science of effective organisation' indicates that either science is a branch of the other.

The Systems Approach is a means to the study of both physical and social systems, which enables complex and dynamic situations to be understood and considered in broad outline. The method focuses on the use of information in decision-making, and is valid whether the topic is a heating system, a company structure, or a project management plan. In the management context, a systems approach is concerned with growth and stability in the system assuming a range of scenarios with varying futures, unpredictable happenings, and alternative policies.

To identify a system it is necessary to distinguish its boundaries, to be aware of its purposes (whether these are a blueprint for its design or inferred from its behaviour), and to define the level to which descriptions or theories may distort in order to simplify. Systems may contain sub-systems, and so on. One of the discoveries made by the systems approach is the extent to which efforts to improve the performance of a sub-system by its own criteria may act to the detriment of the total system, and hence to the defeat of its objectives.

A system may be Open or Closed depending upon its interaction with the environment. Most organic systems are open, whilst many areas of traditional science and industry are closed systems. Closed systems have an inherent tendency to move toward a static equilibrium and ultimately to decay. An open system is in a dynamic relationship with its environment. It receives various inputs, transforms them and exports outputs, and this allows the system to increase its energy and grow. An insular board of directors is an example of the former; whilst re-education and the introduction of 'fresh blood' would open the business to new opportunities in a changing environment.

The major stages in systems analysis are:
1. Interpretation of objectives and requirements.
2. Investigation of factors and influences.
3. Selection from alternative possibilities.
4. Synthesis of chosen plan or design.
5. Verification of developing solutions.
6. Presentation of total proposal.

Since any construction project is itself dynamic and open to changing environmental forces, it is important that solutions are re-checked to verify their aptness. Equally, now that potential building clients are demanding a total package – financial as well as architectural – it is essential that the project is presented as a viable proposition in every way. Each of these major stages will be sub-divided into a number of smaller steps, including all or any of the following:
1. Objectives (refined)
2. Design (spatial, structural, services)

3. Time
4. Cost
5. Quality
6. Economics (cash flow etc.)
7. Risks or uncertainties.

From the foregoing analysis a systems chart is drawn, showing the stages, sequence and approximate timing. This is in effect a network such as Fig. 18.30, which then becomes the monitoring document for the project. Like any other management procedures, the effectiveness of decision and control will depend upon the quality of the communication system. Information must be accurate, complete, real, produced at the right time, relevant, generated economically and be as simple as possible. A good information system should be capable of reporting variances, be flexible, integrated and use standardised terminology.

Whilst the above paragraph applies directly to project management, it must be appreciated that systems analysis is equally applicable to the design of management organisation. In this context, the Linear Responsibility Chart (LRC), adapted by Cleland and King in 1975, is useful for mapping relationships within an organisation. The LRC matrix lists a series of job positions along the top of the chart and a series of responsibilities/tasks down the side of the table. By means of symbols the relationships between horizontal and vertical listings can be explained, e.g. who does the work, who approves etc. The line of balance schedule (Fig. 18.57) is another example of a systems management matrix.

The application of systems management techniques are new to building, and have not yet generally progressed from research to practice. However, the difference between the earlier Operational Research (OR) approach and current Systems Analysis is only a matter of degree. Network Analysis, Queueing Theory, Transportation Studies etc. are individual OR techniques, which Systems Analysis aims to incorporate in a wider examination of a problem and its environment. By taking the broader 'systems view' the possibility of reaching the right answer to the correct question is increased. The systems approach can be especially useful in the management of the large, fast or complex type of building project.

BIBLIOGRAPHY

J. F. Nuttall, 'Operational Research in Building in Europe', *Building Research Current Papers,* Construction Series 6, D.S.I.R.

B. T. Houlden, 'The Contribution of Operational Research to Purchasing and Stores Management', *Purchasing Journal*, February 1964.

C.P.M. in Construction, The Associated General Contractors of America.

H. H. Fairhurst, 'Planning and Control of Engineering and Building Construction Work by use of C.P.M. and P.E.R.T.', *Techn. Rep.* No. 1030 M.P.B.W.

J. F. Nuttall, R. E. Jeanes and E. E. Amos, 'The Critical Path Method and C.P.M. Applied to Building Site Control', *Building Research Current Papers*, Construction Series 3 and 12, D.S.I.R.

'C.P.M. explained', *Building Research Station Digest*, Second Series, 53, H.M.S.O.

B.S. 4335 : 1972 *Glossary of Terms used in Project Network Analysis,* British Standards Institution.

J. F. Nuttall, 'Resource Scheduling: Coping with labour problems as they occur on site', *Building Research Current Papers,* Construction Series 25, Min. Tech.

Programming House Building by Line of Balance, The National Building Agency.

Paul G. Gill, *Systems Management Techniques for Builders and Contractors,* McGraw Hill, 1968.

Peter W. G. Morris, 'Systems Study of Project Management', *Building*, 25 January/1 February 1974.

Walter Mohr, 'The Use of Systems in the Building Industry', *Australian Institute of Building Magazine*, 1979.

Anthony Walker, 'Project Organisation', *Chartered Quantity Surveyor,* February 1984.

Chapter 19

Organisational Development

1. Organisational Development

More recent research and development into management principles and organisation theory have not negated our traditional
ideas, but have transformed them from static two-dimensional
plans to dynamic three-dimensional models. Account has been
taken of the facts of life that all human organisations have to
change with the times if they are to remain viable, and in the
modern social climate they must also be responsive to people –
both inside and outside the enterprise.

Development in the context of industrial or commercial organisations means above all evolution. Evolution may entail growth,
but change rather than mere growth is what it's all about.
However, such organisations unlike biological organisms have no
genetic means of adaption, and the mechanisms of evolution have
to be triggered by constructive criticism. To keep up with the game
through successful evolution, an organisation must therefore be
open to intelligent criticism since this is one of the vital conditions
for survival, and must be able to handle it. At no time is there any
expectation of a perfect solution, even temporarily – only of a
more relevant, better-adjusted instrument for the purpose.

The new philosophy of organisational development (O.D.)
recognises that the objectives of a company and its employees
must be compatible, if effective improvements in performance are
to be achieved. Two principles are fundamental to the achievement of planned change in an organisation. The first is that
significant change must never be applied to one part without due
consideration to the overall effect upon the system as a whole. The
second is that constructive change always requires a positive
change of attitudes. Managers must not only react to the constantly changing external environment, but also to the legitimate
expectations and aspirations of the people comprising the enterprise. The only practicable way to match together the abilities of

397

the work people and the way their jobs are organised, with the physical equipment and material resources of the organisation, is to consult and discuss until acceptance and understanding are reached. The necessary conditions to encourage the full involvement of personnel and create high motivation and commitment to work are only made possible by the understanding leadership provided and the participation allowed.

Amongst business consultants there is a growing understanding of something called O.D., but outside these specialists relatively little is known about it. Moreover, although there are common assumptions shared by most practitioners of O.D., there are great individual variations in the strategies and tactics employed by different consultants. The field is still emerging and new methods are constantly being invented. Of those ideas that focus on total organisation systems and attempt to show how intervention in organisations can lead to constructive change and development, particular mention must be made of the work of Paul Lawrence and Jay Lorsch. In *Organisation and Environment* (1967) they argued that Classical, Human Relations and 'Modern' thought are pointers along the same continuum of management patterns. Stating their case as 'A Contingency Theory of Organizations', it is suggested that the varying patterns related to the environments in which they have operated. Their book *Developing Organizations: Diagnosis and Action* was primarily addressed in 1969 to the managers of organisations, and stressed their need to tackle the three key issues of developing the organisation/environment interface; the group/group interface; and the organisation/individual interface. Their fundamental premise is that 'there is no one best way to organise'; rather, organisations need to be systematically tailored to collective goals and individual human purposes. Moreover, whilst outside consultants can assist, in the final analysis the capacity for organisational development must reside inside the organisation. For this reason, they place great emphasis on the role of internal O.D. specialists, and upon educating managers in the use of the behavioural-science tools that are available to help them work on organisational development issues.

Another very practical handbook is *Career Dynamics* (1978) by Edgar H. Schein of Massachusetts Institute of Technology and Sloan School of Management. With the object of matching individual with organisational needs, Schein surveys (1) the Individual and his Life Cycle with its changing needs; (2) the Individual and Organisational interactions; and (3) ways of managing Human Resource Planning and Development (HRPD).

HRPD is concerned both with organisational efficiency, and individual effectiveness and satisfaction, in both the short and the long terms. Suggestions for improving HRPD systems are listed under three headings:

1. *The Organisation* – activities designed to increase organisational insight, to promote employee involvement in career development, and more flexible management policies and practices.
2. *The Individual* – encouragement to become an effective self-diagnostician, to seek career counselling, and consider changing jobs.
3. *Outside Institutions* – to make career switching easier by helping individuals to make wiser choices, providing financial support during a period of retraining, and the organisation of educational and training programes for mid-life or career changes. However, Schein stresses that ultimate accountability for the total HRPD system must rest with line management.

With the realisation that productive change in any organisation can only be achieved with the parallel education and development of the people comprising the enterprise, it follows that practioners of O.D. must have an appreciation and understanding of:

a. The dynamics and phases of development concerned in the evolution of an organisation;
b. The results of social science research into the behaviour of people at work; and
c. Practical strategies and techniques for the successful integration of individual and group motivation with corporate objectives.

2. The Evolution of an Organisation

Industrial and commercial organisations can be considered as organic systems which move through a life-cycle of growth, in which the various phases of development have vital implications for the behaviour of both management and operatives. It is instructive to study organisational growth and development in terms of a number of distinct stages, although obviously these overlap and merge in practice, and it is also possible that behaviour typical of each phase may co-exist within the same organisation at any one time. It must be remembered that whilst growth signifies numerical increase, development or progressive change has qualitative connotations.

The work of the Nederlands Paedagogisch Instituut (International Institute of Organisation Development), has identified three discrete phases of evolution which are outlined as follows.

a. *The pioneer phase* arising from an economic need. Our capitalist society relies for its success upon private enterprise, an entrepreneur who identifies a need for goods or services and then creates a new organisation specifically to supply that need at the opportune time and a price that people are prepared to pay. To take the initiative and back an untried idea with all that one has requires courage, single-mindedness and strong personality. Goals are clear, leadership is intuitive and autocratic, but accepted because of the drive and prestige of the 'boss'. The organisation structure is typically flat, with the chief executive, often the owner as well, knowing everyone and everything. Planning is informal, dynamic and flexible, whilst improvisation is good. Control tends to be highly personalised, but with high motivation cohesion is good and communications problems minimal. Personal relations with financiers, customers and work people, being centralised and instinctive, may at times be stormy but never inhuman.

There may be an interim 'survival' stage, before the organisation has been fully established and become stabilised, when everyone has to struggle and make sacrifices in order to ensure that the enterprise continues to exist.

Once a firm basis for growth has been built, further expansion may require additional capital, and this may entail bringing in outsiders to have a say in how the business shall be run. Increased size may also necessitate bringing in professional managers and specialists, whose backgrounds, management styles and expectations may contrast sharply with those of the entrepreneur leader, with possible conflicts and misunderstandings. Growing problems indicate that the organisation is ripe to move into a new phase of development – or there is a crisis.

b. *The scientific phase* arises from technical pressures. In an effort to achieve greater stability, the four principles of specialisation, standardisation, mechanisation and co-ordination become the order of the day. Sheer size tends to obscure the fundamental objectives of the business and hence motivation becomes a problem. The need for more delegation and the consequent hierarchy of levels makes control and communications more difficult.

The necessary functional specialisation (hence the alternative title of *differentiated phase*) leading to highly developed 'scientific' departments does increase predictability, but the divorce of planning from execution in turn results in different unwanted symptoms.

Standardisation through systems, procedures, organisation charts, intercommunication networks, cost controls etc. does lead to certain economies, but there are dangers of lost responsibility, empire building and restrictive watertight compartments.

In response to the need for economy the urge for greater mechanisation is natural, since machines do not tire, are more predictable than men and are ideal for continuous, repetitive and identical operations. But rationality and an increase in knowledge can lead to impersonal relations and some lost flexibility.

To counteract these centrifugal tendencies of specialisation, standardisation and mechanisation, it becomes necessary to strengthen co-ordination through committees, reports, memos, house journals etc., by limiting spans of control and the introduction of line and staff relationships. If the era of the 'organisation man' is successfully accomplished, then the firm will gain a reputation and develop a pride in itself that can be used as a base for further expansion and diversification.

But stability can become rigidity, predictability can lead to stagnation, so that survival tactics may have to be employed once again. Companies have been known to oscillate backwards and forwards between these two stages, whilst 'clogs to riches and back to clogs in three generations' is a well-known phenomenon. It can certainly be argued that scientific management has proved its worth over the years, but it seems that yet another stage of development is required in conditions of rapid change.

c. *The integrated phase* is developing in response to social demands. Rapid technological revolutions, the strains of inflation and world recession, combined with society's increased expectations for conservation and participation, call for greater adaptability. A conscious effort is required to develop both people and the organisation together, with a leadership style that better suits the situation. The accent is on handling change, a clearer definition of needs and objectives, and a more enlightened use of human resources. It takes high

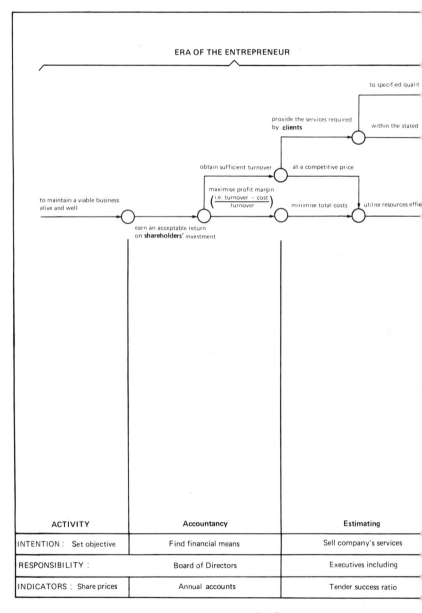

Fig. 19.1. Evolution of a firm

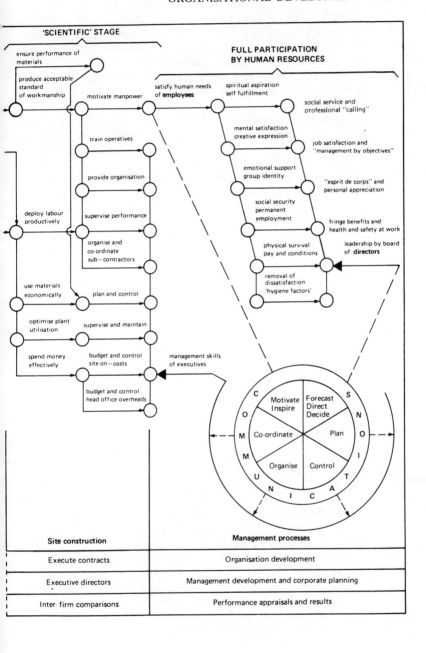

courage to allow work people greater participation – even at the work bench level. Yet it is apparent that only in this way can we gain the motivation and co-operation necessary to deal with present-day problems and opportunities.

No rules have yet been agreed, and no clear blueprints developed, but there have been noteworthy experiments such as Volvo and Glacier Metal which highlight some of the implications for managers. The network in Fig. 19.1 traces the route from the pioneer beginnings through the expertise of scientific management towards the developing system of integrated industrial democracy.

However, the system does not only function in the three-dimensional physical plane illustrated, for the changes of accent from one area of 'What' and 'Why' to another, imply the passage of time. Hence, the network can be thought of as a cross-section at one particular moment of time.

The fourth dimension is more concerned with the 'How', 'When', 'Which' and 'Where' of doing something, and may be considered the mental plane. In the construction context this may be represented in the usual plan and elevations format – see Fig. 19.20.

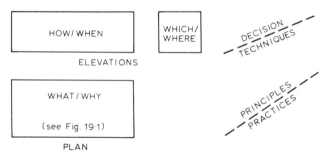

Fig. 19.2. The relationship between management principles/practices and decision techniques

This field of management time utilises decision aids such as method study and work measurement; the application of O.R. to finding optimum solutions to problems; the analysis and interpretation of statistics; and the rapid processing of business data using a computer. Organisational development is also concerned with time, albeit on a much longer scale, since it attempts to rationalise the necessary changes both to organisation structures and individual attitudes, so that the whole living system may evolve in order to survive.

3. Behavioural Science

Behavioural science in the industrial sense concerns the observation, possible explanation and hopeful prediction of the behaviour of individuals and groups of people in the work situation. It is not really a new science but is based upon both psychological and sociological theory and practice, as a result of the concentration by numerous researchers on areas such as management style and job satisfaction which play such a major part in industrial effectiveness. Although the theories of behavioural science are not as exact as the laws of physical science, they nevertheless contain a great deal of valid knowledge which can be applied to our seemingly irrational human behaviour.

The first examples of behavioural science applied to industry were the now classic 'Hawthorne investigations' which began in 1927, and were carried out in the Western Electric Company by Elton Mayo and others. It was demonstrated that the workers perceived themselves as a group, and put their personal advancement as secondary to the interpersonal values laid down by their working group. Some of the more recent ideas with important implications for industrial managers are considered in logical, rather than historical order.

   a. Theory X and Theory Y were formulated by Douglas McGregor in his book *The Human Side of Enterprise* in 1960. Theory X makes the following assumptions:

   i.   The average human being has an inherent dislike of work and will avoid it whenever he can.

   ii.   Because of this objection to work, most people must either be bribed or pressured before they will work harder.

   iii.   The average person is unambitious, dislikes responsibility, prefers to be given instructions, and wants ease and security before all else.

This model ignores the Christian belief that 'man does not live by bread alone', and not surprisingly most employees when treated as morons react in the expected fashion. On the other hand, Theory Y takes the view that:

   i.   Physical and mental work is as natural to man as rest or play.

   ii.   Reward and punishment are not the only ways to make people work, for men will direct themselves if they are committed to the objectives of an organisation.

   iii.   If a job is satisfying in itself, then the workman is more likely to commit himself to the aims of the enterprise.

iv. Given the proper conditions, the average person will learn not only to accept but to seek responsibility.

v. many employees can use their imagination, creativeness, and ingenuity to solve their own work problems.

vi. Under the usual conditions of modern industrial life, the intellectual potentiality of the average workman is only partially realised.

This alternative model approximates to the Christian ideal that 'all men are the children of God, made in His own image'.

Theory Y may be difficult to put into practice in large mass-production operations, where the exercise of managerial authority may be the only way of achieving the desired results. Nevertheless, managers, professionals and staff will certainly do better work and exert self-control if they fully understand the purpose of their labours, and will also contribute more to the organisation if they are treated as responsible and appreciated employees. A manager's belief in either Theory X or Theory Y will largely depend upon his general experience, but whichever he follows will most certainly colour his whole outlook and actions.

b. *The basic human needs* outlined by Abraham Maslow in his book *Motivation and Personality* in 1954 were an attempt to formulate a theory of motivation based upon his observations as a psychologist. He proposed that all human behaviour is motivated by a desire to satisfy certain specific groups of needs, which are almost universal, and are arranged sequentially in hierarchical form. The lowest needs predominate until they are satisfied, when they are replaced by the next higher group of objectives which dominate in turn. He identified five sets of goals as follows, starting from the bottom (see Fig. 19.3).

i. Physiological drives are the most basic: the instinct for survival and the necessities of water, food and shelter to support life. These needs, when satisfied, cease to determine human behaviour, but would again assert dominance if danger, hunger or thirst threatened.

ii. Safety needs are next in priority and lead to efforts to ensure personal security. Men seek stable employment, save money to provide for the unexpected and arrange insurance against known risks. With society protecting everyone's personal safety, and personal security thus assured, the next higher order of needs will become significant; but illness, accident or redundancy will recall

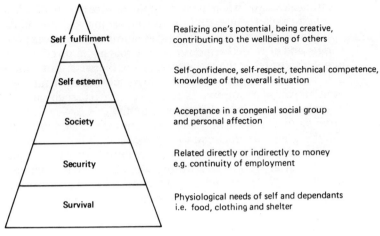

Fig. 19.3. Hierarchy of human needs (after Maslow)

these secondary needs. Much resistance to change at work springs from a real or imagined threat to comfort, safety or security.

iii. The urges to belong and be loved come next: the need to identify and be part of a team, and the desire for affectionate relations with other people. *Esprit de corps*, loyalty and pride in belonging to a successful organisation are very effective motivators. Conversely, it also explains the torture of being 'sent to Coventry'.

iv. Esteem needs comprise self-respect, prestige, status and respect from others. These must be based upon feelings of adequacy and achievement leading to self-confidence; and recognition of one's capability, importance, and individual qualities by superiors, peers and subordinates alike. Lack of esteem may give rise to feelings of inferiority, weakness and helplessness, and lead to general ineffectiveness.

v. The need for self-actualization is the desire for self-fulfilment, personal growth and the realization of one's full potential. Being the highest level this need is least likely to be satisfied fully, except at moments of true creativity or especial achievement. Thus it remains possibly the strongest motivator of all, always drawing men on towards something greater.

Acceptance of Maslow's theory has important implications for managers, who must consider themselves responsible for creating a climate in which their employees are able to develop to their highest potential. This might include providing opportunities for more employee autonomy, greater job variety and increased responsibility, so that higher-order needs may be satisfied in the work situation. Otherwise, frustration and alienation may lead to individuals seeking their satisfactions through disruptive alternative outlets such as the informal group or trade union activities.

c. *Motivation and hygiene* theory was proposed by Frederick Herzberg in *The Motivation to Work* in 1959 in an effort to explain the differences between job dissatisfaction and motivation at work. His research was initially based upon a survey of 200 accountants and engineers, but additional evidence was later collected from employees in various occupations. Respondents were asked to identify those factors which led either to feelings of dissatisfaction or extreme satisfaction. Analysis of his results suggested that job satisfaction and work dissatisfaction arise from two quite different roots. The removal of dissatisfaction produces a neutral state, and new more positive stimuli are required to produce satisfaction and motivational drive. The negative factors associated with the work environment (or context) such as company policy and administration, supervision, interpersonal relationships, working conditions, salary, status and security, which have to be cleared away, he called *hygiene* factors (see Fig. 19.4). The second group of factors intrinsic to the job itself (or content) including achievement, recognition, the work itself, responsibility and growth, he termed *motivators*. By and large these 'hygiene' factors coincide with the three lower levels of Maslow's need hierarchy, and the 'motivators' the upper two. As usual in human behaviour, however, the distinctions are not absolute but blurred, for Fig. 19.4 shows that dissatisfaction comprises 69% context and 31% content, whilst satisfaction is 81% content and 19% context. Moreover, hygiene factors such as pay rises require improvement at regular intervals if they are to continue to allay dissatisfaction. In addition, positive motivation of many employees can only be achieved when their jobs are enriched by the creation of complete and meaningful units of work. This should create opportunities for their psychological growth through increased responsibility, accountability and autonomy, and hence produce changes in behaviour which alone can lead to improved attitudes and performance. Fortunately, there remains a high

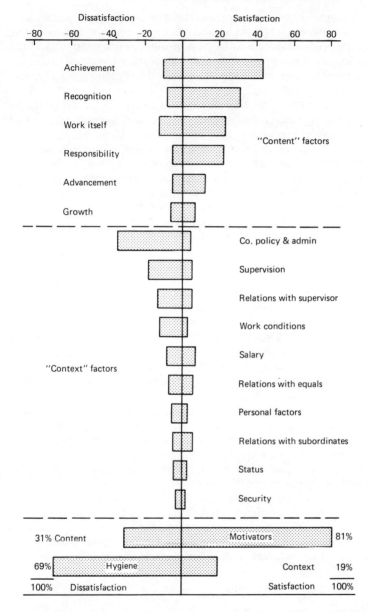

Fig. 19.4. Herzberg's findings: 'context' factors, such as money, alleviate dissatisfaction but 'content' factors motivate

degree of job satisfaction in the building industry, particularly among the craftsmen, and the opportunities for assuming responsibility caused by decentralised work centres, and the constant need for improvisation, still provide ample scope for personal achievement and individual recognition and advancement.

Since the 1928 Hawthorne experiments at Western Electric in Chicago, the behavioural sciences have gained many adherents and considerable legitimacy. But whilst these ideas have certainly gained the greatest ground in some of the large multi-national corporations, precisely those with the greatest problems of controlling and motivating large numbers of workers, there are many more who have not made any major effort to put them to the test. Whilst the majority of executives are reasonably well-versed in the theories, yet a tremendous gap exists between understanding human relations problems and doing something practical about them, and they simply do not know how to bridge that gap.

Much practical research into both the theoretical and applied problems of relating behavioural knowledge to effective action has been carried out by Chris Argyris of the Graduate Schools of Education and Business Administration, Harvard University. His writings have included *Management and Organizational Development* 1971, and *The Applicability of Organizational Sociology* in 1972. The latter considers ways of making Behavioural Science more applicable and applied; the sequences of organisational change and ways of creating such changes; and the effectiveness of various methods of intervention.

Yet even though the number of practical applications is still very small, there is plenty of evidence that many more companies recognise the changing attitudes of both managers and operatives to their work in a situation of rapid, technological change, increasing educational opportunity, and the Welfare State environment. No board of directors can afford to ignore the growing demand for more interest and involvement in the way things are done and in the rewards for doing them. Action needs to be taken to improve motivation and progress towards a more participative style of management, in order to insure against long-term threats to the stability and survival of our business enterprises.

4. Management Leadership

Managers are required to get things done through other people, and must therefore both direct and motivate those whom they manage. Owing to economic and social pressures and physical realities, there is a tendency for many management decisions in large companies to be no longer the prerogative of one individual but rather the collective opinion of all the people concerned, or the work of a team. This concept of a team is probably the only practical way of life in modern society, but it calls for greater qualities of leadership if we are to achieve a higher degree of industrial discipline, and get all to work together. According to Field Marshal Lord Slim, 'There is a difference between leadership and management . . . Leadership is of the spirit, compounded of personality and vision; its practice is an art. Management is of the mind, more a matter of accurate calculation, of statistics, of methods, timetables and routine; its practice is a science'. The qualities may be different, but the objective must be to combine the two if management is to keep in touch with its workpeople. There must be times when it is necessary to 'instruct' for the best results, but it may also inhibit creative energy whilst to 'inspire' will release it, and it is from inspiration that the greatest long-term benefits will come. Much recent research has been in this particular field.

    a. Action-centred leadership, developed by John Adair, emphasises the leadership function of management. Dr. Adair's theories were developed at Sandhurst in order to meet the training needs of the army, but are equally applicable to industrial leadership. He believes that the functions of a leader are not inborn traits, but are skills which can be recognised, practised and developed. As an aid to leadership training he developed a model (see Fig. 19.5) which illustrates how the effectiveness of a leader depends upon his ability to influence, and in turn be influenced by, the group and its members in the accomplishment of a team task. Three overlapping circles represent 'task needs', 'group needs' and 'individual needs', and the interaction of each with the other two. The relative position and importance of the three areas of responsibility will vary with the task and circumstances, and in practice the successful manager must balance correctly the amount of attention he gives to:

    i. ensuring that his business 'tasks' are achieved;

    ii. meeting the needs of his team; and

    iii. supplying the needs of each individual member.

    Achieving the task requires the leader to:

    i. be quite clear what the task is, and to brief the group fully and unmistakeably;

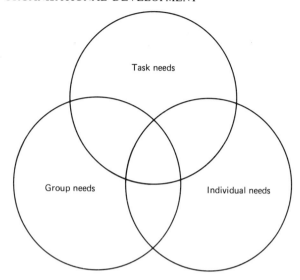

Fig. 19.5. Action-centred leadership (after The Industrial Society)

ii. understand how the particular task fits into the overall
objectives of the organisation, and to plan how best to
accomplish it;
iii. obtain the resources he requires, including the time and
authority needed, and to organise a suitable management
structure;
iv. control progress towards completion of the task;
v. keep everyone informed of developments;
vi. evaluate results.

Team maintenance requires an understanding of the peculiar
personality of the group, its particular attitudes and its own
needs. The key functions of the leader are to:
i. set and maintain group objectives and standards;
ii. involve the group as a whole in the attainment of objectives;
iii. maintain the unity of the group and to minimise disruptive
activity.

Meeting individual needs by providing the right 'climate' and
the opportunities for each member to exert himself and get
involved, is probably the most difficult but certainly the most
rewarding task of the leader. The challenge to achieve
optimum results through the best use of human resources

obliges the effective manager to inspire sufficient motivation for every member of his team. To find personal satisfaction at work, through self-expression, and acceptance by one's mates, industrial man must:

i.   feel that he is making a worthwhile contribution to the objectives of the group, and a sense of personal achievement in his particular job;

ii. find the work itself challenging and demanding, so giving him the opportunity to match his capabilities;

iii. receive proper recognition for his efforts;

iv. have control over those aspects of the task which have been delegated to him;

v.   know that he is developing his individuality, and advancing in experience and ability.

Having completed his analysis of the task, the group, and the individuals, the leader must then make his decision and take action. How he performs these necessary activities, his 'style of leadership', is another factor upon which will depend his acceptance by the group and the response of individuals. He must be sufficiently sensitive to the needs of the situation to know when it would be appropriate, for example, to take decisions for actions directly himself; when to consult others before deciding; or when to delegate. He must learn to be flexible and to suit his approach to the changing requirements of the occasion.

b. *Management style* is concerned with the art rather than the science of management, the manner rather than the matter, or the 'way' in which managing is done. Style is clearly a matter of choice for the manager, and in preferring one style rather than another, the only criterion must be effectiveness. But if there is ever one best answer it can only be for one particular situation: and situations change. The situation at any one time is defined by three things: the position of the company within its own environment, the position of the individual unit within the company, and the calibre and mood of the people being managed.

There has been a great deal of research into the analysis of management styles, in order to guide managers in their choice of the most appropriate style to suit each particular situation, including the following.

i.   Dr. Robert R. Blake and his partner Jane S. Mouton developed a way of identifying and distinguishing various management styles, the *managerial grid* (see Fig. 19.6). The Blake philosophy is that all organisations have a purpose. The goal of industry is production of goods, ideas or services, and these goals are achieved through people. The horizontal axis of the graph represents 'concern for production' whilst the vertical axis represents 'concern for people', each marked on a 1 to 9 scale. With the rectangle completed, four benchmarks are identified in the four corners. The 1.1 manager merely goes through the motions, putting in as little effort as necessary to get the work done, and his main aim is survival. Reading the horizontal

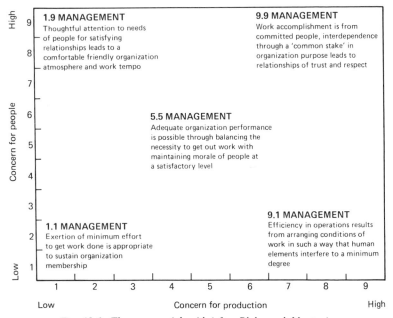

Fig. 19.6. The managerial grid (after Blake and Mouton)

scale first, the 9.1 manager is an autocrat with a total concern for production and minimal interference from the human element. By contrast the 1.9 manager is relaxed and permissive, whose prime concern is to create a friendly, comfortable atmosphere, at the expense of production. In their various ways each of these three are found wanting. The most effective manager, the 9.9, achieves high productivity by the willing and trusting support of his colleagues. People committed to the needs of the organisation, based upon understanding and agreement, make a concerted effort to achieve results. In the middle is the 5.5 manager who attaches equal importance to both aspects of his work, but strives less strenuously for either. Also found wanting, the 'organisation man' compromises and fits into whatever is temporarily required of him. These patterns of management style, when seen in relation to such key concepts as creativity, commitment and conflict, have made a distinctive contribution to management thinking.

ii. Warren G. Schmidt has differentiated between several styles of leadership according to the areas of decision-making either retained or shared with subordinates (see Fig. 19.7). Both the 'autocratic' and 'bureaucratic' managers think, plan and decide, whilst their groups submit, conform and give assent. The 'charismatic' manager thinks out and proposes tentative solutions, then finally decides, whilst his group give their views and eventual assent. The 'diplomatic' manager presents the problem, asks for solutions but still decides himself. His group are allowed to participate in thinking and planning but not in controlling. Only the 'democratic' manager shares control with the group so that together they become an autonomous body.

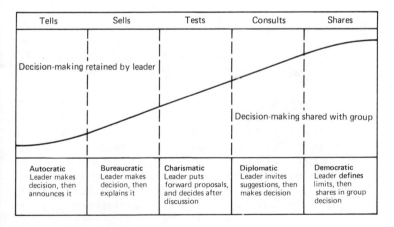

Fig. 19.7. Leadership styles (after W. G. Schmidt)

iii. Dr. Rensis Likert has identified four main types of management style:

The 'exploitive-authoritative' system, where decisions are imposed; where motivation is by threats; where senior levels of management have great responsibility but junior levels none; there is very little communication and no team work.

The 'benevolent-authoritative' system, where leadership has a paternalistic attitude; where motivation is partly by rewards; where managers feel responsible but lower levels do not; there is little communication and a little teamwork.

The 'consultative' system, where superiors have partial trust in their subordinates; where motivation is by rewards with some involvement; where a high proportion of personnel feel responsibility for achieving company goals; and there is more communication and teamwork.

The 'participative' group system, where leadership is by superiors who have complete trust in their subordinates; where motivation is by rewards based upon goals agreed in participation; where all levels of personnel feel real responsibility for the organisation's objectives; there is effective communication and a large amount of co-operative teamwork. This fourth system is considered the optimum solution, ideal for the profit-oriented and human-concerned organisation, which should be adopted despite the painful and lengthy changes involved.

Research has shown that it may be difficult for a manager to modify his natural style to any great extent, but that to the group, consistency of style is more important than a perfect match. Nevertheless, it is possible to get better results from a work group by training the manager to diagnose the demands of his situation, and by encouraging flexibility of style when desirable.

c. *Sensitivity training* of various forms has been offered as a means of encouraging managers to develop their ability to get along with others, and to improve their skills of communication and leadership. Courses in 'group dynamics' have been designed to help trainees to discover ways of forming successful interpersonal relationships, or 'how to make friends and influence people'. Because of their experimental nature it is difficult both to describe their workings and to appraise their value in behaviour modification and consequently there is some sharp disagreement over their effectiveness. Nevertheless, there is a continued and increasing interest in their use as a management development tool.

i. The T-group (T for training) sets out to show each participant how others feel about his behaviour, and to provide an opportunity to examine their reactions to his own actions. The intention is that a man by learning to recognise in himself the kind of 'style' which arouses unproductive responses in others, will have gone some way toward curing those personal defects. Another aim is to discover how and why people are motivated in their actions and decisions. T-groups normally comprise from six to twelve people, usually strangers to one another, with one or two trainers. They stay together for a period of a few days to two weeks in a setting insulated from day-to-day distractions. They meet to talk specifically and freely about one another's behaviour, and analyse the results together. The success of a T-group exercise depends largely upon the 'trainer' who acts as a catalyst, and protector when necessary, and should ideally be a qualified psychologist. An alternative to the 'pure' T-group is the structured group run in-company. Undoubtedly T-groups have their uses, but must be used most carefully; for whilst some executives may be driven to greater things, others may simply be driven insane.

ii. Coverdale Training is another experience-based training system developed by Ralph Coverdale so that managers could learn to perceive and utilise both their own talents and those of their co-workers. At the root of his theory are three basic concepts: (a) the systematic approach to getting things done, the establishment of an objective, the seeking for information, the overcoming of problems and the evaluation of results; (b) the use of differing intellectual skills amongst managers; and (c) the sensitivity element of teaching managers to recognise their own strengths and weaknesses. His training methods concentrate upon personal relationships as a means of achieving goals, but he uses practical exercises rather than theoretical lectures to put them across. Part 1 of the training is a residential course for about 20 managers lasting a week. Participants work in teams of six or seven on a number of repeatable tasks, examine how they have worked together, and plan for better group performance on the next run. The tasks, ranging from building towers with toy bricks to counting windows in a hotel, are not important in themselves, but how the team tackles them against the clock is the key. Individual strengths emerge as the course progresses, and members become more skilful at integrating these talents in teamwork as they gain experience. In part 2 of the training, managers gain further experience of team formation by working in a variety of groups. Advanced courses are also run for key managers and specialists, where issues previously raised are considered more deeply.

Managers who have been through this form of training should become quick to recognise deficiencies in the structure and functioning of their existing organisations, and more prepared to question their own management practices.

iii. The Managerial Grid, devised as a set of simple theories to describe alternative ways of achieving production through people, has been developed by Robert Blake into a complete and sophisticated learning package, and marketed world wide by Scientific Methods Inc. of Texas. The complete Managerial Grid Organisation Development programme may extend over a period of years, and the six-phase approach includes both strategic and tactical considerations. Phase 1 teaches the Grid to a company's entire managerial staff, Phase 2 applies Grid principles to the problems of work teams and departments, Phase 3 improves intergroup co-ordination, Phase 4 designs a blueprint for optimal organisation development, and later phases continue the company policy of achieving corporate excellence.

Basic seminars are organised separately for chief executives and middle and higher levels of management, and advanced seminars for in-company instructors and those responsible for the basic decision to introduce the O.D. programme. Before attending the seminar each participant is expected to put in several hours' reading to familiarise himself with the theory, and to identify his own 'managerial style'. On arrival at the course he is confronted with a test paper on his homework. This is followed by a case study, and later by a film *Twelve Angry Men*.

A Grid seminar is not 'taught' in the usual way, but as teams participants solve complex management problems. Approved 'staff' solutions are presented, and individual and team performance is repeatedly assessed. Various measuring instruments are used to evaluate effectiveness, and these and the intense time pressure introduce a hot-house atmosphere and an element of brainwashing. Whilst some

members may find the strain too much, the majority work
long hours and spend a high level of energy on the discussions
and evaluations.

Although many British companies have initiated Grid
seminars, enthusiasm is variable, and few if any have gone
the full way.

5. Development Programmes

Achieving more profitable business results through improved
managerial performance requires the resolution of two practical
problems: the correct definition of efficiency, and the motivation
of managers to manage more effecively. There may be many ways
of tackling these two factors, but one approach which has become
a widely recognised and accepted management discipline is 'management by objectives'.

a. *Management by objectives* (M.B.O.) was first coined as a
   phrase by Peter F. Drucker in his book *The Practice of
   Management* (1955), to express a general philosophy of
   management. The concepts he put forward under the full title
   'management by objectives and self-control' have widely
   influenced the methods which have been further developed by
   George Ordiorne and William J. Reddin amongst others in
   the U.S.A., and John W. Humble in the U.K. Whilst the
   various authors place a different emphasis upon the twin
   objectives of corporate planning and management development, Humble's claim that 'M.B.O. is a dynamic system
   which seeks to integrate the company's need to clarify and
   achieve its profit and growth goals, with the manager's need
   to contribute and develop himself' seems to be a universally
   acceptable summary. The precise programme for introducing
   the M.B.O. method of management must of course be
   specifically designed for each particular organisation, but its
   distinctive systematic approach will approximate to the following procedure.

   1. The first step is for general management to outline the
      company's strategic objectives and tactical plans, both long-
      and short-term. Drucker has suggested that a business must
      be successful in each of the following vital areas: profitabil-
      ity, productivity, market standing, innovation, uses of
      financial and physical resources, worker performace and
      attitude, manager performance and development, and pub-
      lic responsibility. Information on the present situation

might usefully be gained by taking part in an inter-firm comparison exercise.

2. Top management must also evaluate the corporate organisation structure and its communications network, and where necessary put its house in order. The organisation chart and statements of functions and responsibilities must be checked to ensure that conditions are provided in which it is possible to achieve the key results and improvements planned. Directors must give managers maximum freedom and flexibility in operation, and also ensure that each member's position in the company matches his talents. Effective two-way communication is essential, with top management prepared to listen as well as sharing knowledge. Management control information must be supplied in a form and at a frequency which makes possible both more effective self-control, and better and quicker decisions.

3. Functional objectives must next be prepared for each department, to establish their particular share of the corporate plans from which they are derived. The work of the business must be allocated to profit centres, with each operational area having its own specific standards of performance and criteria of success. Reddin terms these 'effectiveness areas', and suggests as an example that production should concentrate on quality, quantity, timing, scrap, rejects, stock, labour costs, material costs, safety and machine utilization. Goals must be specific and measurable, e.g. 'reduce lost time due to work stoppages by 6%'. Success will depend upon their being orientated towards development rather than by applying pressure, to get results rather than to accomplish tasks.

4. The next step is for the functional manager to pass on the departmental objectives to his unit managers and supervisors. They must be helped to understand the department's goals, to realize how they will contribute to the corporate aims, and to take an active interest in the part which they are asked to play. To ease the difficulties in this area, Ordiorne discriminates between four types of goal: (i) routine goals which relate to the performance of routine responsibilities; (ii) emergency goals which are dictated by outside pressures, e.g. government legislation; (iii) innovations, which demand creative skills, e.g. new processes; (iv)

personnel development goals, e.g. managerial capability or individual attitudes.

5. The next crucial stage requires each line manager and his subordinates to reach joint agreements on their individual goals. Experience with M.B.O. has shown that a manager involved in setting targets for himself, will pursue them with more energy and determination than when they are imposed from outside. The superior must clarify with each junior manager the key results and performance standards that he will aim to achieve, in line with unit and company objectives, and gain his commitment to this contribution. It is essential to determine just how the results will be measured, and the dates by which they should be achieved. The key result areas, perhaps between 3 and 6, are those aspects where a good performance is critical to the job as a whole. The 80/20 rule usually applies, i.e. 20% of the time and activity contributes 80% of the value of the total results.

6. Once attainable objectives have been agreed, the next step is to put into effect the plans necessary to reach each goal. A 'job improvement plan' most frequently derived from the priority plan of the manager's boss, is concerned solely with the redirection of the subordinate's effort. The 'management action plan' lays out a course of action for getting things done, and translates goals into specific projects to be undertaken within agreed times. Whilst the subordinate is given maximum freedom to carry out his tasks, the superior monitors feedback data and gives whatever guidance and assistance becomes necessary.

7. The manager and supervisor should meet frequently to discuss 'how things are going' and 'what needs to be done', and in this way a more positive working relationship may develop. Systematic 'performance reviews' to measure and discuss progress towards results are essential as are also 'potential reviews' to identify those executives with potential for advancement. Each manager is responsible for coaching his subordinates, and for developing their vital potential.

8. As the M.B.O. programme becomes an accepted part of the normal management process, it will become necessary to re-establish goals and perhaps to begin again with a new

set of management objectives. Through the review and evaluation of joint performance and discussion of accomplishments, the ground will have been prepared for decisions on promotions and salary increases. Management training plans will also have been developed to assist each manager to overcome his weaknesses, to build upon his strengths, and to accept a positive role in his self-development.

This formal outline of the implementation of M.B.O. is only half the picture, since its application involves dealing with people. The essential ingredients are teamwork, dedicated encouragement, and uninhibited two-way discussion. The ideal situation for the introduction of M.B.O. is an organisation which is in a sound business situation, and where the chief executive feels strongly that M.B.O. offers a means of long-term improvement. Whilst ideally the start should come from the top, it is possible, however, to implement M.B.O. successfully within a department as a preliminary to expanding it into the larger organisation. It is usual to appoint a specially trained M.B.O. adviser, a company management employee, to help 'unfreeze' the organisation and act as a 'change agent'. The organisational structure may not be flexible enough and the managers' attitudes unsuitable at the outset, so that an educational programme may be necessary as a preliminary stage. People's attitudes and social systems are difficult and time-consuming to change, and managers must therefore be made aware of the nature of the business in which they work. They must learn to appreciate the content of M.B.O. and have the opportunity to discuss with top management the application of M.B.O. philosophy within the company. A number of construction companies have tried the M.B.O. approach for themselves, and it would appear to be eminently suitable for an industry with such real job satisfaction, and managers so used to self-development and with flexible attitudes to new concepts and situations. It is significant that the Construction Industry Training Board grant aid for management development programmes was conditional upon implementation of a scheme that was an M.B.O. procedure in all but name.

b. *Staff appraisal schemes* are one way of realising the untapped potential of employees, which is one of the greatest assets of an organisation. If corporate performance is to be improved, then priority must be given to attempting to improve the people who make it up. Since M.B.O. essentially represents a pragmatic approach to participative management, then any successful staff appraisal must be based on an objective discussion of peformance between manager and subordinate. Some of the objectives of the exercise are to: review the progress of managers in their present jobs; provide pointers to individual needs for further training; determine the capacity of managers for advancement; ensure that the management succession of the organisation is planned ahead; and to shape a positive recruitment policy when vacancies caused by retirements or new opportunities cannot be filled from within the company. Having considered the aims and objectives, let us now look at the methods.

1. Firstly, a policy decision must be made on whether organisations are established primarily to meet corporate objectives or those of the individuals making them up. Clearly some kind of balance must be maintained between these two conflicting needs. Whatever the purposes, all appraisal procedures are aimed at bringing about change in the behaviour of people at work by: sharing out the money, promotions and benefits fairly; motivating staff to reach the required standards and objectives; developing individuals by advice and praise; and checking the effectiveness of personnel practices. No matter how good the procedures, however, it is useless unless the individuals involved are prepared to carry them out. The essential reature of an active scheme, which does add to the level of performance of people within an organisation, is the assembly and sharing of information which provides both the individuals and the company with a 'learning experience'. Appraisal must therefore be seen to be a continuous process, with regular systematic discussion between a manager and his subordinate part of their day-to-day relationship, so that any formal periodic review becomes truly an integral element of management. Since there is no one right style of managing people, the way of appraising subordinates and the sense of occasion necessary at appraisal interviews will depend upon a manager's general relationship with his staff. There are also essential differences between appraisal activities, and 'reward reviews' and 'potential reviews' should be considered as essential precursors to effective 'performance reviews'.

2. Reward reviews concern the distribution of the fruits of organisational activity, such as salary, bonus, status, and all the other kinds of rewards, benefits and perquisites. The purpose is to judge the value of the appointment and the job holder in financial terms Although performance and potential will obviously influence pay, it is better exerted indirectly and at a distance. Effective discussion of personal performance is unlikely to be frank and fruitful when salary is being decided; and reward reviews should therefore be kept separate and distinct from performance and potential, and preferably take place at a point well removed in time from them.

3. Potential reviews are intended for the identification and release of management potential with the emphasis on man's need for self-fulfilment and growth by means of enhanced achievement in his work. The aim must be to assess a manager's potential for promotion, or for another position, according to his capacity and inclination rather than his current level of performance. To do other than this is to risk running foul of the 'Peter Principle', where everyone is eventually promoted to his level of incompetence with calamitous consequences both to the individual and the organisation. The location and development of tomorrow's managers is a key task for industry's leaders of today, for unless existing executives are eventually replaced the company will die out. But how can we pinpoint the candidates for management vacancies, or their training needs, when past job performance will not necessarily be a reliable guide to capacity to fill another position, the demands of which may be very different in character? Inevitably there will then occur a more subjective judgment of his personality traits, as well as a review of his academic qualifications, history, experience and training. Since using measures of past achievement in job performance can mislead in evaluating career potential, it is important to consider the 'quality' and 'style' of performance rather than the 'level of achievement'. The question of whether reports on interviews should be disclosed is another debatable issue; but research suggests that there are fewer problems with standards when potential reports are closed, but performance reports are open. The identification and development of management potential would seem to be an area where more systematic effort could bring great benefits.

4. Performance reviews may be conducted at the same time as assessments of potential, but they must be separate. On the assumption that whilst each individual is getting better at his job, the organisation is also developing and becoming more effective, it becomes necessary to monitor the job performance of each member of staff. With each manager now satisfied with his rewards, and the superior aware of his subordinate's ability and potential, a two-way exchange of information should have been made possible. There are certain well-tried principles for this interview. Both partners should prepare themselves for the meeting; the discussion should not be superficial and must be held on a fairly formal basis; talks should be focused on reviewing performance against previously agreed targets; and the review should culminate in an examination of ways and means of improving future effectiveness. Subordinates must be involved personally in helping to set the standards of their own job performance, for according to the 'self-fulfilling prophecy' concept if we have faith in people and give them the freedom to do what is expected, the majority will conform. Targets should be realistic and quantifiable, and for this reason rating scales and ranking are not satisfactory. Performance must be assessed against specific objectives, definite and closely connected with the critical work tasks.

5. Although a judgement by the superior of his subordinate is an important part of the management appraisal process, it is not the total picture. The subordinate has views of his own about his performance, and both views must be reconciled. Managers must relinquish their formal hierarchical role and learn to perceive situations and problems as they appear to the subordinate. This means that the counsellor must be prepared to listen as well as talk, to understand rather than criticise, and to show that he is mature enough to consider the subordinate's opinions and ideas without feeling insecure or losing his emotional self-control. Only this attitude of mind and this kind of empathy can remove any barriers which may impede the learning process, and so lead to the improvement of the subordinate's performance through the systematic transference of the manager's knowledge, skill and know-how. In this way, the programme will be owned by the subordinate rather than rejected out of hand, and coaching can proceed, in Drucker's phrase, by 'building upon strengths'.

The major development opportunities lie within the job itself, and the most powerfully motivating experiences occur within the work environment. Nevertheless, many of the problems facing a manager stem from the relationships between those who carry out the work, for people don't always 'get on'. He must talk to individuals in order to 'get to the bottom of things', explore reasons for personality clashes and instances of lack of co-operation. In this context, the manager-coach may find it appropriate to advise his subordinate colleague by means of 'non-directive' counselling. Instead of explaining what he considers to be the best solution to the problem, he can help him to come to terms with it and work out the solution himself. The important fact to remember about appraisal schemes is that we are operating in the area of fallible human judgment, not scientific measurement. Moreover, coaching (or counselling) is a continuous, participative process, not an annual occasion; but there is no nobler managerial task than that of helping another human to develop to the limits of his potential.

6. How well a manager develops his staff is the final, and perhaps most important, link in the managerial effectiveness of any organisation. Yet managers often have difficulty in conducting face-to-face reviews with subordinates about their job performance. So many managers actively dislike appraising their immediate subordinates, even when they know they are going to make a complimentary annual report. They are more naturally embarrassed when obliged to tell someone that he has fallen down in some specific manner. Since staff appraisal is such an essential part of a manager's range of skills, he should therefore be given the opportunity to develop those skills, for improvement will only come through training.

Whilst staff appraisal is an essential component of any M.B.O. programme, it is also a valuable management tool in its own right and can be implemented successfully alone. Top management must accept their responsibility to develop a purposeful staff appraisal system and get the coaching climate right, for corporate operating efficiency and the personal development of the company's managers go hand in hand; both are essential to the continuing success of the business.

c. *Action learning* and its associated variants of self-development, on-the-job training, management action groups and problem-centred clinics, are the result of disenchantment with formal classroom teaching and the realisation of a need for an experiential approach to management education and development. In the deeply traditional construction industry many of its managers were 'thrown in at the deep end', and they developed themselves as they struggled along, without finding the time to reflect on what they had learned or how. There must remain a professional responsibility to develop oneself, by improving one's formal qualifications, by gaining knowledge of other specialisms, and an appreciation of the changing structure of the industry. But with changing social values and a need for cost-effectiveness, more intelligent and purposeful development methods, like job rotation and deputising at meetings and during holidays, have been devised to lead to both greater learning and improved motivation through involvement. Courses are excellent for teaching mechanical techniques such as network analysis, but these are minor aspects of a manager's needs, and lectures, case studies, role playing and other classroom activities are not situations where experienced managers learn very much. Learning to manage, i.e. to run things properly, must include discovering how to cope with the unfair pressures of time, the frustration of inadequate information, and the confrontation of one's ability in action, as well as theory.

1. Hawdon Hague, of the management teaching consultancy Context Training Ltd., believes that good management manifests itself in action, and therefore has to be learned in action, i.e. whilst working. He insists that a company must make a firm commitment to job-related training, spread over a number of months or even years, if a training consultancy assignment is to be really worthwhile. Since the definition of learning is 'the modification of behaviour through experience', and if learning by discovery is the most effective method, then the job of the management educator is to design learning situations in which managers can find out things for themselves. The specialist tutor or action trainer is a catalyst who gives on-the-job counselling, as opposed to the coaching which is done by the line boss. Whilst concentrating principally on designing the learning experience, the tutor may intercede with senior managers on behalf of a project team, ask the general manager to

consider their proposals with care, or ensure that time is made available for development exercises. Part of his role is to set up the initial unfreezing of attitudes by means of work diaries, self-assessment questionnaires and group exercises. Managers need to realise that there is room for self improvement, be shown ways and means of becoming bigger people, and provided with good reasons of self-interest to develop themselves. The tutor sets up the projects and is available thereafter to give help when requested, to provoke thought and teach only the habit of learning. He is developing the organisation by developing its managers through a process of action teaching, but his loyalty remains to the company.

2. The Grubb Institute of Behavioural Studies uses the dynamic of 'creative pairing'. The training group consists of members from separate organisations, and one at a time each member is visited by a working colleague who takes with him a live work problem. The group then works on the problem applying the knowledge and insights gained during the course. The individual participant is thus put in the situation of a 'change agent' or catalyst, linking and interpreting the esoteric language of behaviour and process to the problems of his own company. This process is repeated for each member of the group over a period of perhaps six months for the total cycle. This arrangement is intended to overcome the possible problems of experiential learning: either rejection leading to even greater rigidity of mind, or over-enthusiasm creating re-entry difficulties back on the job.

3. Dr. Reginald Revans specifically calls his approach to management development 'action learning'. He believes that a student manager is more likely to learn from doing something himself, than by reading a book or hearing someone else talk about it. He also believes that learning is a social process, and that people gain more from group interchange and debate than from working alone. His method is to take a man away from his own organisation and give him the opportunity to work on a major problem in another company, free from the normal political restraints. By making him accountable for instituting the changes which he reasons out theoretically, he will excel himself in both action and learning. Moreover he has shown that experience can be intensified by the bringing together

of managers and academics in joint exploration, the latter simply finding the problem. In Belgium the programme took the form of an eleven-month exchange of potential top managers from major companies, under the auspices of Revans and the Foundation Industrie-Université at Brussels. In Britain the General Electric Company has adopted action learning through two-week residential courses at Dunchurch Industrial Staff College. The process is essentialy flexible, managers swapping within one company as at G.E.C. or with outsiders at F.I.U. Whatever the variant, Revans' three crucial criteria are: real issues, in a real situation, in real time.

4. At Manchester Business School, Professor John Morris has designed another variant of action learning, which again brings the academics into a realistic collaboration with experienced managers. These 'joint development activities' operate on the principles of real work, the use of teaching staff as resources, and sufficient time to do things properly. Key executives from a single company work together in teams on major company problems, usually part-time over three months or so. The projects on which they work have been carefully chosen by senior management, as real questions to which they earnestly want an answer that can be acted upon within the company's resources. The issues must cut across the different functions of the firm, and also provide challenging work for middle and junior managers on their way up. The key role of the school staff is as 'agents of awareness', working in support as consultants, tutors and research workers.

5. All of these previous examples of the theories and practice of action learning have one essential feature in common; they are all designed around actual life and work experience. This practical 'down to earth' approach should appeal strongly to the entrepreneurial, trouble-shooting, innovative and pragmatic managers of the building industry. Now that its scale of operations is larger and more complex and the environment in which it is operating is more uncertain and demanding, the industry must become more professionally concerned with the quality and quantity of its managers. And in these days when so many interests are debating ways of involving the operatives in decision-making, it is vital that companies should see their main, primary task to be the involvement of their own managers and supervisors first.

BIBLIOGRAPHY

Margaret Brown, *'The Manager's Guide to the Behavioural Sciences'*, The Industrial Society, 1969.

D. W. Birchall, *Employee motivation in the construction industry*, I.O.B. Site Management Information Service, No. 72.

What is Behavioural Science?, B.I.M. Management Information Sheet, No. 6.

R. E. Calvert, 'Improving Site Conditions for Civil Engineering Contracts', Public Works & Municipal Services Congress, 1970.

Likert's Theories on Management, B.I.M. Management Information Sheet, No. 19.

Edwin P. Smith, *'The Manager as an Action Centred Leader'*, The Industrial Society, 1969.

Management by Objectives, B.I.M. Management Information Sheet, No. 14.

A Guide to Coaching for Management, Construction Industry Training Board, 1974.

Employee Counselling, B.I.M. Management Checklist, No. 57.

G.A. Randell, P.M.A. Packard, R.L. Shaw and A.J. Slater, *Staff Appraisal*, Institute of Personnel Management.

Michael Williams, *Training in Performance Appraisal*, The Association of Teachers of Supervisory Studies, 1969.

Training and Development of Managers in the Medium and Large Firms, Construction Industry Training Board, 1968.

John Morris, 'Developing Managers for the Construction Industry', *B.I.M. Management Review & Digest*, January 1978.

The Enterprise and Factors Affecting its Operation, International Labour Office, Geneva, 1965.

Barnes, Fogg, Stephens, Titman of P.A. Management Consultants Ltd., *Company Organisation Theory and Practice*, Geo. Allen and Unwin Ltd. 1970.

Chapter 20

Digital Computing

1. The Computer

The *electronic digital computer* is another piece of office equipment – with a difference. Like the electric typewriter and the
pocket/desk calculator it is electronic, but unlike these and most
mechanical machines which usually perform a single function only,
the computer is most versatile. It can read, write, file, account,
edit, communicate, carry out complex calculations, and make
logical decisions either individually or all within the same system,
at extremely high speeds. Being so flexible, it is also more costly to
acquire and run than other types of equipment. It moreover
requires not one operator but a team to service its operations. A
typical computer department, under the control of a data
processing manager, might include an operations manager responsible for punch operators, data controllers, computer operators and tape librarian; and a systems manager with a team
comprising systems analyst, systems designer and programmers.

Whereas the eighteenth century Industrial Revolution brought
powerful muscles to man's assistance, the new information/
communication revolution has provided an extension to his brain.
However, although the computer by far surpasses any other
machine, in that it can be made to perform some of the boring
routine work of the human brain, it compels its users to think hard
about each application because it possesses no initiative of its own.
In order to realise the full potential of the computer, management
must have a proper understanding of the working of the machine
and the principles of data processing. This is why it warrants a
chapter on its own as a management technique.

There are two main types of computer, *analogue* and *digital*.
The analogue computer has no logical ability and performs its
calculations by representing real-life situations in terms of a
physical analogy by measurement. Thus a car petrol gauge
measures the size of an electric current and indicates the amount

of petrol in the tank upon its dial. Because of its nature the analogue computer only gives approximate answers, but is very useful in mathematical and scientific applications such as weather forecasting. In general, the term 'computer' refers to the digital computer, which is the one used for business systems. The dictionary defines digital as 'pertaining to the fingers', and also has the sense of a figure used to represent a number. The digital computer calculates accurately, representing data in terms of discrete electrical pulses, and can make yes/no logical decisions. An electronic current is either switched 'on' or 'off', a ferrite ring may be magnetized in a clockwise or anticlockwise direction, and a magnetised spot may be present or absent. These alternative states are usually represented by '0' and '1'.

The *hardware* of a computer (see Fig. 20.1) is the physical equipment or machinery, and comprises four groups:

    i.   Central processing unit – the control and operating machine.

   ii.   Peripherals – input, output and storage devices.

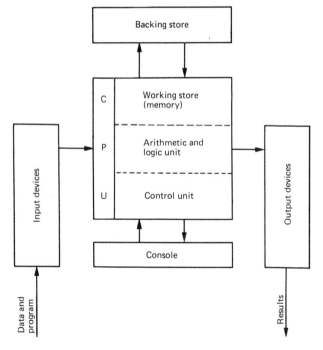

Fig. 20.1. Computer configuration

iii. Data preparation equipment.

iv. Terminals.

A grouping of these machines are inter-connected, and are organised to operate as a total system. The particular layout for a computer installation is referred to as its 'configuration'.

1. *The central processing unit* (C.P.U.) comprises three sections, as follows.

a. *The storage unit or memory* holds information in its magnetic core store. This consists of a closely packed honeycomb of minute iron rings strung on wires in a frame. (More modern machines use electronic circuits on silicon 'chips' about 5 mm square). When an electric current is passed through a ring it is magnetised in either a clockwise or counter-clockwise direction, depending upon the direction of the pulse (see Fig. 20.2). Each ring can thus hold one

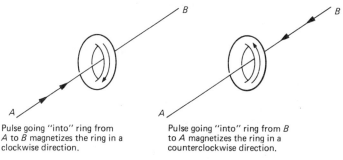

Pulse going "into" ring from *A* to *B* magnetizes the ring in a clockwise direction.

Pulse going "into" ring from *B* to *A* magnetizes the ring in a counterclockwise direction.

Fig. 20.2. Magnetic storage

piece or 'bit' of information – either one of two 'binary' states. The store is used to hold binary coded representations of numbers and letters in groupings of eight digits or a 'byte'. Each character or byte is thus stored in a pigeon hole uniquely identified by a serial number or address, from which it can be transferred on demand. The power of a computer is to some extent dependent upon the size of its memory, which is calculated as so many thousand bytes, e.g. 32 000 or 32K bytes. Another vital factor is the speed of access to or from the store, which is measured in millionths of a second – usually from 8 down to 1 microseconds (μs).

The first use of the internal store is to retain data, both before and after processing. The second use is to hold the program of instructions, which tells the computer precisely what to do and in which particular sequence. These instructions are normally coded in numeric form, and stay in the store until erased and replaced by another program for a new task.

b. *The arithmetic and logic unit* is the place where arithmetic operations are actually carried out. Again the speed is phenomenal, being of the order of $10\mu s$ for adding together two eight-digit numbers.

The unit consists of one or more registers capable of instant access, which may be called accumulators. The numbers to be added together are transferred from their addresses into the accumulator, and the resultant total is then read to another address, so leaving the accumulator free for the next operation.

In addition to the four 'species' of arithmetic, i.e. add, subtract, multiply and divide, other operations may be possible. It is usual to include 'shifting', i.e. moving digits one position to the left or right. The logical operation consists of the ability to differentiate between positive and negative numbers. Thus, depending upon whether a number is more or less than the standard used for comparison, an alternative path in the program may be taken. This facility is of fundamental importance, and a typical program of several thousand instructions will contain many of the 'test and jump if negative' type of directive.

c. *The control unit* functions as the nerve centre of the computer, interpreting the instructions laid down in the program. The various parts of the computer system are connected together by a complex network of wires known as a highway. The job of the control unit is to act as a switching signal box, to see that the information route specified by the program is correctly followed, and to ensure that 'chains of electrical pulses' flow along the prescribed path. The switching elements known as 'gates' allow information to flow when they are closed, but not when they are open. Pulses may flow in serial formation one behind the other on the same path, or in parallel simultaneously on different routes. Instructions are usually transferred sequentially from the store to the control unit, where the instruction register accepts the command, translates it, and operates the appropriate circuits to perform the action required. An instruction must specify both the operation to be performed, and the address of the information to be processed. Whilst both instructions and information are stored in identical numerical form, the computer differentiates between them because the instructions are read to the instruction register for decoding.

A list of instructions, known as the 'instruction code', is specified for each individual computer. These are of three basic types:

i. Arithmetical instructions, e.g. add, subtract, multiply, divide, shift, round off, compare, etc., which are functions of the computer

ii. Data transfer instructions, e.g. read from input, read to output, read a character, read a card, print a line, punch a tape etc. All of these regulate the relations between the C.P.U. and the storage, input and output devices.

iii. Conditional transfers or 'jump instructions'. An unconditional transfer changes the control address at the will of the programmer, and is used to construct loops in a program. A series of operations will be performed over and over again until completed, when the program will jump back to the beginning. A conditional transfer changes the address only when certain conditions are fulfilled. For example, test to see whether there is any taxable pay: if so, proceed to the address containing instructions to perform the P.A.Y.E. calculation; if not, proceed to another address where another part of the program is stored. The conditional jump is therefore a branching instruction which can direct the computer to either of two divergent courses of action.

d. *The console* allows the computer operator to control the central processor and the on-line peripheral units, and to observe and monitor the processing functions. It comprises various switches, control panels etc., and the console typewriter which permits a dialogue between the computer and the operator. For example, through the typewriter the computer can automatically inform the operator when an error in the input data is discovered, e.g. an even number of holes in a frame of a paper tape.

2. *The peripherals* are the machines which feed input to the C.P.U., and collect and/or display the output from the C.P.U. Additional back-up storage devices which supplement the internal storage unit of the C.P.U. are also peripheral units. All are linked directly to the C.P.U. to be called upon as necessary.

Input devices include the card reader, the paper tape reader, the magnetic tape unit, magnetic disc pack, visual display unit (V.D.U.) with light pen, optical reader, magnetic character reader and termiprinter. Output devices include magnetic tape and disc, line printer, computer output microfilm, V.D.U., termiprinter, minicomputer and magnetic drum.

Back-up storage may be on magnetic tape reels, disc pack or magnetic drum.

A list of maximum speeds for various activities is given below for comparative purposes:

Read paper tape: 300 characters per second.
Read punch card: 1 200 characters per second.
Read magnetic tape: 80 000 characters per second.
Read magnetic disc: 416 000 characters per second.
Line printer: 2 700 characters per second.

3. *Data preparation* equipment caters for both input and output. Input machines punch information onto cards, paper tape or magnetic tape. All such input information has to be 'punched' twice, once by the machine that actually prepares the message carrier, and again by a separate machine called a verifier that checks the punched data. Examples of the three forms are shown in Figs. 20.3, 20.4 and 20.5.

Output machines handle the computer printout and include the decollator-guillotine for separating continuous stationery, and facilities for cutting off sprocket hole margins, and centre slicing when output is printed 'two up'.

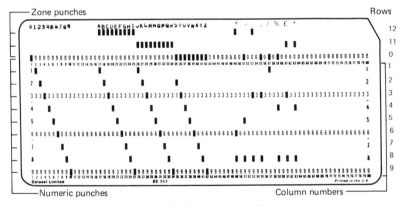

Fig. 20.3. Punched card

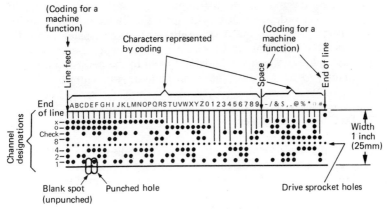

Fig. 20.4. Section of a punched paper tape

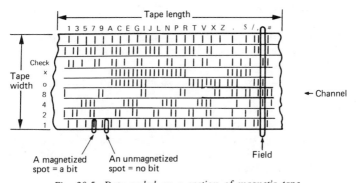

Fig. 20.5. Data coded on a section of magnetic tape

4. **Terminals** are of two basic categories both linked to the main computer. The first type have keyboards which can communicate with the C.P.U. control unit and are described as having 'on-line access'. They display information provided by the main computer, either on a television screen (V.D.U.s) or by means of a line printer (termiprinters.) These machines can also be used to input information and so update the computer files immediately. This is the 'real-time system' such as is used for booking airline passages. The second type of terminal is in effect a smaller computer which can interact with the mainframe computer. At the smaller end of the scale they merely have input/output facilities and are dependent upon the main computer for processing. At the larger end of the

scale they may have sufficient peripherals to be capable of working independently, but using the facilities of the mainframe for additional working space and also using centrally located information files. This is the type that might be available in the site office and linked to the main computer at Head Office: hence the term 'remote job entry'.

2. Data Processing – Means

A typical *data processing operation* will follow these stages:
Stage 1. The raw (i.e. unprocessed) data is prepared in written or typewritten form. This is not a machine-sensible form and so in:
Stage 2 the recorded data is translated by means of an automatic writing machine into punched cards, paper tape or magnetic tape, in which form they are intelligible to a machine.
Stage 3. The data is translated by means of the input device into electrical pulse form, either by mechanical probes or electrical/magnetic sensors.
Stage 4. The data now in electrical pulse form is processed by the computer C.P.U.
Stage 5. The processed data is translated back into punched tape form by means of the output device.
Stage 6. The processed data is translated once again from machine-sensible form by means of the automatic writing machine into typewritten form, which thus communicates the result to the human operator.
The binary system of notation has to be used by the computer for all of its workings, since it can only differentiate between the two states of off/on, left/right, yes/no etc. The symbols traditionally used for the representation of binary numbers are (0) and (1). These basic symbols are called binary digits, usually abbreviated to 'bits' from the first and last pairs of letters. All data is stored inside the computer in binary form, either by magnetizing a tiny iron ring in the memory store in either a clockwise or anticlockwise direction, or on 'chips'. However, by using different patterns or codes we can represent data that is numeric, alphabetic or symbolic.

In the punched card the binary digits are represented by a punched hole or no hole (see Fig. 20.3). The numbers are shown directly by a single hole in one of the numeric rows 0 to 9.

Alphabetic characers are also shown in a single column, by a combination of one hole in a zone row and one in a numeric row. Special characters or symbols are shown by one, two or three punches in each column. Note the clipped corner which is used to check that the cards are not stacked upside down or back-to-front. These are the same (Hollerith) cards as were used in the electro-mechanical systems described in Chapter 10.5.

Just as in the decimal system the columns of figures are weighted 10^0, 10^1, 10^2, 10^3, etc., so the binary system column weights are 2^0, 2^1, 2^2, 2^3 etc. In the computer it is usual to store information in blocks of eight bits, called a 'byte'. Fig. 20.6 shows that a byte can thus hold 256 messages in binary form. A typical binary addition and subtraction and their decimal equivalents are also illustrated.

A punched paper tape (see Fig. 20.4) has eight channels and represents numbers in this same binary form. Letters and characters are similarly coded as shown. Note that the channels are three on one side and five on the other side of the drive sprocket holes, so that the tape cannot be transposed. Moreover, each letter or character is represented by an uneven number of punched holes, an additional hole being added to the 'check' channel where necessary. If an additional hole is punched, or one omitted by accident, then an automatic check will throw up the error indicated by the even number of holes.

The magnetic tape shown in Fig. 20.5 carries coded information in columns known as 'fields', each containing up to eight bits. The illustration shows nine channels, an extra one having been added for 'parity checking'. In high-speed data processing the computer can occasionally drop one bit out of a byte. It is, however, extremely unlikely to drop two bits from the same byte. To insure against the accidental loss of a bit, parity checking is performed by adding when necessary an extra bit to each byte to ensure that the total number of bits is either odd or even. The process is called either 'odd' or 'even' parity checking.

Because pure binary results in the handling of large quantities of digits, both in the preparation of the input data and in the receipt of output data from the computer, alternative systems have been devised to make the input and output processes less cumbersome for the user. The binary coded decimal (B.C.D.) notation is one of these simplified systems. In the B.C.D. system each digit of a decimal number is represented by a group of four bits, as in the examples shown in Fig. 20.7.

Another alternative system is the 'hexadecimal' arithmetic, with a base of $6 + 10 = 16$. The sixteen symbols required are the

	Representation	
	Decimal	*Binary*
Column weights	100.10.1	128.64.32.16.8.4.2.1
	0	0
	1	1
	2	1 0
	3	1 1
	4	1 0 0
	5	1 0 1
	6	1 1 0
	7	1 1 1
	8	1 0 0 0
	9	1 0 0 1
	1 0	1 0 1 0
	3 0	1 1 1 1 0
	6 3	1 1 1 1 1 1
	6 4	1 0 0 0 0 0 0
	1 2 7	1 1 1 1 1 1 1
	1 2 8	1 0 0 0 0 0 0 0
	2 5 5	1 1 1 1 1 1 1 1
Addition	8 9	1 0 1 1 0 0 1
	+ 2 8	+1 1 1 0 0
	1 1 7	1 1 1 0 1 0 1

$$0 + 1 = 1$$
$$0 + 0 = 0$$
$$1 + 0 = 1$$
$$1 + 1 = 0 \text{ and carry } 1$$
$$(1 + 1) + 1 = 1 \text{ and carry } 1$$
$$(0 + 1) + 0 = 1$$
$$0 + 1 = 1$$

Subtraction	8 9	1 0 1 1 0 0 1
	− 2 8	− 1 1 1 0 0
	6 1	1 1 1 1 0 1

$$0 \text{ from } 1 = 1$$
$$0 \text{ from } 0 = 0$$
$$1 \text{ from } 0 = 1 \text{ and borrow } 1$$
$$(1 + 1) \text{ from } 1 = 1 \text{ and borrow } 1$$
$$(1 + 1) \text{ from } 1 = 1 \text{ and borrow } 1$$
$$(0 + 1) \text{ from } 0 = 1 \text{ and borrow } 1$$
$$(0 + 1) \text{ from } 1 = 0$$

Fig. 20.6

numbers from 0 to 9 plus the letters A to F. Thus a single hexadecimal digit can have sixteen different values from O to F, whereas the binary system requires four bits to represent the sixteen numerical values from 0000 to 1111. Therefore, a single hexadecimal digit can be used to represent the same value as each group of four bits (see Fig. 20.8). This provides us with a convenient shorthand for representing long binary numbers, simply by separating them into groups of four bits, starting from the right (see example in Fig. 20.8).

| | Binary coded decimal notation | | | |
Decimal notation	4 bit group	4 bit group	4 bit group	4 bit group
0				0000
1				0001
1 2			0001	0010
1 2 3		0001	0010	0011
2 3 4 5	0010	0011	0100	0101
9 8 7 6	1001	1000	0111	0110

Fig. 20.7

Although the contents of a computer store are in binary numbers, nevertheless we can represent those contents in abbreviated form by using hexadecimal digits.

Software is a collective name for all the intangibles of a computer installation, as opposed to the visible hardware described earlier. All computer operations are based upon 'files', broken down into 'records', and the machine performs exactly the same functions as most clerical assistants, and in a very similar fashion. Processing involves updating the records, creating new and deleting old records, extracting selected information from its records, and performing basic calculations on selected fields of information. The advantage of the computer stems from the fact that it can perform these functions remarkably quickly. But unlike the human clerk, a computer is totally lacking in enterprise and initiative, and literally does everything it is told to do, and nothing more. The software provides the computer instructions, and thus complements the hardware by making the machinery work.

There are three types of instruction:

a. the operating system;

b. the application program, properly spelt the American way to distinguish it from other forms of programme;

c. software packages.

1. *The operating system* is provided by the computer manufacturer, and is held in the central storage unit and back-up peripheral storage devices. It is able to call any peripheral, or other part of the C.P.U. whenever they are required; and it is able to maximise the utilisation of the various parts of the system, in order that a series of jobs being handled at the same time may be completed in the quickest possible time.

The console operator has to stand over the machine, prepared to instruct it 'what to do next' whenever it finishes one part of a job or encounters some exceptional condition. But human operators are very slow by comparison with a computer, and are also prone to errors. Consequently

Decimal numbers	Hexadecimal numbers	Binary numbers
0	00	00000000
1	01	00000001
2	02	00000010
3	03	00000011
4	04	00000100
5	05	00000101
6	06	00000110
7	07	00000111
8	08	00001000
9	09	00001001
10	0A	00001010
11	0B	00001011
12	0C	00001100
13	0D	00001101
14	0E	00001110
15	0F	00001111
16	10	00010000
17	11	00010001
18	12	00010010
⋮	⋮	⋮
253	FD	11111101
254	FE	11111110
255	FF	11111111

Decimal number 1980
Binary number 11110111100
Groups of four bits   0111   1011   1100
Hexadecimal number   7   B   C
Binary calculation   Hexadecimal calculation

$1024 \times 1 = 1024$ $256 \times 7 = 1792$
$\ 512 \times 1 = \ 512$ $\ 16 \times 11 = \ 176$
$\ 256 \times 1 = \ 256$ $\ \ 1 \times 12 = \ \ 12$
$\ 128 \times 1 = \ 128$ ————
$\ \ 64 \times 0 = \ \ \ -$ 1980
$\ \ 32 \times 1 = \ \ 32$ ————
$\ \ 16 \times 1 = \ \ 16$
$\ \ \ 8 \times 1 = \ \ \ 8$
$\ \ \ 4 \times 1 = \ \ \ 4$
$\ \ \ 2 \times 0 = \ \ \ -$
$\ \ \ 1 \times 0 = \ \ \ -$

$\ \ \ \ \ \ \ \ \ \ \ 1980$

Fig. 20.8. Equivalent numbers in the decimal, hexadecimal and binary systems

computer time could be wasted simply waiting for the operator to interpret its questions, to take a decision and implement appropriate action. The purpose of this particular software is to enable the computer to undertake as much as possible of the routine work connected with its own control and programming. The efficiency and therefore the value to the user of a computer installation, is judged as much by the quality of the software offered with it as by the technical specification of the hardware.

Thus the operating system organises the processing, but the operating system itself needs to be told the things that require doing.

2. *The application program* contains the detailed instructions necessary to carry out a particular task or 'job'. Because of the primitive nature of the computer, even the most simple operation usually requires several step-by-step instructions to perform. The following BASIC program illustrates the need for strict adherence to formal rules, and the necessity to include every detail, including stop. The language used, BASIC (Beginners All purpose Symbolic Instruction Code,) is widely available from most manufacturers.

```
10 REM EXAMPLE OF A BASIC PROGRAM
20 FOR A = 1 TO 10
30 PRINT A;
40 NEXT A
50 END
RUN
```

Line 10 is a Remark, requiring the computer to retain the line of program code.

Line 20 is a 'loop' type instruction to give 'A' the values from 1 to 10.

Line 30 commands the computer to print the contents of the variable 'A', the ';' suppresses any spaces.

Line 40 returns control to line 20 where 'A' will take its new value.

Line 50 informs the computer that the program has finished.

RUN is the command given by the operator to 'run the program'.

The resulting output is a line of figures 1 2 3 4 5 6 7 8 9 10

Individual programs are written by the user, and hence tailor-made to suit his particular requirements and organisation. Programs are usually stored on magnetic discs, and the computer operator, through the C.P.U.'s console, tells the operating system to call in the relevant disc and read the instructions contained.

One job, e.g. stocktaking, may consist of several programs, and within each job there is a section called the job control language (J.C.L.) This is a series of definitive statements informing the operating system which particular files the job will need, and which peripherals and programs it will need to use in order to perform the instructions contained in the programs. The J.C.L., in effect, is the link between the programs and the operating system.

3. *Software packages* are provided by the computer manufacturer to serve a general need (such as a payroll suite), or a type of sub-operating system to control certain items of hardware via the main operating system.

A suite of programs which can be taken off the shelf and used immediately has its attractions. Unfortunately, such a package may not satisfy the individual idiosyncrasies of an organisation, and it is usually more trouble to amend than write from scratch.

The latter type of package would be essential, if for example one wished to use an on-line system requiring a telecommunications package.

Programme languages are the result of the great effort that has been made towards communicating with the computer in everyday English. The only language that the computer can interpret directly is 'machine-code', a purely numeric form of 'low-level' language that is unique to each series of machines, e.g. ASSEMBLER and PLAN. These machine or 'assembly' languages provide a direct translation of the program written by the user (the 'source' program) into a machine-coded program (the 'object' program) understood by the computer: more or less instruction by instruction. Since every single step in the logic is represented by a separate numeric instruction, the machine program is very lengthy, takes a long time to write, and is difficult to check and amend. The trend has therefore been towards 'high-level' languages which are much like everyday English. But in order to provide a greater precision in instruction, because of the consequences of misinterpretation, programs are written in 'symbolic' languages composed of letters of the alphabet, numbers and other characters.

Because much of the early work with computers was done by scientists, mathematicians and engineers, the first high-level language was FORTRAN (*for*mula *tran*slation.) This proved to be a very useful method of translating algebraic formulas and mathematical equations into machine-readable form and was easy to learn because its instructions closely resembled the mathematical formulas. For example, A = B + C/D means 'Get the sum of B and quotient of C and D and use that value for A'. Another internationally accepted high-level language intended primarily for research purposes is ALGOL (*Algo*rithmic *L*anguage.)

However, for business applications where the calculations are simple but a great deal of input/output activity is involved, FORTRAN is not suitable. The high-level language developed primarily for commercial use is COBOL (*Co*mmon *B*usiness-*O*riented *L*anguage.) COBOL programs are written in the form of basic English statements, such as 'read time-sheets' or 'print pay-slips'. A vocabulary of 'reserved' words e.g. read, multiply, and, or, giving, etc., are precisely and unequivocally defined. Others are defined by the user specifically for each program and include such terms as time-sheet, pay-slip etc. If these are the names given to particular records, then a 'picture' of the record is included that defines the format and contents. Information of this type is contained in that part of the progam called the data division, whilst the actual processing is given in the procedure division. This separation enables the description of a new record to be added to the data division, and an additional segment inserted into the procedure division, without touching the rest of the program. Despite the limited vocabulary and strict rules of grammatical arrangement, COBOL is easy to understand and follow, even by those not involved in writing the original program, and this results in easier supervision.

Eventually business managers began to use more sophisticated mathematics, whilst scientists and engineers found that they were handling problems which required increasing masses of data. At the same time general-purpose computer systems were developed that could be used by both the business and the scientific worlds. A new high-level multipurpose language developed for use by both commercial and scientific programmers is PL/1. This incorporates features of both FORTRAN and COBOL but is free of many of the constraints of language and format in the originals.

In order to 'convert' these high-level languages into machine language, an intermediary program called a 'compiler' is used. In addition to translating the instructions it also prints them out in a report called a 'program compilation'. The COBOL compiler, for instance, takes only five minutes to interpret a source program of say 500 statements, and generate a series of machine-coded instructions to carry out the tasks specified, i.e. the object program.

Since each program is written for a particular type of computer, it may be necessary to rewrite the program completely if the user wishes to use a different computer. However, specially developed programs called 'simulators' are available, so that certain other types of computer may be made to understand and obey programs written for any of a group of different manufacturers.

3. Data Processing – Method

Solving a data-processing problem by means of a computer, must be tackled in five steps.

1. Define the problem: describe the problem and the required results as clearly and completely as possible.
2. Analyse the problem: decide how to proceed and list the operations that are necessary.
3. Programme the solution: expand and re-state the list of operations to be performed by the computer.
4. Implement the solution: run the computer through the series of operations specified in the computer program. Review the results, and make decisions or carry out additional actions as required.
5. Complete the documentation: verify all the documents produced in the earlier steps; write final instructions for the computer operator; and gather all documents into a 'run book'.

1. *Defining the problem* begins with the description of the task given by the person requesting the data-processing job. Additional information and clarification will probably be necessary before a complete 'outline or narrative' is produced containing all the relevant facts for the eventual solution of the problem. This 'problem statement' contains four elements:

   a. Job description: a summary of what the data processing is to accomplish.
   b. Input information: a description of the kind of data going into the computer, the medium (paper, punch card etc.) on which the data is recorded, and the format in which the data appears.

    c. Output information: a description of the kind of data required in the results, the medium upon which the data is to be recorded, and the format in which it is to be presented.

    d. Processing information: (i) the calculations or processes to be performed on the input data, and (ii) the conditions of the problem which will determine which calculations are to be effected.

2. *Analysing the problem* to arrive at a possible solution involves examining the problem statement, in order to identify the specific conditions upon which the actions to be taken will depend. In order to correlate conditions with their appropriate actions, it is necessary to recognise and differentiate between an 'action statement' and a 'condition statement'. The latter describes the situation that must exist (or the condition that must be present), before a certain action is appropriate (or something else can take place). Rather as we try to decide, in a network analysis, which comes first and what may then follow, we endeavor to associate the words IF and THEN. IF this (condition statement) is present, THEN this (action statement) must be done as a consequence. The words IF and THEN are not always explicit in the problem statement, but if their presence may be implied then this is a clue. For example: IF a building labourer works after 4.30 p.m. THEN he is entitled to be paid overtime. Sometimes it is apparent from the problem statement that a particular action is dependent upon two or more conditions. Such a situation is termed an AND problem statement. For example: you must possess a current driving licence AND an H.G.V. licence before you may drive a heavy goods vehicle. When one or more of the conditions of an AND problem statement are missing/or not met, then an alternative course of action must be taken. To identify this action, we look for the word OTHERWISE, or its implied presence to provide the cue. For example: IF brick stocks are available AND we are able to recruit additional bricklayers, THEN we may complete ahead of time. If not (OTHERWISE) we must proceed as planned.

If a problem statement contains two or more alternative conditions, any one of which will allow action to be taken, then it is termed an OR problem statement. For example: IF you are short of labour OR materials THEN you must advise Head Office.

Depending upon the complexity of the problem, a programmer might find that a decision table is a convenient tool when careful discrimination is required. The decision table shown in Fig. 20.9 is divided into four sections by means of double vertical and horizontal lines. In section 1 (upper left) are listed the conditions outlined in the problem statement. In

Cost code begins with prefix L	Y	N	Y	N
Last card	Y	Y	N	N
Record on labour report	X		X	
Add to oncost summary		X		X
Stop	X	X		
Read another card			X	X

Fig. 20.9. Decision table for cost analysis program

section 2 (bottom left) are listed the various actions described in the problem statement. Section 3 (top right) contains a pattern of yes (Y) and no (N) answers to the conditions, covering all the practicable permutations. In section 4 (bottom right) are recorded (X) the appropriate action/s that should be taken beneath each single or combination of conditions. Each set of conditions is carefully considered using the techniques of IF/THEN etc. described earlier, and the correct action/s deduced logically.

Another aid to the analysis of a problem statement is the 'flowchart'. It is sometimes difficult to keep the step-by-step development of a solution in an orderly fashion, or to relate condition to action statements clearly. The flowchart uses a series of conventional symbols (see Fig. 20.10) to represent the sequence in which a combination of operations is to be performed. It also shows what happens to the data from input, through processing to output. Flowlines are drawn from symbol to symbol to show the reading order, and arrowheads are used to indicate the direction of flow when necessary. In the absence of arrows, a flowchart is normally read from top to bottom, and from left to right.

In addition to the program flowchart symbols, a group of system flowchart symbols (see Fig. 20.10) may also be used to indicate the type of medium being used, or to show the configuration of hardware devices in the data-processing operation.

S/P	**Processing** A group of program instructions that performs a processing function	**Predefined process** A group of operations not detailed in the particular flowchart P
S/P	**Input/Output** Any function of an input/ output device (making information available for processing, recording processing information, tape positioning etc.)	**Terminal interrupt** The beginning, end, or a point of interruption in a program P
P	**Decision** The decision function used to document points in the program where a branch to alternate paths is possible based upon variable conditions	**Connector** An entry from, or an exit to, another part of the program flowchart P
P	**Preparation** An instruction or group of instructions that changes the program	**Offpage connector** A connector used instead of the connector symbol to designate entry to or exit from a page P
S	**Punched card** All varieties of punched card, including stubs	**Punched tape** Paper or plastic S
S	**Document** Paper documents and reports of all kinds	**Transmittal tape** A proof or adding machine tape or similar batch-control information S
S	**Magnetic tape**	**Online storage** Input/output using any kind of online storage — magnetic tape, drum, or disc S
S	**Offline storage** Offline storage of paper or cards or magnetic or perforated tape	**Display** Information displayed by plotters or video devices S
S	**Manual input** Information input by online keyboards, switch settings, pushbuttons	**Sort** An operation to arrange a set of items into sequence S

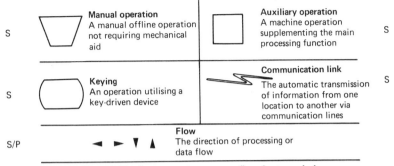

S

S

S

S

S/P

Fig. 20.10. System and program flowchart symbols

3. ***Programming the chosen solution*** to a problem involves writing a series of detailed instructions that the computer will execute one by one as it processes data and finally discharges the result through an output device. The program is written in one of the symbolic (high level) languages which, when translated by the compiler into machine language, will describe explicitly how the computer will receive, process and return the data. Since instructions must be followed one at a time, in sequence, each instruction is given an identifying 'label', so that it can be referred to later in the program if necessary. These may be simple reference numbers, or certain instructions may be labelled with words, perhaps foreshortened like CALC for a computational calculation. Firstly in the input section the computer is told what to name things, what space to set aside for them i.e. the expected number of digits, and what values to put in them. Similarly, at the end of the program the form and method of output will be specified. In between, the details of processing will be given in precise logical detail. There is usually more than one way to accomplish a specific task, some obviously more efficient than others. This is where experience counts, but some of the most basic concepts of programming technique include conditional and unconditional branching, and loops.

Sometimes a particular series of mathematical processes is required to be repeated again and again, for example if we are producing the squares of a list of numbers. We may therefore make use of a conditional branching, by instructing the computer to test for a certain condition. If this is fulfilled then the logic goes straight ahead; otherwise the program loops (goes back) to an earlier instruction so that the process is repeated. In order to control the looping we may use the device of establishing an index somewhere before the beginning of the loop such as $I = 0$. At the end of each loop we insert an instruction such as $I = I + 1$. Thus every time the loop is completed I will grow larger, and we can therefore set a predetermined value which will operate the conditional branch and move out of the loop.

Alternatively, several sections of a larger program may all end in performing an identical calculation. Each section may therefore branch unconditionally to the same instruction like GO TO CALC which has been labelled for this purpose. After this operation has been completed another instruction will return the process to another part of the program.

4. *Implementation of the solution* to the problem is then tested by running the full computer system.

The symbolic-language program, written on coding sheets, is copied by a keypunch operator onto punched cards and thus translated into machine-sensible information. These source-language data cards are fed into a card reader and hence put into storage. The compiler then translates the source program into an object program in machine-language form that the computer can understand, and this now exists in storage. The raw data is then fed into storage in a similar fashion, and processed in accordance with the written program. The processed data is finally output, usually in the form of a printed report.

The total input-process-output system begins with data stored in a physical form, such as a hole in a punched card or a magnetised spot on tape. Information in its external medium is then converted into electrical pulses which are stored in the main memory. The object program processes the data held in storage and assembles it in the required form for output. Data stored magnetically in the memory is changed back to electrical pulses and fed to an output device for conversion again to a permanent physical form.

After correction of the inevitable flaws in the program logic, we may proceed to the final phase.

5. *Completing the documentation* brings to a conclusion what has been a continuing process since the initial problem statement. Collecting, organizing, and storing all the recorded information and evidence culminating in the final solution is an essential task, vital for program development and improvement, for instruction of operating personnel, and future

programming assistance. Most of the documents developed during the problem solution and program implementation are filed in the run manual, primarily for use by the programmer. Documents relating to the operation of the computer console, including the vital input and output data layouts and punching instructions are kept in the console run book for the benefit of the systems operators. Finally the user manual is written, with examples of all input documents with their completion instructions, and examples of outputs. It also provides guidance notes on the use of the system, how it works, and code lists to assist with the completion of documents.

4. Applications to Construction

The advantage of a computer over a manual system is its ability to carry out simple operations at phenomenal speeds. It follows therefore that effective computerised systems are those that can benefit from speed and repetition. They usually have the following characteristics:

a. a large volume of individual operations;
b. a large volume of simple calculations;
c. a large number of variables;
d. frequent use of logic;
e. a lot of information to be sorted;
f. a large information base; and
g. a large amount of useful output is required.

It should also be remembered that a computer has limitations: it is inflexible, cannot think for itself, and lacks common sense, intuition and experience. The saying 'garbage in, garbage out' underlines the fact that results can only be as good as the raw data provided by the people in an organization. The National Computing Centre, a non-profit-distributing organisation backed by government and industry, exists to develop techniques and provide aids for the more effective use of computers, including the education and training of members staff.

The *general types of applications* in the commercial fields were therefore initially in office administration: accounting, stock control and sales. Of course many of these are of immediate interest to a building company, including weekly payroll, monthly salaries, cash flow, management ratios, plant spares and suppliers accounts.

There are two basic types of computer processing, batch and real-time. Batch processing means that input is batched, and programs run to a schedule. Runs are carried out at particular times, perhaps the same day each week, and the relevant files and programs are set up beforehand and removed afterwards. Real-time processing means that the files and programs are continally on call, thus enabling data to be fed in at any time, with immediate updating and output. This usually involves the use of terminals, such as would be used in airline booking offices.

Computers may be bought or rented from the manufacturers; or facilities may be hired on someone else's installation, i.e. time sharing. Alternatively one can make use of the all-in service provided by bureaux, who will charge by the computer time used and the services involved. Several bureaux specialise in construction industry requirements.

Specific building and civil engineering uses are now well developed, and this progress has been fostered by the Design Office Consortium (D.O.C.), an association of users of computers in construction. With over 100 members including educational establishments, architects, consulting engineers, quantity surveyors, contractors, government departments, local authorities and computer organisations, all concerned with providing information and exchange of experience on using computers, D.O.C. has provided impartial advice to first-time users in the construction industry since 1973. Supported by the Department of the Environment, together with the professional institutes and trade associations representing the construction industry, D.O.C. was expanded in 1980 to form the Construction Industry Computing Association.

Computer-aided design systems have already proved their value in architectural practices; and depending on size, design offices may have either a large in-house time-sharing minicomputer, possibly with interactive terminals serving many people, or desktop programmable machines.

Typical of the impact on structural engineering is the Genesys Centre (*GEN*eral *E*ngineering *SYS*tem) at the University of Technology, Loughborough, which under the auspices of the Department of the Environment has produced a vast library of programs, all able to work on most makes of computer.

A British Integrated Highway Design Suite of programs, produced initially by the County Surveyors Society and the Ministry of Transport, covers survey, design, setting out and measurement, and is compatible with several makes of computer. The range of software packages and bureaux services is well demonstrated in the Services and Products Directory published in *New Civil Engineer* and the CIOB quarterly *Construction Computing*.

With the backing of the Committee for the Application of Computers in the Construction Industry (CACCI), quantity surveying was one of the earlier disciplines to take up computing, and the preparation of bills of quantities is well advanced, and several programs exist to handle formula price adjustment.

Although not yet so well advanced, limited but successful attempts have been made to harness the computer to estimating.

The most obvious application of the computer to construction problems is that of network analysis and production control. The National Building Agency has been active in the project planning and progressing aspect, whilst many of the major contractors have attempted most areas of design, financial management, planning and forecasting, production control and other technical systems.

The many reasons delaying the pace of acceptance must be attributed to both the computer manufacturers and the industry itself. Despite the obvious advantages of standard software packages, instruction manuals are frequently inadequate, C.P.M. programs are much too complex, and programs for calculating earthwork quantities do not always accept information in the form issued by the consultant. Designers have a healthy fear of distancing themselves from their structures and losing that 'feel' of the manual process. Even the 'holy grail' of an effective site cost control system can be aborted by the stumbling block of reliable and speedy time allocations.

Developments and future applications are certain to accelerate because of the remarkable miniaturisation and even more astounding reduction in price brought about by the technological revolution of the semiconductor or microprocessor 'chip'. These tiny silicon chips, each a complete circuit in itself, have produced first minicomputers and then microcomputers. The different categories tend to overlap and cannot be clearly distinguished by a simple definition. However, approximate price ranges (1979) are : mainframe £100 000 to, say, £5 000 000; mini £20 000 to £150 000; and micro £200 to £20 000. Moreover, mainframe computers require air-conditioning, which may be optional for mini and unnecessary for micro hardware. Microcomputers are usually characterised by floppy disc and cassette tapes, but whilst comparatively cheap and powerful, their processing speed is slower and their data-storage capacity is much lower than that of the minis.

The advent of the microcomputer in 1977 has allowed even small businesses to contemplate their use, and at the same time has broadened the field of applications. The general concentration upon BASIC has simplified the writing of programs, whilst the introduction of VDUs has allowed greater interaction between machine and user. 1983 proved to be a record year for micro-computer sales, culminating in the Christmas rush for home computers. With a personal computer costing as little as £100, Technology Intelligence list their national sales figures for micro-computers in bands £500 to £1500, £1500 to £3500 and £3500 to £6262; which may be compared with those ranges shown earlier for 1979. But the cost of buying the basic hardware – the processor, disc drives and display – rarely accounts nowadays for more than 25% of the total expense of acquiring and installing a stand-alone, single-user, business microcomputer.

There is a positive trend towards the so-called 'electronic office' with the advent of word processors which could radically improve the productivity of typists. This should have direct implications for the producers of contract documents, offering improved accuracy and a reduction in the time required to correct or revise specifications, bills of quantities etc.

Another recent innovation is the emergence of information-handling telecommunications facilities, and the use of television to operate public data networks. This potential is now being developed by the Post Office (Prestel), British Broadcasting Corporation (Ceefax), and the Independent Broadcasting Authority (Oracle.) The Post Office has arranged with the Department of the Environment for the National Building Agency to compile a service for the construction industry within Prestel named Contel. This viewdata system is intended to replace the office library of material and component directories, British Standards and Codes of Practice, standard contracts, industrial and legislative regulations, statistics and current prices etc., which could revolutionise the business information world.

The future does indeed offer great opportunities for the construction industries, but the potential can only be tapped and developed by disciplined thought, logical application, imagination and enthusiasm. It is essential to prevent the tail from wagging the dog, producing mountains of unusable information or shaping systems to suit the machine rather than the business. For that reason, the builder must understand sufficient about the digital computer to be able to control and direct the computer technicians. Under economic pressure there is already a general quickening in the tempo of construction projects, and as clients realise even more that time truly is money, there will be considerable commercial advantage for those firms who can provide rapid estimates, designs and erection programmes within an integrated management system. Computers can make this possible.

BIBLIOGRAPHY

Rodney Revell, *Computers and the Management Services Officer,* Institute of Management Services, 1978.

'Computer Services', five articles in *Contract Journal,* 12 October 1978.

'Survey: Computers in Construction', *Construction News Magazine,* February 1975.

Plain Builders' Guide to Computing, Institute of Building, 1978.

Computer Programs for Construction Management, Evaluation Report No. 4, Design Office Consortium, 1979.

'Computers in Construction', series of articles in *New Civil Engineer,* 14 February 1980.

'Can Viewdata replace the printed word?', *New Civil Engineer,* 22 November 1979.

Computing and Communications in the Building Industy, N.C.C. of the Building and Civil Engineering Industries (Property Services Agency).

Computer Program User Report No. 5 (Network Analysis Techniques), Loughborough University of Technology, 1968.

R. A. Reynolds, *Computer Methods for Architects,* Butterworths, 1980

Chartered Quantity Surveyors and the Microcomputer, Royal Institution of Chartered Surveyors, 1981.

Construction Computing, a quarterly journal launched by the Chartered Institute of Building, 1983.

Appendix 1

Terms used in CPM

Activity. A time-consuming operation or job. Represented by an arrow.

Arrow Diagram. A representation of a project, in which the relationship of the arrows indicates the sequence in which the constituent activities will be performed. Also known as a network.

Critical Path. The longest chain of activities connecting the beginning and the completion of a project. Along this path the earliest and latest times for each event are identical, and the sum total of the critical activity durations is equal to the minimum period required for the execution of the project.

Dummy. A restraint relationship between activities which requires no time. Indicated by a dotted arrow.

Duration. The time necessary to complete an activity. Usually shown within brackets below the arrow.

Earliest Event Time. The earliest possible time by which all the activities terminating at the event can be completed. Shown within a square on the 'head' side of the event.

Earliest Finish Time. The earliest time by which an activity can be completed.

Earliest Start Time. The earliest time at which an activity can start – controlled by the earliest event time at its 'tail'.

Event. A moment in time when all preceding activities have been completed, and before any succeeding activities have started. Represented by a circle, sometimes known as a node.

Float. The difference between the amount of time available to accomplish an activity and the time actually necessary. There are four types of float: *total, free, independent* and *interfering,* as illustrated in Fig. 18.6. Total float is the maximum amount of leeway available for all the activities in a particular chain, and the more it is used up for any one activity, the less there will be left for the others. Free and independent float are available exclusively to

457

a particular activity, without delaying the start of any subsequent activity. When it is necessary to defer the start of non-critical activities to level out demands for resources or to provide continuity of work for a particular trade, the first choice would be those with independent float following by those with free float. Interfering float is equal to the slack in the subsequent event.

Interface. An event occurring identically in two or more networks so that they are interconnected. Usually identified by an additional concentric circle or other similar device.

i.   The event at the tail of an activity arrow.

j.   The event at the head of an activity arrow.

Ladder. A convention for representing overlapping activities where sections of the work are released progressively. The head event is shown by a square node (see Fig. 18.12).

Latest Event Time. The latest possible time by which all the activities terminating at the event must be completed, if they are not to cause a delay to the project completion time. Shown within a triangle on the tail side of the event. Alternatively, both earliest and latest event times may be displayed in a double box.

Latest Finish Time. The latest time by which an activity can be completed – controlled by the latest event times at its head.

Latest Start Time. The latest time at which an activity can start if it is not to delay the project completion time.

Lag. The time required to perform that last portion of an overlapping activity which remains after completion of the preceding activity (see Fig. 18.12).

Lead. The time required to perform the first portion of an overlapping activity, after which the succeeding activity may begin (see Fig. 18.12).

Resource Aggregation. Listing the total requirements of a resource for each time period.

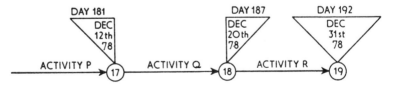

P MUST BE FINISHED NOT LATER THAN 12th DEC 78.
R CANNOT START EARLIER THAN 20th DEC 78.
(19) OCCURS ON 31st DEC 78

Fig. A.1. Scheduled or imposed dates

Resource Levelling. Rearranging a schedule of activities so that a predetermined limit or level for a resource is not exceeded, while the project duration is minimised.

Resource Smoothing. Rearranging a schedule of activities within the limits of their total floats so that the fluctuations in resource requirements are minimised, while the project duration is unaffected.

Scheduled Date. A specified date or time imposed upon an event or activity by an agency or circumstance outside the network. An early scheduled date may prevent an activity from starting before an authorised commencement, or a late scheduled date may establish a target by which an event must be attained. Usually indicated by a triangular flag (see Fig. A.1).

Slack. The difference between latest and earliest event times, see Fig. 18.6.

Appendix 2

Metric Conversion Factors

	British unit	British unit to metric	Metric unit	Metric unit to British
Length	Mile	1.609 km	Kilometre	0.621 mile
	Yard	0.914 m	Metre	1.093 yd
	Foot	305 mm	Metre	3.281 ft
	Inch	25.4 mm	Millimetre	0.039 in
Area	Square mile	2.590 km^2	Square kilometre	0.386 mile^2
	Acre	0.405 ha	Hectare	2.471 acre
	Square yard	0.836 m^2	Square metre	1.196 yd^2
	Square foot	0.093 m^2	Square metre	10.764 ft^2
	Square inch	645.16 mm^2	Square millimetre	0.00155 in^2
Volume	Cubic yard	0.764 m^3	Cubic metre	1.308 yd^3
	Cubic foot	0.028 m^3	Cubic metre	35.315 ft^3
	Cubic inch	16387.1 mm^3	Cubic millimetre	0.000061 in^3
Mass	Ton	1.016 t	Tonne	0.984 ton
	Pound	0.454 kg	Kilogram	2.205 lb
	Ounce	28.350 g	Gram	0.035 oz
Force	Pound-force	4.448 N	Newton	0.225 lbf
Stress	Tonf/sq.foot	107.252 kN/m^2	Kilonewton/sq. metre	0.00932 tonf/ft^2
	Pound f/sq. inch	0.00689 N/mm^2	Newton/sq. mm.	145.038 lbf/in^2
Density	Pound/cubic foot	16.019 kg/m^3	Kilogram/cu. metre	0.062 lb/ft^3
	Pound/cubic inch	0.0277 g/mm^3	Gram/cu. mm.	36.1 lb/in^3
Capacity	Gallon	4.546 ℓ	Litre	0.220 gal

Notes: nano = 10^{-9}; micro = 10^{-6}; milli = 10^{-3}; kilo = 10^3; mega = 10^6; giga = 10^9
tonne = 10^3 kg; hectare = 10^4 m^2; kg = 9.81N

460

Appendix 3

Definitions of Computer Terms

Access Time. The time taken to retrieve data from a storage device or peripheral.

Address. Is the identification of a given location within the computer's store, or memory.

ALGOL. ALGOrithmic Language. A high-level programming language for mathematical and scientific use.

Application Program. A specific program developed by the user to solve his particular problem.

Available Time. Period during which computer is ready for use.

Backing Store. An auxiliary store of large capacity.

BASIC. Beginners All-purpose Symbolic Instruction Code. A high-level language mainly used for on-line programming.

Batch Processing. A method of processing data in which input is prepared and processed without interaction with the user.

Baud. In computer telecommunications, the transmission of one 'bit' per second.

Bit. An abbreviation of 'binary digit'. The smallest unit of information, having one of two values: 'on' or 'off', 1 or 0, etc. Also used to describe an element of core storage.

'Bubble' Memory. A device which, like a floppy disc, stores work and programs. It continues to store the data even when the power supply is disconnected.

Bug. An error in a program or system.

Bureau Service. A service for running programs on behalf of a user, or for selling computer resources so that the user can run his own programs.

Byte. A set of binary digits considered as a unit, usually a subdivision of a word; now generally accepted as 8 bits and storing one character.

COBOL. COmmon Business Oriented Language. The language most commonly used in business.

461

Code. Symbolic representation of data or instruction.

Compatibility. If the same programs can be used on different computers then the computers are said to be compatible.

Communications. Describes the methods of transmitting data from remote locations to the computer and vice versa. Communications channels are a hardware feature of the computer. Telecommunications refers to the more involved systems where Post Office telephone lines, or direct lines, are used in conjunction with a modem.

Compiler. A program which takes as input another program, written in a language meaningful to people, and produces as output another program which is meaningful to the computer.

Configuration. A description of the physical units comprising a computer system.

Console. The control device used by computer operators, usually a teletype or visual display unit, enabling the operator to input messages to the computer and receive messages back.

Conversational Mode. A method of operation in which the user is in direct communication with the computer and is able to obtain immediate response to his input messages.

Core Storage. A type of computer memory in which data is held in binary form.

Core Store. The computer's main memory.

CPS. Characters per second.

CPU. See *Processor.*

Data. Raw information which is input to the machine.

Databank. A collection of data, usually stored on magnetic tape or disc, and available to users via remote terminals. The data tend to be limited to a particular application area over a particular time period (say, a traffic survey.)

Database. An organised pool of shareable data, typically a series of regularly updated applications files related through one or more indexes which permit the direct retrieval of information for a wide range of purposes.

Data Preparation. The process of organising data so that all transactions entering a system are transcribed into some medium suitable for input.

Data Structure. A group of items of information ordered or related in a specific manner.

Digitiser. Machine used to convert physical quantities into computer code.

Direct Access. The storage and retrieval of data in such a way that each record's storage location is completely unconnected with the previous record stored. Contrasts with 'serial access' and is associated with magnetic discs.

Disc. A storage device, peripheral, consisting of flat circular plates, coated on both surfaces with magnetised material.

Duplexing. System of data transmission which enables instantaneous two-way transmission between terminals.

Fields. Part of a record, used to hold one item of data (e.g. a reference number or a design parameter).

File. An organised collection of data on a storage device, tape or disc.

Fixed Format. A layout of data (particularly for card input) where items must be specified in pre-determined character positions.

Floppy Disc. A single flexible circular plate with magnetised material forming a coating; used as backing store on microcomputers.

Flowchart. A diagrammatic presentation of the sequence of events of a program.

FORTRAN. FORmula TRANslation. A problem-oriented high-level programming language primarily for scientific and mathematical use. Used extensively in civil engineering.

Free Format. A method of specifying data, particularly for paper input, where a series of numerical data times or text is provided sequentially with each item separated from its neighbours by a space, comma or other delimiter.

General-purpose Computer. Computer able to handle a wide range of programs.

Hard Copy. A printed output or 'permanent' message, as opposed to a 'temporary' display as seen on a video monitor.

Hardware. The physical units making up a computer system: the apparatus as opposed to the programs.

High-level Language. A language which can be readily understood by a programmer. Each statement may correspond to several machine code instructions.

Housekeeping. Standard routines incorporated into a program to perform procedures such as input and output.

Implementation. (i) A version of a program on a particular type of computer; (ii) the process of installing a program.

Information Technology. Embraces microelectronics, software technology, advanced information processing, and office and factory computerisation.

Input. The process of passing data or instructions from a remote device to the computer's memory.

Integrated Circuit. Usually a piece of silicon on which all the necessary components of an electronic circuit, such as resistors and capacitors, have been etched in miniature and then packaged as a plug-in device.

Intelligent Terminal. A terminal with its own processor and memory. Its function is to carry out simple tasks locally, using the more expensive time of the computer with which it is linked for tasks beyond the terminal's capability.

Interactive. A method of operation in which the user is in direct communication with the computer but in which his decisions and the flow of the conversation are influenced by results obtained.

Interactive Display. A display which allows the operator to input data in response to displayed questions.

Interface (User-Machine). The common frontier between the user and the computer. The form that the exchange of information between them takes.

Interpreter. A program which takes as input one statement of another program written in a language meaningful to people, and produces as output a series of instructions which are then obeyed by the computer.

Job Control Language. The specialised language to inform the computer about the systems software it will need in order to run a piece of work.

kb. Kilobyte, or $1024(2^{10})$ bytes.

Length. The number of bits which make up a unit of data or record.

Library. A collection of subroutines which can be automatically incorporated within a program without adjustment.

Line Printer. The main output device which prints results, one line at a time, on continuous paper.

Line Speed. The rate at which information passes between a computer and a terminal.

Low-level Language. One in which one program statement corresponds to a single machine-code instruction.

Machine Code. Instructions needed to tell a computer how to handle data.

Machine-independent. Describes a program for use on any system.

Magnetic Disc. Similar to a gramophone record, but each surface is coated with magnetisable material. Data is stored in the form of magnetic pulses.

Main Frame. Name given to central processor. Often used to describe more powerful computers.

Matrix printer. Printing device which formulates an image out of a series of dots.

Memory. Those storage locations in the internal working storage that can be immediately addressed by the control unit; backing stores (i.e. disc, tape) are sometimes referred to as 'memory units', in which case the internal working storage would be referred to as 'main memory'.

Memory Size. Number of storage locations available in a memory, e.g. a million bits (megabit).

Microcomputer. A fully operational computer, in its simplest form consisting of central processing unit and memory, but also available up to a complete configuration. It is characterised by small size, lower power consumption, and low cost.

Mode. Way in which hardware or software operates, e.g. binary mode.

Modem. The acoustic coupler (or faster modem) provides a means of connecting a computer with the telephone lines, by converting the electric signals into burps and beeps.

Monitor. A visual display unit specifically designed for use with a computer only, which by obviating the necessity to code and uncode, as with a normal television set, increases the strength of illumination. Also available with green lettering on a black background which further enhances the definition.

Mouse. A hand-held device connected to the computer, which with the right program can be used to manipulate screen displays without any need for the keyboard.

Multiplex. Transmission of several messages simultaneously within the same system.

Off-line. Peripheral equipment not under the direct control of the Central Processor. Also used loosely to include peripheral-to-peripheral transfers, e.g. magnetic tape listing.

On-line. Any device directly connected to the Central Processor. Often applied to terminal devices that employ a keyboard for direct input of data.

Operating System. The procedures which control resources within a computer system.

Output. The results produced by the computer.

Package. A generalised program written so that a user's particular problems will not make the package any less useful.

Paging. Operation used to store data in the virtual storage method; data is divided into 'pages'.

Paper Tape. A means of preparing data as a pattern of holes punched across a paper tape. The *Paper Tape Reader* detects the holes with light rays.

Pascal. A most sophisticated and efficient language that has become increasingly popular for writing large programs such as business applications by reason of its structured nature. Named after the 17th century mathematician Blaise Pascal.

Peripherals. Supporting devices which can be operated under computer control, e.g. teletypes, line printers, card readers.

Plotter. A device for drawing under computer control; e.g. a graph plotter depicts output results in the form of graphs on paper.

Processor (or CPU). The Central Processing Unit of the computer. The nerve centre of the system which controls and carries out arithmetical and logical operations on data as dictated by the computer program.

Program. A sequence of instructions to be performed by an electronic computer in processing a given class of data.

Program Documentation. Information written for the user to tell him how to handle computer input and output data and enable him to run his program.

Programming Language. A means for specifying instructions to a computer.

Punched Cards. A means of input and output, data being represented as holes punched into cards. The card reader detects the holes with light rays.

Random Access Memory (RAM). Computer memory which the program can use to store and manipulate data: so structured that the time to access every item is the same.

Raw Time. Any time sold on a computer with no applications software included.

Read Only Memory (ROM). Memory containing data – usually a program – which is built into the hardware and can be read or executed, but cannot be altered by the user.

Real Time. Describes a system in which responses to data input are produced almost simultaneously.

Record. A set of one or more fields containing related information.

Recording Density. The number of binary digits that can be stored per unit length.

Response Time. The total time from the initiation of an operation at a computer terminal, transmission of data to the distant computer, processing, file access and transmission back to the terminal.

Run Time. The time required to complete a single, continuous execution of a program.

Software. The programs. Systems software is the software for internal workings of the machine, such as communications handling. Applications software is user-oriented, like a payroll.

Software House. An organisation specialising in the production of software.

Source (Program). A program which cannot be processed by the hardware of a computer without compilation.

Storage tube. A form of visual display terminal on which can be drawn lines as well as characters.

Subroutine. A program that can only be used directly by another program.

Syntax. A mistake in writing a particular instruction into a program is referred to as an error of Syntax.

Teletype. An automatic typewriter communicating with a computer direct or via telephone lines. The keyboard layout for letters and numbers is the same as that of the standard typewriter, but the position of symbols etc. vary with the particular machine.

Terminal. A device by which data may be input to (by keyboard), or output from (by automatic typewriter), a computer system; terminals may be remote from the computer linked over telephone lines.

Timesharing. A system in which several users or peripherals may be connected to the computer simultaneously.

Transportability. The ability to move software from one type or model of computer to another.

User Friendly. A computer that uses a relatively simple operating language, such as BASIC, is called 'User Friendly'. This means that it is easier to operate than other machines, because it uses words taken from everyday language rather than cryptic expressions.

Variable. A programming term to denote a storage location of an item of data.

VDU. Visual Display Unit; a terminal with a cathode-ray-tube display screen in place of a print-out device.

Visual Record System. An accounting-machine-like computer which inputs and outputs data on to cards.

Virtual Storage. Device which enables the user to run programs without being constrained by the size of the main store.

Word. A basic unit of data in a computer memory consisting of a predetermined number of bits.

Index